■ PRINCIPLES
OF MODERN
HETEROCYCLIC CHEMISTRY

∎ PRINCIPLES
OF MODERN
HETEROCYCLIC
CHEMISTRY

LEO A. PAQUETTE THE OHIO STATE UNIVERSITY

W. A. BENJAMIN, INC. ∎ New York   Amsterdam

1968

PRINCIPLES OF MODERN
HETEROCYCLIC CHEMISTRY

Library of Congress Catalog Card Number 68-11542
Manufactured in the United States of America

*The manuscript was put into production on June 15, 1967;
This volume was published on June 9, 1968*

W. A. BENJAMIN, INC., *New York, New York 10016*

12345K321098

TO ESTELLE,

AND RONALD, DONNA, SUSAN, LINDA, AND LISA

■ EDITOR'S FOREWORD

UNDERGRADUATE education in chemistry is in the midst of a major revolution. Sophisticated material, including extensive treatment of current research problems, is increasingly being introduced into college chemistry courses. In organic chemistry, this trend is apparent in the new "elementary" textbooks. However, it has become clear that a single text, no matter how sophisticated, is not the best medium for presenting glimpses of advanced material in addition to the necessary basic chemistry. A spirit of critical evaluation of the evidence is essential in an advanced presentation, while "basic" material must apparently be presented in a relatively dogmatic fashion.

Accordingly, we have instituted a series of short monographs intended as supplements to a first-year organic text; they may, of course, be used either concurrently or subsequently. It is our hope that teachers of beginning organic chemistry courses will supplement the usual text with one or more of these intermediate level monographs and that they find use in secondary courses as well. In general the books are designed to be read independently by the interested student and to lead him into the current research literature. It is hoped that they will serve their intended educational purpose and will help the student to recognize organic chemistry as the vital and exciting field it is.

We welcome any suggestions or comments about the series.

RONALD BRESLOW

New York, New York
December, 1964

■ PREFACE

THE estimate has been made that approximately 65% of the published work in organic chemistry can be classified as heterocyclic. Because of the rather extensive nature of this field, exposure of advanced undergraduate and beginning graduate students of organic chemistry to a broad survey of the synthetic approaches to, and reactions of, the fundamental heterocyclic systems would seem to be highly desirable. This text has been written with the goal of providing an introduction to such subject matter.

Because of the severe limitations imposed by a monograph of this length, my aims have been to simplify the major features of heterocyclic chemistry. My intention has not been to offer an exhaustive survey of all the synthetic methods available, nor to account for all of the reactions characteristic of a particular heterocyclic nucleus. Rather, the inclusion or exclusion of topics has been designed to present to the reader an overall view of the field. Naturally, the individual chapters necessarily reflect certain personal preferences of the author, and he accepts sole responsibility for the tone of the book.

In this regard, a number of significant deviations from the customary presentation of heterocyclic subject matter have been instituted herein. For instance, discussions of a particular heterocyclic group have not been fractionated into separate sections according to the nature of the hetero atom wherever this has proved feasible. Thus, in Chapter 1 the synthetic approaches to oxirans, aziridines, and episulfides are presented according to general methods of formation. The reactions are treated in a similar manner. Chapter 10 reflects an even greater alteration in the style of presentation. I welcome at any time constructive comments and suggestions about these innovations.

Problem exercises, which have been culled from the available literature, have been included after each chapter, except for Chapter 11. It will be found that many of them can be worked out from a knowledge of the text material, although an approximately equal number are more difficult. In short, the exercises are meant to be interesting, stimulating, and challenging; in order that frustration does not overcome some students, literature references have been provided in each instance.

The writing of this book would have proved very tedious were it not for the many specialized works in heterocyclic chemistry which are available. Extensive references to all such reviews have been incorporated in order that easy access to more advanced subject matter be at hand.

I am particularly indebted to Professor James A. Moore who read the entire manuscript and who contributed significantly to the final version of the text with his innumerable penetrating and keen comments. The task of proofreading the manuscript in various stages of preparation was lightened significantly by the efforts of Messrs. Donald Kuhla and Robert J. Haluska, both of whom are presently graduate students in the Chemistry Department. Finally, I am especially grateful to Miss Donna Winkel who not only typed the manuscript in its entirety, but also checked many references and offered useful suggestions.

LEO A. PAQUETTE

Columbus, Ohio
December 1967

▪ CONTENTS

1

■ THREE-MEMBERED RINGS WITH
ONE HETERO ATOM

THE OUTSTANDING CHARACTERISTIC of the three-membered hetero rings is their reactivity to a wide variety of reagents, an effect undoubtedly resulting from the necessary compression of bond angles in these molecules. The introduction of a double bond serves to further increase the strain of the particular system under study. Thus, aziridines are far more reactive than ordinary amines, and 1H-azirines remain to be synthesized (although 2H-azirines are known, see pp. 16–19).

Of the three saturated analogs, epoxides, aziridines, and episulfides, the second group is intrinsically interesting because the substituent on nitrogen does not lie in the plane of the ring, leading to the possibility that suitably constructed derivatives may be subject to resolution into optically active enantiomers, for example, [1a] and [1b]. However, because of the ease with which nitrogen undergoes inversion of configuration, [1] exists at room temperature as a rapidly interconverting mixture[1]; in fact, the rate of the inversion process is such that

[1a]   [1b]

substituted aziridines with molecular asymmetry attributable to trivalent nitrogen are likely only to be resolvable at temperatures below $-50°$.[2] On the other hand, nitrogen inversion in aziridines occurs sufficiently slowly (in a relative sense) below room temperature that direct determination of the inversion frequency by nuclear magnetic resonance (n.m.r.) spectroscopy is feasible.[2, 3]

SYNTHETIC APPROACHES
Direct Insertion of the Hetero Atom into a Carbon-Carbon Double Bond

The direct preparation of epoxides [2] from olefins can be carried out by a number of methods, the most frequently employed and generally applicable of which is peracid oxidation.[4]   Of the variety

[2]

of peracids that have been used for this purpose, *m*-chloroperbenzoic acid has recently emerged as the most convenient oxidizing agent.[5] This reagent is commercially available,[6] reacts at a somewhat faster rate than either peracetic or perbenzoic acids, and is ideally suited for epoxidations which require long reaction times due to its excellent stability.   Because epoxides readily undergo ring cleavage (see p. 25) in the presence of sufficiently acidic carboxylic acids, reactions performed with performic, trifluoroperacetic, monopermaleic, and peracetic acids (in nonbuffered solutions) generally result in the formation of monoesters of 1,2-diols[7]; these reagents are therefore less satisfactory.

The epoxidation reaction proceeds by an electrophilic attack of the peracid upon the double bond as indicated above.[8]   In agreement with this mechanism, it has been widely demonstrated that the rate of epoxidation is very sensitive to the electron density at the olefinic site (Table 1–1). Thus, whereas, alkyl substitution is attended by pronounced rate enhancement (cyclic olefins are epoxidized at rates comparable to open chain analogs), double bonds which are conjugated with aromatic rings react more slowly. Selectivity is therefore very easily achieved.

TABLE I–I ▪

Rate Sequence for Reaction with Peracetic Acid[9]

Compound	Rate	Compound	Rate
$CH_2=CH_2$	1	$R_2C=CH_2$	500
$RCH=CH_2$	24	$R_2C=CHR$	6500
$RCH=CHR$	500	$R_2C=CR_2$	Very fast

(61%)   (*Ref. 10*)

The peracid oxidation of olefins is highly stereospecific as demonstrated by the fact that *cis*-cyclooctene affords [3] and *trans*-cyclooctene gives rise to [4].[11]

[3]   [4]

Because of the bulkiness of the peracid in the transition state leading to epoxidation, attack generally proceeds from the less hindered side (e.g., [5]).[12]   However, the direction of attack by the peracid may be influenced by polar groups.   In the case of [6], for example, hydrogen bonding between the hydroxyl group and the peracid not only reverses the stereochemistry of the electrophilic attack, but also results in a significant rate increase.[12a, b]

When the olefinic bond is conjugated with a strongly electron-withdrawing group such as carbonyl or cyano, the rate of epoxidation is either slow or fails completely.   For such systems, epoxidation by means of alkaline hydrogen peroxide is very useful.   The reaction

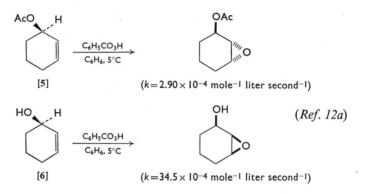

[5]

$(k=2.90 \times 10^{-4}$ mole^{-1} liter second$^{-1})$

[6]

$(k=34.5 \times 10^{-4}$ mole^{-1} liter second$^{-1})$

(*Ref. 12a*)

proceeds by Michael addition of hydroperoxide anion to the unsaturated system followed by intramolecular displacement of hydroxide ion,[14] as illustrated in the case of [7]. A fundamental difference exists between alkaline hydrogen peroxide oxidation and

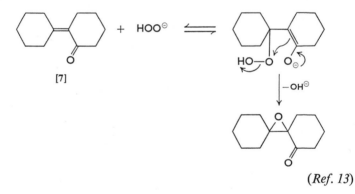

[7]

(*Ref. 13*)

peracid epoxidation. Whereas, the latter is stereospecific, the former is not; generally, however, a single epoxide is formed, but it bears no stereochemical relationship to the reactant[4c]; for example, the alkaline peroxide oxidation of the isomeric ketones [8] and [9] gives rise to the same epoxide.[4c,15]

With α,β-unsaturated nitriles under these conditions, α,β-epoxy-amides (e.g., [10]) generally result. The reaction very likely proceeds via a peroxyimidic acid intermediate which functions as the electrophilic reagent.[16] The intermediate peroxyimidic acid derived from benzonitrile readily epoxidizes olefins under neutral conditions and shows promise in the preparation of acid-sensitive epoxides.[16]

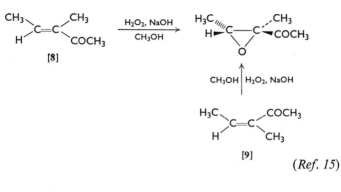

(*Ref. 15*)

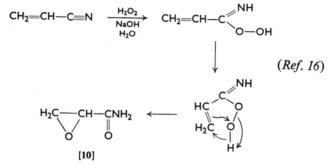

(*Ref. 16*)

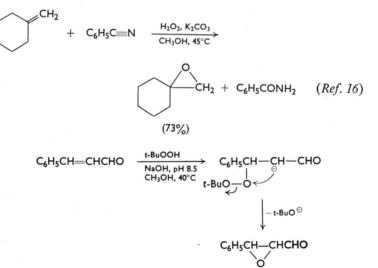

(73%) (*Ref. 16*)

An important variation of the alkaline hydrogen peroxide method makes use of *tert*-butyl hydroperoxide.[16, 17] With this reagent, epoxidation of α,β-unsaturated nitriles does not result in hydration of the cyano function.

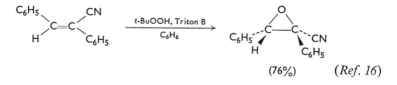

(76%)   (*Ref. 16*)

Aziridines can be prepared by the direct insertion of nitrenes (e.g., [11]) into olefinic linkages.[18] However, the use of such energy-rich nitrenes results in the formation of substantial quantities of side

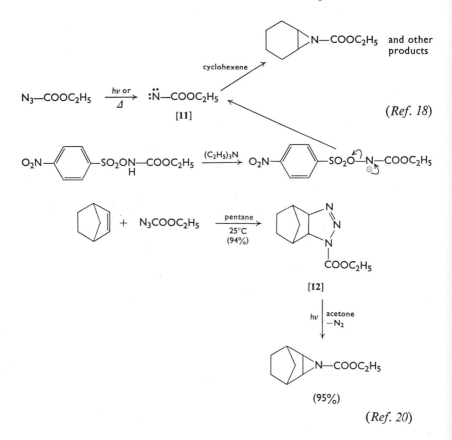

and other products

(*Ref. 18*)

[12]

(*Ref. 20*)

products. By contrast, a pure aziridine can be prepared by initially permitting the azide to react with the olefin by 1,3-dipolar addition[19] to afford a 1,2,3-triazoline (e.g., [12]) which subsequently can be decomposed quantitatively by ultraviolet irradiation.[20]

Methylene Insertion Reactions

The reaction of dimethyloxosulfonium methylide [13a] with aromatic and nonconjugated aldehydes and ketones results in the

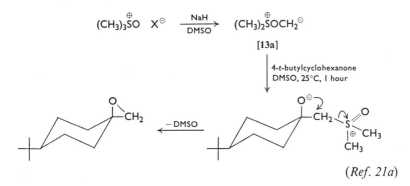

(*Ref. 21a*)

transfer of a methylene group from the ylide to the carbonyl group and yields epoxides.[21]   Methylene transfer likewise occurs with the more reactive dimethylsulfonium methylide [13b], but an important

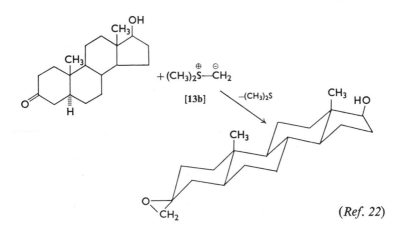

(*Ref. 22*)

difference is observed between the two reagents. Whereas nucleophilic attack by [13a] upon the carbonyl group generally proceeds from the less hindered side to produce a new carbon-carbon bond which is equatorial, [13b] reacts stereospecifically in the opposite direction. This reversal in stereochemistry has been attributed to the greater stability, lesser reactivity, and greater bulk of [13a] relative to [13b].[22]

An additional fundamental divergence of these ylides appears in their reaction with α,β-unsaturated ketones. Thus, reaction of [13b] with benzalacetophenone leads only to the corresponding epoxide; however, [13a] gives exclusively the cyclopropyl ketone because of its preference to undergo initial Michael addition.[21]

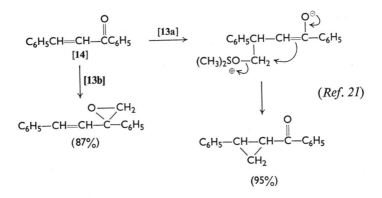

(Ref. 21)

Episulfides can be prepared by methylene transfer to thioketones, but similar attempts with $>C=N-$ bonds has given several products only one of which is an aziridine.[21a]

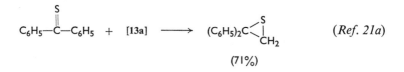

(Ref. 21a)

Diazomethane and its derivatives react with many aldehydes and ketones to produce epoxides, but longer-chained aldehydes and ketones are also formed and the desired oxide may be difficult to separate from the mixture. The reaction is very sensitive to the nature of the substituent and prediction of the products is often difficult. The procedure has seen widespread use, however, and the

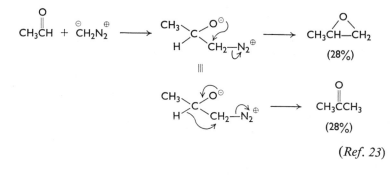

(*Ref. 23*)

results have been extensively summarized.[7a, 24] Treatment of α,β-unsaturated aldehydes with diazomethane does not result in epoxide formation but generally yields pyrazolines.

Schiff bases usually yield 1,2,3-triazolines when treated with diazomethane,[25] but aromatic thioketones have been successfully converted to episulfides by interaction with aryldiazomethanes.[26a]

$$(C_6H_5)_2C{=}S \ + \ (C_6H_5)_2C{=}N_2 \ \xrightarrow{-N_2} \ (C_6H_5)_2\overset{\displaystyle S}{\overset{\diagup\diagdown}{C{-}C}}(C_6H_5)_2$$

(100%)   (*Ref. 26a*)

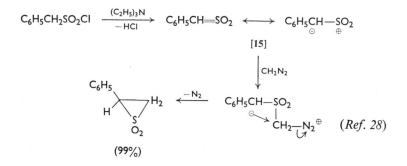

(99%)

The generation of sulfenes (e.g., [15]), a group of reactive intermediates known to undergo nucleophilic attack by electron-rich reagents,[27] in the presence of diazomethane leads to the formation of episulfones.[28] Episulfones can, moreover, be produced directly by reaction of diazomethane and its derivatives with sulfur dioxide.[29] The mechanism of this latter condensation probably involves initial formation of a sulfene, followed by a similar nucleophilic addition of a second molecule of the diazo compound.

$(p\text{-}CH_3OC_6H_4)_2C{=}N_2 \xrightarrow[-N_2]{SO_2} (p\text{-}CH_3OC_6H_4)_2C{=}SO_2 \longrightarrow$

$$
\begin{array}{c}
SO_2 \\
\diagup \quad \diagdown \\
(p\text{-}CH_3OC_6H_4)_2C\text{---}C(C_6H_4OCH_3\text{-}p)_2
\end{array}
$$

(70%)

(*Ref. 29b*)

Treatment of ternary iminium perchlorates (e.g., [16]) and fluoro-borates with diazomethane yields aziridinium salts.[30] The per-chlorate and fluoroborate anions were selected because of their low order of nucleophilicity which results in their inability to open the

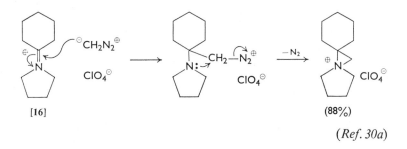

[16]   (88%)

(*Ref. 30a*)

very reactive positively charged three-membered ring (see p. 35). The reaction is of wide applicability, and can be used to prepare a variety of aziridinium salts.[30]

Cyclization Methods

The preparation of three-membered heterocycles by a variety of cyclization reactions is convenient, general, and, often (except perhaps

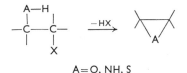

A=O, NH, S

in the case of epoxides)[31] the method of choice.   Although a wide range of such reactions are available, they all proceed according to the same mechanistic scheme; that is, cyclization occurs by backside attack of the hetero atom (O⁻, NH₂, S⁻, etc.) at the carbon atom bearing the leaving group.   Therefore, inversion of configuration takes place at the latter site.

The reaction of a halohydrin with alkali is kinetically second order, first order in each component, and proceeds by rapid formation of an alkoxide anion followed by the slower rate-determining cyclization.[32]

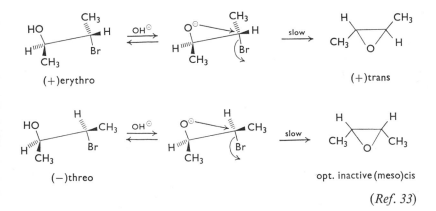

(*Ref. 33*)

The displacement reaction is not limited to halogen atoms, but may be effected with any good leaving group such as tosylate or trimethylamine.   However, since *trans*-halohydrins are readily available through the addition of hypohalous acids[34] to olefins, such substances are most often employed.   The hypohalogenation reaction is believed to proceed by an electrophilic attack of the positively charged halogen atom upon the site of unsaturation and results in the formation of a halonium ion intermediate (e.g., [17]), which is subsequently attacked by water at the site of greatest incipient carbonium ion stabilization to give *trans*-halohydrins.   The reaction is stereospecific and proceeds by addition of halonium ion from the less hindered side[36, 37]; since subsequent epoxide formation results in inversion of configuration at one center, the overall result locates the oxygen atom on the more hindered side (e.g., [18]).   This result is in direct contrast to peracid oxidation which generally (see p. 4) inserts the oxygen from the less hindered side (e.g., [19]).[38, 39]

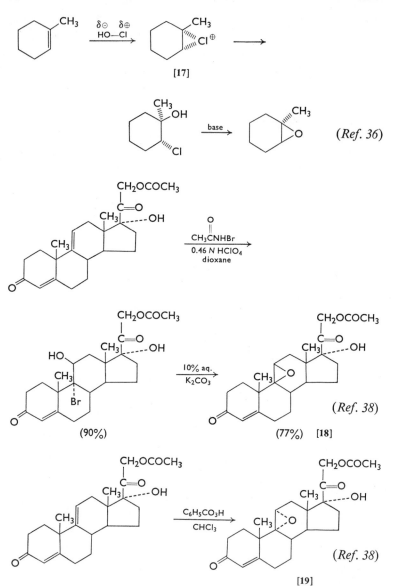

(*Ref. 36*)

(*Ref. 38*)

(90%)   (77%)   [18]

(*Ref. 38*)

[19]

The rate of formation of epoxides from halohydrins can be enhanced by the introduction of substituents (Table 1–2). That the
closure of small rings is favored by such substitution is made evident

TABLE I-2 ▪

Rate Sequence for Reaction with Alkali[40]

Compound	Rate	Compound	Rate
HO—CH$_2$CH$_2$Cl	0.31	HO—CH$_2$C(CH$_3$)$_2$Cl (CH$_3$ above and below C)	77
HO—CH$_2$CHClCH$_3$ (CH$_3$ above)	1.7	HO—C(CH$_3$)$_2$—CHClCH$_3$	424
HO—CHClCH$_2$Cl (CH$_3$ above)	6.5	HO—CH(CH$_3$)—CCl(CH$_3$)$_2$	633
HO—C(CH$_3$)$_2$CH$_2$Cl	78	HO—C(CH$_3$)$_2$—C(CH$_3$)$_2$Cl	3600

in the case of [20].[41] The nature of the halohydrin-epoxide reaction is most dramatically demonstrated by halohydrins derived from cyclic olefins. Thus, epoxide formation occurs several thousand

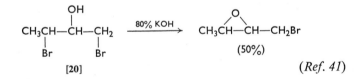

times faster in the diaxial isomer [21] than in the diequatorial isomer [22].[42] Whereas *trans*-halohydrins of the above type cyclize via trans ring closure and Walden inversion at the site of displacement to the *cis*-epoxide, *cis*-halohydrins react only very slowly with alkalies, and the reaction when it does occur gives rise to carbonyl compounds.[43]

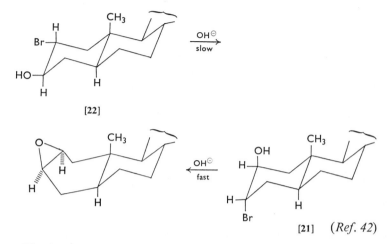

[22]

[21]   (*Ref. 42*)

The best preparative methods for aziridines involve cyclization reactions. The time-honored syntheses consist in the conversion of a β-amino alcohol (available generally from the reaction of epoxides with ammonia or primary amines, see p. 25) to a β-haloamine (Gabriel method[44]) or to a β-amino hydrogen sulfate (Wenker method[45]) followed by treatment with alkali.[46] The Gabriel synthesis fails,

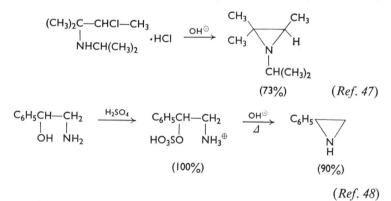

(73%)   (*Ref. 47*)

(100%)   (90%)

(*Ref. 48*)

however, in the preparation of 2,2,3,3-tetraalkylaziridines because of the difficulty of obtaining the necessary chloroamines. A unique preparation of such heterocycles (which, however, appears to fail when less substituted alkenes are used) consists in a three-step sequence involving chloronitrosation of a tetraalkylethylene, reduction of the nitrosochloride, and cyclization with base.[49] A more recent

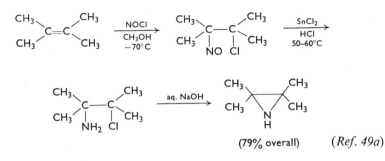

(79% overall)   (*Ref. 49a*)

preparative scheme, which appears to be of general utility, is effective in converting olefins of any degree of substitution to aziridines.[50] The olefin is treated with iodine isocyanate, a reagent which is known to react via an iodonium ion and to give rise to the trans-diaxial β-iodo isocyanate [23]; the latter substance on heating with methanol

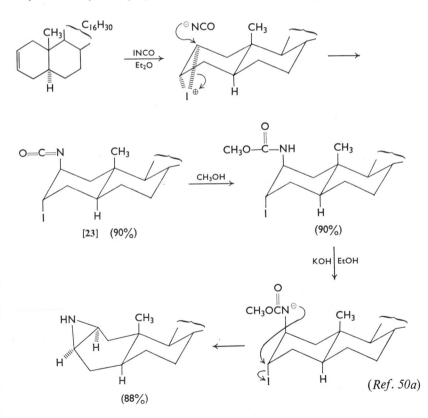

(*Ref. 50a*)

affords the related β-iodocarbamate. Treatment of the β-iodo-carbamate with alcoholic alkali results in aziridine formation in good yield. The kinetics of this cyclization indicate[50c] that ring formation proceeds by rapid abstraction of the carbamate proton followed by the rate-determining ring closure. The intermediate N-carbalkoxy aziridine is rapidly saponified and decarboxylated as it is formed.

The Gabriel ring closure proceeds according to first-order kinetics, in agreement with an intramolecular displacement of the halogen atom by the free amino group.[51] The cyclizations are stereospecific and occur with inversion at the carbon bearing the leaving group.[52]

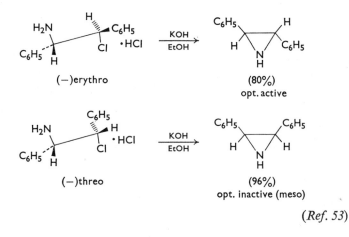

(*Ref. 53*)

Several variants of the Gabriel synthesis are illustrated in the following reactions. The physical and chemical properties of the resulting benzoylaziridines have been summarized.[56]

Stable aziridinium perchlorates have been synthesized from β-chloroethylamines by treatment with silver perchlorate[57] (for further discussion, see p. 35).

A ketoxime arylsulfonate (e.g., [24]), when treated with base followed by acid hydrolysis, is transformed into an α-aminoketone (the Neber rearrangement).[58, 59] The mechanistic course of this rearrangement is believed to involve initial α-proton abstraction by base to give a carbanion, followed by loss of tosylate affording an α,β-unsaturated nitrene (e.g., [26]), which then attacks the double bond to give an azirine (e.g., [27]).[60, 61] The Neber rearrangement, therefore, does not conform to the general mechanistic trends for

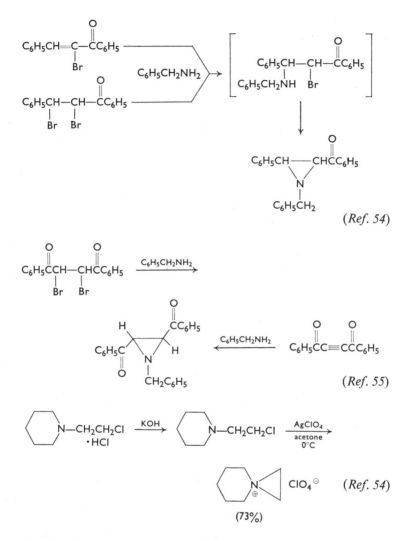

(*Ref. 54*)

(*Ref. 55*)

(*Ref. 54*)

(73%)

cyclization reactions outlined earlier (see p. 10). The above scheme is required by the observation that the configuration of the ketoxime tosylate (syn or anti) has little, if any, influence upon the direction of reaction.[59b, 60] As is illustrated in the cases of [24] and [25], the incipient amino group is inserted exclusively upon that carbon bearing the more acidic hydrogen atom (i.e., the more stable enolate carbanion).[62]

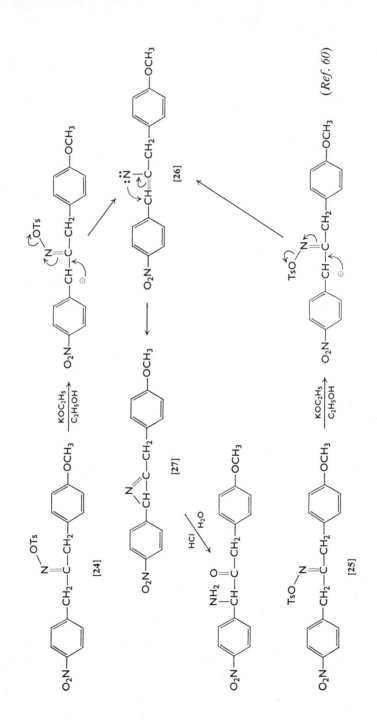

(*Ref. 60*)

From the synthetic point of view, it appears difficult to isolate azirines from the Neber rearrangement; this is also the case in the base-catalyzed rearrangement of N-chloroketimines (e.g., [28]) to

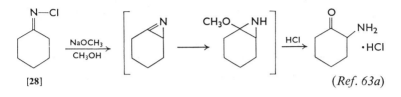

[28]   (*Ref. 63a*)

α-aminoketones.[63]   More recently, however, a modification of these reactions has been introduced in which a methiodide salt of a ketone dimethylhydrazone (e.g., [29] and [30]) is used rather than an oxime tosylate or N-chloroketimine.[64]   Because of the highly activated nature of the leaving group, this reaction can be performed under conditions sufficiently mild to permit isolation of the azirine.[64]

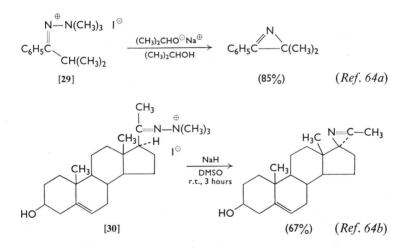

α-Lactams, or aziridinones, can be prepared by the cyclization of N-halo- or α-halo *tert*-butylamides with strong base.[65]   This reaction may be considered formally analogous to the Favorskii reaction.[66, 67] When [31] was prepared in optically active form, it was possible to obtain an optically active aziridinone.[65b]

A variety of cyclization reactions leading to episulfides has been reported, among which may be cited the dehydrohalogenation of

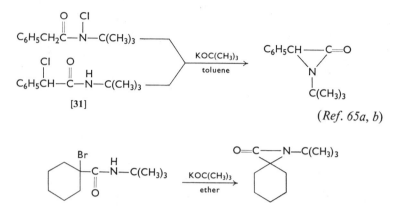

(*Ref. 65a, b*)

(*Ref. 65c*)

2-haloethanethiols and the dehydration of 2-hydroxyethanethiols[68]; however, the most widely used synthesis is the direct conversion of epoxides to episulfides with thiocyanate salts.[69] The illustrated mechanism has been suggested for this transformation, and has

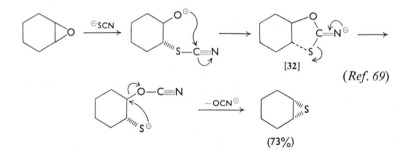

(*Ref. 69*)

(73%)

received strong corroboration from the observation that cyclopentene oxide is unaffected by the customary reaction conditions because of the considerable strain required to form a trans-fused bicyclo[3.3.0] intermediate analogous to [32].[69, 70] Epoxides react with thiourea by a mechanism analogous to the above sequence.[71] Both mechanisms demand that the resultant episulfide possess a configuration opposite to that of the starting epoxide.

In situations where the above reactions fail or give low yields, it has proven advantageous to initially cleave the epoxide ring to an α-hydroxy xanthate, thiocyanate, or thiol acetate.[72, 73] However, in

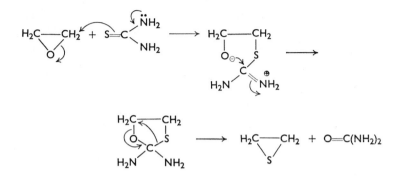

certain cases, such as with [33], direct treatment of the hydroxy thiocyanate with base results in the displacement of the thiocyanate group by the oxide anion in a manner analogous to the reaction of halohydrins and the starting epoxide is recovered. This situation

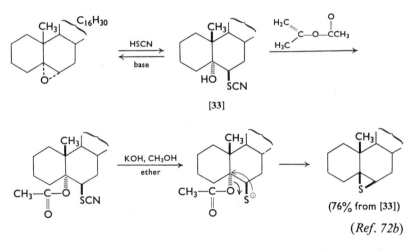

[33]

(76% from [33])

(*Ref. 72b*)

can be easily remedied by first converting the hydroxyl group to its acetate ester; subsequent base treatment results in the kinetically preferred hydrolysis of the thiocyanate moiety to produce the sulfide anion which displaces the acetate ion to furnish the episulfide of inverted configuration.

Condensation Reactions

The condensation of a ketone or aromatic aldehyde with an α-halo ester or ketone[74] in the presence of a strong base (the Darzens reaction) yields an α,β-epoxy carbonyl derivative.[75]　The reaction is kinetically third order, first order in each of the three components.[76] The Darzens reaction proceeds in a stereoselective manner to yield

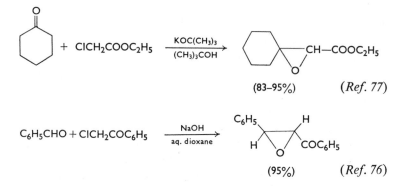

(83–95%)　　　　　(*Ref. 77*)

(95%)　　　　　(*Ref. 76*)

trans-epoxides.　Although the trans-isomers are the kinetically favored products, prolonged exposure of such compounds to alkali may result in epimerization to the *cis*-epoxides.[78]　This stereochemistry has been most recently justified on the basis of stereoelectronic control in the rate-determining collapse of the α-halohydrin anion[79]; thus, in the condensation of benzaldehyde with chloroacetone, the carbonyl group assists in the ring-closure step (e.g., [34]).

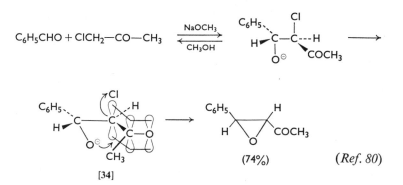

(74%)　　　　　(*Ref. 80*)

[34]

When the resulting epoxide has three substituents, the stereoisomer which results generally possesses the carbonyl function trans to the larger group at the β-carbon atom.　In both of the above situations, the stereoelectronic assistance in the cyclization reaction is sterically unfavorable when the carbonyl function and a large β-substituent are cis to each other.

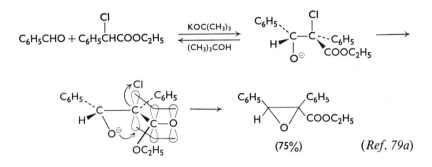

(75%) (*Ref. 79a*)

The reaction of α-haloketones with Grignard reagents and subsequent dehydrohalogenation of the resulting halohydrins with alkali also affords epoxides.[81] The process often, however, gives rise to abnormal rearrangement products.[43, 81b, 83] Furthermore, branched

$$ClCH_2COCH_3 + C_6H_5MgBr \longrightarrow$$

$$ClCH_2{-}\underset{\underset{CH_3}{|}}{\overset{\overset{OH}{|}}{C}}{-}C_6H_5 \xrightarrow{OH^{\ominus}} \underset{\underset{CH_3}{|}}{CH_2{-}\overset{O}{\overset{\triangle}{C}}{-}C_6H_5} \quad (Ref.\ 82)$$

α-haloketones with hindered carbonyl groups do not furnish the desired chlorohydrin, but rather undergo simple halide displacement.[81a] It is evident, therefore, that this approach to the synthesis of 1,1-disubstituted epoxides lacks generality.

Other reactions which proceed by analogous mechanisms are found in the addition of cyanide and alkoxide ions to α-halocarbonyl compounds; several examples are described by the accompanying equations.

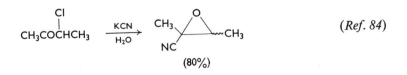

(80%)

(*Ref. 84*)

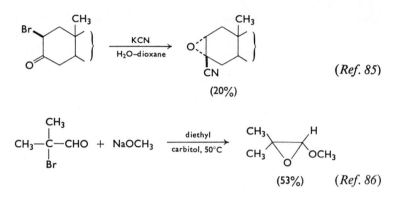

(Ref. 85)

(20%)

(53%)   (Ref. 86)

Finally, the reaction of aromatic aldehydes with phosphorus triamides has been observed to furnish epoxides.[87] The following mechanism has been proposed for the transformation. The presence

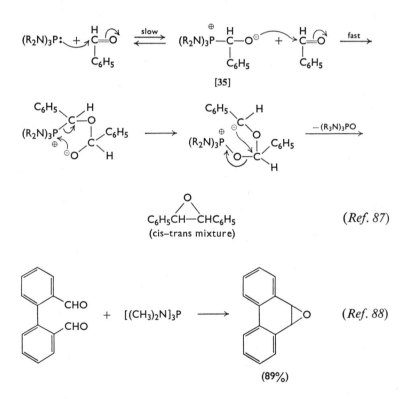

[35]

(Ref. 87)

(cis–trans mixture)

(Ref. 88)

(89%)

of an electronegative group on the aromatic ring enhances epoxide formation, whereas electron-releasing substituents favor instead the formation of intermediate adducts of type [35].[87]

REACTIONS

The monohetero atomic, three-membered rings are extremely susceptible to cleavage reactions because of the favourable release of strain energy involved. For this reason, these substances may be converted to a wide variety of functionalized compounds. With the exceptions to be noted below, aziridines exhibit behavior characteristic of secondary aliphatic amines; such reactions, because they are not peculiar to the three-membered ring, will not be considered here.[89]

Nucleophilic Ring Openings

Ring opening processes initiated by nucleophilic reagents have been shown to proceed with extensive, if not complete, inversion of configuration at the point of attack:

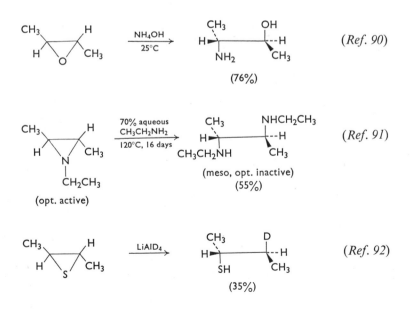

In certain situations, further reactions of the reactive ring-opened intermediates may occur, for example:

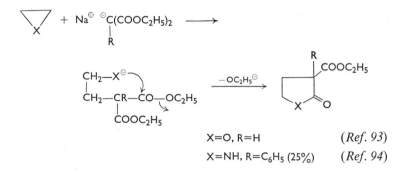

$$X=O, R=H \qquad (Ref.\ 93)$$
$$X=NH, R=C_6H_5\ (25\%) \qquad (Ref.\ 94)$$

When unsymmetrical three-membered rings are involved, ring opening can occur in either of two different directions. Frequently, the nucleophile attacks the less hindered carbon atom preferably with

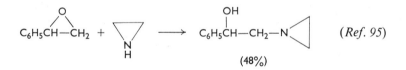

$$(Ref.\ 95)$$

the result that one direction of ring opening is predominant.[7b] However, such reactions are generally difficult to predict because the product ratio can easily be affected by changes in the solvent and in

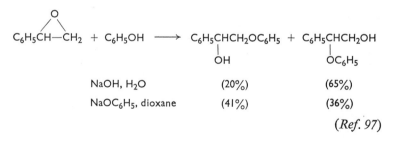

	(20%)	(65%)
NaOH, H₂O		
NaOC₆H₅, dioxane	(41%)	(36%)

$$(Ref.\ 97)$$

the proportion of the reagents.[96] The diverse and often seemingly contradictory facts relating to the opening of these strained rings can be correlated in terms of a "push-pull" mechanism.[98] According to this concept, the major factors involved in such processes are approach

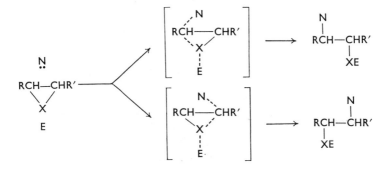

of the nucleophilic reagent (N), the rupture of the C—X bond, and the effect of the electrophilic reagent (E, solvent in nucleophilic displacements or proton in electrophilic reactions). As a result, steric factors are less influential than usual, while sensitivity to factors such as solvent, resonance, and the presence of electron-releasing substituents is substantially increased. In 1,1-diphenylethylene oxide, for example, steric considerations would promote attack at the methylene carbon, but bond breaking is facilitated by resonance stabilization of the incipient carbonium ion and renders attack at the tertiary carbon very feasible.[96] The latter mode of reaction is, as

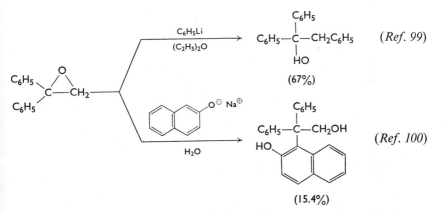

expected, enhanced by solvents of high ionizing power. Of a similar nature, lithium aluminum hydride reduction of unsymmetrical epoxides affords the more highly substituted carbinols, whereas similar reduction in the presence of aluminum halides gives the less highly substituted carbinols.[101]

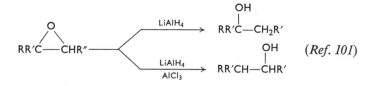

(*Ref. 101*)

Rigid systems (steroids have been most widely studied) containing three-membered hetero rings are attacked by nucleophilic reagents in a remarkable conformationally-specific manner from the axial side to give rise to products arising from trans-diaxial addition.[102]   Such

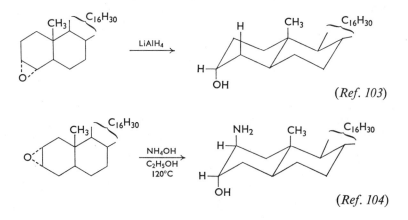

(*Ref. 103*)

(*Ref. 104*)

diaxial cleavages presumably result because they proceed by way of a favorable linear distribution of charge in the transition state.   In systems which are not rigid, and interconversion of chair forms is occurring, prediction of the product by the principle of axial attack is clearly impossible since either point of attachment of the heterocyclic ring may become axial.

A series of interesting and synthetically useful processes is embodied in the conversion of epoxides to cyclopropanes upon reaction with carbalkoxymethylenephosphoranes [36],[105] or with phosphonate [37],[106] phosphinate [38],[107] and phosphine oxide [39] carbanions.[107, 108]   Phosphonate carbanions [37] are more reactive than [36], thus enabling syntheses to be carried out at considerably lower temperatures (85°C instead of 200°C) with the result that higher yields are generally achieved with the former reagents.   The use of nucleophiles of types [36], [37], and [38] is restricted to those derivatives

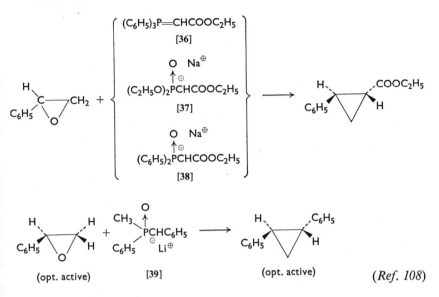

(opt. active) [39] (opt. active) (*Ref. 108*)

which contain a carbanion-stabilizing substituent such as carbethoxy or cyano. The utility of phosphine oxide carbanions [39], where such restrictions are not present, is immediately apparent. Of particular importance in these reactions is the finding that optically active epoxides yield optically active cyclopropane derivatives; furthermore, as illustrated below, the overall reaction proceeds

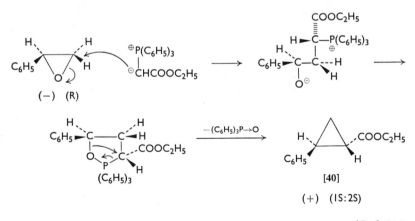

[40]

(+) (1S:2S)

(*Ref. 110*)

predominantly with inversion of configuration.[109, 110] The mechanism of this group of reactions which involve the same fundamental processes (although, some differences in transient electronic distributions undoubtedly exist) involves initial S_N2 attack at the less hindered epoxide carbon by the nucleophilic carbanion to cause ring cleavage. The resulting zwitterion probably undergoes ring closure to a five-membered, phosphorus-containing ring which subsequently collapses (in one or more steps) to give the observed product. The formation of cyclopropanes is not stereospecific, but trans isomers do predominate and, in the case of [40], the trans isomer is the only cyclopropane observed.

The reaction of Grignard reagents with epoxides has been employed extensively as a route to primary alcohols containing two additional carbon atoms[111]; however, rearrangements under these conditions are very commonly observed.[7c] Such rearrangements have been found to result because of the halide component of the Grignard reagent

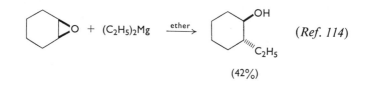

$$CH_3CH_2MgBr \xrightarrow{\text{ether}} (CH_3)_3C-\overset{\overset{\displaystyle OH}{|}}{\underset{\underset{\displaystyle CH_3}{|}}{C}}-CH_2CH_3 \qquad (Ref.\ 112)$$

(38%)

which isomerizes (see p. 41) the epoxide to an aldehyde or ketone which subsequently reacts normally with the Grignard reagent. Replacement of the Grignard reagent with a dialkylmagnesium usually eliminates such rearrangements when they are prone to occur.[113]

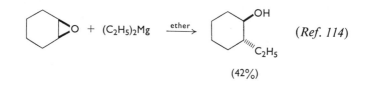

$+ (C_2H_5)_2Mg \xrightarrow{\text{ether}}$ ... OH ... C₂H₅ $\qquad (Ref.\ 114)$

(42%)

Electrophilic Ring Openings

Ring opening reactions of monohetero atomic, three-membered rings are greatly accelerated in acidic media as exemplified by the observations that hydrobromic acid adds readily to ethylene oxide at

−78°C to yield ethylene bromohydrin[115] and that ethyleneimine and ethylene sulfide polymerize readily, and sometimes explosively, in the presence of acids under noncontrolled conditions. From the stereochemical point of view, these processes generally occur stereospecifically with inversion of configuration at the point of attack Such evidence reflects the fact that fully developed carbonium ions are customarily not generated in such electrophilic processes,[116] and agrees with a mechanistic interpretation based on the "push-pull" theory described earlier (see p. 26).

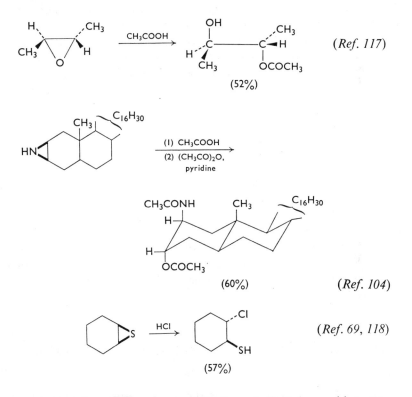

(*Ref. 117*)

(52%)

(*Ref. 104*)

(60%)

(*Ref. 69, 118*)

(57%)

In reactions with unsymmetrically substituted epoxides, two products are possible and the mode of ring cleavage is again strongly controlled by such factors as solvent and electron distribution in the substrate (see p. 27). In the following example, the product ratio is markedly altered in favor of the more highly substituted carbon atom on passing from nonpolar ether to polar water as the reaction medium:

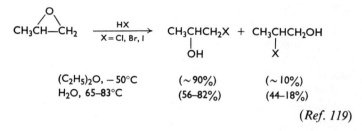

$$(C_2H_5)_2O, -50°C \qquad (\sim 90\%) \qquad (\sim 10\%)$$
$$H_2O, 65-83°C \qquad (56-82\%) \qquad (44-18\%)$$

(Ref. 119)

Substituents exert a powerful effect on the course of ring opening as illustrated by the cleavage of styrene oxide with hydrogen iodide in the direction of the incipient benzylic carbonium ion. In contrast, hydrochloric acid adds to *o*-nitrostyrene oxide in the opposite sense because of the powerful electron-withdrawing capability of the nitro group, which raises the activation energy of the transition state in

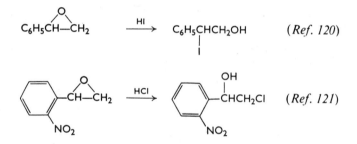

which the benzylic carbon atom exhibits partial positive character above that for reaction at the primary carbon atom. A similar phenomenon has been observed in the aziridine series as demonstrated by the following examples:

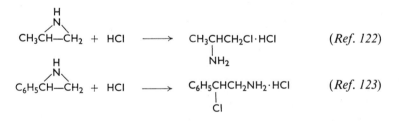

The principle of axial attack in ring-opening processes is also operative under electrophilic conditions (see also aziridine example, p. 31).

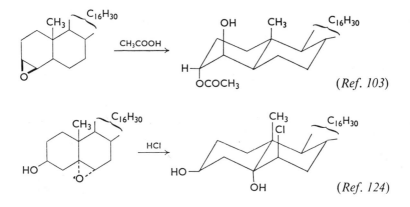

(Ref. 103)

(Ref. 124)

It may be readily seen that epoxides, aziridines, and episulfides are cleaved by hydrohalogen acids to halohydrins, haloethylamines, or haloethylmercaptans, respectively, from which the respective heterocycles can be resynthesized on treatment with base. This stereospecificity has been utilized advantageously in the case of epoxides, to prepare glycols which are isomeric with those glycols which result from treatment of olefins with such reagents as potassium permanganate (which give *cis* addition). Such an application is shown below.

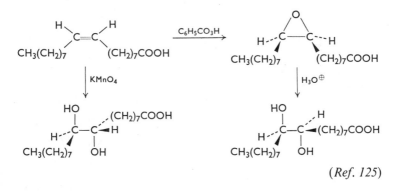

(Ref. 125)

The reaction of epoxides and episulfides with acid chlorides is believed to proceed by electrophilic attack of the latter reagent at the hetero atom to produce an intermediate onium salt which, because of its extremely high reactivity, is easily and rapidly attacked by the anion at the carbon atom with rupture of the ring. The stereochemical course of such reactions follows the usual pattern of trans

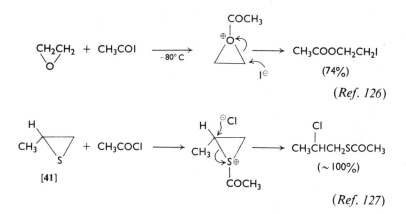

(74%)

(*Ref. 126*)

(~100%)

(*Ref. 127*)

addition.[69] It is interesting to note that the episulfide [41] reacts with acetic anhydride in pyridine to open in the direction opposite to

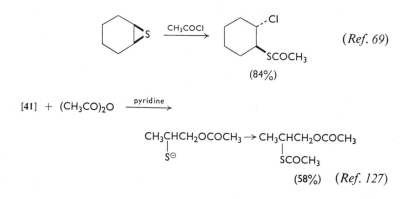

(84%)

(*Ref. 69*)

(58%) (*Ref. 127*)

that encountered with acetyl chloride. It appears that, in contrast to the latter situation in which the onium salt is probably directly involved and therefore the transition state favoring attack at the more highly substituted carbon atom is preferred, the reaction in pyridine proceeds by direct attack of acetate ion on the free episulfide and steric hindrance becomes the important criterion.

Other Ring Opening Processes

Protonated aziridines or quaternary aziridinium salts are exceptionally reactive toward nucleophiles, and attempts to prepare them generally result in ring cleavage (see [42], for example). Generally, however, isolation of such compounds has proven feasible when anions of low nucleophilicity such as picrylsulfonate,[128] perchlorate,[30] fluoroborate,[30] and *p*-toluene sulfonate[129] are employed, although a few examples of stable monomeric aziridine methiodides have been cited.[130]

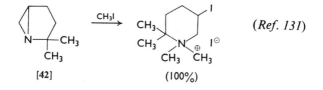

[42]   (100%)   (*Ref. 131*)

The reverse process, namely the cyclization of a β-haloethylamine to an aziridinium cation, has been found by kinetic methods to occur during the solvolysis of such amines.[132] In addition, other reactions of these substances such as the rearrangements shown below can only be explained as proceeding through aziridinium intermediates.

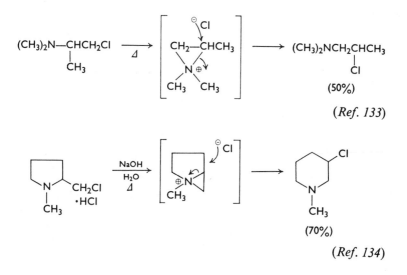

(*Ref. 133*)

(*Ref. 134*)

Furthermore, the mechanism of biological action of nitrogen mustards is believed to involve the alkylation of functional groups of metabolic importance by intermediate aziridinium salts.[135] In fact, stable aziridinium perchlorates can be readily isolated from the reaction of β-chloroethylamines with silver perchlorate in cold acetone (see p. 17).[57, 136]

The reaction of aziridinium salts with various nucleophilic reagents results as expected in the formation of ring cleavage products. Several examples are given below.

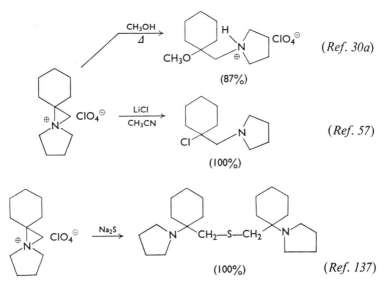

(*Ref. 30a*)

(87%)

(*Ref. 57*)

(100%)

(*Ref. 137*)

Epoxides and aziridines condense readily with carbonyl compounds to give dioxolanes [43] and oxazolidines [44], respectively.[138, 139] By analogy, aziridinium salts likewise condense with aldehydes, ketones, and nitriles at moderate temperatures with expansion of the aziridinium ring.[30c, d] The reactions of aziridinium salts can be generally described according to the nucleophilicity of the attacking reagent. If the attacking species is very nucleophilic, the product will be that in which cleavage of the less substituted C—N bond of the three-membered ring occurs. If the attacking species is a relatively poor nucleophile, the reaction can be viewed as an ionization with cleavage of the three-membered ring to yield the most stable carbonium ion (e.g., [45]) which then reacts with the poor nucleophile.

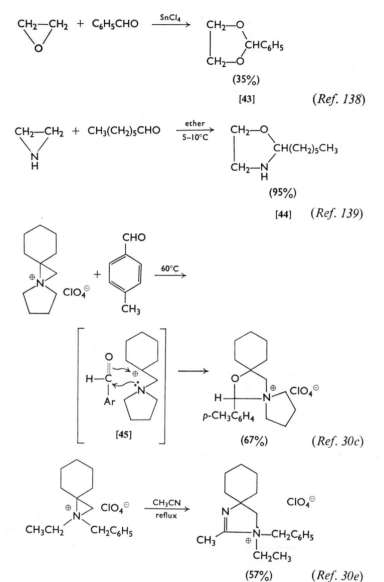

(35%)

[43]   (*Ref. 138*)

(95%)

[44]   (*Ref. 139*)

[45]

(67%)   (*Ref. 30c*)

(57%)   (*Ref. 30e*)

Ring cleavages have also been observed during the attempted alkylation of episulfides with methyl iodide; olefins generally result (see p. 40 for a further discussion of this reaction). Stable episulfonium salts can be isolated, however, by again resorting to anions of low nucleophilicity such as the 2,4,6-trinitrobenzenesulfonate anion.[141] Such salts are rapidly cleaved by nucleophilic reagents with net trans addition.[142]

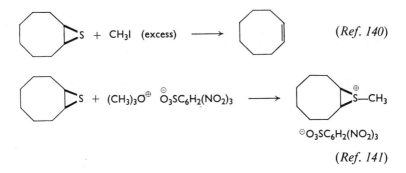

(*Ref. 140*)

(*Ref. 141*)

Reactions Involving Extrusion of the Hetero Atom

Epoxides are smoothly deoxygenated by tertiary phosphines at elevated temperatures (150–200°C) and give rise to olefins.[143]. Pre-

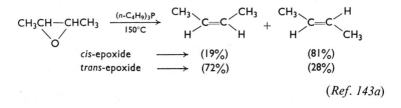

(*Ref. 143a*)

sumably, the reaction occurs by nucleophilic attack of the tertiary phosphine at an epoxide carbon atom, thus affording a betaine of type [46] which, after rotation of the central carbon-carbon bond by 180°, collapses with the liberation of *tert*-phosphine oxide to yield as the predominant product an olefin of configuration opposite to that of the starting epoxide.   The minor olefinic product probably arises because of the propensity of ylids to form betaines reversibly[144]; thus, decomposition of [46] to an ylide and an aldehyde followed by a Wittig-type recombination of these two moieties would be expected to lead to a certain amount of *cis*-olefin formation.[145]   Control experiments showed that isomerization of the 2-butenes did not occur under the reaction conditions.[143a]

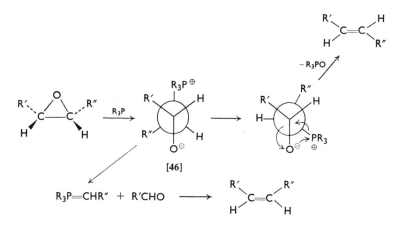

[46]

$R_3P{=}CHR'' + R'CHO \longrightarrow$

In contrast, the treatment of episulfides with tertiary phosphines[143a, 146b] or phosphites[146a, c, d] leads to greater than 97% stereospecific removal of sulfur from the three-membered ring with the formation of olefins possessing the original configuration of the

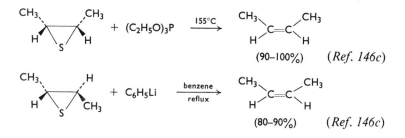

(90–100%)   (Ref. 146c)

(80–90%)   (Ref. 146c)

heterocycle. Similar stereospecificity was obtained with phenyllithium.[146c, 147] The reaction of tertiary phosphines with episulfides is bimolecular, first order in each reactant, and the rate is unaffected by solvents of varying dielectric constant, thus indicating that charge separation is of little importance in the transition state of the rate-controlling step. These results rule out a mechanism such as that which prevails in the case of epoxides, but favor a concerted process involving nucleophilic attack by phosphorus on sulfur as pictured in [47]. The organolithium desulfurization reaction has been formulated as proceeding through [48],[147] but because the geometry of the starting heterocycle is maintained, this postulated intermediate must have a very brief lifetime, if it exists at all.

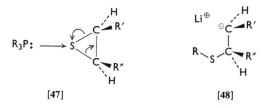

[47]   [48]

It has already been mentioned (p. 37) that the reaction of episulfides with methyl iodide results in the formation of olefins. Of
intrinsic interest is the fact that this reaction proceeds with greater
than 97% stereoselectivity.[140] The principal route for this transformation involves the initial formation of an episulfonium salt, and
is illustrated in the accompanying equations. Firm evidence for this

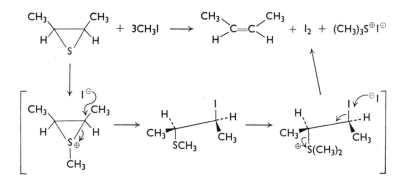

mechanistic pathway has been obtained by utilizing methyl bromide
as the alkylating agent which permits the isolation of the β-bromo-
sulfide and β-bromosulfonium bromide; these latter substances can in
turn be converted to olefin when treated with iodide ion or iodine
under the original reaction conditions.[148]
    The reaction of aziridines with nitrosating agents such as nitrosyl
chloride or methyl nitrite results in the formation of olefins with
greater than 99% stereoselective deamination.[149, 150] Such trans-

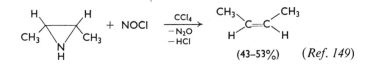

(43–53%)   (*Ref. 149*)

formations proceed via N-nitrosoaziridine intermediates which are isolable at temperatures below −20°C, but which decompose to the observed products at higher temperatures.

Rearrangements

Although certain simple epoxides are known to undergo thermal isomerization to carbonyl compounds, epoxide rearrangements are, in general, most readily and conveniently effected with such acid catalysts as aqueous mineral acid, boron trifluoride etherate in benzene, or anhydrous magnesium bromide in benzene or ether.[7] These conversions are of special interest since they provide a simple means of converting olefins to carbonyl compounds. Which carbonyl-containing product is formed from a particular epoxide is dependent

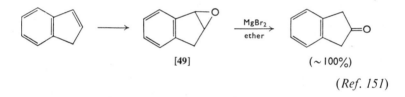

[49]   (∼100%)

(*Ref. 151*)

upon the ease of cleavage of one or the other of the carbon-oxygen bonds, and on the relative migratory aptitudes of the different substituent groups. For example, in indene oxide [49] rupture of the C—O bond which leads to an incipient benzylic carbonium ion is to be preferred and therefore, 2-indanone results.[152] In fact, monoaryl-substituted epoxides invariably rearrange to give non-conjugated ketones. The relative migratory aptitudes of groups appears generally to be in the order of aryl>acyl>H>ethyl>methyl (note that hydride shifts are favored by a considerable margin over migration of alkyl groups). In certain cases, the rearrangement may be accompanied by ring expansion or contraction.

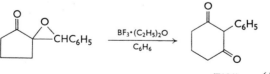

(71%)   (*Ref. 153*)

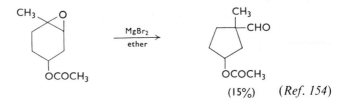

(15%)   (*Ref. 154*)

The rearrangement of epoxides to ketones under the influence of Lewis acids has been shown to be stereospecific.[155] For example, the steroidal epoxide [50] gives only the less stable 5β,6-ketone on treatment with boron trifluoride etherate in benzene.

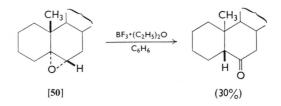

[50]   (30%)

Strong bases may also effect the rearrangement of certain epoxides (bases must not be those which will preferentially rupture the ring by nucleophilic attack at an epoxide carbon atom), and the products frequently differ from those isolated under acidic conditions, as

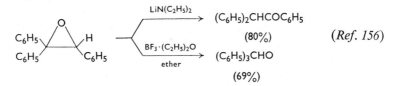

illustrated below. The course of such base-catalysed isomerizations may be depicted as follows:

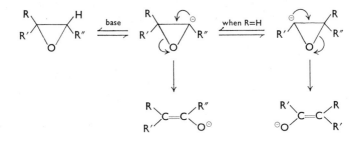

N-Acyl derivatives of ethyleneimine are readily converted upon distillation to 2-substituted-2-oxazolines (e.g., [51]). The rearrange-

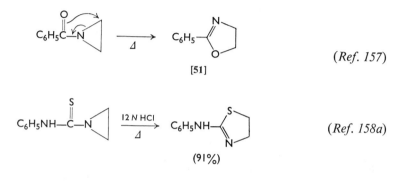

(Ref. 157)

[51]

(Ref. 158a)

(91%)

ment occurs by intramolecular attack of the carbonyl oxygen at a ring carbon to cause rupture of the system. The driving force for this process is found in the relief of strain which the opening of the three-membered ring provides. Similar rearrangements occur under the influence of acid catalysts.[158] Pyrolysis of N-acyl derivatives of homologous aziridines, in contrast, results in isomerization to N-allyl amides.[159] Sucn rearrangements proceed via transition states in which intramolecular proton transfer from a side chain carbon to oxygen occurs concomitantly with cleavage of the three-membered hetero ring (as depicted), and involve stereospecific cis-elimination (see [52]) as is observed in the Chugaev reaction and the Cope amine oxide pyrolysis.

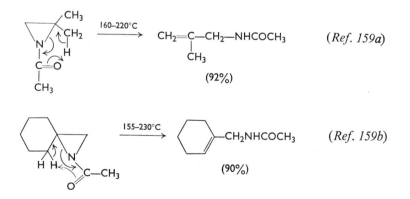

$CH_2=C-CH_2-NHCOCH_3$
$\quad\quad\;\; |$
$\quad\quad\; CH_3$

(92%)

(Ref. 159a)

—$CH_2NHCOCH_3$

(90%)

(Ref. 159b)

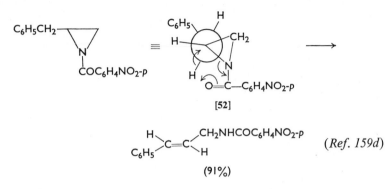

[52]

(*Ref. 159d*)

(91%)

Iodide ion (and thiocyanate ion) is an effective catalyst for the isomerization of aziridine derivatives.[160] Such rearrangements are envisioned as proceeding by nucleophilic attack on the least substituted aziridinyl carbon atom by iodide ion to give an iodoethyl

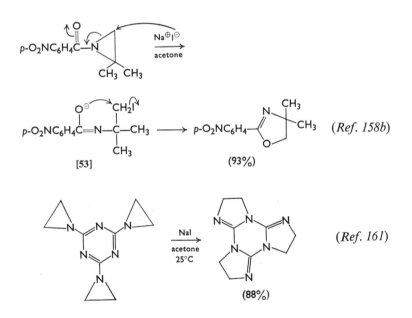

[53]   (93%)   (*Ref. 158b*)

(*Ref. 161*)

(88%)

intermediate such as [53] which is converted to product in the manner shown. When an intermediate such as [53] is difficult to form, dimerization generally occurs.

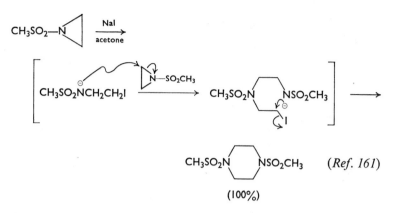

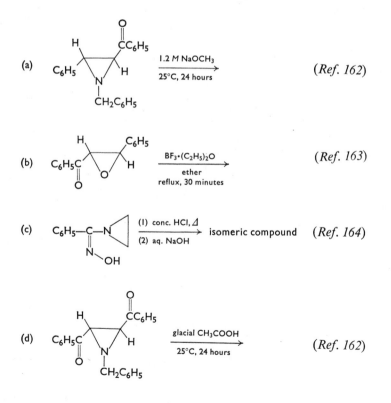

CH_3SO_2N⎯⎯⎯NSO_2CH_3 (*Ref. 161*)

(100%)

Exercises

1. Predict the major product of the following reactions:

(a) $\xrightarrow[\text{25°C, 24 hours}]{\text{1.2 M NaOCH}_3}$ (*Ref. 162*)

(b) $\xrightarrow[\substack{\text{ether}\\\text{reflux, 30 minutes}}]{\text{BF}_3 \cdot \text{(C}_2\text{H}_5)_2\text{O}}$ (*Ref. 163*)

(c) C_6H_5-C-N $\xrightarrow[\text{(2) aq. NaOH}]{\text{(1) conc. HCl, }\Delta}$ isomeric compound   (*Ref. 164*)

(d) $\xrightarrow[\text{25°C, 24 hours}]{\text{glacial CH}_3\text{COOH}}$ (*Ref. 162*) (e)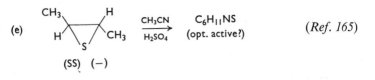

$$\xrightarrow[\text{H}_2\text{SO}_4]{\text{CH}_3\text{CN}} \quad \text{C}_6\text{H}_{11}\text{NS} \quad \text{(opt. active?)} \qquad (Ref.\ 165)$$

(f)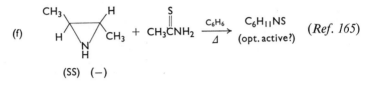

$$+ \text{CH}_3\overset{\text{S}}{\overset{\|}{\text{C}}}\text{NH}_2 \xrightarrow[\Delta]{\text{C}_6\text{H}_6} \quad \text{C}_6\text{H}_{11}\text{NS} \quad \text{(opt. active?)} \qquad (Ref.\ 165)$$

(g)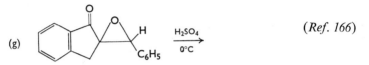

$$\xrightarrow[0°\text{C}]{\text{H}_2\text{SO}_4} \qquad\qquad (Ref.\ 166)$$

(h)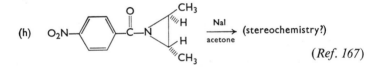

$$\xrightarrow[\text{acetone}]{\text{NaI}} \quad \text{(stereochemistry?)} \qquad (Ref.\ 167)$$

(i) $\quad \text{ClCH}_2\text{SO}_2\text{Cl} + \text{CH}_2\text{N}_2 \xrightarrow[\text{ether, } -10°\text{C}]{(\text{C}_2\text{H}_5)_3\text{N}}$ $\qquad (Ref.\ 168)$

(j) $\quad \text{C}_6\text{H}_5\text{CH}=\text{N}-\text{N}=\text{CHC}_6\text{H}_5 + (\text{CH}_3)_2\overset{\oplus}{\text{S}}\text{CH}_2^{\ominus} \xrightarrow{(\text{CH}_3)_2\text{S}=\text{O}}$

$$\text{(1 equiv.)} \qquad (Ref.\ 169)$$

(k) $\quad$ $\xrightarrow[10-15°\text{C}]{48\%\ \text{HBr}}$ $\qquad (Ref.\ 170)$

(l) $\quad \text{C}_6\text{H}_5\text{C}\equiv\text{N} + $ ⬡ $\text{BF}_4^{\ominus} \xrightarrow{100°\text{C}}$

$$(Ref.\ 171)$$

(m) $\quad \text{C}_6\text{H}_5\text{CHBr}-\text{SO}_2-\text{CHBrC}_6\text{H}_5 + (\text{C}_2\text{H}_5)_3\text{N} \xrightarrow{\text{CH}_2\text{Cl}_2} \qquad (Ref.\ 172)$

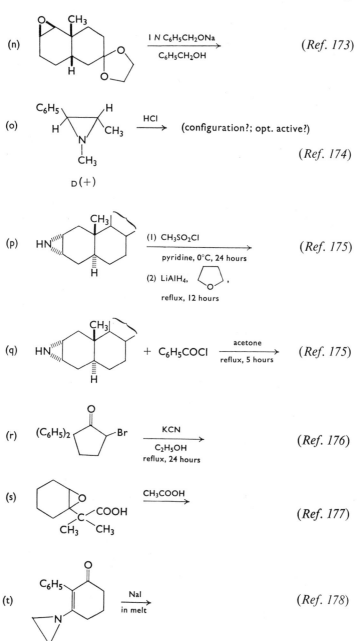

(n) $\xrightarrow{\substack{1\ N\ C_6H_5CH_2ONa \\ C_6H_5CH_2OH}}$ (*Ref. 173*)

(o) $\xrightarrow{HCl}$ (configuration?; opt. active?)

(*Ref. 174*)

D(+)

(p) $\xrightarrow{\substack{(1)\ CH_3SO_2Cl \\ \text{pyridine, 0°C, 24 hours} \\ (2)\ LiAlH_4,\ \text{reflux, 12 hours}}}$ (*Ref. 175*)

(q) $+\ C_6H_5COCl\ \xrightarrow{\substack{\text{acetone} \\ \text{reflux, 5 hours}}}$ (*Ref. 175*)

(r) $(C_6H_5)_2$ ...Br $\xrightarrow{\substack{KCN \\ C_2H_5OH \\ \text{reflux, 24 hours}}}$ (*Ref. 176*)

(s) $\xrightarrow{CH_3COOH}$ (*Ref. 177*)

(t) $\xrightarrow{\substack{NaI \\ \text{in melt}}}$ (*Ref. 178*)

(u) 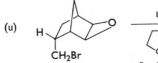 $\xrightarrow[\text{reflux, 24 hours}]{\text{Li}}$ (*Ref. 179*)

(v) 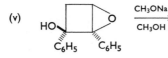 $\xrightarrow[\text{CH}_3\text{OH}]{\text{CH}_3\text{ONa}}$ (*Ref. 180*)

(w) 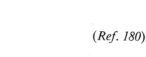 $\xrightarrow[\text{H}_2\text{O}]{\text{HCl}}$ $C_{16}H_{12}O$ (*Ref. 180*)

(x) 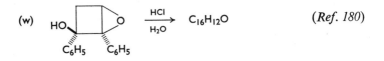 $\xrightarrow[\text{reflux, 2 hours}]{\text{CH}_3\text{OH}}$ (*Ref. 181*)

(y) 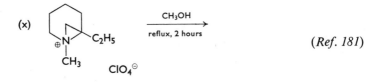 $\xrightarrow[\text{10–20 hours}]{\text{reflux}}$ (*Ref. 182*)

(z) 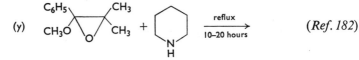 $+ \text{CH}_3\text{OOCC}\equiv\text{CCOOCH}_3$ $\xrightarrow[\text{reflux, 11 hours}]{\text{toluene}}$ (*Ref. 183*)

(a′) 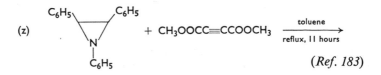 $+ \text{CH}_2(\text{COOC}_2\text{H}_5)_2$ $\xrightarrow[\substack{\text{C}_2\text{H}_5\text{OH} \\ 70°\text{C, 3 hours}}]{\text{NaOC}_2\text{H}_5}$ (*Ref. 184*)

(b′) 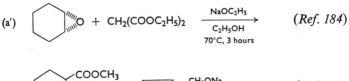 $+$  $\xrightarrow[\text{CH}_3\text{OH}]{\text{CH}_3\text{ONa}}$ (*Ref. 185*)

2. Suggest a reasonable mechanism for each of the following transformations:

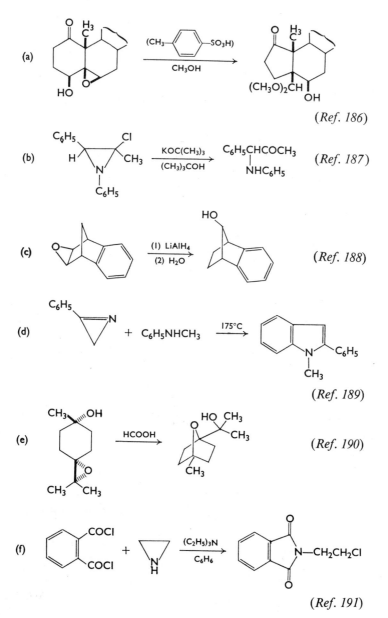

(a)   (*Ref. 186*)

(b)   (*Ref. 187*)

(c)   (*Ref. 188*)

(d)   (*Ref. 189*)

(e)   (*Ref. 190*)

(f)   (*Ref. 191*)

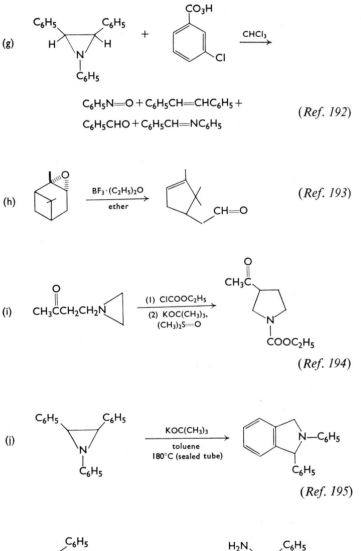

(g)

$$C_6H_5N{=}O + C_6H_5CH{=}CHC_6H_5 +$$
$$C_6H_5CHO + C_6H_5CH{=}NC_6H_5$$

(*Ref. 192*)

(h) (*Ref. 193*)

(i) (*Ref. 194*)

(j) (*Ref. 195*)

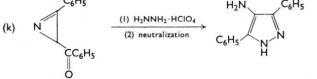

(k) (*Ref. 196*)

3. Explain each of the following results:

(a) Reaction (1) proceeds with first-order dependence on the organic substrate and zero-order dependence on alkali, while reaction (2) is first-order in each component:

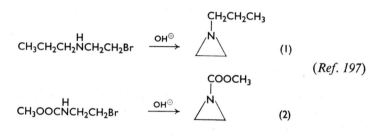

(1)

(Ref. 197)

(2)

(b) Epoxyketone [I] upon irradiation or heating is converted to an isomeric red compound.   When either source of energy is removed, the colorless [I] is reformed.   What is the structure of the red isomer?

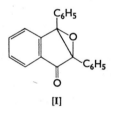

(Ref. 198)

[I]

(c) Ring cleavage of epoxyketone [II] proceeds with *retention* of configuration instead of the usual inversion of configuration.

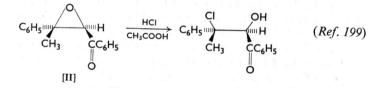

(Ref. 199)

[III]

(d) Treatment of [III] with excess *m*-chloroperbenzoic acid in methylene chloride results in the uptake of *two* atoms of oxygen to give [IV] ($\nu_{max}^{CCl_4}$ 1754 and 1709 cm^{-1}).   In base, [IV] undergoes a facile rearrangement to [V].   What is the structure of [IV], and depict the mechanism by which it is transformed to [V].

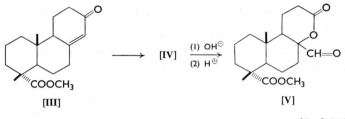

[III] → [IV] $\xrightarrow[(2)\ H^{\oplus}]{(1)\ OH^{\ominus}}$ [V]

(*Ref. 200*)

References and Notes

(1) The reader should satisfy himself that inversion in configuration of the nitrogen atom in [1a] followed by rotation of the resulting structure by 180° gives [1b].

(2) A. T. Bottini and J. D. Roberts, *J. Am. Chem. Soc.*, **78**, 5126 (1956); *ibid.*, **80**, 5203 (1958); A. Loewenstein, J. F. Neumer, and J. D. Roberts, *ibid.*, **82**, 3599 (1960); A. T. Bottini, R. L. VanEtten, and A. J. Davidson, *ibid.*, **87**, 755 (1965).

(3) A similar examination of the n.m.r. spectra of azetidine, pyrrolidine, piperidine, and morpholine derivatives showed that inversion of nitrogen configuration in these larger rings was too rapid for measurement even at −77°C.

(4) (a) D. Swern, *Chem. Revs.*, **45**, 1 (1949); (b) D. Swern, *Org. Reactions*, **7**, 378 (1953); (c) H. O. House, *Modern Synthetic Reactions*, W. A. Benjamin, Inc., New York, 1965, Chapter 5.

(5) N. N. Schwartz and J. H. Blumbergs, *J. Org. Chem.*, **29**, 1976 (1964).

(6) The F.M.C. Corp., New York, N.Y.

(7) (a) A. Rosowsky in A. Weissberger (ed.), *The Chemistry of Heterocyclic Compounds*, Vol. 19, Part I, Interscience, New York, 1964, Chapter 1; (b) R. E. Parker and N. S. Isaac, *Chem. Revs.*, **59**, 737 (1959); (c) S. Winstein and R. B. Henderson in R. C. Elderfield (ed.), *Heterocyclic Compounds*, Vol. 1, Wiley, New York, 1950, Chapter 1.

(8) (a) P. D. Bartlett, *Rec. Chem. Progr.* (*Kresge-Hooker Sci. Lib.*), **11**, 51 (1950); (b) B. M. Lynch and K. H. Pausacker, *J. Chem. Soc.*, **1955**, 1525.

(9) D. Swern, *J. Am. Chem. Soc.*, **69**, 1692 (1947).

(10) W. Hückel and V. Wörffel, *Chem. Ber.*, **88**, 338 (1955).

(11) A. C. Cope, S. W. Fenton, and C. F. Spencer, *J. Am. Chem. Soc.*, **74**, 5884 (1952); A. C. Cope, A. Fournier, Jr., and H. E. Simmonds, Jr., *ibid.*, **79**, 3905 (1957).

(12) (a) H. B. Henbest and R. A. L. Wilson, *J. Chem. Soc.*, **1957**, 1958; (b) H. B. Henbest, *Proc. Chem. Soc.*, **1963**, 159; (c) B. Rickborn and S. Y. Lwo, *J. Org. Chem.*, **30**, 2212 (1965).

(13) J. Reese, *Chem. Ber.*, **75**, 384 (1942).

(14) C. A. Bunton and G. J. Minkoff, *J. Chem. Soc.*, **1949**, 665.

(15) H. E. Zimmerman, L. Singer, and B. S. Thyagarajan, *J. Am. Chem. Soc.*, **81**, 108 (1959); H. O. House and R. S. Ro, *ibid.*, **80**, 2428 (1958).

(16) G. B. Payne and P. H. Williams, *J. Org. Chem.*, **26**, 651 (1961); G. B. Payne, P. H. Deming, and P. H. Williams, *ibid.*, **26**, 659 (1961); G. B. Payne, *ibid.*, **26**, 663, 668 (1961); G. B. Payne, *Tetrahedron*, **18**, 763 (1962); Y. Ogata and Y. Sawaki, *ibid.*, **20**, 2065 (1964).

(17) N. C. Yang and R. A. Finnegan, *J. Am. Chem. Soc.*, **80**, 5845 (1958).

(18) W. Lwowski and T. W. Mattingly, Jr., *ibid.*, **87**, 1947 (1965); W. Lwowski and T. J. Maricich, *ibid.*, **86**, 3164 (1964); K. Hafner and C. König, *Angew. Chem.*, **75**, 89 (1963) and references cited therein.

(19) R. Huisgen, *Angew. Chem. Intern. Ed.*, **2**, 565, 633 (1963).

(20) P. Scheiner, *J. Org. Chem.*, **30**, 7 (1965).

(21) (a) E. J. Corey and M. Chaykovsky, *J. Am. Chem. Soc.*, **87**, 1345, 1353 (1965) and references cited therein; (b) V. Franzen and H. E. Driessen, *Tetrahedron Letters*, 661 (1962).

(22) C. E. Cook, R. C. Corley, and M. E. Wall, *ibid.*, 891 (1965).

(23) P. Pöhls, Inaug. diss. Univ. Marburg, Germany, 1934.

(24) B. Eistert in *Newer Methods of Preparative Organic Chemistry*, Interscience, New York, 1948, pp. 513–570; C. D. Gutsche, *Org. Reactions*, **8**, 364 (1954).

(25) A. Mustafa, *J. Chem. Soc.*, **1949**, 234; G. D. Buckley, *ibid.*, **1954**, 1850; see, however, A. L. Logothetis, *J. Org. Chem.*, **29**, 3049 (1964) where the reaction of diazomethane with fluoro-substituted imines has been found to occur readily and give rise to aziridines.

(26) (a) H. Staudinger and J. Siegwart, *Helv. Chim. Acta*, **3**, 833 (1920); (b) the direct interaction of diazo compounds with sulfur also yields episulfides: N. Latif and I. Fathy, *J. Org. Chem.*, **27**, 1633 (1962); N. Latif, I. Fathy, and B. Haggag, *Tetrahedron Letters*, 1155 (1965). It is likely that such condensations occur via the intermediacy of a thioketone.

(27) L. A. Paquette, *J. Org. Chem.*, **29**, 2851 (1964) and references cited therein.

(28) G. Opitz and K. Fischer, *Angew. Chem.*, **77**, 41 (1965).

(29) (a) H. Staudinger and F. Pfenninger, *Chem. Ber.*, **49**, 1941 (1916); (b) L. v. Vargha and E. Kovacs, *ibid.*, **75**, 794 (1942); (c) G. Hesse, E. Reichold, and S. Majmudar, *ibid.*, **90**, 2106 (1957); (d) G. Hesse and S. Majmudar, *ibid.*, **93**, 1129 (1960); (e) N. P. Neureiter and F. G. Bordwell, *J. Am. Chem. Soc.*, **85**, 1209 (1963).

(30) (a) N. J. Leonard and K. Jann, *ibid.*, **82**, 6418 (1960); **84**, 4806 (1962); (b) N. J. Leonard, K. Jann, J. V. Paukstelis, and C. K. Steinhardt, *J. Org. Chem.*, **28**, 1499 (1963); (c) N. J. Leonard, E. F. Kiefer, and L. E. Brady, *ibid.*, **28**, 2850 (1963); (d) N. J. Leonard, J. V. Paukstelis, and L. E.

Brady, *ibid.*, **29**, 3383 (1964); (e) N. J. Leonard and L. E. Brady, *ibid.*, **30**, 817 (1965); (f) N. J. Leonard, *Rec. Chem. Progr.* (*Kresge-Hooker Sci. Lib.*), **26**, 211 (1965).

(31) The epoxidation of olefins is sometimes preferred; however, this reaction and the cyclodehydrohalogenation of ethylene halohydrins constitute the majority of epoxide syntheses.

(32) For a summary of various kinetic investigations, see ref. 7a, p. 94.

(33) S. Winstein and H. J. Lucas, *J. Am. Chem. Soc.*, **61**, 2845 (1939).

(34) The reagents which have emerged as those of choice for generating hypohalous acids *in situ* are the N-haloacetamides and N-halosuccinimides in the presence of aqueous perchloric acid, see R. Filler, *Chem. Revs.*, **63**, 21 (1963).

(35) (a) S. Winstein and L. Goodman, *J. Am. Chem. Soc.*, **76**, 4368, 4373 (1954) and references cited therein; (b) Unusual effects have, however, been noted: J. G. Traynham and O. S. Pascual, *ibid.*, **79**, 2341 (1957); J. G. Traynham and O. S. Pascual, *Tetrahedron*, **7**, 165 (1959).

(36) P. D. Bartlett and R. H. Rosenwald, *J. Am. Chem. Soc.*, **56**, 1990 (1934); P. D. Bartlett, *ibid.*, **57**, 224 (1935).

(37) P. D. Bartlett and R. V. White, *ibid.*, **56**, 2785 (1934); S. Winstein and R. E. Buckles, *ibid.*, **64**, 2780, 2787, 2791, 2796 (1942); S. Winstein and L. L. Ingraham, *ibid.*, **74**, 1160 (1952); S. Winstein and H. J. Lucas, *ibid.*, **61**, 1576, 2845 (1939); R. A. Raphael, *J. Chem. Soc.*, **1952**, 401.

(38) J. Fried and E. F. Sabo, *J. Am. Chem. Soc.*, **79**, 1130 (1957).

(39) E. L. Eliel, N. L. Allinger, S. J. Angyal, and G. A. Morrison, *Conformational Analysis*, Interscience, New York, 1965, p. 284.

(40) H. Nilsson and L. Smith, *Z. Physik. Chem.*, **166A**, 136 (1933) and earlier references cited therein.

(41) A. A. Petrov, *J. Gen. Chem.* (*U.S.S.R.*), **11**, 713 (1941); *Chem. Abstr.*, **36**, 404 (1942).

(42) D. H. R. Barton, D. A. Lewis, and J. F. McGhie, *J. Chem. Soc.*, **1957**, 2907.

(43) See, for example, D. Y. Curtin and R. J. Harder, *J. Am. Chem. Soc.*, **82**, 2357 (1960).

(44) S. Gabriel, *Chem. Ber.*, **21**, 1049 (1888); S. Gabriel and R. Stelzner, *ibid.*, **28**, 2929 (1895).

(45) H. Wenker, *J. Am. Chem. Soc.*, **57**, 2328 (1935).

(46) (a) J. S. Fenton in R. C. Elderfield (ed.), *Heterocyclic Compounds*, Vol. 1, Wiley, New York, 1950, Chapter 2; (b) P. E. Fanta in A. Weissberger (ed.), *The Chemistry of Heterocyclic Compounds*, Vol. 19, Part I, Interscience, New York, 1964, Chapter 2.

(47) G. F. Hennion and P. E. Butler, *J. Org. Chem.*, **27**, 2089 (1962).

(48) S. J. Brois, *ibid.*, **27**, 3532 (1962).

(49) (a) G. L. Closs and S. J. Brois, *J. Am. Chem. Soc.*, **82**, 6068 (1960); (b) J. Meinwald, Y. C. Meinwald, and T. N. Baker, III, *ibid.*, **86**, 4074

(1964); E. Vogel, M. Biskup, W. Pretzer, and W. A. Böll, *Angew. Chem. Intern. Ed.*, **3**, 642 (1964).

(50) (a) A. Hassner and C. Heathcock, *Tetrahedron Letters*, 393 (1963); 1125 (1964); (b) A. Hassner and C. Heathcock, *Tetrahedron*, **20**, 1037 (1964); (c) A. Hassner and C. Heathcock, *J. Org. Chem.*, **29**, 3640 (1964).

(51) H. Freundlich and G. Salomon, *Z. Physik. Chem.*, **166A**, 161, 179 (1933) and previous papers; G. Salomon, *Helv. Chim. Acta*, **16**, 1361 (1933); **19**, 743 (1936); P. L. Levins and Z. B. Papanastassiou, *J. Am. Chem. Soc.*, **87**, 826 (1965) and pertinent references cited therein.

(52) The Wenker synthesis has been found not to be stereospecific when the hydroxyl group of the amino alcohol is on a benzyl-type carbon atom, see ref. 46b, p. 534.

(53) A. Weissberger and H. Bach, *Chem. Ber.*, **64**, 1095 (1931); **65**, 631 (1932).

(54) N. H. Cromwell, R. D. Babson, and C. E. Harris, *J. Am. Chem. Soc.*, **65**, 312 (1943).

(55) A. B. Turner, H. W. Heine, J. Irving, and J. B. Bush, Jr., *ibid.*, **87**, 1050 (1965).

(56) N. H. Cromwell, *Rec. Chem. Progr.* (*Kresge-Hooker Sci. Lib.*), **19**, 215 (1958).

(57) N. J. Leonard and J. V. Paukstelis, *J. Org. Chem.*, **30**, 821 (1965).

(58) (a) C. O'Brien, *Chem. Revs.*, **64**, 81 (1964); (b) D. J. Cram and M. J. Hatch, *J. Am. Chem. Soc.*, **75**, 33 (1953).

(59) Aldoxime tosylates on reaction with base undergo *E2* elimination of *p*-toluenesulfonic acid with the formation of nitriles or isonitriles: (a) E. Mueller and B. Narr, *Z. Naturforsch.*, **16B**, 845 (1961); (b) M. S. Hatch and D. J. Cram, *J. Am. Chem. Soc.*, **75**, 38 (1953).

(60) H. O. House and W. Berkowitz, *J. Org. Chem.*, **28**, 2271 (1963).

(61) The insertion of unsaturated nitrenes into double bonds as a preparative route to azirines has been reported: G. Smolinsky, *J. Am. Chem.*

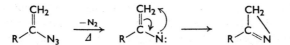

Soc., **83**, 4483 (1961); G. Smolinsky, *J. Org. Chem.*, **27**, 3557 (1962); L. Horner, A. Christmann, and A. Gross, *Chem. Ber.*, **96**, 399 (1963).

(62) Although a direct 1,3-displacement of tosylate by the carbanion in a concerted process has not been definitely ruled out,[60] the process may be considered unlikely because (a) an S_N2 displacement at a multiply bonded atom would be involved, and (b) frontside displacements, as would be required in the case of [25], are quite unfavorable.

(63) (a) G. H. Alt and W. S. Knowles, *J. Org. Chem.*, **25**, 2047 (1960); (b) H. E. Baumgarten and J. M. Petersen, *ibid.*, **28**, 2369 (1963); H. E.

Baumgarten, J. E. Dirks, J. M. Petersen, and D. C. Wolf, *J. Am. Chem. Soc.*, **82**, 4422 (1960); H. E. Baumgarten and J. M. Petersen, *ibid.*, **82**, 459 (1960); H. E. Baumgarten and F. A. Bower, *ibid.*, **76**, 4561 (1954).

(64) (a) R. F. Parcell, *Chem. Ind. (London)*, **1963**, 1396; (b) D. F. Morrow, M. E. Butler, and E. C. Y. Huang, *J. Org. Chem.*, **30**, 579 (1965).

(65) (a) H. E. Baumgarten, *J. Am. Chem. Soc.*, **84**, 4975 (1962); (b) H. E. Baumgarten, J. F. Fuerholzer, R. D. Clark, and R. D. Thompson, *ibid.*, **85**, 3303 (1963); (c) J. C. Sheehan and I. Lengyel, *ibid.*, **86**, 746 (1964) and other pertinent references cited in these papers.

(66) A. S. Kende, *Org. Reactions*, **11**, 261 (1960).

(67) Another process related in nature to the Favorskii reaction is the Ramberg-Bäcklund rearrangement of α-halosulfones, for example,

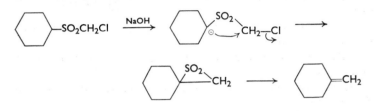

which proceeds via an episulfone intermediate to an olefin. This reaction cannot be used for the synthesis of episulfones, however, because the latter compounds lose rapidly the elements of sulfur dioxide (to produce olefins) in the alkaline medium required for the rearrangement; see L. A. Paquette, *J. Am. Chem. Soc.*, **86**, 4085, 4089, 4383 (1964) for leading references.

(68) (a) D. D. Reynolds and D. L. Fields in A. Weissberger (ed.), *The Chemistry of Heterocyclic Compounds*, Vol. 19, Part I, Interscience, New York, 1964, Chapter 3; (b) A. Schönberg in E. Müller (ed.), *Methoden der Organischen Chemie (Houben-Weyl)*, Georg Thieme Verlag, Stuttgart, Germany, 1955, pp. 153 ff.

(69) E. E. Van Tamelen, *J. Am. Chem. Soc.*, **73**, 3444 (1951).

(70) The fusion of ethylene carbonate with potassium thiocyanate yields ethylene sulfide: S. Searles and E. F. Lutz, *J. Am. Chem. Soc.*, **80**, 3168 (1958). A similar mechanistic sequence has been proposed:

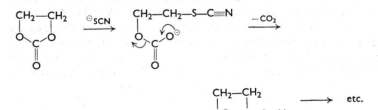

(71) C. C. J. Culvenor, W. Davies, and W. E. Savige, *J. Chem. Soc.*, **1952**, 4480, and references cited in this paper.

(72) (a) L. Goodman, A. Benitez, and B. R. Baker, *J. Am. Chem. Soc.*, **80**, 1680 (1958); (b) D. A. Lightner and C. Djerassi, *Tetrahedron*, **21**, 583 (1965).

(73) This procedure is also advisable for minimizing the formation of mixtures when higher molecular weight epoxides are involved. For example, reaction of (+)-*trans*-9-methyldecalin-2α,3α-epoxide with potassium thiocyanate in refluxing ethanol proceeds slowly to give a 4 : 1 mixture of the episulfides shown. The latter substance most probably arises from reaction of the initially formed episulfide with thiocyanate.

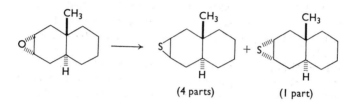

(4 parts)   (I part)

(74) As a general rule, α-chloro derivatives are preferred to the bromo or iodo analogs because they give rise to fewer side products. In situations where the chloro derivative yields cleanly the desired epoxy compound, the bromo and iodo counterparts give alkylation products or result in the formation of a mixture of the two.

(75) (a) M. S. Newman and B. J. Magerlein, *Org. Reactions*, **5**, 413 (1949); (b) M. Ballester, *Chem. Revs.*, **55**, 283 (1955).

(76) M. Ballester and P. D. Bartlett, *J. Am. Chem. Soc.*, **75**, 2042 (1953).

(77) R. H. Hunt, L. J. Chinn, and W. S. Johnson, *Org. Syn.*, **Coll. Vol. 4**, 459 (1963).

(78) J. A. Berson, *J. Am. Chem. Soc.*, **74**, 5175 (1952); H. H. Wasserman, N. E. Aubrey, and H. E. Zimmerman, *ibid.*, **75**, 96 (1953); H. H. Wasserman and J. B. Brows, *J. Org. Chem.*, **19**, 515 (1954); C. L. Stevens, R. J. Church, and V. J. Traynelis, *ibid.*, **19**, 522 (1954); C. L. Stevens and V. Traynelis, *ibid.*, **19**, 533 (1954); N. H. Cromwell and R. A. Setterquist, *J. Am. Chem. Soc.*, **76**, 5752 (1954).

(79) (a) H. E. Zimmerman and L. Ahramjian, *ibid.*, **82**, 5459 (1960); (b) C. C. Tung, A. J. Speziale, and H. W. Frazier, *J. Org. Chem.*, **28**, 1514 (1963).

(80) H. Kwart and L. G. Kirk, *ibid.*, **22**, 116, 1755 (1957).

(81) (a) M. S. Kharasch and O. Reinmuth, *Grignard Reactions of Non-Metallic Compounds*, Prentice-Hall, New York, 1954, pp. 181 *et seq.*, (b) T. A. Geissman and R. I. Akawie, *J. Am. Chem. Soc.*, **73**, 1993 (1951);

(c) R. L. Huang, *J. Org. Chem.*, **19**, 1363 (1954); (d) R. L. Huang, *J. Chem. Soc.*, 2539 (1954); (e) F. Ya. Perveev and F. Ya. Statsevich, *Zh. Obshch. Khim.*, **30**, 3558 (1960) and earlier papers.

(82) M. Tiffeneau, *Compt. Rend.*, **134**, 774 (1902).

(83) Compare (a) H. O. House, *J. Am. Chem. Soc.*, **77**, 3070, 5083 (1955); (b) S. M. Naqvi, J. P. Horwitz, and R. F. Filler, *ibid.*, **79**, 6283 (1957).

(84) R. Justoni, *Gazz. Chim. Ital.*, **69**, 378 (1939).

(85) F. Winternitz, C. Menon, and E. Arnal, *Bull. Soc. Chim. France*, **1960**, 505.

(86) C. L. Stevens and B. T. Gillis, *J. Am. Chem. Soc.*, **79**, 3448 (1957).

(87) V. Mark, *ibid.*, **85**, 1884 (1963).

(88) M. S. Newman and S. Blum, *ibid.*, **86**, 5598 (1964).

(89) For a comprehensive review of this subject, see ref. 46.

(90) F. H. Dickey, W. Fickett, and H. J. Lucas, *J. Am. Chem. Soc.*, **74**, 944 (1952).

(91) R. Ghirardelli and H. J. Lucas, *ibid.*, **79**, 734 (1957).

(92) G. K. Helmkamp and N. Schnantz, *Tetrahedron*, **2**, 304 (1958).

(93) W. Traube and E. Lehmann, *Chem. Ber.*, **32**, 720 (1899).

(94) H. Stamm, *Angew. Chem.*, **74**, 694 (1962).

(95) A. Funke and G. Benoit, *Bull. Soc. Chim. France*, **1953**, 1021.

(96) For a more comprehensive discussion of this point, see E. L. Eliel in M. S. Newman (ed.), *Steric Effects in Organic Chemistry*, Wiley, New York, 1956, pp. 106–114.

(97) C. O. Guss, *J. Am. Chem. Soc.*, **71**, 3460 (1949); C. O. Guss and H. R. Williams, *J. Org. Chem.*, **16**, 1809 (1951).

(98) A. Feldstein and C. A. Vanderwerf, *J. Am. Chem. Soc.*, **76**, 1626 (1954); R. Fuchs and C. A. Vanderwerf, *ibid.*, **76**, 1631 (1954).

(99) S. J. Cristol, J. R. Douglass, and J. S. Meek, *ibid.*, **73**, 816 (1951).

(100) C. O. Guss, R. Rosenthal, and R. F. Brown, *ibid.*, **75**, 2393 (1953).

(101) M. N. Rerick and E. L. Eliel, *ibid.*, **84**, 2356 (1962); E. L. Eliel and M. N. Rerick, *ibid.*, **82**, 1362 (1960); E. L. Eliel and D. W. Delmonte, *ibid.*, **80**, 1744 (1958).

(102) A. Fürst and Pl. A. Plattner, *Helv. Chim. Acta*, **32**, 275 (1949).

(103) A. Fürst and R. Scotoni, Jr., *ibid.*, **36**, 1332 (1953).

(104) A. Hassner and C. Heathcock, *J. Org. Chem.*, **30**, 1748 (1965).

(105) D. B. Denney and M. J. Boskin, *J. Am. Chem. Soc.*, **81**, 6330 (1959); D. B. Denney, J. J. Vill, and M. J. Boskin, *ibid.*, **84**, 3944 (1962).

(106) W. S. Wadsworth, Jr., and W. D. Emmons, *ibid.*, **83**, 1733 (1961).

(107) L. Horner, H. Hoffmann, and V. G. Toscano, *Chem. Ber.*, **95**, 536 (1962); see also L. Horner, H. Hoffmann, W. Klink, H. Ertel and V. G. Toscano, *ibid.*, **95**, 581 (1962).

(108) I. Tömösközi, *Chem. Ind. (London)*, 689 (1965).

(109) I. Tömösközi, *Tetrahedron*, **19**, 1969 (1963).

(110) Y. Inouye, T. Sugita, and H. M. Walborsky, *ibid.*, **20**, 1695 (1964).

(111) N. G. Gaylord and E. I. Becker, *Chem. Revs.*, **49**, 413 (1951).

(112) F. H. Norton and H. B. Hass, *J. Am. Chem. Soc.*, **58**, 2147 (1936).

(113) For a comprehensive discussion of the reaction of epoxides with organometallic reagents, see ref. 7a, pp. 386 ff.

(114) P. D. Bartlett and C. M. Berry, *J. Am. Chem. Soc.*, **56**, 2683 (1934).

(115) O. Mass and E. H. Boomer, *ibid.*, **44**, 1709 (1922); for kinetic evidence on this point, see J. N. Brønsted, M. Kilpatrick, and M. Kilpatrick, *ibid.*, **57**, 428 (1929).

(116) A frequently quoted exception to this rule is found in the report that hydrochloric acid reacts with either *cis*- or *trans*-2,3-diphenylethylene-imine to afford a mixture of the two isomeric α-amino-β-chlorodibenzyls (suggesting, of course, that both cis and trans additions have occurred): A. Weissberger and H. Bach, *Chem. Ber.*, **65**, 631 (1932). Such is, however, not the case with the related *cis*- and *trans*-stilbene oxides which open stereospecifically: D. Reulos, *Compt. Rend.*, **216**, 714 (1943); **218**, 795 (1944).

(117) S. Winstein and H. J. Lucas, *J. Am. Chem. Soc.*, **61**, 1581 (1939).

(118) C. C. J. Culvenor, W. Davies, and N. S. Heath, *J. Chem. Soc.*, **1949**, 282.

(119) C. A. Stewart and C. A. Vanderwerf, *J. Am. Chem. Soc.*, **76**, 1259 (1954).

(120) M. Tiffeneau and E. Fourneau, *Compt. Rend.*, **146**, 697 (1908); A. Orekhoff and M. Tiffeneau, *Bull. Soc. Chim. France*, **37**, 1410 (1925).

(121) F. Arndt, J. Amende, and W. Ender, *Monatsh. Chem.*, **59**, 202 (1932).

(122) S. Gabriel and H. Ohle, *Chem. Ber.*, **50**, 804 (1917).

(123) F. Wolfheim, *ibid.*, **47**, 1440 (1914).

(124) R. A. Baxter and F. S. Spring, *J. Chem. Soc.*, **1943**, 613; P. N. Chakravorty and R. H. Levin, *J. Am. Chem. Soc.*, **64**, 2317 (1942).

(125) D. Atherton and T. P. Hilditch, *J. Chem. Soc.*, **1943**, 204.

(126) E. L. Gustus and P. G. Stevens, *J. Am. Chem. Soc.*, **55**, 378 (1933).

(127) W. Davies and E. W. Savige, *J. Chem. Soc.*, **1950**, 317.

(128) C. Golumbic, J. S. Fruton, and M. Bergmann, *J. Org. Chem.*, **11**, 518 (1946); N. B. Chapman and J. W. James, *J. Chem. Soc.*, **1954**, 2103; J. F. Allen and N. B. Chapman, *ibid.*, **1960**, 1482.

(129) A. T. Bottini, B. F. Dowden, and R. L. Van Etten, *J. Am. Chem. Soc.*, **87**, 3250 (1965).

(130) P. E. Fanta, L. J. Pandya, W. R. Groskopf, and H.-J. Su, *J. Org. Chem.*, **28**, 413 (1963); A. T. Bottini and R. L. Van Etten, *ibid.*, **30**, 575 (1965); G. K. Helmkamp, R. D. Clark, and J. R. Koskinen, *ibid.*, **30**, 666

(1965). Note especially the fact that such methiodides undergo rapid equilibration with the corresponding 2-iodoalkylamines: A. T. Bottini, B. F. Dowden, and L. Sousa, *J. Am. Chem. Soc.*, **87**, 3249 (1965).

(131) A. L. Logothetis, *ibid.*, **87**, 749 (1965).

(132) P. D. Bartlett, S. D. Ross, and C. G. Swain, *ibid.*, **69**, 2971 (1947); P. D. Bartlett, J. W. Davis, S. D. Ross, and C. G. Swain, *ibid.* **69**, 2977 (1947); P. D. Bartlett, S. D. Ross, and C. G. Swain, *ibid.*, **71**, 1415 (1949).

(133) E. M. Schultz and J. M. Sprague, *ibid.*, **70**, 48 (1948).

(134) R. C. Fuson and C. L. Zirkle, *ibid.*, **70**, 2760 (1948).

(135) W. C. G. Ross, *Biological Alkylating Agents*, Butterworths, London, England, 1962.

(136) N. J. Leonard and J. V. Paukstelis, *J. Org. Chem.*, **28**, 3021 (1963).

(137) J. V. Paukstelis, Ph.D. Thesis, University of Illinois, Urbana, 1964.

(138) M. T. Bogert and R. L. Roblin, Jr., *J. Am. Chem. Soc.*, **55**, 3741 (1933).

(139) J. B. Doughty, C. L. Lazell, and A. R. Collett, *ibid.*, **72**, 2866 (1950).

(140) G. K. Helmkamp and D. J. Pettitt, *J. Org. Chem.*, **25**, 1754 (1960), see also ref. 141.

(141) D. J. Pettitt and G. K. Helmkamp, *ibid.*, **28**, 2932 (1963).

(142) G. K. Helmkamp, B. A. Olsen, and D. J. Pettitt, *ibid.*, **30**, 676 (1965), see also D. J. Cram, *J. Am. Chem. Soc.*, **71**, 3883 (1949); N. Kharasch and A. J. Havlik, *ibid.*, **75**, 3734 (1953); N. R. Slobodkin and N. Kharasch, *ibid.*, **82**, 5837 (1960).

(143) (a) M. J. Boskin and D. B. Denney, *Chem. Ind. (London)*, 330 (1959); (b) D. E. Bissing and A. J. Speziale, *J. Am. Chem. Soc.*, **87**, 2683 (1965).

(144) A. J. Speziale and D. E. Bissing, *ibid.*, **85**, 1888, 3878 (1963).

(145) H. O. House and G. Rasmusson, *J. Org. Chem.*, **26**, 4278 (1961), see also ref. 4c, p. 253.

(146) (a) R. E. Davis, *J. Org. Chem.*, **23**, 1767 (1958); (b) D. B. Denney and M. J. Boskin, *J. Am. Chem. Soc.*, **82**, 4736 (1960); (c) N. P. Neureiter and F. G. Bordwell, *ibid.*, **81**, 578 (1959); (d) R. D. Schultz and R. L. Jacobs, *J. Org. Chem.*, **23**, 1799 (1958).

(147) F. G. Bordwell, H. M. Andersen, and B. M. Pitt, *J. Am. Chem. Soc.*, **76**, 1082 (1954).

(148) G. K. Helmkamp and D. J. Pettitt, *J. Org. Chem.*, **29**, 3258 (1964).

(149) R. D. Clark and G. K. Helmkamp, *ibid.*, **29**, 1316 (1964).

(150) Aziridines can also be deaminated readily with 3-nitro-N-nitrosocarbazole: C. L. Bumgardner, K. S. McCallum, and J. P. Freeman, *J. Am. Chem. Soc.*, **83**, 4417 (1961).

(151) B. Tchoubar, *Compt. Rend.*, **214**, 117 (1942), see also J. E. Horan and R. W. Schiessler, *Org. Syn.*, **41**, 53 (1961).

(152) Magnesium bromide is known to initially convert epoxides to bromohydrin derivatives prior to rearrangement.[83]

(153) H. O. House and R. L. Wasson, *J. Am. Chem. Soc.*, **78**, 4394 (1956).

(154) E. A. Braude, A. A. Webb, and M. V. S. Sultanbawa, *J. Chem. Soc.*, **1958**, 3328.

(155) H. B. Henbest and T. I. Wrigley, *ibid.*, **1957**, 4596.

(156) A. C. Cope, P. A. Trumbull, and E. R. Trumbull, *J. Am. Chem. Soc.*, **80**, 2844 (1958).

(157) S. Gabriel and R. Stelzner, *Chem. Ber.*, **28**, 2929 (1895).

(158) (a) A. S. Deutsch and P. E. Fanta, *J. Org. Chem.*, **21**, 892 (1956); (b) H. W. Heine and Z. Proctor, *ibid.*, **23**, 1554 (1958); (c) H. W. Heine, M. E. Fetter, and E. M. Nicholson, *J. Am. Chem. Soc.*, **81**, 2202 (1959).

(159) (a) P. E. Fanta and A. S. Deutsch, *J. Org. Chem.*, **23**, 72 (1958); (b) P. D. Talukdar and P. E. Fanta, *ibid.*, **24**, 526 (1959); (c) D. V. Kashelikar and P. E. Fanta, *J. Am. Chem. Soc.*, **82**, 4927 (1960); (d) D. V. Kashelikar and P. E. Fanta, *ibid.*, **82**, 4930 (1960).

(160) For a review of aziridine rearrangements, see H. W. Heine, *Angew. Chem.*, **74**, 772 (1962); *Angew. Chem. Intern. Ed.*, **1**, 528 (1962). More recent examples have been described by: H. W. Heine and A. C. Brooker, *J. Org. Chem.*, **27**, 2943 (1962); H. W. Heine, *J. Am. Chem. Soc.*, **85**, 2743 (1963); H. W. Whitlock, Jr., and G. L. Smith, *Tetrahedron Letters*, 1389 (1965).

(161) H. W. Heine, W. G. Kenyon, and E. M. Johnson, *J. Am. Chem. Soc.*, **83**, 2570 (1961).

(162) A. B. Turner, H. W. Heine, J. Irving, and J. B. Bush, Jr., *ibid.*, **87**, 1050 (1965).

(163) H. O. House, *ibid.*, **76**, 1235 (1954).

(164) P. Rajagopalan and C. N. Talaty, *ibid.*, **88**, 5048 (1966).

(165) J. R. Lowell, Jr., and G. K. Helmkamp, *ibid.*, **88**, 768 (1966).

(166) J. W. Ager, F. A. Eastwood, and R. Robinson, *Tetrahedron*, **Suppl. No. 7**, 277 (1966).

(167) H. W. Heine, D. C. King, and L. A. Portland, *J. Org. Chem.*, **31**, 2662 (1966).

(168) L. A. Paquette and L. S. Wittenbrook, *Chem. Commun.*, **1966**, 471.

(169) R. Huisgen, R. Sustmann, and K. Bunge, *Tetrahedron Letters*, **1966**, 3603.

(170) H. M. Walborsky and D. F. Loncrini, *J. Org. Chem.*, **22**, 1117 (1957).

(171) E. Pfeil and U. Harder, *Angew. Chem. Intern. Ed.*, **4**, 518 (1965).

(172) L. A. Carpino and L. V. McAdams, III, *J. Am. Chem. Soc.*, **87**, 5804 (1965).

(173) C. Heathcock, *ibid.*, **88**, 4110 (1966).

(174) S. J. Brois and G. P. Beardsley, *Tetrahedron Letters*, **1966**, 5113.

(175) K. Ponsold and D. Klemm, *Chem. Ber.*, **99**, 1502 (1966).

(176) S. S. Kulp, V. B. Fish, and N. R. Easton, *J. Med. Pharm. Chem.*, **6**, 516 (1963).

(177) J. Falbe, H.-J. Schulze-Steinen, and F. Korte, *Chem. Ber.*, **97**, 1096 (1964).

(178) H. W. Whitlock, Jr., and G. L. Smith, *Tetrahedron Letters*, **1965**, 1389.

(179) R. R. Sauers, R. A. Parent, and S. B. Damle, *J. Am. Chem. Soc.*, **88**, 2257 (1966).

(180) A. Padwa, *ibid.*, **87**, 4205 (1965).

(181) N. J. Leonard, K. Jahn, J. V. Paukstelis, and C. K. Steinhardt, *J. Org. Chem.*, **28**, 1499 (1963).

(182) C. L. Stevens and C. H. Chang, *ibid.*, **27**, 4392 (1962).

(183) H. W. Heine and R. Peavy, *Tetrahedron Letters*, **1965**, 3123; A. Padwa and L. Hamilton, *ibid.*, **1965**, 4363.

(184) J. A. Marshall and N. Cohen, *J. Org. Chem.*, **30**, 3475 (1965).

(185) F. Jakob and P. Schlack, *Chem. Ber.*, **96**, 88 (1963).

(186) D. Lavie, Y. Kashman, E. Glotter, and N. Danielli, *J. Chem. Soc.* (*C*), **1966**, 1757.

(187) J. A. Deyrup and R. B. Greenwald, *Tetrahedron Letters*, **1966**, 5091.

(188) P. D. Bartlett and W. P. Giddings, *J. Am. Chem. Soc.*, **82**, 1240 (1960).

(189) G. Smolinsky and B. I. Feuer, *J. Org. Chem.*, **31**, 1423 (1966).

(190) R. M. Bowman, A. Chambers, and W. R. Jackson, *J. Chem. Soc.* (*C*), **1966**, 1296.

(191) H. W. Heine, *J. Am. Chem. Soc.*, **85**, 2743 (1963).

(192) A. Padwa and L. Hamilton, *J. Org. Chem.*, **31**, 1995 (1966).

(193) M. P. Hartshorn, D. N. Kirk, and A. F. A. Wallis, *J. Chem. Soc.*, **1964**, 5494.

(194) J. E. Dolfini and D. M. Dolfini, *Tetrahedron Letters*, **1965**, 2053.

(195) H. W. Heine and F. Scholer, *ibid.*, **1964**, 3667.

(196) E. F. Ullman and B. Singh, *J. Am. Chem. Soc.*, **88**, 1844 (1966).

(197) W. J. Gensler and B. A. Brooks, *J. Org. Chem.*, **31**, 568 (1966).

(198) E. F. Ullman and J. E. Milks, *J. Am. Chem. Soc.*, **86**, 3814 (1964).

(199) H. H. Wasserman and N. E. Aubrey, *ibid.*, **78**, 1726 (1956).

(200) C. W. J. Chang and S. W. Pelletier, *Tetrahedron Letters*, **1966**, 5483.

2

▪ THREE-MEMBERED RINGS WITH

TWO HETERO ATOMS

WHEREAS THE MONOHETERO ATOMIC three-membered ring systems were known in the nineteenth century, no three-membered rings with two hetero atoms had been prepared prior to 1950. Since this date, however, the chemistry of the oxaziranes [1], diaziridines [2], and diazirines [3] has rapidly developed.[1] As will be seen in the ensuing section, the unfavorable strain energy in these molecules is not reflected in the ease with which they can be prepared. They are nonetheless highly reactive and possess certain unusual properties.

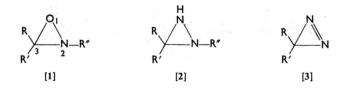

[1]   [2]   [3]

SYNTHETIC APPROACHES

The preparation of the title compounds can be readily achieved by the direct insertion of an appropriate hetero atom into a carbonyl or imine double bond. Thus, the oxaziranes are conveniently synthesized by the oxidation of imines with organic peracids.[2, 3] Because a large variety of imines are amenable to synthesis (from primary amines and ketones or aldehydes), and because the oxidation step is

$$C_6H_5CH=NC(CH_3)_3 + CH_3\overset{O}{\overset{\|}{C}}OOH \xrightarrow[10-20°C]{CH_2Cl_2}$$

(90%)　　(Ref. 2a)

general in nature, this reaction represents an oxazirane synthesis of wide applicability. The main limitations of the process reside in the instability of certain imines and a few oxaziranes under the acidic conditions. This oxidation is remarkably selective for it can be performed in the presence of functional groups which normally react with peracids.

The reaction of ketones and aldehydes with hydroxylamine-O-sulfonic acids or chloramines in alkaline solution provides a useful alternative route to oxaziranes.[4] The formation of the three-

$$\bigcirc=O + CH_3NHOSO_3H \xrightarrow[\text{(45%)}]{OH^{\ominus}}$$

$$\xleftarrow[\text{(81%)}]{} CH_3NHCl + \bigcirc=O \quad (Ref.\ 4a)$$

membered ring is believed to proceed by initial 1,2-addition of the nitrogen-containing component to the carbonyl group, followed by an intramolecular S_N2 displacement as depicted below:

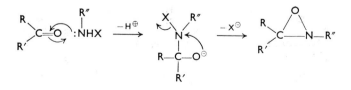

Although many oxaziranes have limited stability in alkaline media (see p. 70), such reactions go to completion rapidly at 0°C (often within 1 minute) and, therefore, can in general compete successfully with decomposition of the product. This synthetic scheme is a valuable addition to the peracid-imine reaction for it permits the preparation of oxaziranes without a substituent on nitrogen.

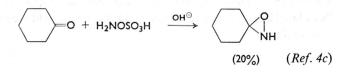

$$(20\%) \qquad (Ref.\ 4c)$$

The addition of ozone[5] and hydrogen peroxide[6] to Schiff bases has also been found to produce oxaziranes, but details of such studies are limited.

A reaction closely related in mechanistic detail is the addition of hydroxylamine-O-sulfonic acids or chloramines to Schiff bases which yields diaziridines.[7] Several variations of this reaction are known, including generation of the imine *in situ*, and a few examples are given below.

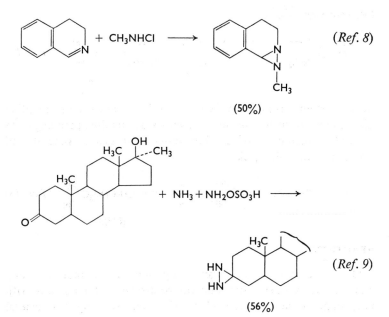

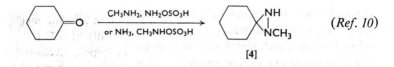

(*Ref. 10*)

[4]

The preparation of [4] by two routes clearly establishes the equivalence of the two nitrogen atoms. When aldehydes are treated with ammonia and chloramine, the resulting diaziridines frequently cannot be isolated because of further rapid condensation to yield triazolidines such as [5].

$$CH_3CHO \xrightarrow[NH_2Cl]{NH_3} \left[CH_3CH\!\!\begin{array}{c}NH\\|\\NH\end{array} \right] \longrightarrow CH_3CH\!\!\begin{array}{c}CH_3\\|\\CH\\N\diagdown\\ \quad NH\\N\diagup\\CH\\|\\CH_3\end{array}$$

[5]   (*Ref. 11*)

Diazirine [6] can be prepared by the reaction of dichloramine with *tert*-octylazomethine[12]; generally, however, when diazirines are

$$CH_2{=}N\text{-}t\text{-octyl} \xrightarrow{HNCl_2}$$

$$\left[CH_2\!\!\begin{array}{c}NHR\\ \diagdown NCl_2\end{array} \right] \xrightarrow{-HCl^{\oplus}} CH_2\!\!\begin{array}{c}N{-}R\\|_{\kappa}\\N{-}Cl\end{array} \xrightarrow[(25-33\%)]{-RCl} CH_2\!\!\begin{array}{c}N\\\|\\N\end{array} \quad (\textit{Ref. 12})$$

[6]

needed recourse is made to the facile oxidation of the corresponding diaziridines by such reagents as silver oxide, alkaline permanganate or yellow mercuric oxide. The latter synthesis is general and proceeds with a high yield.

$$(CH_3CH_2CH_2)_2C\!\!\begin{array}{c}NH\\|\\NH\end{array} \xrightarrow[H_2O]{Ag_2O} (CH_3CH_2CH_2)_2C\!\!\begin{array}{c}N\\\|\\N\end{array} \quad (\textit{Ref. 13})$$

(81%)

REACTIONS

Oxaziranes are active oxygen compounds, comparable in many ways to organic peroxides, and can be assayed iodometrically with potassium iodide in acetic acid.[14] The oxazirane ring is in general slowly decomposed by strong acids, but is stable to weakly basic reagents (however, see p. 70). The stability of this group of heterocycles varies considerably with the nature and number of substituents.

The diaziridines, likewise a class of oxidizing agents, are usually more stable than the oxaziranes[15]; they are weakly basic and form salts, but are also rather readily hydrolyzed in acid solution to a carbonyl component and a hydrazine.[16] The diaziridine ring is stable to alkaline reagents.

The diazirines, although isomeric with the aliphatic diazo compounds, display considerable differences (more stable and much less reactive) in their properties from the latter class of substances, except in their explosive nature (in the lower molecular weight derivatives). Acid[13] and alkali[17] have no effect on the ring at room temperature.

Reactions Involving Fission of the Ring

The three-membered ring of the oxaziranes is cleaved in all of its reactions, in contrast to the diaziridine and diazirine rings where

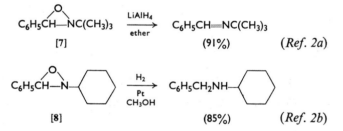

substitution on nitrogen is possible (see p. 71). For example, reduction of [7] with lithium aluminum hydride or of [8] with hydrogen gives the corresponding imine and secondary amine, respectively.[18] The catalytic hydrogenation of diaziridines results in the uptake of two moles of hydrogen and two amines are formed.

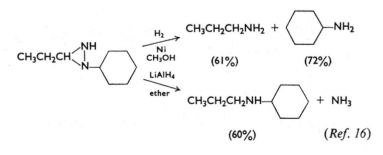

Lithium aluminum hydride, in contrast, will only reduce diaziridines that have at least one unsubstituted nitrogen atom[19]; again in this case, N—N bond cleavage occurs, but the products generally differ from those formed under hydrogenative conditions.

The acid hydrolysis of 3-aryloxaziranes occurs with the formation of an aromatic aldehyde and alkyl hydroxylamine. This reaction is thought to involve protonation on oxygen, followed by rupture of the C—O bond to produce a stabilized benzylic carbonium ion which reacts further as shown. In the case of alkyl oxaziranes, a different

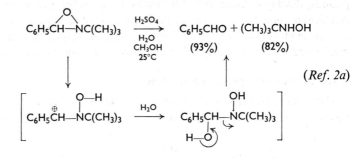

(Ref. 2a)

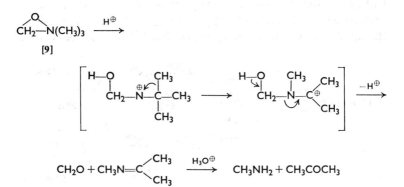

course is followed which probably involves the formation of an electron-deficient nitrogen species. When a hydrogen atom is present on the neighboring carbon atom, a hydride shift occurs; but if such is not the case, as in [9], then alkyl group migration is observed.

The acid hydrolysis of diaziridines has been found to follow first order kinetics[20]; although the influence of substitution on nitrogen has a negligible effect on the rate, an increase in the number of substituents on the carbon atom greatly accelerates the hydrolytic process, Table 2–1. These data provide strong evidence for a

TABLE 2–I ▪

Half-lives of Some Aziridines in $2NH_2SO_4$ at $35°C$[20]

Compound	Half-life, minutes
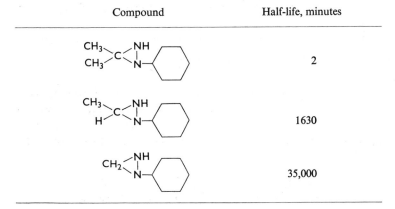	2
	1630
	35,000

mechanism involving a rate-determining ionic rupture of the diaziridinium ion as given below:

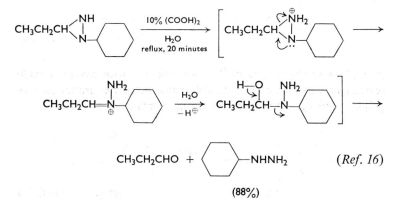

Although the oxazirane ring itself is unreactive toward basic reagents, oxaziranes with a 2-methylene or 2-methinyl substituent such as [10] react vigorously with aqueous alcoholic alkali to evolve ammonia quantitatively. This reaction is believed to proceed by carbanion formation on the substituent group which is subsequently degraded to carbonyl products.

$$C_6H_5\overset{\displaystyle O}{\overset{\diagup\diagdown}{CH}-N}-CH_3 \quad \xrightarrow{\;OH^{\ominus}\;}$$

[10]

$$\left[C_6H_5\overset{\displaystyle O}{\overset{\diagup\diagdown}{CH}-N}-CH_2^{\ominus} \longrightarrow C_6H_5CH-\overset{O^{\ominus}}{\underset{}{N}}{=}CH_2 \right] \xrightarrow{\;H_2O\;}$$

$$C_6H_5CHO + CH_2O + NH_3 \qquad\qquad (Ref.\ 1a)$$

(91%)　　(71%)　(80%)

The rearrangement of oxaziranes under thermal conditions is interesting; here again, the aryl- and alkyl-substituted derivatives differ in their behavior. Whereas the former are isomerized at elevated temperatures to nitrones (e.g., [11]) in good yield, the latter

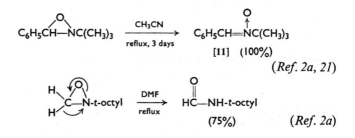

$$C_6H_5\overset{\displaystyle O}{\overset{\diagup\diagdown}{CH}-N}C(CH_3)_3 \quad \xrightarrow[\text{reflux, 3 days}]{\;CH_3CN\;} \quad C_6H_5CH{=}\overset{\displaystyle O}{\underset{}{N}}C(CH_3)_3$$

[11]　(100%)

(Ref. 2a, 21)

(75%)　　　　(Ref. 2a)

generally give rise to amides.[21]　As in the case with certain epoxide rearrangements (see p. 41), suitably constructed oxaziranes such as [12] can undergo ring expansion during rearrangement.

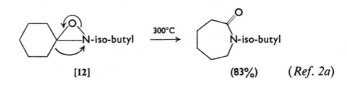

[12]　　　　　　　　　　(83%)　　(Ref. 2a)

Thermal or photochemical decomposition of diazirines proceeds with the evolution of nitrogen and the formation of carbenoid intermediates[22]; the ultimate fate of the carbene is, of course, a function of the molecular structure.[23]   Examples of some of the cases studied are illustrated in the following equations.

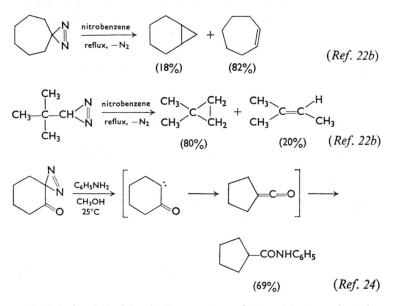

(Ref. 22b)

(Ref. 22b)

(Ref. 24)

Photolysis of diazirine in the presence of *trans*-2-butene gives rise predominantly to the *trans*-cyclopropane; because the addition to the double bond is stereospecific, the methylene generated from the diazirine is presumed to be in the singlet state.

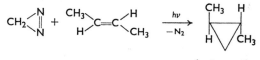

(major product)

(Ref. 22a)

Reactions Involving Retention of the Ring

An interesting and useful synthetic procedure in this category is the addition of Grignard reagents to diazirines.   The reaction is general and proceeds instantly at 0°C.

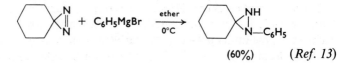

(60%)   (*Ref. 13*)

Diaziridines which contain at least one N—H group undergo certain reactions typical of secondary amines, of which the condensation with chloral is but an example.[1a]

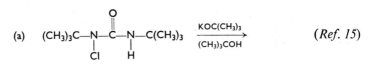

(*Ref. 17*)

Exercises

1. Predict the major product of the following reactions:

(a) $(CH_3)_3C—N—C—N—C(CH_3)_3$ $\xrightarrow[\text{(CH}_3)_3\text{COH}]{\text{KOC(CH}_3)_3}$ (*Ref. 15*)

(b) 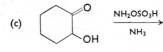 $\xrightarrow{\text{NaOCl}}$ $C_5H_{10}N_2$ (*Ref. 25*)

(c) $\xrightarrow[\text{NH}_3]{\text{NH}_2\text{OSO}_3\text{H}}$ (*Ref. 24*)

(d) $\xrightarrow[\text{CH}_3\text{OH}]{\text{KOH}}$ (*Ref. 26*)

2. Suggest a reasonable mechanism for each of the following transformations:

(a) $\xrightarrow[\substack{1\ N\ H_2SO_4 \\ CH_3OH}]{\text{FeSO}_4}$ $CH_3NHCO(CH_2)_8CONHCH_3$ (*Ref. 27*)

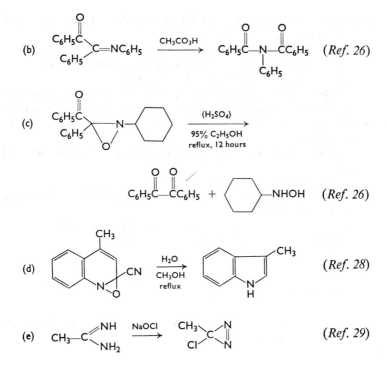

(b)

(c)

(*Ref. 26*)

(*Ref. 26*)

(d)   (*Ref. 28*)

(e)   (*Ref. 29*)

References and Notes

(1) (a) E. Schmitz in A. R. Katritzky (ed.), *Advances in Heterocyclic Chemistry*, Vol. 2, Academic Press, New York, 1963, p. 83; (b) E. Schmitz, *Angew. Chem. Intern. Ed.*, **3**, 333 (1964); (c) W. D. Emmons in A. Weissberger (ed.), *The Chemistry of Heterocyclic Compounds*, Vol. 19, Part I, Interscience, New York, 1964, Chapter 4.

(2) (a) W. D. Emmons, *J. Am. Chem. Soc.*, **78**, 6208 (1956); **79**, 5739 (1957); (b) L. Horner and E. Jürgens, *Chem. Ber.*, **90**, 2184 (1957); (c) H. Krimm, K. Hamann, and K. Bauer, U.S. Pat. No. 2,784,182 dated March 5, 1957.

(3) The peracid-imine reaction probably proceeds via a transition state similar to that previously discussed in the case of epoxidations (see p. 2).

(4) (a) E. Schmitz, R. Ohme, and D. Murawski, *Chem. Ber.*, **98**, 2516 (1965); (b) E. Schmitz, R. Ohme, and S. Schramm, *ibid.*, **97**, 2521 (1964); (c) E. Schmitz, R. Ohme, and D. Muraswki, *Angew. Chem.*, **73**, 708 (1961).

(5) M. Schulz, D. Becker, and A. Rieche, *Angew. Chem. Intern. Ed.*, **4**, 525 (1965); A. H. Riebel, R. E. Erickson, C. J. Abshire, and P. S. Bailey,

J. Am. Chem. Soc., **82**, 1801 (1960); J. S. Belew and J. T. Person, *Chem. Ind.* (*London*), **1959**, 1246.

(6) E. Höft and A. Rieche, *Angew. Chem. Intern. Ed.*, **4**, 524 (1965).

(7) For a summary of references in this area, see reference 1a.

(8) E. Schmitz, *Angew. Chem.*, **71**, 127 (1959).

(9) R. F. R. Church, A. S. Kende, and M. J. Weiss, *J. Am. Chem. Soc.*, **87**, 2665 (1965). These authors found that steroid diaziridines are formed if at all, only in moderate yields and that ring formation was subject to electronic and steric restrictions.

(10) E. Schmitz, R. Ohme, and R. D. Schmidt, *Chem. Ber.*, **95**, 2714 (1962).

(11) E. Schmitz, *ibid.*, **95**, 688 (1962).

(12) W. H. Graham, *J. Org. Chem.*, **30**, 2108 (1965), see also *J. Am. Chem. Soc.*, **84**, 1063 (1962).

(13) E. Schmitz and R. Ohme, *Chem. Ber.*, **94**, 2166 (1961).

(14) According to the following stoichiometry:

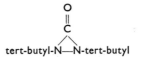

(15) Most diaziridines can be heated to 100°C without change; di-*tert*-butyldiaziridinone

$$
\begin{array}{c}
\text{O} \\
\parallel \\
\text{C} \\
\diagup\diagdown \\
\text{tert-butyl-N——N-tert-butyl}
\end{array}
$$

undergoes only slight decomposition in 2 hours at 175°C [F. D. Greene and J. C. Stowell, *J. Am. Chem. Soc.*, **86**, 3569 (1964)].

(16) E. Schmitz and D. Habisch, *Chem. Ber.*, **95**, 680 (1962).

(17) E. Schmitz and R. Ohme, *ibid.*, **95**, 795 (1962).

(18) Lithium aluminum hydride reduction of 2-substituted oxaziranes, for steric or electronic reasons, yields only secondary amines.[2a]

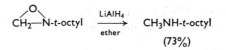

(19) 1,2-Dialkylaziridines are not attacked by this reagent.

(20) Cs. Szántay and E. Schmitz, *Chem. Ber.*, **95**, 1759 (1962).

(21) (a) M. F. Hawthorne and R. D. Strahm, *J. Org. Chem.*, **22**, 1263 (1957); (b) J. S. Splitter and M. Calvin, *ibid.*, **30**, 3427 (1965).

(22) (a) H. M. Frey and I. D. R. Stevens, *J. Chem. Soc.*, **1965**, 3101; **1964**, 4700; **1963**, 3514; *Proc. Chem. Soc.*, **1962**, 79; *J. Am. Chem. Soc.*, **84**, 2647 (1962); (b) E. Schmitz, D. Habisch, and A. Stark, *Angew. Chem.*, **75**, 723 (1963).

(23) J. Hine, *Divalent Carbon*, Ronald Press, New York, 1964; W. Kirmse, *Carbene Chemistry*, Academic Press, New York, 1964.

(24) E. Schmitz, A. Stark, and C. Horig, *Chem. Ber.*, **98**, 2509 (1965).

(25) R. Ohme, E. Schmitz, and P. Dolge, *ibid.*, **99**, 2104 (1966).

(26) A. Padwa, *J. Am. Chem. Soc.*, **87**, 4365 (1965).

(27) E. Schmitz and D. Murawski, *Chem. Ber.*, **98**, 2525 (1965).

(28) C. Kaneko and S. Yamada, *Chem. Pharm. Bull. (Tokyo)*, **14**, 555 (1966).

(29) W. H. Graham, *J. Am. Chem. Soc.*, **87**, 4396 (1965).

3

■ THE FOUR-MEMBERED
HETEROCYCLES

THE FOUR-MEMBERED HETERO RINGS possess chemical properties that differ to a significant extent from those of smaller and larger rings. For example, oxetane [1], azetidine [2], and thietane [3] are, in general, more stable than their three-membered ring congeners, and more

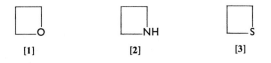

[1]   [2]   [3]

vigorous conditions are required to cause ring cleavage. β-Lactams and β-lactones, on the other hand, are considerably more reactive than analogous systems of greater ring size. The latter group of compounds are very susceptible to reactions involving the carbonyl group and generally undergo ring cleavage quite readily. These phenomena will be illustrated below.

Spectroscopic investigations of [1] and [3][1] indicate that these molecules are virtually planar (C_{2v} symmetry) and are not square (because of the larger size of the hetero atom relative to carbon). The propensity of such heterocycles for coplanarity, when compared to cyclobutane which is puckered, has been attributed to a reduction in the number of nonbonded interactions between methylene groups. Restoration of this steric factor as, for example, in the thietane dioxides, results in a pronounced puckering of the ring as evidenced by the fact that cis-2,4-diphenylthietane dioxide [4] is more stable than the trans-isomer.[2]

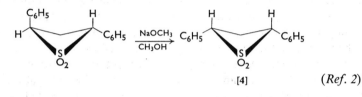

[4] (Ref. 2)

SYNTHETIC APPROACHES
Cyclization Reactions

The method most frequently employed at the present time for the preparation of the four-membered heterocycles is cyclization. Typically, however, the rates of such processes are very slow, Table 3–1. Second-order rate constants, determined for the intramolecular cyclization of a number of chloroalcohols in alkaline solution, suggest that γ-chloroalcohols at 80°C cyclize 10^{-2} times slower than comparable β-chloroalcohols at 20°C.[3] Many complications were therefore encountered in early synthetic schemes. More recently, however, a number of variations have been developed which improve not

TABLE 3–I ▪

First-Order Rate Constants (25°C) for Cyclization of Bromoalkylamines[4]

Amine	Rate constant
$Br(CH_2)_2NH_2$	0.036
$Br(CH_2)_3NH_2$	0.0005
$Br(CH_2)_4NH_2$	~30
$Br(CH_2)_5NH_2$	0.5
$Br(CH_2)_6NH_2$	0.001

only the yields, but also the scope of this chemical approach, thereby rendering it fairly general.

For example, whereas oxetanes were initially prepared in low yield by the cyclization of 1,3-halohydrins with alkali, better yields of oxetanes can be obtained by prior acetylation of the halohydrins followed by reaction of the derived acetates with base.[5] The acetate

$$ClCH_2CH_2CH_2OH \xrightarrow[\substack{H_2O,\ 140°C \\ (20\text{--}25\%)}]{KOH} [1] \xleftarrow[\substack{H_2O,\ 140°C \\ (42\text{--}44\%)}]{KOH} ClCH_2CH_2CH_2OCOCH_3$$

(*Ref. 6*)

group perhaps serves merely to limit the concentration of alkoxide anion present in solution at any instant, thus favoring cyclization over intermolecular polymerization. In contrast to the situation in the analogous preparations of epoxides where substitution invariably enhances the cyclization process (see p. 13), the effect of alkyl substitution on oxetane synthesis is markedly dependent upon the position of attachment of such groups. Yields are increased by alkyl substitution on the carbinol carbon, but markedly decreased on the halogen-bearing (because E_2 elimination predominates) or central carbon atoms.[7]

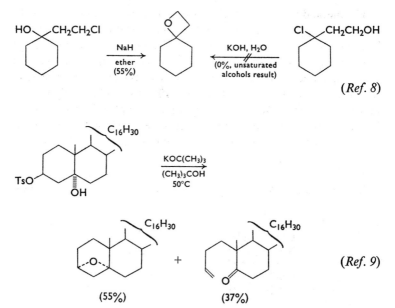

(*Ref. 8*)

(*Ref. 9*)

Occasionally, monotosylates and monobrosylates of 1,3-diols are more accessible, and such functionalized molecules can be converted successfully to oxetanes.

Azetidines are frequently prepared by the intramolecular nucleophilic displacement of a suitable leaving group in the γ-position of a three-carbon chain by an amino group, or the anion of a sulfonamido group.[10] No single method is appropriate for all azetidines because of different problems which arise with different substituents. The alkaline cyclization of [5] exclusively to an aziridine (no azetidine observed) again demonstrates the rate differences discussed above.

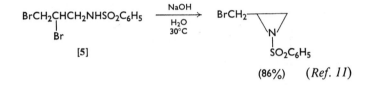

(86%)   (Ref. 11)

Azetidine [2] is best prepared by the dialkylation of trimethylene chlorobromide with p-toluenesulfonamide,[12] followed by reduction of [6] with sodium and amyl alcohol. The conversion of [6] to [2]

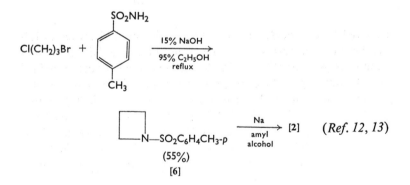

can be achieved only by such a reductive procedure because azetidine rings do not, in general, survive drastic hydrolytic treatment. Several other approaches to azetidines are exemplified in the accompanying equations.

Although thietane syntheses are subject to problems similar to those evidenced with [1] and [2], improved yields can, in general, be

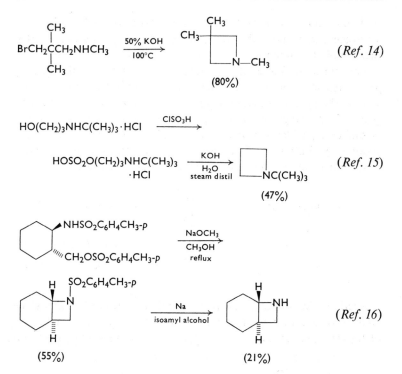

achieved by appropriate modifications.　For example, whereas 1,3-dichloropropane reacts with anhydrous sodium sulfide in ethanol solution to yield [3] in 20–30 % yield, the same product can be obtained consistently in good yield by prior conversion of 1-bromo-3-chloropropane into its monothiouronium salt followed by alkaline decomposition of this intermediate.[17]　Again in this instance, the success of the scheme may perhaps be due to the progressive liberation of the highly nucleophilic mercaptide ion in solution.　The condensation of epichlorohydrin with barium hydrosulfide leads to the formation

ClCH$_2$CH$_2$CH$_2$Br $\xrightarrow[\text{H}_2\text{O}]{\overset{\text{S}}{\overset{\|}{\text{H}_2\text{NCNH}_2}}}$

ClCH$_2$CH$_2$CH$_2$SC$\overset{\oplus}{\underset{\diagdown \text{NH}_2}{\diagup \text{NH}_2}}$ Br$^{\ominus}$ $\xrightarrow[\text{H}_2\text{O}]{\text{NaOH}}$ ☐—S (Ref. 17)

(45%)

of 3-thietanol [7].[18]   Since 3-chloro-2-hydroxy-1-propanethiol is isolated readily under the same conditions at 0°C, a mercaptide intermediate can be implicated with certainty in this conversion.

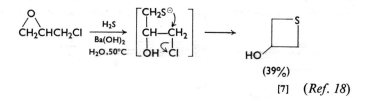

(39%)

[7]   (*Ref. 18*)

The direct preparation of β-lactones or β-lactams by the thermal dehydration of the corresponding β-hydroxy- or β-aminopropionic acids, respectively, is not generally successful, principally because of the ease with which such substances undergo β-elimination.[19]   However, the reaction of β-haloacids with one equivalent of base at or near room temperature under strictly controlled pH conditions may be used to generate β-lactones, although this method is sometimes complicated by the formation of an alkene via a decarboxylative elimination pathway.   This complication, which is heavily favored when the haloacid is di-α-substituted, results from an internal elimination in which carbon dioxide and halide ion are lost, as in [8].   That

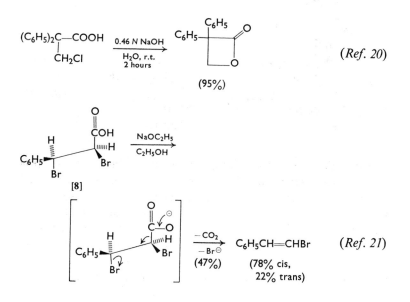

the cyclizations are stereospecific and occur with inversion of configuration at the carbon bearing the halogen atom is demonstrated dramatically in the behavior of [9] and [10]. In the latter example, since the carboxylate anion cannot approach for steric reasons the backside of the neighboring carbon atom, normal solvolysis occurs.

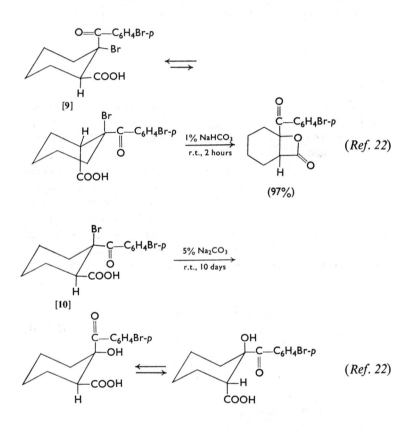

(*Ref. 22*)

(*Ref. 22*)

Although β-aminopropionic acids do not yield β-lactams upon heating, acyl derivatives of many such acids can be transformed thermally into these four-membered heterocycles. The success of this method has been attributed to the intermediacy of hydroxylactones such as [11].[19b] Reagents such as acetyl chloride, phosphorus trichloride, and thionyl chloride have been successful on occasion in effecting the ring closure of β-amino acids; however, these reagents have been displaced almost totally in recent years since the

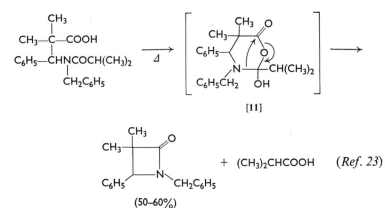

[11]

(50–60%)

appearance of the carbodiimides. Most notable of the accomplishments with this latter group of reagents has been the total synthesis of penicillin V [12].[25]

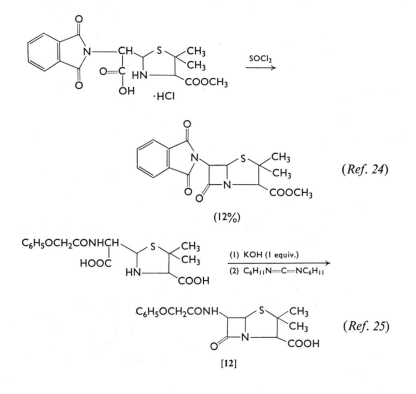

(12%)   (Ref. 24)

[12]   (Ref. 25)

The reaction of β-amino acid esters with Grignard reagents is often employed to prepare β-lactams and, in fact, represents the best method for preparing the parent compound of the series. The

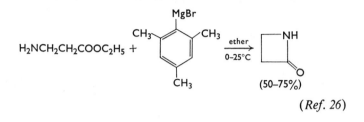

(*Ref. 26*)

hindered nature of mesityl magnesium bromide prevents further condensation at the reactive carbonyl group. Several other procedures involving intramolecular alkylation have been developed, the two most important of which involve the base-catalyzed ring closure of N-substituted diethyl chloroacetamidomalonates[27, 28] and the intramolecular Michael-type addition of substituted acylamides of type [13].[29] Although both procedures generally produce β-lactams in high yield, the processes suffer from the fact that the resulting

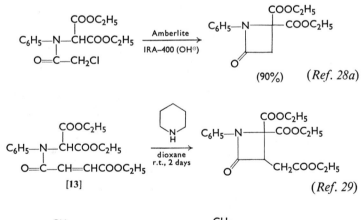

(90%)   (*Ref. 28a*)

(*Ref. 29*)

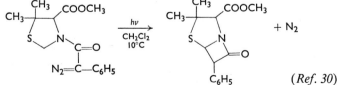

(*Ref. 30*)

heterocycles possess one or two carboalkoxy groups in the 4-position which fact serves to limit the generality of the methods.

A new synthetic approach to the β-lactam system which makes use of α-diazoamides may prove of wide utility.[30]

Direct Combination Pathways

Alternative preparative methods which lead to certain four-membered heterocyclic systems proceed via the combination of two appropriately constructed difunctional components. For example, photocycloaddition of carbonyl compounds to olefins leads via the carbonyl $n \rightarrow \pi^*$ state to oxetane formation.[31] Competing reactions are observed if the olefin contains easily abstractable hydrogen atoms (carbinols or pinacols result) or when products derived from the $\pi \rightarrow \pi^*$ triplet of the diene are formed. It has been generalized that

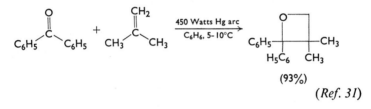

(93%)

(Ref. 31)

ketones which are not reduced to carbinols upon irradiation in isopropyl alcohol are incapable of forming oxetanes.[31]

The condensation of ketenes with carbonyl compounds, generally, in the presence of catalysts such as boric acid, zinc chloride, or boron trifluoride etherate, gives good yields of β-lactones. The reaction conditions, especially pH, often must be carefully controlled to

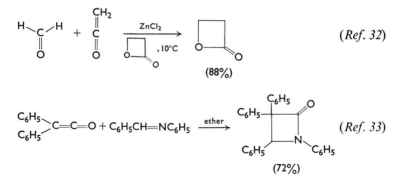

(88%)

(Ref. 32)

(72%)

(Ref. 33)

minimize a number of possible side reactions. Ketoketenes also react quite readily with imines at ordinary temperatures to produce β-lactams in good yields, but substitution of monosubstituted ketenes in this cycloaddition has not proved successful because of their extremely slow reaction and their great propensity for polymerization.[19b] Acyl aminoketenes, generated *in situ* by the reaction of an acid chloride with a tertiary amine, condense with imines to afford acyl amino-β-lactams in good yield.[19b] The scope of this cycloaddition reaction has not been established, but it is clear that the process is not general for all acid chlorides or imines.

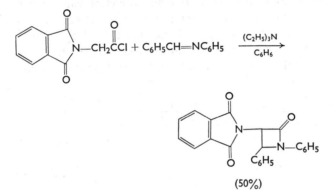

(*Ref. 34*)

(50%)

Chlorosulfonyl isocyanate reacts with a number of olefins to form the corresponding N-chlorosulfonyl-β-lactams[35] from which the chlorosulfonyl group may be removed with relative ease. The cycloaddition product may be contaminated frequently with straight chain

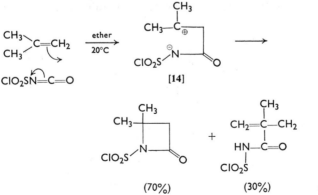

(70%)   (30%)   (*Ref. 36b*)

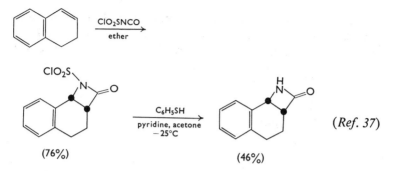

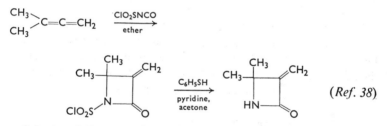

(*Ref. 37*)

isomers; in certain cases, the latter reaction pathway may pre-dominate.[36] In agreement with the observed products, the mechan-ism appears to involve electrophilic attack at the olefinic site by the isocyanate grouping; a dipolar species such as **[14]** probably results. This zwitterion may react further by simple collapse to the heterocyclic ring or by a prototropic shift to afford open chain N-chlorosulfonyl amides. A further useful synthetic application of this reaction is the addition of chlorosulfonyl isocyanate to allenes.[38]

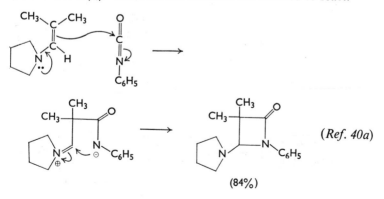

β-Amino-β-lactams result when equimolar quantities of an iso-cyanate and a β,β'-disubstituted enamine are allowed to react.[39, 40]

(*Ref. 40a*)

(84%)

The enamine structural requirements are very specific, however, since β-monosubstituted enamines apparently do not afford stable β-lactams; only ring opened products are observed. It is possible that

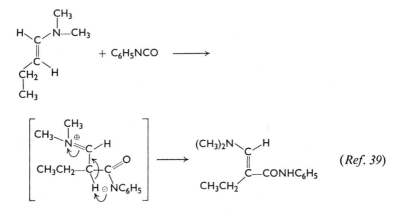

(*Ref. 39*)

a mechanism involving β-hydrogen abstraction (as shown) occurs exclusively.[39, 40b]

Enamines and other appropriately activated olefins such as ketene acetals and ketene aminals react with sulfenes (see p. 9) presumably by a cycloaddition pathway[41] to give rise to derivatives of thietane dioxide. Although the reaction has seen considerable use since its discovery,[45] especially because the 3-aminothietane dioxides serve as

$$CH_3SO_2Cl + (C_2H_5)_3N \xrightarrow[\text{solvent}]{\text{appropriate}} (CH_2{=}SO_2) + (C_2H_5)_3N \cdot HCl$$

(*Ref. 42*)

(73%)

(*Ref. 43*)

(65%)

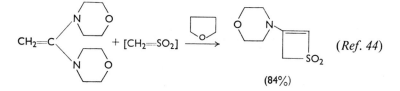

excellent precursors for the corresponding thiete sulfones such as [15],[46] the scope of the reaction does not appear to be entirely general, since open chain compounds are obtained with some reactants and in certain solvent systems.[47]

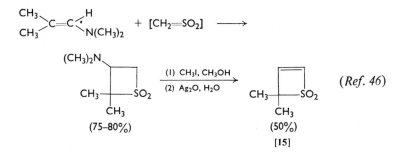

REACTIONS

The four-membered heterocycles display many of the transformations characteristic of their lower homologs (Chapter 1), but generally with a lesser degree of reactivity because of the decrease in ring strain. The chemistry peculiar to these systems, therefore, resides predominantly in ring cleavage reactions. Again, processes which are not particularly characteristic of such four-membered rings will not be discussed.

Electrophilic Ring-Openings

In general, oxetanes, azetidines, and thietanes are particularly susceptible to attack by electrophilic reagents and the rates of ring cleavage are rapid. Noncatalyzed reactions, in contrast, proceed extremely slowly. The direction of ring cleavage of unsymmetrically substituted oxetanes does not always occur in a manner predictable from a purely S_N1 process; such evidence indicates the operation of a "push-pull mechanism" (see p. 26) in which fully developed carbonium ions are not always generated. Not unlike the analogous epoxides

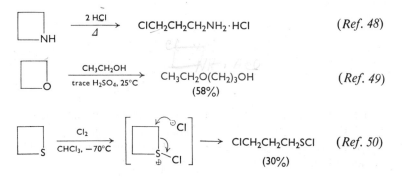

$$CH_3CH_2OH \xrightarrow{\text{trace } H_2SO_4, 25°C} \quad$$

(see p. 32), 2-methyloxetane [16] appears to react with hydrogen chloride or acetyl chloride via an intermediate oxonium ion which is subsequently attacked at the least hindered α-carbon atom, while

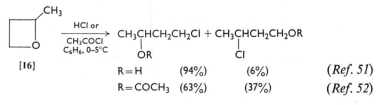

2-phenyloxetane [17] gives only products resulting from the generation of the benzylic carbonium ion. In contrast, the Friedel-Crafts reaction of [16] and [17] with benzene in the presence of aluminum

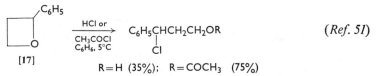

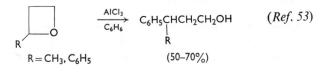

chloride gives the corresponding 3-aryl-1-propanols exclusively.[53] Obviously, in these latter examples, the necessity for cationic intermediates is reflected in the identity of the ring opening modes which favor the more stable carbonium ion.

Although β-lactones as expected are rapidly hydrolyzed to β-hydroxyacids in aqueous media, the mechanism of this hydration varies with the pH employed. For example, in strong acid such heterocycles are cleaved via the customary (for esters and γ-lactones) bimolecular acyl oxygen heterolysis (A_{AC2}) while in neutral or slightly acidic solution a bimolecular alkyl oxygen heterolysis (B_{AL2}) occurs.[54] The differing modes of cleavage are apparent when H_2O^{18} is employed,[55] or when optically active 3-substituted β-lactones are submitted to hydrolysis.[56] As the accompanying equation illustrates, certain β-lactones are converted exothermically to substituted acrylic acids with concentrated sulfuric acid or boron trifluoride.

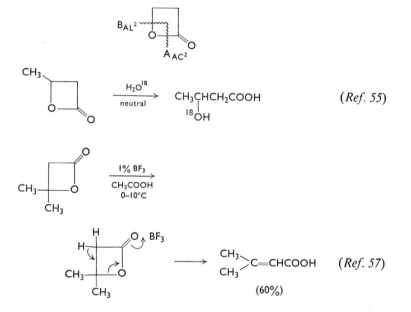

As would be expected from the above discussion, alcohols react with β-lactones under neutral (extremely slowly) or weakly acidic (rapidly) conditions by means of alkyl oxygen cleavage to yield β-alkoxypropionic acids and their esters, hydracrylic esters, and polyesters.[58] Phenol and β-propiolactone react slowly at room temperature to give β-phenoxypropionic acid. However, in the presence of catalytic amounts of sulfuric acid a striking change in the reaction occurs; phenyl hydracrylate, which arises from acyl oxygen

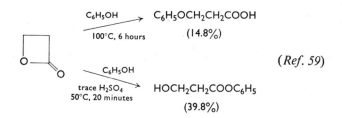

(*Ref. 59*)

fission, is isolated.[59]   The apparent paradox results because the basicity of phenol is much lower than that of methanol.   As a result an acid concentration which in methanol still reflects the uncatalyzed attack of solvent on the four-membered ring ester will in phenol reveal the limiting acid-catalyzed mechanism as is observed in very strongly acidic aqueous or methanolic solutions.[60]

Finally, the acid-catalyzed hydrolysis of β-lactams has been claimed to be slower than alkaline hydrolysis (see p. 95), and for this reason has received much less attention.   Such heterocycles, although less reactive than β-lactones, are nevertheless far more reactive than normal amides, with the exception of highly substituted β-lactams which are particularly stable to acid hydrolysis.

Nucleophilic Ring-Openings

Four-membered heterocycles react with nucleophiles at markedly reduced rates when compared to the three-membered rings.   For example, oxetane is cleaved by hydroxide ion 10^3 times more slowly than ethylene oxide[61]; with other anions, the reactions must be

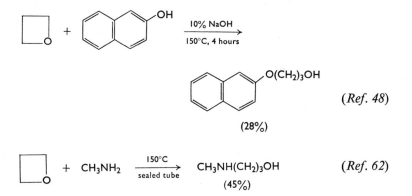

☐O + C₆H₅CH₂SH $\xrightarrow[\text{reflux, 6 hours}]{10\% \text{ NaOH}}$ C₆H₅CH₂S(CH₂)₃OH (*Ref. 63*)

(63%)

allowed to proceed for relatively long periods of time at high temperatures in order to achieve moderate yields.   Unlike their smaller sized counterparts, azetidines and thietanes are quite resistant to the action of bases and nucleophiles, a property which is reflected in the synthetic approaches utilized successfully in their preparation (see earlier). Furthermore, a number of functionalized thietanes have been treated with nucleophilic reagents without evidence of ring cleavage.

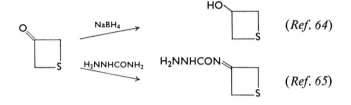

(*Ref. 64*)

(*Ref. 65*)

When unsymmetrical four-membered rings are involved, the less hindered carbon atom is attacked by the nucleophile so that one product predominates.

C₆H₅ ☐O $\xrightarrow[\text{(2) H}_2\text{O}]{\text{(1) CH}_3\text{MgBr, ether}}$ C₆H₅CHCH₂CH₂CH₃ (*Ref. 1a*)
                                    |
                                   OH

CH₃ ☐ CH₃ $\xrightarrow[\text{(2) H}_2\text{O}]{\text{(1) LiAlH}_4,\ \text{reflux, 26 hours}}$ CH₃CHCHCH₃
 O | |
                                         HO CH₃

(58%) (*Ref. 66*)

The reaction of β-lactones with nucleophilic reagents (including alkaline hydrolysis) proceeds in general by the bimolecular alkyl oxygen heterolysis mechanism to give a β-substituted propionate salt. The following examples illustrate this phenomenon.   However, such reactions are often complicated by reaction of the heterocycle with the solvent, polymerization of the β-lactone, or polyaddition resulting

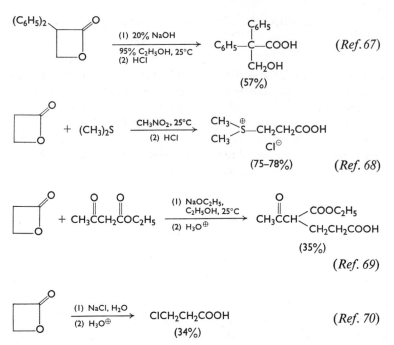

$$(C_6H_5)_2 \quad \xrightarrow[\substack{95\% \ C_2H_5OH, \ 25°C \\ (2) \ HCl}]{(1) \ 20\% \ NaOH} \quad C_6H_5-\overset{\overset{\displaystyle C_6H_5}{|}}{\underset{\underset{\displaystyle CH_2OH}{|}}{C}}-COOH \qquad (Ref.\ 67)$$

(57%)

$$+ \ (CH_3)_2S \quad \xrightarrow[(2) \ HCl]{CH_3NO_2, \ 25°C} \quad \overset{CH_3}{\underset{CH_3}{>}}\overset{\oplus}{S}-CH_2CH_2COOH \atop Cl^{\ominus}$$

(75–78%) \qquad (Ref. 68)

$$+ \ CH_3CCH_2COC_2H_5 \quad \xrightarrow[(2) \ H_3O^{\oplus}]{\substack{(1) \ NaOC_2H_5, \\ C_2H_5OH, \ 25°C}} \quad CH_3CCH\overset{COOC_2H_5}{\underset{CH_2CH_2COOH}{<}}$$

(35%)

(Ref. 69)

$$\xrightarrow[(2) \ H_3O^{\oplus}]{(1) \ NaCl, \ H_2O} \quad ClCH_2CH_2COOH \qquad (Ref.\ 70)$$

(34%)

from nucleophilic attack of the newly generated carboxylate anions upon unchanged β-lactone.

In contrast, in the reaction of β-lactones with ammonia or amines, neither polymer or oligomer results in a significant quantity. In such cases, however, cleavage occurs in both possible directions, and the relative proportions of the two products depends, in the order of importance, upon the nature of the amine employed, the reaction medium, and the order of addition of the reactants. A suitable

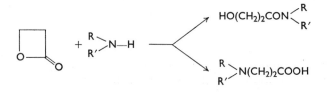

interpretation of these results is lacking, but certain empirical rules have evolved. For example, although the course of the ring cleavage cannot be related to the basic strength of the amine, it is known that with water as solvent hydracrylamide formation is favored, whereas in acetonitrile or *tert*-butyl alcohol amino acids are the major products. Also, when the amine is added to the β-lactone, the major product is the amino acid, whereas the reverse mode of addition leads to the formation of the amide.[71]

The alkaline hydrolysis of β-lactams is widely applicable and β-amino acids are generally obtained in high yields. The rate of such reactions varies widely with the nature and number of ring substituents. In Table 3–2, N-methylacetamide has been included to facilitate comparison with a strain-free system.

TABLE 3–2 ▪

Apparent Second-Order Rate Constants for the Hydrolysis of β-Lactams (0.5 N NaOH in 85% Ethanol, 50°C)[72]

Substituents	$10^{-2} k_2$ (liter mole^{-1} second^{-1})
None	13.0
1-Benzyl	1.7
1-Benzyl-4-phenyl	1.0
1-Benzyl-3,3-dimethyl-4-phenyl	0.04
N-Methylacetamide	0.03

Exercises

1. Predict the major product of the following reactions:

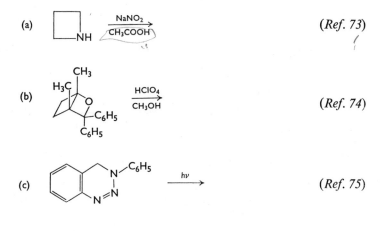

(a)   NaNO₂ / CH₃COOH   (*Ref. 73*)

(b)   HClO₄ / CH₃OH   (*Ref. 74*)

(c)   hν   (*Ref. 75*)

(d) 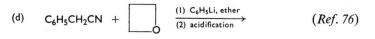   (*Ref. 76*)

(e)    (*Ref. 77*)

(f) 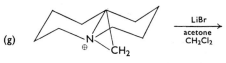   (*Ref. 78*)

(g) 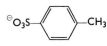   (*Ref. 79*)

(h)    (*Ref. 30*)

(i) 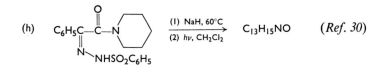   (*Ref. 80*)

(j) 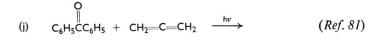   (*Ref. 81*)

(k) 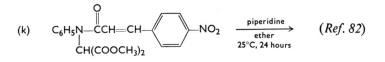   (*Ref. 82*)

(l) 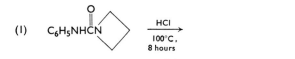   (*Ref. 83*)

2. Suggest a reasonable mechanism for each of the following transformations:

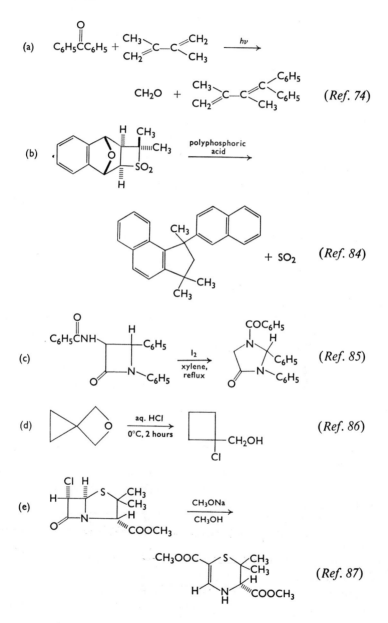

(a) $C_6H_5\overset{\underset{\displaystyle O}{\|}}{C}C_6H_5$ + ... $\xrightarrow{h\nu}$

CH_2O + ... (*Ref. 74*)

(b) ... $\xrightarrow{\text{polyphosphoric acid}}$

... + SO_2 (*Ref. 84*)

(c) ... $\xrightarrow[\text{xylene, reflux}]{I_2}$ ... (*Ref. 85*)

(d) ... $\xrightarrow[\text{0°C, 2 hours}]{\text{aq. HCl}}$ ... (*Ref. 86*)

(e) ... $\xrightarrow[\text{CH}_3\text{OH}]{\text{CH}_3\text{ONa}}$ ... (*Ref. 87*)

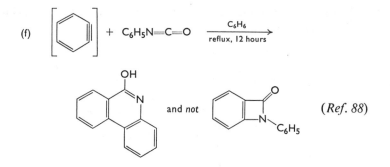

(f) ... C_6H_6, reflux, 12 hours ... and *not* ... (*Ref. 88*)

References and Notes

(1) (a) Oxetane: S. Searles, Jr., in A. Weissberger (ed.), *The Chemistry of Heterocyclic Compounds*, Vol. 19, Part II, Interscience, New York, 1964, Chapter 9; (b) Thietane: Y. Etienne, R. Soulas, and H. Lumbroso, in A. Weissberger (ed.), *ibid.*, Chapter 5; M. Sander, *Chem. Rev.*, **66**, 341 (1966).

(2) R. M. Dodson and G. Klose, *Chem. Ind.* (*London*), 450 (1963).

(3) (a) G. Forsberg, *Acta Chem. Scand.*, **8**, 135 (1954); (b) W. P. Evans, *Z. Physik. Chem.*, **7**, 337 (1891).

(4) H. Freundlich and H. Kroepelin, *ibid.*, **122**, 39 (1926).

(5) (a) S. Searles, Jr., K. A. Pollart, and F. Block, *J. Am. Chem. Soc.*, **79**, 952 (1957); (b) D. C. Dittmer, W. R. Hertler, and H. Winicov, *ibid.*, **79**, 4431 (1957).

(6) C. R. Noller, *Org. Syn.*, **Coll. Vol. 3**, 835 (1955).

(7) This latter type of substitution promotes the following fragmentation reaction:

$$R_2C \overset{CH_2OH}{\underset{CH_2Br}{\big\langle}} \xrightarrow{OH^{\ominus}} R_2C \overset{CH_2 \cdots O^{\ominus}}{\underset{CH_2 \cdots Br}{\big\langle}} \longrightarrow R_2C{=}CH_2 + CH_2O + Br^{\ominus}$$

S. Searles, Jr., and M. J. Gortatowski, *J. Am. Chem. Soc.*, **75**, 3030 (1953); S. Searles, Jr., R. G. Nickerson, and W. K. Witsiepe, *J. Org. Chem.*, **24**, 1839 (1959).

(8) A. Rosowsky and D. S. Tarbell, *ibid.*, **26**, 2255 (1961).

(9) R. B. Clayton, H. B. Henbest, and M. Smith, *J. Chem. Soc.*, **1957**, 1982.

(10) (a) J. A. Moore, in A. Weissberger (ed.), *The Chemistry of Heterocyclic Compounds*, Vol. 19, Part II, Interscience, New York, 1964, Chapter 7; (b) S. A. Ballard and D. S. Melstrom in R. C. Elderfield (ed.), *Heterocyclic Compounds*, Vol. 1, Wiley, New York, 1950, Chapter 3.

(11) W. J. Gensler, *J. Am. Chem. Soc.*, **70**, 1843 (1948).

(12) S. Searles, Jr., M. Tamres, F. Block, and L. A. Quaterman, *ibid.*, **78**, 4917 (1956).

(13) F. C. Schaeffer, *ibid.*, **77**, 5928 (1955).

(14) C. Mannich and G. Baumgarten, *Chem. Ber.*, **70**, 210 (1937).

(15) A. T. Bottini and J. D. Roberts, *J. Am. Chem. Soc.*, **80**, 5203 (1958).

(16) E. J. Moriconi and P. S. Mazzocchi, Abstr. 150th Meeting Am. Chem. Soc., Sept. 1965, p. 18S.

(17) F. G. Bordwell and B. M. Pitt, *J. Am. Chem. Soc.*, **77**, 572 (1955).

(18) D. C. Dittmer and M. E. Christy, *J. Org. Chem.*, **26**, 1324 (1961).

(19) (a) β-Lactones: H. E. Zaugg, *Org. Reactions*, **8**, 305 (1954); Y. Etienne and N. Fischer, in A. Weissberger (ed.), *The Chemistry of Heterocyclic Compounds*, Vol. 19, Part II, Interscience, New York, 1964, Chapter 6; (b) β-Lactams: J. C. Sheehan and E. J. Corey, *Org. Reactions*, **9**, 388 (1957).

(20) H. E. Zaugg, *J. Am. Chem. Soc.*, **72**, 2998 (1950).

(21) E. Grovenstein, Jr., and D. E. Lee, *ibid.*, **75**, 2639 (1953).

(22) P. D. Bartlett and P. N. Rylander, *ibid.*, **73**, 4275 (1951); E. P. Kohler and J. E. Jansen, *ibid.*, **60**, 2142 (1938).

(23) H. Staudinger, H. W. Klever, and P. Kober, *Ann. Chem.*, **374**, 1 (1910).

(24) J. C. Sheehan, K. R. Henery-Logan, and D. A. Johnson, *J. Am. Chem. Soc.*, **75**, 3292 (1953).

(25) J. C. Sheehan and K. R. Henery-Logan, *ibid.*, **81**, 3089 (1959).

(26) S. Searles, Jr., and R. E. Wann, *Chem. Ind. (London)*, 2097 (1964).

(27) J. C. Sheehan and A. K. Bose, *J. Am. Chem. Soc.*, **73**, 1761 (1951); **72**, 5158 (1950).

(28) (a) B. G. Chatterjee, V. V. Rao, and B. N. G. Mazumdar, *J. Org. Chem.*, **30**, 4101 (1965); (b) see also A. K. Bose, B. N. G. Mazumdar, and B. G. Chatterjee, *J. Am. Chem. Soc.*, **82**, 2382 (1960).

(29) A. K. Bose, M. S. Manhas, and R. M. Ramer, *Tetrahedron*, **21**, 449 (1965).

(30) E. J. Corey and A. M. Felix, *J. Am. Chem. Soc.*, **87**, 2518 (1965).

(31) D. R. Arnold, R. L. Hinman, and A. H. Glick, *Tetrahedron Letters*, **No. 22**, 1425 (1964) and leading references cited therein.

(32) H. J. Hagemeyer, Jr., *Ind. Eng. Chem.*, **41**, 765 (1949).

(33) H. Staudinger, *Ann. Chem.*, **356**, 51 (1907).

(34) J. C. Sheehan and J. J. Ryan, *J. Am. Chem. Soc.*, **73**, 1204 (1951).

(35) H. Ulrich, *Chem. Rev.*, **65**, 369 (1965).

(36) (a) R. Graf, *Chem. Ber.*, **89**, 1071 (1956); (b) R. Graf, *Ann. Chem.*, **661**, 111 (1963); (c) H. Hoffmann and H. J. Diehr, *Tetrahedron Letters*, **No. 27**, 1875 (1963).

(37) E. J. Moriconi and P. H. Mazzochi, *J. Org. Chem.*, **31**, 1372 (1966).

(38) E. J. Moriconi and J. F. Kelly, *J. Am. Chem. Soc.*, **88**, 3657 (1966).

(39) M. Perelman and S. A. Mizsak, *ibid.*, **84**, 4988 (1962).

(40) (a) G. Opitz and J. Koch, *Angew. Chem.*, **75**, 167 (1963); (b) S. Hünig, *ibid.*, **71**, 312 (1959); D. Clemens and W. Emmons, *J. Org. Chem.*, **26**, 767 (1961); G. Berchtold, *ibid.*, **26**, 3043 (1961); S. Hünig, H. Hubner, and E. Benzing, *Chem. Ber.*, **95**, 926 (1962).

(41) I. J. Borowitz, *J. Am. Chem. Soc.*, **86**, 1146 (1964).

(42) L. A. Paquette, *J. Org. Chem.*, **30**, 629 (1964).

(43) W. E. Truce and J. R. Norell, *J. Am. Chem. Soc.*, **85**, 3231 (1963).

(44) R. H. Hasek, P. G. Gott, R. H. Meen, and J. C. Martin, *J. Org. Chem.*, **28**, 2496 (1963).

(45) G. Stork and I. J. Borowitz, *J. Am. Chem. Soc.*, **84**, 313 (1962); G. Opitz and H. Adolph, *Angew. Chem.*, **74**, 77 (1962).

(46) W. E. Truce, J. R. Norell, J. E. Richman, and J. P. Walsh, *Tetrahedron Letters*, **No. 25**, 1677 (1963).

(47) L. A. Paquette and M. Rosen, *ibid.*, **No. 3**, 311 (1966); W. E. Truce and P. N. Son, *J. Org. Chem.*, **30**, 71 (1965); G. Opitz and H. Schemp, *Ann. Chem.*, **684**, 103 (1965).

(48) S. Searles and C. F. Butler, *J. Am. Chem. Soc.*, **76**, 56 (1954).

(49) S. A. Ballard and D. S. Melstrom in R. C. Elderfield (ed.), *Heterocyclic Compounds*, Vol. 1, Wiley, New York, 1950, Chapter 3.

(50) J. M. Stewart and C. H. Burnside, *J. Am. Chem. Soc.*, **75**, 243 (1953).

(51) S. Searles, Jr., K. A. Pollart, and E. F. Lutz, *J. Am. Chem. Soc.*, **79**, 952 (1959).

(52) C. G. Derick and D. W. Bissell, *ibid.*, **38**, 2478 (1916).

(53) S. Searles, Jr., and co-workers, unpublished work.

(54) (a) F. A. Long and M. Purchase, *J. Am. Chem. Soc.*, **72**, 3267 (1950); (b) P. D. Bartlett and G. Small, *ibid.*, **72**, 4867 (1950); (c) A. R. Olson and P. V. Youle, *ibid.*, **73**, 2468 (1951); (d) J. O. Edwards, *ibid.*, **76**, 1540 (1954).

(55) A. R. Olson and R. J. Miller, *ibid.*, **60**, 2687 (1938).

(56) A. R. Olson and J. L. Hyde, *ibid.*, **63**, 2459 (1941).

(57) R. Hart, *Bull. Soc. Chim. Belges*, **58**, 255 (1949).

(58) T. L. Gresham, J. E. Jansen, F. W. Shaver, J. T. Gregory, and W. L. Beears, *J. Am. Chem. Soc.*, **70**, 1004 (1948).

(59) T. L. Gresham, J. E. Jansen, R. A. Bankert, W. L. Beears, and M. G. Prendergast, *ibid.*, **71**, 661 (1949).

(60) P. D. Bartlett and P. N. Rylander, *ibid.*, **73**, 4273 (1951).

(61) J. G. Pritchard and F. A. Long, *ibid.*, **80**, 4162 (1960).

(62) S. Searles and V. P. Gregory, *ibid.*, **76**, 2789 (1954).

(63) S. Searles, *ibid.*, **73**, 4515 (1951).

(64) R. Mayer and K. F. Funk, *Angew. Chem.*, **73**, 578 (1961).

(65) H. Prinzbach and G. V. Veh, *Z. Naturforsch.*, **16b**, 763 (1961).

(66) S. Searles, Jr., K. A. Pollart, and E. F. Lutz, *J. Am. Chem. Soc.*, **79**, 948 (1957).

(67) H. Zaugg, *ibid.*, **72**, 3001 (1950).

(68) N. F. Blau and C. G. Stuckwisch, *ibid.*, **73**, 2355 (1951).

(69) T. L. Gresham, J. E. Jansen, F. W. Shaver, M. R. Frederick, and W. L. Beears, *ibid.*, **73**, 2345 (1951).

(70) T. L. Gresham, J. E. Jansen, F. W. Shaver, and J. T. Gregory *ibid.*, **70**, 999 (1948).

(71) T. L. Gresham, J. E. Jansen, F. W. Shaver, R. A. Bankert, and F. T. Fiedorek, *ibid.*, **73**, 3168 (1951).

(72) A. D. Holley and R. W. Holley, *ibid.*, **72**, 2771 (1950); **71**, 2124, 2129 (1949).

(73) C. L. Bumgardner, K. S. McCallum, and J. P. Freeman, *ibid.*, **83**, 4417 (1961).

(74) J. Saltiel, R. M. Coates, and W. G. Dauben, *ibid.*, **88**, 2745 (1966).

(75) E. M. Burgess and L. McCullagh, *ibid.*, **88**, 1580 (1966).

(76) L. L. Darko and J. G. Cannon, *Tetrahedron Letters*, **No. 4**, 423 (1966).

(77) L. W. Deady, G. J. Leary, R. D. Topsom, and J. Vaughan, *J. Org. Chem.*, **28**, 511 (1963).

(78) P. Yates and A. G. Szabo, *Tetrahedron Letters*, **No. 9**, 485 (1965).

(79) G. Fodor, *J. Am. Chem. Soc.*, **88**, 1040 (1966).

(80) D. C. Dittmer and M. E. Christy, *ibid.*, **84**, 399 (1962).

(81) D. R. Arnold and A. H. Glick, *Chem. Commun.*, **1966**, 813.

(82) A. K. Bose, M. S. Manhas, and R. M. Ramer, *Tetrahedron*, **21**, 449 (1965).

(83) Y. Iwakura, A. Nabeya, T. Nishiguchi, and Y. Ichikawa, *J. Org. Chem.*, **30**, 3410 (1965).

(84) L. A. Paquette and T. R. Phillips, *ibid.*, **30**, 3883 (1965).

(85) C. W. Bird, *Tetrahedron*, **22**, 2489 (1966).

(86) S. Searles, Jr., and E. F. Lutz, *J. Am. Chem. Soc.*, **81**, 3674 (1959).

(87) I. McMillan and R. J. Stoodley, *Tetrahedron Letters*, **No. 11**, 1205 (1966).

(88) J. C. Sheehan and G. D. Daves, Jr., *J. Org. Chem.*, **30**, 3247 (1965).

4

■ FURAN, PYRROLE, AND
THIOPHENE

THE UNSATURATED MONOHETERO ATOMIC five-membered ring systems, namely, furan [1], pyrrole [2], and thiophene [3], although embodying a cis-dienoid component in their structures, do not in general display

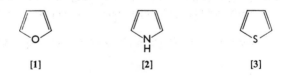

[1]   [2]   [3]

reactivities characteristic of analogous molecules such as cyclopentadiene. Rather, the reactions of these heterocycles (see below) suggest that they are endowed with considerable aromatic character, although there exists a wide variation in their chemical properties.[1]

From the molecular orbital point of view, these molecules are described as consisting of planar pentagons with sp^2-hybridized carbon atoms. Each of the four carbon atoms has 1 electron remaining in a p_z orbital, while the hetero atom has two such p-electrons. These p orbitals overlap to give rise to π-clouds above and below the ring (as exemplified for pyrrole in [4]); since the π-clouds contain 6 electrons, a stable closed shell of electrons ("aromatic sextet") exists and renders stability to the ring.

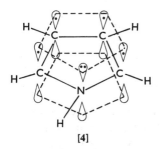

[4]

In the alternative valence-bond description, these molecules are considered as resonance hybrids of a number of contributing structures. This approach describes pictorially the result of the delocalization of the hetero atomic lone pair of electrons, namely, the acquisition

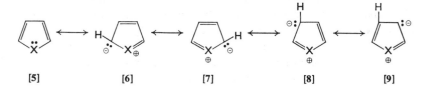

[5]   [6]   [7]   [8]   [9]

by the ring carbons of a degree of negative character. Structure [5] ·is the major contributor because no separation of charge is involved; of the remaining resonance structures, [6] and [7] would be expected to outweigh [8] and [9] in importance because of the smaller charge separation involved and because the chromophore is conjugated (as opposed to the cross-conjugation in the latter two formulas). Of considerable importance is the fact that, whereas two uncharged resonance structures may be written for benzene, for furan, pyrrole, and thiophene only one valence-bond structure with no charge separation is possible. This limitation is reflected in the experimental and calculated heats of combustion which demonstrate that the stabilization energies of the heterocycles are approximately half that of benzene, Table 4–1. Also, because the electronegativities of the

TABLE 4–I ■

Heats of Combustion and Stabilization Energies of the Five-Membered Heterocycles[2]

| Compound | ΔH, kcal/mole | | S.E. |
	Exptl.	Calcd.	
Benzene	789	827	37.9
Furan	507	523	16
Pyrrole	578	594	16
Thiophene	612	623	11

hetero atoms are in the order oxygen > nitrogen > sulfur, resonance structures [6]–[9] are less important in the case of furan relative to pyrrole and thiophene (oxygen is most resistant to releasing its pair of electrons) and, in consequence, furan is the least "aromatic" of the three heterocycles.

Additional evidence in support of the delocalized structures is available from bond length measurements (the bonds of the heterocycles are intermediate in length between the usual single and double bonds), microwave and ultraviolet spectra, and dipole moments. In the latter studies, comparison of the dipole moments of the heterocycles with those of appropriate reference compounds with known dipole vectors (arrow tip points to negative end of dipole) indicates electron pair delocalization into the ring and thus, significant contributions of the polar resonance structures.

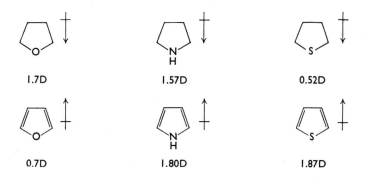

1.7D   1.57D   0.52D

0.7D   1.80D   1.87D

The aromaticity of these heterocycles is therefore dependent upon the two electrons which the hetero atom contributes to the π-system. In the case of pyrrole, this requirement deprives the nitrogen atom of the pair of electrons commonly associated with organic amines, and therefore pyrrole can form a salt only at the expense of its aromatic character. Pyrrole, therefore, is a very weak base ($pK_a = 0.4$) which in fact is protonated preferably at a ring carbon in strong acid,[3] and which is polymerized under such conditions presumably by attack of a nonprotonated pyrrole molecule upon its conjugated acid.[4]

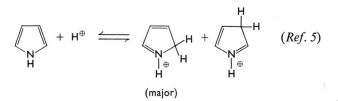

(major)   (*Ref. 5*)

Furans react violently with strong acids, but careful hydrolysis in dilute mineral acids can produce 1,4-dicarbonyl compounds in good yield. The presence of electron-withdrawing substituents on the

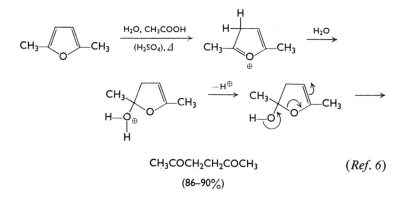

$CH_3COCH_2CH_2COCH_3$ (*Ref. 6*)

(86–90%)

furan nucleus lowers the basicity of the heterocycle and renders it more stable to mineral acid.

Thiophene, although virtually devoid of basic properties, does react with Meerwein's reagent [10] to yield a stable S-methylthiophenium salt.[7] Apparently, therefore, the "extra" lone electron pair

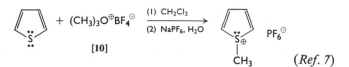

[10]

(Ref. 7)

on sulfur can become coordinated in certain cases without destruction of the ring. Attempts to oxidize thiophene leads to **[11]** which presumably results via a Diels-Alder reaction of the intermediate

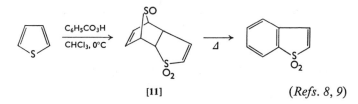

[11]   *(Refs. 8, 9)*

thiophene sulfoxide to thiophene sulfone. Thiophene-1,1-dioxide **[12]** has been synthesized in six steps from butadiene sulfone[10a] and was found to be stable only in dilute solution. It is extremely reactive and may function as a diene or dienophile in the Diels-Alder reaction. Several examples are given below. The reactions of **[12]** are thus

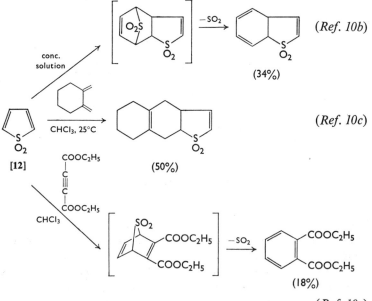

characteristic of an unsaturated compound, not of an aromatic species. Thiophene-1-oxide has also been obtained in solution, but is even less stable than [12], and dimerizes spontaneously by a similar diene-type reaction.[11]

SYNTHETIC APPROACHES

Furan [1] is available cheaply from its 2-aldehyde derivative, furfural, which in turn is obtained readily by acid hydrolysis of the polysaccharides in oat hulls or other naturally occurring substances which contain pentose fragments such as corncobs[12] and straw. Passage of the aldehyde in the vapor phase over catalysts such as nickel (280°C)[13] or lime (350°C)[14] gives furan in high yields. Al-

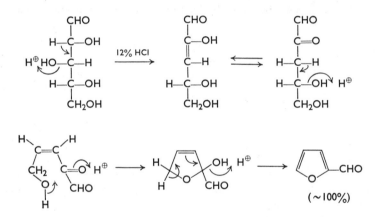

ternatively, furfural can be converted to furoic acid by the Cannizzaro reaction,[15] or preferably by air oxidation in the presence of alkaline cuprous and silver salts[16]; the acid can then be thermally decarboxylated to furan.[17]

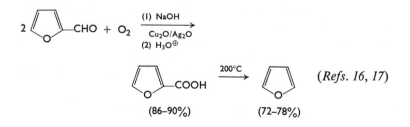

(*Refs. 16, 17*)

Pyrrole [2] is prepared commercially by the fractional distillation of coal tar and bone oil or by the passage of furan, ammonia, and steam over an alumina catalyst at 400°C. In the latter process, a primary amine may be substituted for the ammonia in which case a

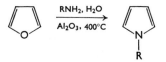

1-substituted pyrrole is obtained. An improved method for preparing pyrroles from furans involves the intermediate 2,5-dialkoxy-tetrahydrofurans (see p. 135). Pyrrole may also be obtained conveniently in the laboratory by heating ammonium mucate[18]; at the

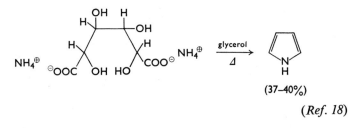

(37–40%)

(*Ref. 18*)

elevated temperature, the ammonium salt dissociates into the free acid, which undergoes dehydration, decarboxylation, and finally cyclization with the ammonia.

The commercial synthesis of thiophene [3] involves the cyclization of butane, butadiene, or butenes with sulfur; the constituents are preheated to 600°C and passed rapidly (contact time about 1 second) through a reaction tube, the exit gases from which are cooled rapidly. The unreacted materials are recycled, and the redistilled thiophene is of 99% purity.[19] On a laboratory scale, thiophene is prepared by heating an intimate mixture of sodium succinate and phosphorus trisulfide.[20] This method finds utility in the fact that the position of

$$CH_2COO^\ominus Na^\oplus \atop CH_2COO^\ominus Na^\oplus + P_2S_3 \xrightarrow{\Delta}$$

(*Ref. 20a*)

(25–30%)

substituents on the heterocycle can be controlled by proper selection of the substituted succinic acid.[20b, 21]

The Paal-Knorr Synthesis[22]

The general procedure whereby an enolizable 1,4-dicarbonyl compound is heated either with a dehydrating agent (H_2SO_4, P_2O_5, $ZnCl_2$, etc.), ammonia or a primary amine, or an inorganic sulfide is known as the Paal-Knorr synthesis. Because of the ready availability of a wide variety of such dicarbonyl compounds, the reaction is of very wide applicability. The mechanistic aspect of this group of reactions has been little studied, but probable reaction pathways are suggested below. The driving force in all of these processes

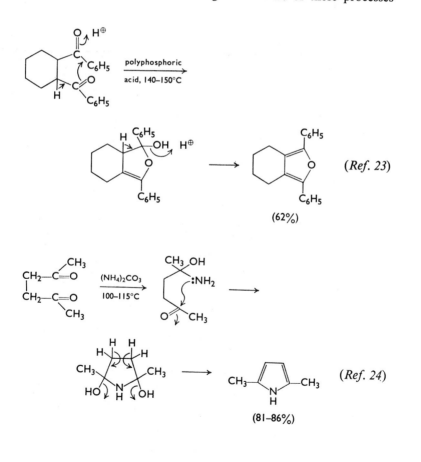

(*Ref. 23*)

(62%)

(*Ref. 24*)

(81-86%)

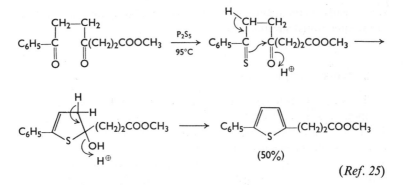

(Ref. 25)

results from the stabilization gained in formation of the aromatic heterocycle.

The Feist-Benary Furan Synthesis[26] and the Hantzsch Pyrrole Synthesis[27]

The reaction of an α-haloketone or aldehyde with a β-keto ester (or β-diketone) in the presence of a base such as sodium hydroxide or pyridine leads to the formation of furans. When a nitrogen base such as ammonia or a primary amine is employed, reaction with the keto ester generally precedes condensation with the halocarbonyl component, and a pyrrole results predominantly. The first reaction very likely proceeds by means of initial O-alkylation followed by

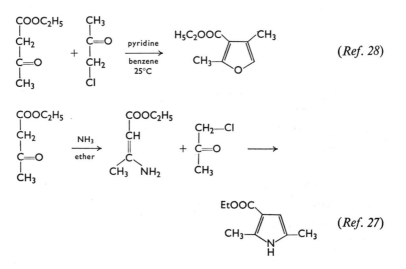

C_3—C_4 ring closure.   Pyrroles result when formation of intermediate enamines is possible in which case the usual enamine C-alkylation pathway is operative and is followed by N—C_2 cyclization.

The Knorr Pyrrole Synthesis[29]

The condensation of an α-aminoketone or α-amino-β-keto ester with a ketone or keto ester in the presence of such reagents as acetic acid (frequently) or alkali (less frequently) gives rise to pyrroles in good yields.   The Knorr reaction represents the most general and widely applicable pyrrole synthesis.   The α-aminoketones are usually

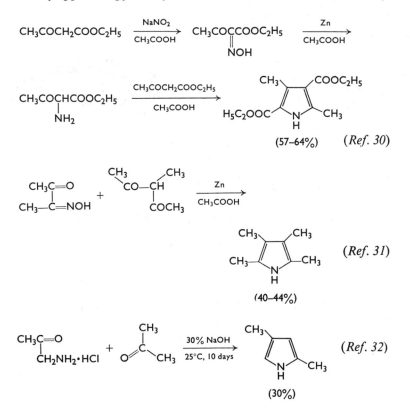

prepared by nitrosation of β-keto esters or β-diketones to give the related oxime which is reduced subsequently with zinc in acetic acid. Generally, the ring closure is effected most conveniently by preparing and condensing the α-aminoketone in the same operation[33]; the reductive conditions do not affect the coreactant. Numerous variations of this reaction have been used; the primary limitation resides in the propensity of the α-aminoketone to dimerize,[34] if the ketone or keto ester is not sufficiently reactive to condense at an appreciable rate. The mechanistic details of the Knorr synthesis have not been investigated, but the following sequence appears likely:

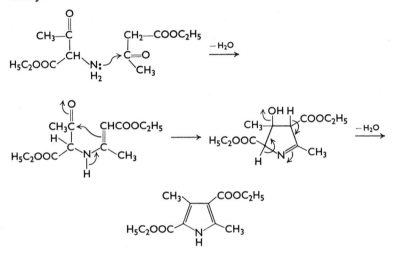

In the second example selected above, intermediate [13] is formed and deacylation leads to the pyrrole, probably as shown below:

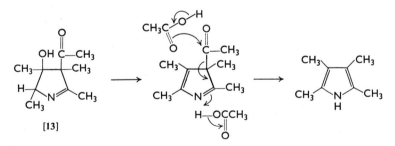

The Hinsberg Thiophene Synthesis[35]

The reaction of α-diketones, α-haloesters, and oxalic esters with diethyl thiodiacetate [14] under Claisen-type conditions (usually sodium alkoxide in alcohol) produces thiophene derivatives in good yields and has proved to be quite general.[20b]   Usually, the reaction is worked up by diluting the alcoholic alkaline mixture with water, refluxing the solution briefly, and isolating the free dicarboxylic acid

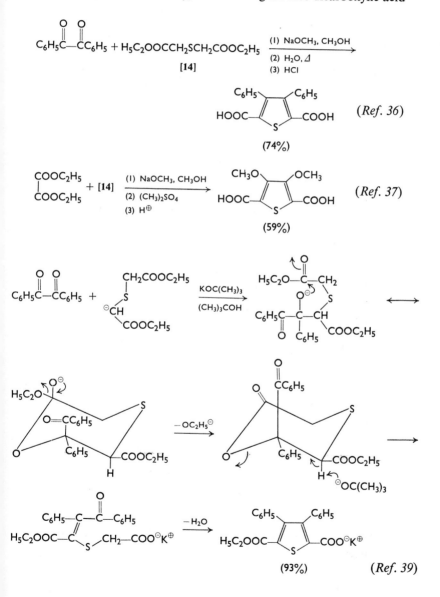

thus formed.   This method is of special interest because the thiophene dicarboxylic acids are readily decarboxylated (by pyrolysis) to produce the 3,4-disubstituted thiophenes.   Furthermore, by varying the ester component from the sulfur to the oxygen, selenium, and nitrogen analogs, the appropriate corresponding heterocycles can be prepared.[38]

Although the implication that diesters are the primary products in the Hinsberg reaction is rampant in the literature,[20b] it is now known that half-acid half-esters actually result, and that they result from a process which is mechanistically analogous to the Stobbe condensation.[39]

Use of Acetylenedicarboxylic Esters

The reaction of acetylenedicarboxylic esters with a variety of nucleophiles yields furan, pyrrole, and thiophene derivatives.   The mechanistic course of the additions obviously involves Michael addition followed by cyclization as outlined below.

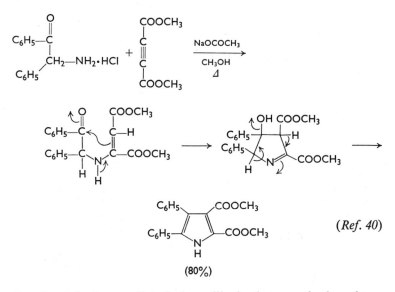

(*Ref. 40*)

(80%)

Certain of the intermediate hydroxydihydro heterocycles have been isolated and independently "aromatized."[40]   This latter step is reminiscent of the mechanism of the Knorr pyrrole synthesis (see p. 111).

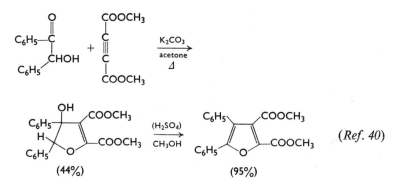

(Ref. 40)

(44%)   (95%)

REACTIONS

Electrophilic Substitution

Furan, pyrrole, and thiophene are very reactive toward the usual electrophilic reagents; in fact, their reactivity is in many ways reminiscent of the most reactive benzene derivatives, namely phenols and anilines. This enhanced susceptibility to electrophilic attack is due to the unsymmetrical charge distribution in these heterocycles, whereby the ring carbon atoms are endowed with greater negative charge than in benzene (see p. 103). Of the three systems, furan is slightly more reactive than pyrrole, while thiophene is the least reactive; the following competitive reaction illustrates this point to some degree:

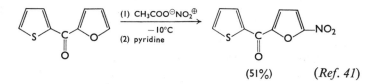

(51%)   (Ref. 41)

In this regard, the higher reactivity of the 2- and 3-positions of thiophene relative to a single position in benzene is known with some accuracy; the ratio of the rate of protodesilylation (exemplified for the 2-isomer below) for the 2- and 3-substituted thiophene derivatives (k_2/k_3) is 43.5. When compared to benzene, the partial rate factors become 5000 and 115 for the 2- and 3-positions, respectively.[42]

Thiophene is much more stable than furan or pyrrole to acids; this single fact allows greater latitude when selecting conditions for electro-

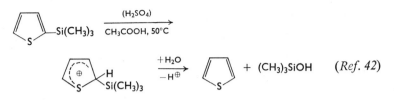

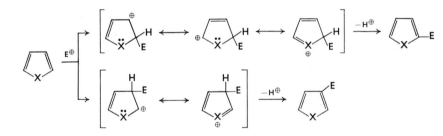

philic substitution of thiophene, whereas with the other two hetero-cycles strongly acidic conditions, which would lead to polymerization, must be avoided.

Electrophilic substitution of the title compounds occurs pre-ferentially at the 2-position because the transition state for attack at this site is of lower energy (due to greater resonance stabilization) than that at the 3-position.   Since the rate of substitution at either position

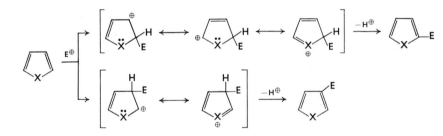

is dependent upon the energy difference between ground state of reactants and the particular transition state, that process which passes through the more stable transition state will occur more rapidly (see Figure 4–1).

The sulfonation of thiophene proceeds readily in 95% sulfuric acid at room temperature to give thiophene-2-sulfonic acid in 69–76% yield.[43]   Such strongly acidic conditions cannot be utilized for furan and pyrrole, but with 1-proto-1-pyridinium sulfonate [15] the respec-tive 2-sulfonic acids can be obtained in 90% yields.[44]   It should be noted that benzene and its homologs are not sulfonated by this reagent which is, however, sufficiently reactive to effect substitution of anisole and thiophene (86%).[45]

The direct halogenation of furan is extremely vigorous and useful products rarely are isolated because the liberated hydrogen halide causes polymerization.[46]   Under very mild conditions, however, bromine adds to furan to afford the unstable intermediate [16] which

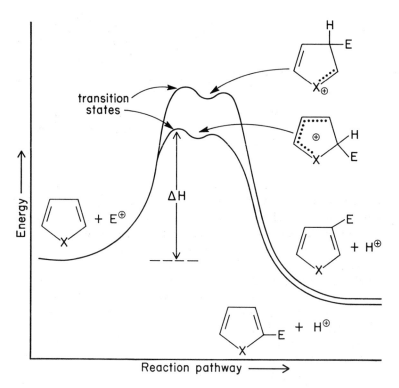

FIGURE 4-1. Energy diagram for the electrophilic substitution of the five-membered unsaturated heterocycles at the 2- and 3-positions.

is solvolyzed rapidly by the medium employed. Furan is brominated by dioxane dibromide at 0°C to give 2-bromofuran in good yield[49]; the mechanism by which this reaction occurs is not known with

[15]   (90%)   (*Ref. 44*)

certainty. By comparison, pyrrole also reacts very readily with halogenating agents, and perhalogenated pyrroles are invariably obtained. Thiophene reacts so vigorously with chlorine and bromine

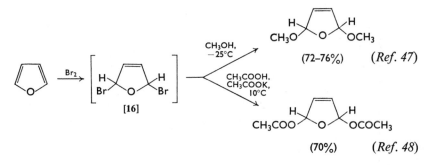

(72–76%)   (*Ref. 47*)

(70%)   (*Ref. 48*)

that pure monosubstituted thiophenes are difficult to prepare; contamination with polyhalogenated derivatives generally prevails. The iodination of thiophene proceeds very slowly, but 2-iodothiophene results in good yields from iodination in the presence of mercuric oxide in benzene (75%)[50] or aqueous nitric acid (70%).[51]

Attempts to nitrate [1], [2], or [3] under conditions normally employed for benzene and its derivatives invariably result in destruction of the heterocycle and tar formation. Instead, successful nitration is achieved with acetyl nitrate (i.e., the mixed anhydride generated from fuming nitric acid and acetic anhydride) at low temperatures. Under these conditions at 5°C, pyrrole affords mainly 2-nitropyrrole (83%), but some (5–7%) of the 3-isomer also is isolated.[52] Similarly at 10°C, thiophene gives rise to 2-nitrothiophene (70%) and 3-nitrothiophene (5%).[53] Furan, on the other hand, reacts initially with this reagent to give the addition compound [17][54]; treatment of [17] with pyridine removes the elements of

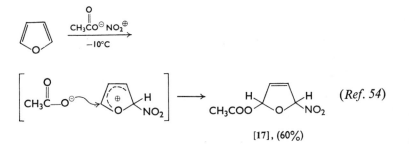

[17], (60%)

acetic acid and generates 2-nitrofuran.[55] Again in this instance a clear distinction in reactivity is apparent; whereas electrophilic substitution of pyrrole and thiophene are direct and parallel in type what is observed in benzenoid systems, several such reactions with furan proceed through the formation of 2,5-dihydrofuran derivatives.

Attempts to alkylate furan by the Friedel-Crafts method have proved uniformly unsuccessful because catalysts required for the reaction also catalyze polymerization. Because furans bearing electron-withdrawing groups are more stable to electrophilic attack, acylation of [1] can be achieved readily with a mild Lewis acid since the products are relatively stable to such acids. Best results are obtained when interaction of the unreacted furan with the catalyst

$$\text{furan} + (CH_3CO)_2O \xrightarrow[CH_3COOH]{BF_3} \text{2-acetylfuran—COCH}_3$$

(75–92%) (*Ref. 56*)

is kept at a minimum. 2-Acetylpyrrole may be obtained merely by heating pyrrole with acetic anhydride in the absence of catalyst.[57] Because of the high stability of thiophene to acidic conditions, Friedel-Crafts acylation of [3] can be achieved with a wide variety of catalysts with excellent results. In the Friedel-Crafts alkylation of

$$\text{thiophene} + CH_3COCl \xrightarrow[C_6H_6]{SnCl_4} \text{2-acetylthiophene—COCH}_3 \quad (Ref. 58)$$

(79–83%)

thiophene, both the 2- and 3-positions are attacked in ratios varying from 1:1 to 3:1 depending upon the reagent and catalyst employed.[59] This poor selectivity is due to the highly reactive nature of the electrophilic alkyl cations which attack the heterocycle in rather indiscriminate fashion.

Examples of various other electrophilic substitutions are illustrated in the following equations.

$$\text{furan} \xrightarrow[\substack{CH_3COONa \\ H_2O,\ C_2H_5OH}]{HgCl_2} \text{—HgCl} + ClHg\text{—furan—HgCl} \quad (Ref. 60)$$

(33.5%)

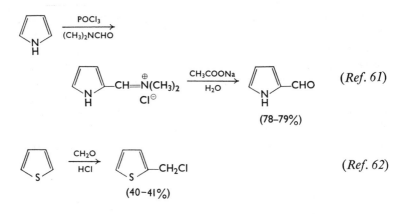

(*Ref. 61*)

(78–79%)

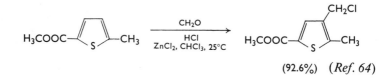

(40–41%)   (*Ref. 62*)

When the 2- and 5-positions of the above heterocycles already carry substituents, the electrophile will attack at one or the other, or both, of the available β-positions (carbon atoms 3 and 4). The particular entry position of the electrophile generally is controlled by electronic considerations, that is, that reaction pathway will be favored which will proceed through the transition state of lowest energy. For example, nitration of [18] gives rise exclusively to [21] by virtue of the fact that intermediate [19] is endowed with more resonance stabilization than [20], in which the positive charge is located in an energetically unfavorable close proximity to the ester carbonyl group.

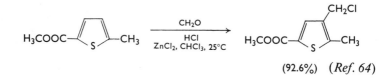

(92.6%)   (*Ref. 64*)

A rather common phenomenon observed in electrophilic substitution of certain 2,5-disubstituted derivatives of furan, pyrrole, and thiophene is the displacement of an atom or group already attached to the nucleus by the entering electrophile. Such substitution with elimination of substituents is more prevalent than in the benzene series because of the much higher relative reactivity of the α-positions in the heterocyclic systems due to stabilization of intermediates such as [22] by the hetero atom. This stabilization lowers the energy of the

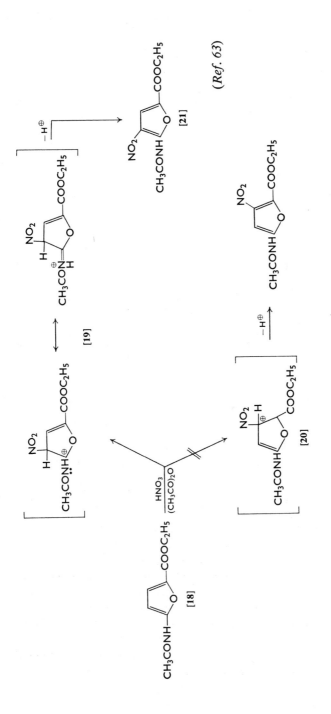

(Ref. 63)

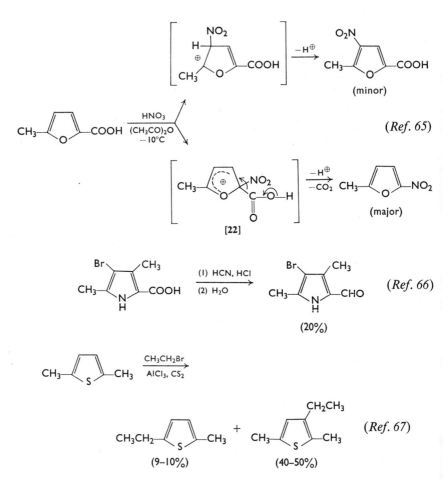

(Ref. 65)

[22]

(Ref. 66)

(Ref. 67)

transition state leading to attack at the substituted α-position with the resulting effect that the rate of this process becomes competitive with the rate of substitution at a β-position.

An analysis of the orientation or directive effects of substituents in relation to the introduction of a second substituent into the heterocyclic nucleus is somewhat more complex than in benzene derivatives. In the latter series, the position attacked by an electrophile is determined largely by the electronic characteristics of the group already present. With furan, pyrrole, and thiophene, although the substituent plays a decisive role in the substitution process, the ring

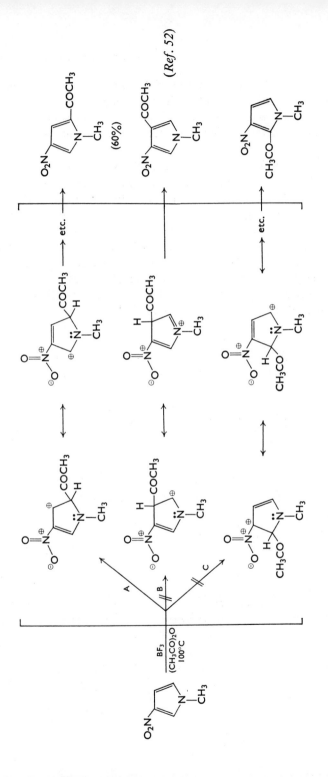

(Ref. 52)

hetero atom also exerts a profound directing influence in the manner outlined in earlier examples. The complicating factor is that the oxygen, nitrogen, and sulfur atoms differ substantially in the magnitude of their α-directing effect. These points are illustrated below

(a) ELECTRON-WITHDRAWING 3-SUBSTITUENT. As might be expected from the combined "meta-directing" influence of an electron-withdrawing substituent and the α-directing influence of the hetero atom, the entering group will enter the α-position most remote to the 3-substituent. Of the three possibilities in the acetylation of 1-methyl-3-nitropyrrole, path A is favored heavily over the alternative routes because of the extensive relative stabilization in the cationic intermediate; path C is especially unfavorable because of the proximity of positive charges in one of the resonance contributors. This mechanistic rationale is applicable to all three heterocyclic systems.

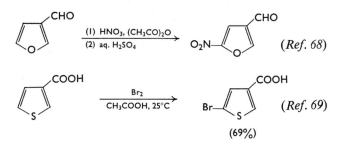

(b) ELECTRON-DONATING 3-SUBSTITUENT. Such substituents direct the incoming electrophile to the adjacent 2-position because of the

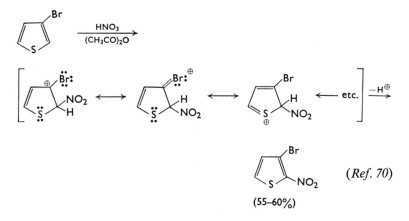

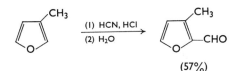

(57%)

(Ref. 71)

lower energy of the intermediates along that particular reaction pathway. However, in certain derivatives, especially the 3-alkyl heterocycles, the difference in reactivity of the 2- and 5-positions is small; product distribution often is altered by such secondary effects as the relative steric bulk of the alkyl group and/or the entering electrophile. For example, whereas 3-methylthiophene gives upon acylation (92% yield) a mixture consisting of about 80% of the 2,3-isomer and 20% of the 3,5-isomer,[72] acylation of 3-isopropyl-thiophene affords an isomer ratio of 31:48, respectively,[73] and 3-*tert*-butylthiophene gives rise exclusively to 4-*tert*-butyl-2-acetylthio-phene.[74]

(c) ELECTRON-WITHDRAWING 2-SUBSTITUENT. An electronegative substituent in the 2-position will tend to favor electrophilic substitution in the 4-position; however, this effect is in direct competition with the α-directing effect of the hetero atom which dictates attack at the 5-position. Actually, the ratio of products obtained is a result of the relative capabilities of the two opposing factors to control the substitution reaction and of the selectivity of the electrophilic reagent. Thus, it has been found that nitration of 2-nitrofuran yields only the 2,5-dinitro compound,[75] that 2-nitrothiophene leads to a mixture of 85% of 2,4-dinitro- and 15% of 2,5-dinitro-isomers,[76] and that 2-nitropyrrole gives the dinitro derivatives in a ratio of about 4:1, respectively.[77] Similarly, nitration of 2-acetylfuran furnishes only 2-acetyl-5-nitrofuran,[78] but upon nitration of the corresponding 2-acetylthiophene and 2-acetylpyrrole the 2,4- and 2,5-dinitro derivatives are isolated in ratios of roughly 1:1[79] and 2:1,[77, 80] respectively. The above examples show the overwhelming α-directing effect of the hetero oxygen atom of furan, which influence is much less domineering in the case of the sulfur and nitrogen atoms of thiophene and pyrrole. Several exceptions to this pattern of reactivity are known, but will not be discussed here.

(d) ELECTRON-DONATING 2-SUBSTITUENT. When analyzing the energetics of electrophilic attack at the various positions of [1], [2], or [3] substituted with an electropositive substituent at the 2-position in the manner outlined for the nitration of 2-bromothiophene, it

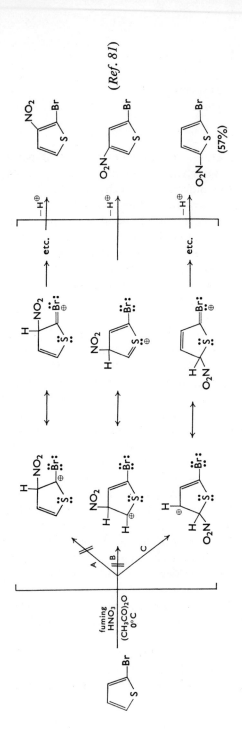

(Ref. 81)

becomes apparent that the substituent can stabilize the intermediates formed in routes A and C. However, if the 2-substituent is weakly directing as in the case of halogen and alkyl groups, the α-directing capability of the hetero atom is the prevailing effect and substitution at the 5-position is favored heavily. When the activating influence of a 2-substituent is more pronounced, such as, for example, with —OCH$_3$, —SCH$_3$, and —NHCOCH$_3$ groups, substitution at the 3-position is often more prevalent. The nature of the electrophilic reagent also plays a role in the isomer distribution, but this effect has not yet been studied systematically.[82]

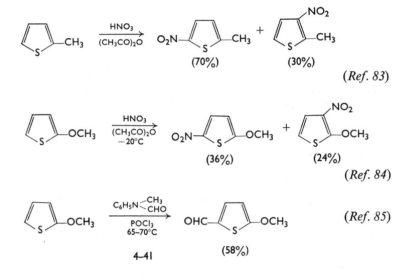

(*Ref. 83*)

(*Ref. 84*)

(*Ref. 85*)

4–41

Nucleophilic and Radical Substitutions

Nucleophilic and radical substitution reactions of the five-membered unsaturated monohetero atomic ring systems has been investigated much less than electrophilic substitution, especially in the case of pyrroles, and are not as well understood.[86]

Although the halogen-substituted furans and thiophenes are relatively inert to nucleophilic substitution (for example, neither 2-bromo- nor 2-iodofuran react with sodium methoxide at 100°C),[87] their reactivity is somewhat greater than that of the corresponding aryl halides. With reference to Table 4–2, it is evident from an examination of the values of the rate-controlling free energy of

TABLE 4–2 ▪

Activation Parameters for Nucleophilic Displacement in Piperidine at 200°C [88]

Compound	ΔE^*, kcal	ΔF^*, kcal	ΔS^*, e.u.
2-Chlorofuran	22	41.2	−42
Chlorobenzene	27	43.3	−42
2-Bromofuran	22	39.1	−39
Bromobenzene	24	41.4	−42
2-Iodofuran	31	38.7	−19
2-Iodo-5-methylfuran	26	39.5	−29
Iodobenzene	23.6	40.7	−38.2

activation that the furans have a slightly more reactive carbon-halogen bond than the benzene analogs. Of some interest is the fact that a 5-methyl group in this series causes a 2.2-fold decrease in rate.

As in the benzene series, the introduction of powerful electron-withdrawing groups, such as the nitro substituent, greatly facilitates nucleophilic substitution. In such examples, the activated halogen-substituted five-membered ring heterocycles are far more reactive than their benzenoid counterparts (see Table 4–3). Because the

TABLE 4–3 ▪

Relative Pseudo First Order Rates of Displacement with Piperidine at 25°C [89]

Compound	Rate
m-Bromonitrobenzene	1
p-Bromonitrobenzene	185
o-Bromonitrobenzene	1620
5-Bromo-2-nitrothiophene	2.84×10^4
2-Bromo-3-nitrothiophene	6.32×10^5
5-Bromo-3-nitrothiophene	Very fast
4-Bromo-2-nitrothiophene	1360
3-Bromo-3-nitrothiophene	2.5×10^6
4-Bromo-3-nitrothiophene	Very fast [90]

rates of such displacement processes are sufficiently rapid, such reactions find considerable synthetic utility. The most useful activating group is the carboxy or carboalkoxy function because of the ease with which it can be removed, as shown in the following examples. Halothiophenes and furans which are not activated by an electron-withdrawing substituent, often can be made to undergo substitution under forcing conditions as, for example, in [23].

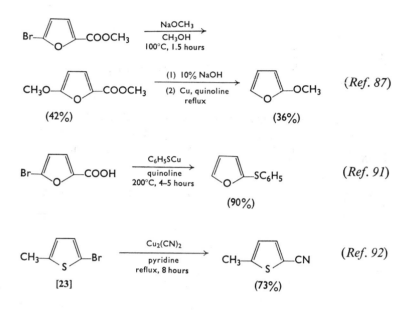

The greater reactivity of the heteroaromatics can be attributed to the inductive effect of the hetero atom which increases slightly the electron deficiency at the halogen-bearing carbon (relative to benzene); however, this effect must be small because it is opposed by resonance effects and the possible repulsion of the approaching nucleophile by the *p*-electrons of the oxygen or sulfur atom.

Relatively little attention has been directed to radical substitution of the five-membered heterocycles. However, it has been established that homolytic attack at the 2-position predominates or is exclusive, as illustrated in the following examples. When thiophene is treated

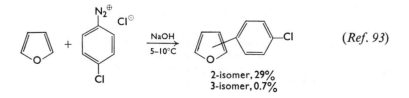

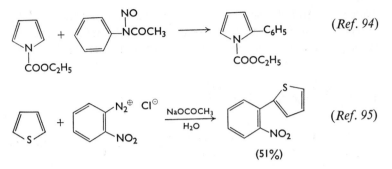

(*Ref. 94*)

(*Ref. 95*)

with radical sources which can readily yield stable anions (e.g., benzoate or iodide, see Table 4–4), results suggest that in these instances a 1-electron transfer process is favored; that is, an initially formed

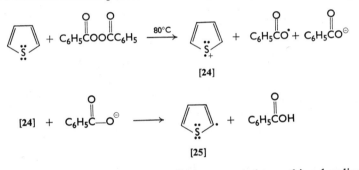

radical cation (e.g., [24]) eventually is converted to a thienyl radical (e.g., [25]), and ultimately to products. In cases where stable

TABLE 4-4 ▪

Biaryl Fractions from Homolytic Phenylations of Thiophene[96]

Product, mole %	Radical source[a]			
	A	B	C	D
2-Phenylthiophene[b]	22.8	86.7	63.0	63.1
3-Phenylthiophene	—	13.3	37.0	5.5
2,2′-Bithienyl	15.8	—	—	24.5
2,3′-Bithienyl	18.3	—	—	6.8

[a] Source: A, dibenzoyl peroxide; B, phenylazotriphenylmethane in air; C, phenylazotriphenylmethane in nitrogen; D, iodobenzene.

[b] Yield of 2-phenylthiophene (based on radical source): A, 3.75%; B, 0.91%; C, 0.58%; D, 3.25%.

nucleophiles cannot form (generally the situation in the examples studied to date), direct substitution of the heterocycle apparently occurs. Under such circumstances bithienyls would not be expected, and indeed are not observed (see Table 4–4 for example).

Thiophene can be converted conveniently to 2-bromothiophene through the agency of N-bromosuccinimide by a process which is believed to be radical in nature.[97] Bromination of 2-methylthiophene with the same reagent under conditions which, in the case of

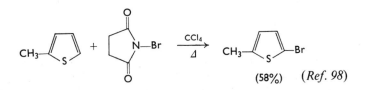

(58%)   (*Ref. 98*)

toluene, would lead to halogenation of the methyl substituent gives 5-bromo-2-methylthiophene and only very small amounts of 2-bromomethylthiophene. Such behavior reflects the greater reactivity of the thiophene ring relative to a similarly substituted benzene ring toward homolytic substitution.

Furan and thiophene undergo normal addition reactions with carbenes. The photolytic decomposition of diazoacetic ester or the cuprous bromide-catalyzed reactions of diazomethane with these

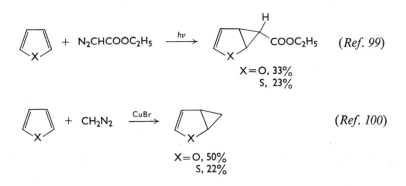

heterocycles gives the anticipated cyclopropane derivatives. Pyrroles, on the other hand, when subjected to the copper-catalyzed decomposition of diazoacetic ester give the normal product of electrophilic substitution. Examples of α- and β-attack are known.

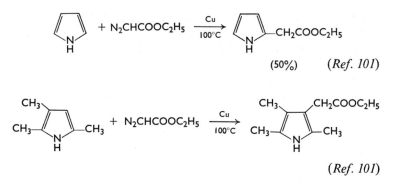

(50%)   (*Ref. 101*)

(*Ref. 101*)

Submission of pyrrole to the Reimer-Tiemann reaction (strong base and CHCl$_3$),[102] conditions which are known to favor dichlorocarbene formation, yields 3-chloropyridine or pyrrole-2-aldehyde depending upon the particular reagents employed.   The bicyclic intermediate [26] has been postulated in these transformations.

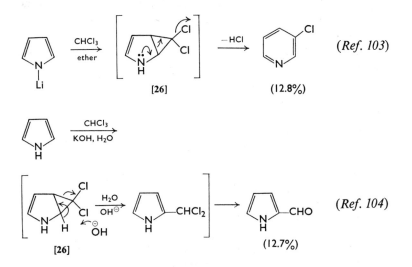

Metalations and halogen-metal interconversion reactions of [1] [2], and [3] may be considered as nucleophilic substitution on hydrogen and halogen, respectively, and therefore will be discussed here. Furan[105] and thiophene[106] are metalated in high yield when treated with *n*-butyllithium; 2-furyllithium and 2-thienyllithium result.   The metalation reaction is believed to proceed via a four-centered process in which almost complete carbon-hydrogen bond cleavage occurs in the transition state. This mechanism is in accord with the large

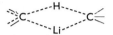

isotope effects observed with thiophenes labeled in the 2-position, that is, $k_H/k_D = 6.6$ and $k_H/k_T = 16$.[107] The high selectivity for α-attack is evidenced by the fact that 2-substituted furans and thiophenes are metalated exclusively in the 5-position. When both

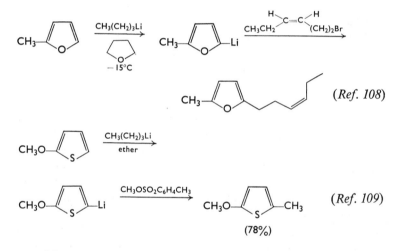

(Ref. 108)

(Ref. 109)

(78%)

α-positions carry substituents, this specificity obviously cannot be operative; in fact, metalation of 2,5-disubstituted derivatives may or may not occur, the reactivity apparently being dependent upon the nature of these substituents. Thus, although 2-methoxy-5-methyl-thiophene is metalated in the 3-position, 2,5-dimethylthiophene does not react.[84] For purposes of comparison, it should be noted that benzene is metalated extremely slowly and to a very small extent by *n*-butyllithium in ether.[110] Metalation studies of 3-substituted thiophenes have shown that substituents also exert a directive effect in this process. For example, whereas 3-methylthiophene is metalated predominantly in the 5-position,[109, 111] the 3-methoxy,[112] 3-methylthio-,[113] and 3-bromo-derivatives[111a] are metalated in the

2-position. These data can be interpreted on the basis of the inductive effect of the particular substituent on the acidity of the 2- or 5-hydrogen; as a result of the electron-releasing effect of the 3-methyl group, the 2-hydrogen is relatively less acidic than the 5-hydrogen while the reversal of this situation occurs with the electronegative substituents.

Pyrrole reacts readily with a wide variety of Grignard reagents to give the pyrrole Grignard reagent,[114] the structure of which has been the subject of much controversy. Recent physical evidence suggests that pyrrylmagnesium chloride consists predominantly of an N—MgX [27] or ionic species [28].[115] Alkylation of pyrrylmagnesium bromide with a series of alkyl halides results in the

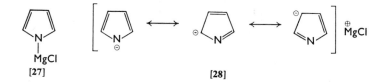

[27]   [28]

formation of isomeric 2- and 3-alkylpyrroles (generally with the former predominating to the extent of 1.5–3.0 to 1) and polyalkyl-pyrroles.[116] Only 2-acylpyrroles result from the acylation of the same reagent with acyl halides or esters.[116] Thus, magnesium (and also lithium) salts of pyrrole give mainly products of C-alkylation. In contrast, the sodium and potassium salts of pyrrole form predominantly N-alkylated products.[117] Because the percentage of N-alkylation decreases with the coordinating ability of the metal ion and increases with the solvating power of the medium, dissociation of the pyrryl-metal ion pair is believed to favor N-alkylation.[117]

Bromo- and iodo-substituted furans and thiophenes undergo halogen-metal interconversion with n-butyl- or phenyllithium and

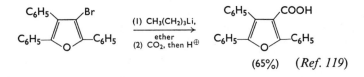

(65%)   (Ref. 119)

give rise to the corresponding heterocyclic lithium derivatives in high yield.[118] Such conversions are especially important from a synthetic viewpoint in the case of the 3-halo-derivatives because they yield

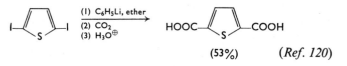

(53%)   (*Ref. 120*)

Grignard reagents only with difficulty or not at all.   Because an acidic
(NH) hydrogen remains in N-unsubstituted 3-halogeno pyrroles, and
therefore prototropic shifts can be expected, such 3-lithium derivatives
are generally only stable at $-70°C$ for several hours.[121]

Ring Cleavage and Addition Reactions[122]

Furan, pyrrole, and thiophene vary considerably in the ease with
which they undergo ring cleavage reactions.   The opening of the
furan ring, for example, can be effected with a wide variety of reagents.
The conversion of furans to 1,4-dicarbonyl compounds with dilute
mineral acids has been discussed earlier (see p. 105).   2,5-Dialkoxy-
and 2,5-diacyloxydihydrofurans, which result in high yield from
1,4-additions to furan (see p. 118), have proven to be very useful
synthetic intermediates.[123]

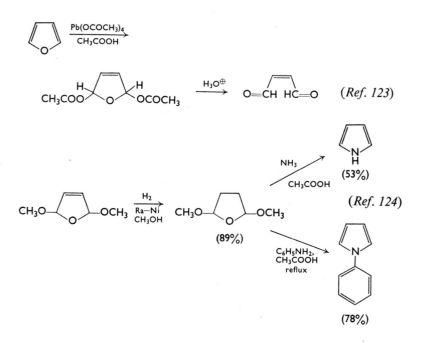

In contrast, the pyrrole ring is not cleaved readily by acids (see p. 105) or bases, but when pyrrole is refluxed with an alcoholic solution of hydroxylamine hydrochloride, succindialdoxime is obtained. Δ^3-Pyrrolines are formed in the reduction of pyrroles with zinc and acid.

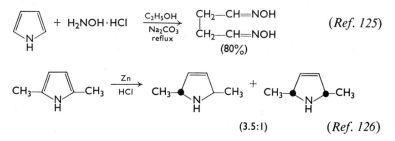

Being the most "aromatic" of the three systems (see p. 104), thiophene is the most resistant to ring-opening reactions. A uniquely important cleavage of thiophenes, however, is embodied in the Raney nickel desulfurization procedure,[127] which has received wide application as a synthetic pathway to a variety of compounds. Several examples are given below.

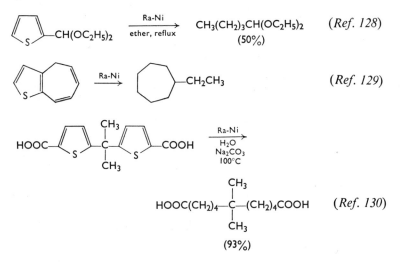

The same wide variety in reactivity of [1], [2], and [3] is observed in addition reactions. Whereas furan and its derivatives behave as typical dienes in the Diels-Alder reaction, pyrroles undergo such condensations with considerable difficulty, it at all. For example pyrrole reacts with maleic anhydride to give only a product of substitution [29],[132] and acetylenedicarboxylic acid adds to 1-benzyl-pyrrole to afford [30] in 8.5% yield, together with α-substituted

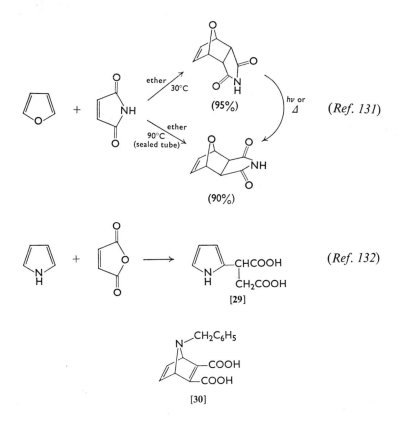

(Ref. 131)

(Ref. 132)

[29]

[30]

products.[133] Thiophene does not enter into reaction with dienophiles.[134, 135]

The addition of benzyne to furans has been found to proceed readily and in good yield.[136] Substituted pyrroles have been found generally to give N-substituted 1- and 2-naphthylamines, and not the expected 1,4-imines.[137] Apparently, the Diels-Alder reaction occurs to form the imines, but the latter immediately rearrange to the naphthylamines. This theory is substantiated by the isolation of the stable imines [31] and [32].

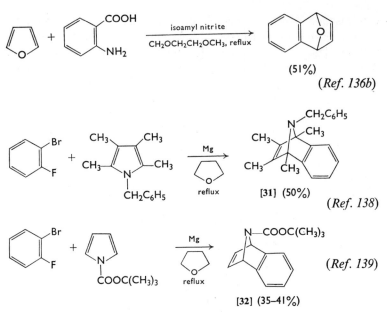

(51%)

(*Ref. 136b*)

[31] (50%)

(*Ref. 138*)

(*Ref. 139*)

[32] (35–41%)

Exercises

1. Predict the major product of the following reactions:

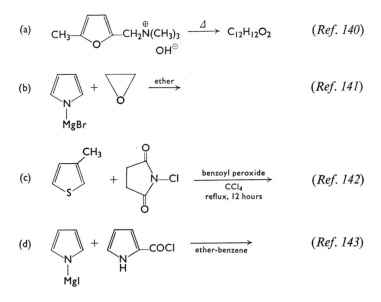

(a) CH_3 — furan — $CH_2\overset{\oplus}{N}(CH_3)_3$ $OH^{\ominus}$ $\xrightarrow{\Delta}$ $C_{12}H_{12}O_2$ (*Ref. 140*)

(b) pyrrole-N-MgBr + ethylene oxide $\xrightarrow{\text{ether}}$ (*Ref. 141*)

(c) 3-methylthiophene + N-chlorosuccinimide $\xrightarrow[\text{reflux, 12 hours}]{\substack{\text{benzoyl peroxide} \\ CCl_4}}$ (*Ref. 142*)

(d) pyrrole-N-MgI + pyrrole-2-$COCl$ $\xrightarrow{\text{ether-benzene}}$ (*Ref. 143*)

(e) 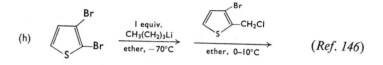 (*Ref. 144*)

(f) 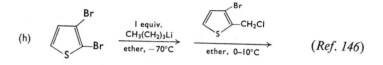 (*Ref. 144*)

(g) $CH_3OOCCH_2NHC_2H_5 + CH_3OOC—C≡C—COOCH_3$

$$\xrightarrow[\substack{(2)\ K,\ toluene \\ (3)\ neutralization}]{(1)\ ether}} C_{10}H_{13}NO_5$$ (*Ref. 145*)

(h) 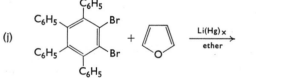 (*Ref. 146*)

(j) 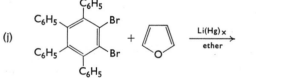 (*Ref. 148*)

(i) 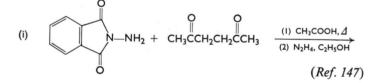 (*Ref. 147*)

(k)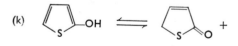

$$CH_3\overset{O}{\overset{\|}{C}}CH_2COOC_2H_5 \xrightarrow[C_2H_5OH]{NaOC_2H_5} C_{10}H_{14}O_4S$$ (*Ref. 149*)

(l) 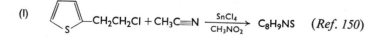 (*Ref. 150*)

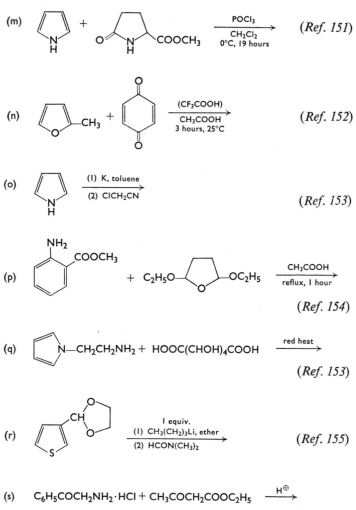

(m) ... $\xrightarrow[\substack{CH_2Cl_2 \\ 0°C, 19 \text{ hours}}]{POCl_3}$ (*Ref. 151*)

(n) ... $\xrightarrow[\substack{CH_3COOH \\ 3 \text{ hours, } 25°C}]{(CF_3COOH)}$ (*Ref. 152*)

(o) ... $\xrightarrow[\text{(2) ClCH}_2CN]{\text{(1) K, toluene}}$ (*Ref. 153*)

(p) ... $+ \ C_2H_5O\text{—}\underset{O}{\overset{}{}}\text{—}OC_2H_5 \xrightarrow[\text{reflux, 1 hour}]{CH_3COOH}$ (*Ref. 154*)

(q) $\begin{array}{c}\text{N—CH}_2\text{CH}_2\text{NH}_2\end{array} + HOOC(CHOH)_4COOH \xrightarrow{\text{red heat}}$ (*Ref. 153*)

(r) ... $\xrightarrow[\text{(2) HCON(CH}_3)_2]{\substack{1 \text{ equiv.} \\ \text{(1) CH}_3(\text{CH}_2)_3\text{Li, ether}}}$ (*Ref. 155*)

(s) $C_6H_5COCH_2NH_2 \cdot HCl + CH_3COCH_2COOC_2H_5 \xrightarrow{H^{\oplus}}$ (*Ref. 156*)

2. Suggest a reasonable mechanism for each of the following transformations:

(a) 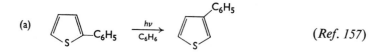 $\xrightarrow[C_6H_6]{h\nu}$ (*Ref. 157*)

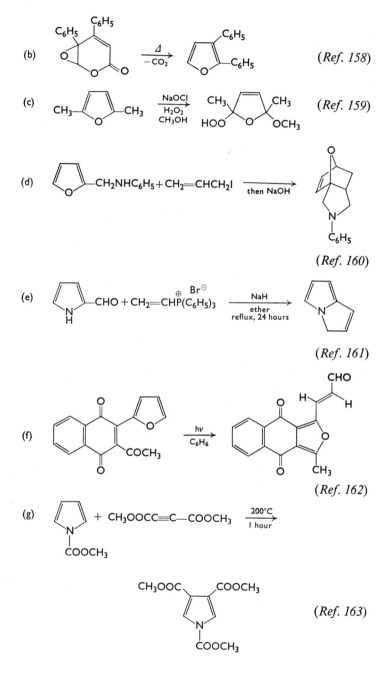

(b) $\xrightarrow[-CO_2]{\Delta}$ (*Ref. 158*)

(c) $\xrightarrow[\substack{H_2O_2 \\ CH_3OH}]{NaOCl}$ (*Ref. 159*)

(d) $\xrightarrow{\text{then NaOH}}$ (*Ref. 160*)

(e) $\xrightarrow[\substack{\text{ether} \\ \text{reflux, 24 hours}}]{NaH}$ (*Ref. 161*)

(f) $\xrightarrow[C_6H_6]{h\nu}$ (*Ref. 162*)

(g) $\xrightarrow[\text{I hour}]{200°C}$

(*Ref. 163*)

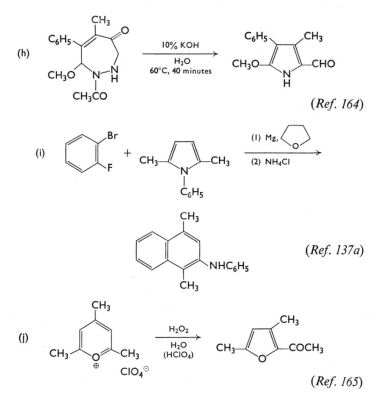

(h) ... *(Ref. 164)*

(i) ... *(Ref. 137a)*

(j) ... *(Ref. 165)*

3. Devise synthetic pathways by which each of the denoted starting materials may be converted to the indicated products:

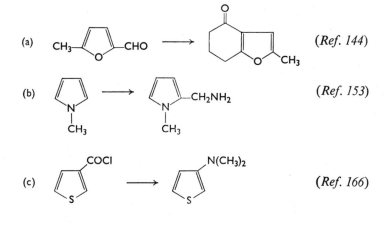

(a) CH₃—furan—CHO ⟶ ... *(Ref. 144)*

(b) ... *(Ref. 153)*

(c) ... *(Ref. 166)*

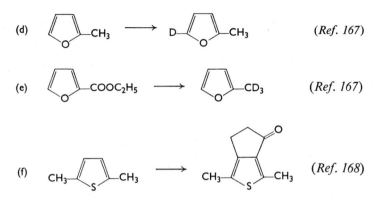

(d) ⟶ (*Ref. 167*)

(e) ⟶ (*Ref. 167*)

(f) ⟶ (*Ref. 168*)

References and Notes

(1) For this reason, the extrapolation of an observation made, for example, with a furan derivative to a prediction of the behaviour of a related pyrrole or thiophene derivative *under the same conditions* may be erroneous.

(2) J. D. Roberts and M. C. Caserio, *Basic Principles of Organic Chemistry*, W. A. Benjamin, Inc., New York, 1964, p. 981.

(3) Substitution of the pyrrole nucleus serves to increase the basicity of the heterocycle. Certain heavily substituted pyrroles are known to yield relatively stable hydrochloride salts: R. J. Abraham, E. Bullock, and S. S. Mitra, *Can. J. Chem.*, **37**, 1859 (1959).

(4) G. F. Smith, *Adv. Heterocyclic Chem.*, **2**, 287 (1963).

(5) M. Koizumi and T. Titani, *Bull. Chem. Soc. Japan*, **12**, 107 (1937); **13**, 85, 298 (1938).

(6) D. M. Young and C. F. H. Allen, *Org. Syn.*, **Coll. Vol. II**, 219 (1943).

(7) G. C. Brumlik, A. L. Kosak, and R. Pitcher, *J. Am. Chem. Soc.*, **86**, 5360 (1964).

(8) J. L. Melles and H. J. Backer, *Rec. Trav. Chim.*, **72**, 491 (1953).

(9) W. Davies and F. C. James, *J. Chem. Soc.*, **1954**, 15.

(10) (a) W. J. Bailey and E. W. Cummins, *J. Am. Chem. Soc.*, **76**, 1932 (1954); (b) **76**, 1936 (1954); (c) **76**, 1940 (1954).

(11) M. Prochazka, *Collection Czech. Chem. Commun.*, **30**, 1158 (1965).

(12) R. Adams and V. Voorhees, *Org. Syn.*, **Coll. Vol. 1**, 280 (1941).

(13) C. L. Wilson, *J. Chem. Soc.*, **1945**, 61.

(14) For a review, see D. G. Jones and A. W. C. Taylor, *Quart. Rev. (London)*, **4**, 195 (1950).

(15) W. C. Wilson, *Org. Syn.*, **Coll. Vol. 1**, 276 (1941).

(16) R. J. Harrison and M. Moyle, *ibid.*, **Coll. Vol. 4**, 493 (1963).

(17) W. C. Wilson, *ibid.*, **Coll. Vol. 1**, 274 (1941), see also, D. M. Burness, *ibid.*, **Coll. Vol. 4**, 628 (1963).

(18) S. M. McElvain and K. M. Bolliger, *ibid.*, **Coll. Vol. 1**, 473 (1941).

(19) H. D. Hartough, *Thiophene and Its Derivatives*, in A. Weissberger (ed.), *The Chemistry of Heterocyclic Compounds*, Interscience, New York, 1952.

(20) (a) R. Phillips, *Org. Syn.*, **Coll. Vol. 2**, 578 (1943); (b) for extensions of this reaction to the synthesis of substituted thiophenes, see D. E. Wolf and K. Folkers, *Org. Reactions*, **6**, 410 (1951).

(21) R. F. Feldkamp and B. F. Tullar, *Org. Syn.*, **Coll. Vol. 4**, 671 (1963).

(22) C. Paal, *Chem. Ber.*, **17**, 2757 (1884); L. Knorr, *ibid.*, **17**, 2863 (1884).

(23) G. Nowlin, *J. Am. Chem. Soc.*, **72**, 5754 (1950).

(24) D. M. Young and C. F. H. Allen, *Org. Syn.*, **Coll. Vol. 2**, 219 (1943).

(25) R. Robinson and W. M. Todd, *J. Chem. Soc.*, **1939**, 1743.

(26) (a) F. Feist, *Chem. Ber.*, **35**, 1545 (1902); (b) E. Benary, *ibid.*, **44**, 493 (1911).

(27) A. Hantzsch, *ibid.*, **23**, 1474 (1890).

(28) A. T. Blomquist and H. B. Stevenson, *J. Am. Chem. Soc.*, **56**, 146 (1934).

(29) L. Knorr, *Chem. Ber.*, **17**, 1635 (1884); *Ann. Chem.*, **236**, 290 (1886).

(30) H. Fischer, *Org. Syn.*, **Coll. Vol. 2**, 202 (1943); for a modification, see H. Fischer, *ibid.*, **Coll. Vol. 3**, 513 (1955).

(31) A. W. Johnson and R. Price, *ibid.*, **42**, 92 (1962); A. W. Johnson, E. Markham, R. Price, and K. B. Shaw, *J. Chem. Soc.*, **1958**, 4254.

(32) O. Piloty and P. Hirsch, *Ann. Chem.*, **395**, 63 (1913).

(33) For a modification of the reductive step which is claimed to lead to improved yields, see A. Treibs and R. Schmidt, *Ann. Chem.*, **577**, 105 (1952).

(34) See Chapter 1, ref. 63.

(35) O. Hinsberg, *Chem. Ber.*, **43**, 901 (1910).

(36) H. J. Backer and W. Stevens, *Rec. Trav. Chim.*, **59**, 423 (1940).

(37) E. W. Fager, *J. Am. Chem. Soc.*, **67**, 2217 (1945).

(38) See, for example, H. J. Backer and W. Stevens, *Rec. Trav. Chim.*, **59**, 899 (1940); K. Dimroth and H. Freyschlag, *Chem. Ber.*, **89**, 2602 (1956); K. Dimroth and V. Pintschovius, *Ann. Chem.*, **639**, 102 (1961).

(39) H. Wynberg and H. J. Kooreman, *J. Am. Chem. Soc.*, **87**, 1739 (1965).

(40) J. B. Hendrickson, R. Rees, and J. F. Templeton, *ibid.*, **86**, 107 (1964).

(41) H. Gilman and R. V. Young, *J. Am. Chem. Soc.*, **56**, 464 (1934).

(42) F. B. Deans and C. Eaborn, *J. Chem. Soc.*, **1959**, 2303.

(43) W. Steinkopf and W. Ohse, *Ann. Chem.*, **437**, 14 (1924).

(44) For a summary of references to this work, see A. P. Dunlop and F. N. Peters, *The Furans*, Reinhold, New York, 1953, p. 72.

(45) L. A. Kazitsyna, *Vestn. Mosk. Univ.*, **1947**, No. 3, 109; *Chem. Abstr.*, **42**, 3751 (1948).

(46) G. F. Wright and H. Gilman, *Ind. Eng. Chem.*, **40**, 1517 (1948).

(47) D. M. Burness, *Org. Syn.*, **40**, 29 (1960).

(48) N. Clauson-Kaas, *Acta Chem. Scand.*, **1**, 379 (1947).

(49) A. P. Terent'ev, L. I. Belen'kii, and L. A. Yanovskaya, *Zh. Obshch. Khim.*, **24**, 1265 (1954); *Chem. Abstr.*, **49**, 12327 (1955).

(50) W. Minnis, *Org. Syn.*, **Coll. Vol. 2**, 357 (1943).

(51) H. Y. Lew and C. R. Noller, *ibid.*, **Coll. Vol. 4**, 545 (1963).

(52) H. G. Anderson, *Can. J. Chem.*, **35**, 21 (1957).

(53) (a) W. Steinkopf, *Ann. Chem.*, **403**, 17 (1914); (b) W. Steinkopf and T. Höpner, *ibid.*, **501**, 174 (1933).

(54) N. Clauson-Kaas and J. Farlstrop, *Acta Chem. Scand.*, **1**, 210 (1947); J. G. Michels and K. J. Hayes, *J. Am. Chem. Soc.*, **80**, 1114 1958).

(55) R. Marquis, *Compt. Rend.*, **132**, 140 (1902); *Ann. Chim. (Paris)*, (**8**), **4**, 196 (1905).

(56) R. Levine, J. V. Heid, and M. W. Farrar, *J. Am. Chem. Soc.*, **71**, 1207 (1949).

(57) G. L. Ciamician and M. Dennstedt, *Gazz. Chim. Ital.*, **13**, 455 (1883).

(58) J. R. Johnson and G. E. May, *Org. Syn.*, **Coll. Vol. 2**, 8 (1943).

(59) W. M. Kutz and B. B. Corson, *J. Am. Chem. Soc.*, **71**, 1503 (1949); W. G. Appleby, A. F. Sartor, S. H. Lee, and S. W. Kapranos, *ibid.*, **70**, 1552 (1948); P. Cagniant and D. Cagniant, *Bull. Soc. Chim. France*, **1956**, 1152; M. Sy, N. P. Buu-Hoi, and N. D. Xuong, *J. Chem. Soc.*, **1954**, 1975.

(60) H. Gilman and G. F. Wright, *J. Am. Chem. Soc.*, **55**, 3302 (1933).

(61) R. M. Silverstein, E. E. Ryskiewicz, and C. Willard, *Org. Syn.*, **Coll. Vol. 4**, 831 (1963).

(62) K. B. Wiberg and H. F. McShane, *ibid.*, **Coll. Vol. 3**, 197 (1955), see also W. S. Emerson and T. M. Patrick, Jr., *ibid.*, **Coll. Vol. 4**, 980 (1963).

(63) H. Gilman and G. F. Wright, *Iowa State Coll. J. Sci.*, **5**, 85 (1931).

(64) M. Janda, *Collection Czech. Chem. Commun.*, **26**, 1889 (1961).

(65) I. J. Rinkes, *Rec. Trav. Chim.*, **49**, 1118 (1930).

(66) H. Fischer and P. Ernst, *Ann. Chem.*, **447**, 148 (1926).

(67) N. Messina and E. V. Brown, *J. Am. Chem. Soc.*, **74**, 920 (1952).

(68) H. Gilman and R. R. Burtner, *ibid.*, **55**, 2903 (1933).

(69) E. Campaigne and R. C. Bourgeois, *ibid.*, **76**, 2445 (1954).

(70) C. D. Hurd and H. J. Anderson, *ibid.*, **75**, 3517 (1953).

(71) T. Reichstein, H. Zschokke, and A. Georg, *Helv. Chim. Acta*, **14**, 1277 (1933).

(72) H. D. Hartough and A. I. Kosak, *J. Am. Chem. Soc.*, **69**, 3093 (1947).

(73) E. C. Spaeth and C. B. Germain, *ibid.*, **77**, 4066 (1955).

(74) M. Sy, N. P. Buu-Hoi, and N. D. Xuong, *J. Chem. Soc.*, **1955**, 21.

(75) B. Oddo and C. Dainotti, *Gazz. Chim. Ital.*, **42**, 727 (1912).

(76) A. H. Blatt, S. Bach, and L. W. Kresch, *J. Org. Chem.*, **22**, 1693 (1957); J. Tirouflet and P. Fournari, *Compt. Rend.*, **246**, 2003 (1958).

(77) I. J. Rinkes, *Rec. Trav. Chim.*, **53**, 1167 (1934).

(78) I. J. Rinkes, *ibid.*, **51**, 352 (1932).

(79) I. J. Rinkes, *ibid.*, **52**, 538 (1933), see also ref. 53b.

(80) By comparison, nitration of 1-methyl-2-acetylpyrrole yields the 4-nitro- and 5-nitro-derivatives in a ratio of 6:1.[52]   Such a result probably reflects the decreased stabilizing influence of the nitrogen electron pair in 1-alkylpyrroles.

(81) A. L. Stone and R. R. Estes, *J. Am. Chem. Soc.*, **74**, 2691 (1952).

(82) For a more extensive discussion of directing effects in thiophenes, see S. Gronowitz, *Adv. Heterocyclic Chem.*, **1**, 1 (1963).

(83) R. A. Hoffman and S. Gronowitz, *Arkiv Kemi*, **16**, 563 (1960).

(84) J. Sicé, *J. Am. Chem. Soc.*, **75**, 3697 (1953).

(85) E. Profft, *Ann. Chem.*, **622**, 196 (1959).

(86) For a broad survey of nucleophilic heteroaromatic substitution, refer to G. Illuminati, *Adv. Heterocyclic Chem.*, **3**, 285 (1964).

(87) D. G. Manly and E. D. Amstutz, *J. Org. Chem.*, **21**, 516 (1956).

(88) D. G. Manly and E. D. Amstutz, *ibid.*, **22**, 133 (1957).

(89) R. Motoyama, S. Nishimura, Y. Murakami, K. Hari, and E. Imoto, *Nippon Kagaku Zasshi*, **78**, 954 (1957); *Chem. Abstr.*, **54**, 14224 (1960).

(90) This rate cannot be explained readily; however, it does indicate that the positions occupied by the activating nitro group cannot be considered comparable to *o*-, *m*- and *p*-positions in benzene derivatives.

(91) R. Adams and A. Ferretti, *J. Am. Chem. Soc.*, **81**, 4927 (1959).

(92) A. Vecchi and G. Melone, *J. Org. Chem.*, **22**, 1636 (1957).

(93) A. W. Johnson, *J. Chem. Soc.*, **1946**, 895, see also K. B. L. Mathur and H. S. Mehra, *ibid.*, **1961**, 2576.

(94) I. J. Rinkes, *Rec. Trav. Chim.*, **62**, 116 (1943).

(95) P. A. S. Smith and J. H. Boyer, *J. Am. Chem. Soc.*, **73**, 2626 (1951).

(96) C. E. Griffin and K. R. Martin, *Chem. Commun.*, **1965**, 154.

(97) N. P. Buu-Höi, *Ann. Chem.*, **556**, 1 (1944); S. Gronowitz, N. Gjös, R. M. Kellogg, and H. Wynberg, *J. Org. Chem.*, **32**, 463 (1967).

(98) S. Gronowitz, P. Moses, and R. Hakansson, *Arkiv Kemi*, **16**, 267 (1960), see also P. Cagniant and P. Cagniant, *Bull. Soc. Chim. France*, **1952**, 713.

(99) G. O. Schenck and R. Steinmetz, *Ann. Chem.*, **668**, 19 (1963).

(100) E. Müller, H. Kessler, H. Fricke, and H. Suhr, *Tetrahedron Letters*, No. **16**, 1047 (1963).

(101) C. D. Nenitzescu and E. Solomonica, *Chem. Ber.*, **64**, 1924 (1931).

(102) H. Wynberg, *Chem. Rev.*, **60**, 169 (1960).

(103) E. R. Alexander, A. B. Herrick, and J. M. Roder, *J. Am. Chem. Soc.*, **72**, 2760 (1950).

(104) E. Bamberger and G. Djierdjian, *Chem. Ber.*, **33**, 536 (1900).

(105) V. Ramanathan and R. Levine, *J. Org. Chem.*, **27**, 1216 (1962), and references cited therein.

(106) For a summary of work in this area, see ref. 84, p. 73 ff.

(107) D. A. Shirley and K. R. Barton, *Tetrahedron*, **22**, 515 (1966), see also S. Gronowitz and K. Halvarson, *Arkiv Kemi*, **8**, 343 (1955).

(108) G. Büchi and H. Wüest, *J. Org. Chem.*, **31**, 977 (1966).

(109) S. Gronowitz, P. Moses, A.-B. Hörnfeldt, and R. Hakansson, *Arkiv Kemi*, **17**, 165 (1961).

(110) H. Gilman and J. W. Morton, Jr., *Org. Reactions*, **8**, 258 (1954).

(111) (a) S. Gronowitz, *Arkiv Kemi*, **7**, 361 (1954); (b) J. Sicé, *J. Org. Chem.*, **19**, 70 (1954).

(112) S. Gronowitz, *Arkiv Kemi*, **12**, 239 (1958).

(113) S. Gronowitz, *ibid.*, **13**, 269 (1958).

(114) M. S. Kharasch and O. Reinmuth, *Grignard Reactions of Non-metallic Substances*, Prentice-Hall, Inc., New York, 1954, pp. 75–78.

(115) M. G. Reinecke, H. W. Johnson, Jr., and J. F. Sebastian, *J. Am. Chem. Soc.*, **85**, 2859 (1963).

(116) P. S. Skell and G. P. Bean, *ibid.*, **84**, 4655 (1962).

(117) C. F. Hobbs, C. K. McMillin, E. P. Papadopoulos, and C. A. VanderWerf, *ibid.*, **84**, 43 (1962), and references cited therein.

(118) For an extensive discussion of the halogen-metal interconversion reaction, refer to R. G. Jones and H. Gilman, *Org. Reactions*, **6**, 339 (1951).

(119) H. Gilman and D. S. Melstrom, *J. Am. Chem. Soc.*, **68**, 103 (1946).

(120) E. Campaigne and W. O. Foye, *ibid.*, **70**, 3941 (1948).

(121) P. Moses and S. Gronowitz, *Arkiv Kemi*, **18**, 119 (1961).

(122) This and other phases of the chemistry of the five-membered heterocyclics have been reviewed: furan, R. C. Elderfield and T. N. Dodd, Jr., in R. C. Elderfield (ed.), *Heterocyclic Compounds*, Vol. 1, Wiley, New York, 1950, Chapter 4; pyrrole, A. H. Corwin, *ibid.*, Chapter 6; thiophene F. F. Blicke, *ibid.*, Chapter 5.

(123) For a recent review of the synthetic utility of dialkoxy- and diacyloxy-dihydrofurans, see N. Elming, *Adv. Org. Chem.*, **2**, 67 (1960).

(124) N. Elming and N. Clauson-Kaas, *Acta Chem. Scand.*, **6**, 867 (1952).

(125) G. Ciamician and C. U. Zanetti, *Chem. Ber.*, **22**, 1968 (1889), see also R. Willstätter and W. Heubner, *ibid.*, **40**, 3871 (1907).

(126) D. M. Lemal and S. D. McGregor, *J. Am. Chem. Soc.*, **88**, 1335 (1966); G. G. Evans, *ibid.*, **73**, 5230 (1951), and references cited therein.

(127) G. R. Pettit and E. E. van Tamelen, *Org. Reactions*, **12**, 356 (1962).

(128) Ya. L. Gol'dfarb and P. A. Konstantinov, *Izv. Akad. Nauk SSSR, Otd. Khim. Nauk*, **1957**, 217; *Chem. Abstr.*, **51**, 10474 (1957).

(129) D. Sullivan and R. Pettit, *Tetrahedron Letters*, **No. 6**, 401 (1963).

(130) G. M. Badger, H. J. Rodda, and W. H. F. Sasse, *J. Chem. Soc.*, **1954**, 4162.

(131) H. Kwart and I. Burchuk, *J. Am. Chem. Soc.*, **74**, 3094 (1952).

(132) O. Diels and K. Alder, *Ann. Chem.*, **490**, 267 (1931); **486**, 211 (1931).

(133) L. Mandell and W. A. Blanchard, *J. Am. Chem. Soc.*, **79**, 6198 (1957).

(134) J. F. Scully and E. V. Brown, *ibid.*, **75**, 6329 (1953).

(135) D. D. Callander, P. L. Coe, and J. C. Tatlow, *Chem. Commun.*, **1966**, 143 have reported recently that thiophene and tetrafluorobenzyme react to produce *inter alia* 5% of an unstable substance which may be the product of 1,4-addition.

(136) (a) G. Wittig and L. Pohmer, *Chem. Ber.*, **89**, 1334 (1956); (b) L. F. Fieser and M. J. Haddadin, *J. Am. Chem. Soc.*, **86**, 2081 (1964).

(137) (a) E. Wolthuis, D. VanderJagt, S. Mels, and A. DeBoer, *J. Org. Chem.*, **30**, 190 (1965); (b) G. Wittig and B. Reichel, *Chem. Ber.*, **96**, 2851 (1963); (c) G. Wittig and W. Behnisch, *ibid.*, **91**, 2358 (1958).

(138) E. Wolthuis and A. DeBoer, *J. Org. Chem.*, **30**, 3225 (1965).

(139) L. A. Carpino and D. E. Barr, *ibid.*, **31**, 764 (1966).

(140) H. E. Winberg, F. S. Fawcett, W. E. Mochel, and C. W. Theobald, *J. Am. Chem. Soc.*, **82**, 1428 (1960).

(141) Y. H. Wu, J. R. Corrigan, and R. F. Feldkamp, *J. Org. Chem.*, **26**, 1531 (1961).

(142) J. Lamy, D. Lavit, and N. P. Buu-Höi, *J. Chem. Soc.*, **1958**, 4202.

(143) H. Rapoport and C. D. Willson, *J. Am. Chem. Soc.*, **84**, 630 (1962).

(144) D. A. H. Taylor, *J. Chem. Soc.*, **1959**, 2767.

(145) E. Winterfeldt and H.-J. Dillinger, *Chem. Ber.*, **99**, 1558 (1966).

(146) H. Wynberg and A. Kraak, *J. Org. Chem.*, **29**, 2455 (1964).

(147) R. Epton, *Chem. Ind. (London)*, **1965**, 425.

(148) D. Seyferth and H. H. A. Menzel, *J. Org. Chem.*, **30**, 649 (1965).

(149) H. J. Jakobsen, E. H. Larsen, and S.-O. Lawesson, *Rec. Trav. Chim.*, **82**, 791 (1963).

(150) M. Lora-Tamayo, R. Madronero, and M. G. Perez, *Chem. Ber.*, **95**, 2188 (1962).

(151) H. Rapoport, N. Castagnoli, Jr., and K. G. Holden, *J. Org. Chem.*, **29**, 883 (1964).

(152) N. Baumann, S. Fumagalli, G. Weisgerber, and C. H. Eugster, *Helv. Chim. Acta*, **49**, 1794 (1966).

(153) R. J. Gritter and R. J. Chriss, *J. Org. Chem.*, **29**, 1163 (1964).

(154) A. D. Josey and E. L. Jenner, *ibid.*, **27**, 2466 (1962).

(155) D. W. H. MacDowell and T. B. Patrick, *ibid.*, **31**, 3592 (1966).

(156) H. Nakano, *et al.*, *Tetrahedron Letters*, **No. 7**, 737 (1966).

(157) H. Wynberg and H. van Driel, *J. Am. Chem. Soc.*, **87**, 3998 (1965).

(158) A. Padwa and R. Hartmann, *Tetrahedron Letters*, **No. 21**, 2277 (1966).

(159) C. S. Foote and S. Wexler, *J. Am. Chem. Soc.*, **86**, 3879 (1964).

(160) D. Bilovic, Z. Stojanac, and V. Hahn, *Tetrahedron Letters*, **No. 31**, 2071 (1964).

(161) E. E. Schweizer and K. K. Light, *J. Am. Chem. Soc.*, **86**, 2963 (1964).

(162) G. Weisgerber and C. H. Eugster, *Helv. Chim. Acta*, **49**, 1806 (1966).

(163) R. M. Acheson and J. M. Vernon, *J. Chem. Soc.*, **1961**, 457.

(164) R. L. Wineholt, E. Wyss, and J. A. Moore, *J. Org. Chem.*, **31**, 48 (1966).

(165) A. T. Balaban and C. D. Nenitzescu, *Chem. Ber.*, **93**, 599 (1960).

(166) J. B. Sullivan and W. C. McCarthy, *J. Org. Chem.*, **30**, 662 (1965).

(167) S. Saltzer, *J. Am. Chem. Soc.*, **87**, 1534 (1965).

(168) W. Steinkopf, I. Poulsson, and O. Herdey, *Ann. Chem.*, **536**, 128 (1938).

5

■ CONDENSED FIVE-MEMBERED
HETEROCYCLES

THE MAJOR EFFECT of fusing a benzene ring onto the 2,3-positions of furan, pyrrole, and thiophene, leading to benzofuran [1], indole [2], and benzo[b]thiophene [3] respectively, is to alter several of the

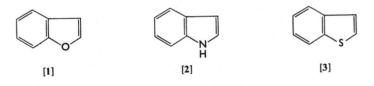

[1]   [2]   [3]

chemical properties of the basic heterocyclic system. Certain of these intrinsic differences will be made evident in this chapter.

The molecular orbital description of [1], [2], and [3] is very similar to that of furan, pyrrole, and thiophene (see p. 102), the only added feature being the distribution of 10 π-electrons over the cyclic framework instead of the previous six such electrons. From the valence-bond point of view, a variety of contributing structures such as [4]–[8]

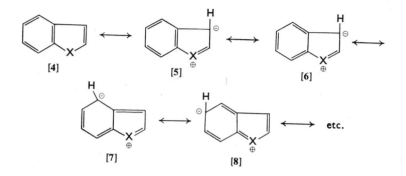

can be written for the resonance hybrid, but structures such as [4]–[6] are far more important than contributors such as [7] and [8] in which benzenoid resonance has been destroyed and charge separation is large. The increased electron density at the 3-position of these condensed heteroaromatics may be contrasted with the increase of negative character at the 2-position of their monocyclic counterparts (see p. 103).

The stability of these heterocycles likewise is dependent upon the 2 electrons which the hetero atom contributes to the π-system. For example, indole is very weakly basic and only a few simple alkyl derivatives of indole are known to form isolable salts with strong acids.[1] Furthermore, 1,1-dimethylindolinium perchlorate [9], prepared by an indirect synthetic procedure,[2] undergoes remarkably

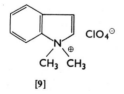

[9]

facile demethylation in the presence of weak nucleophiles such as chloride ion; undoubtedly, the driving force of this process is the formation of the aromatic indole ring.

Also benzo[b]thiophene 1,1-dioxide [10], which can be prepared readily by the hydrogen peroxide oxidation of [3] in acetic acid and acetic anhydride,[3] is not endowed with aromatic properties and reacts as a simple vinyl sulfone.

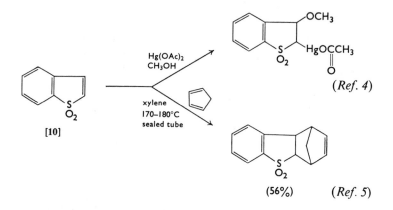

(*Ref. 4*)

(56%)   (*Ref. 5*)

SYNTHETIC APPROACHES

Parent substances **[1]**, **[2]**, and **[3]** all have been isolated from coal tar; indole **[2]** and its derivatives, however, hold a far more important place in organic chemistry than their oxygen and sulfur analogs because of the high incidence of indoles in natural products and because of the intensive studies effected on the dyestuff indigo. For this reason, the chemistry of indoles has been investigated much more thoroughly than that of **[1]** and **[3]**.

The majority of the more general methods for the synthesis of the title compounds involve procedures which form the heterocyclic ring through ring closure. Because of the greater importance of indoles, their syntheses will be discussed first.

The Fischer Indole Synthesis[6]

The general procedure by which a phenylhydrazone of an aldehyde or ketone is heated in the presence of a catalyst such as zinc chloride, boron trifluoride, or polyphosphoric acid (many other catalysts have been employed) to produce an indole is the single most important method for the synthesis of this class of compounds, although the reaction fails for indole itself.

Formally, the Fischer synthesis involves rearrangement with the loss of a molecule of ammonia; the mechanism by which such a

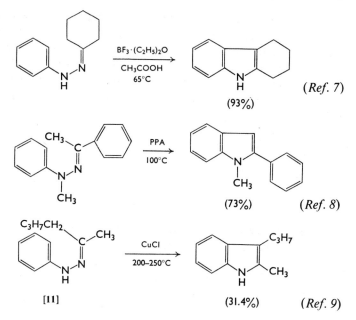

(93%) (*Ref. 7*)

(73%) (*Ref. 8*)

[11]   (31.4%)   (*Ref. 9*)

molecular manipulation occurs has been the object of much study. The scheme[10] which most satisfactorily explains the various known aspects is outlined below and is seen to involve an *o*-benzidine rearrangement of a tautomer of the hydrazone. In support of this

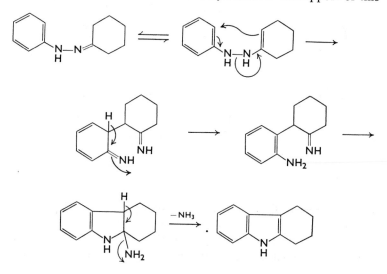

$-NH_3$

mechanism may be cited the observations that (1) the reaction is acid-catalyzed, (2) the reaction proceeds normally in the presence of foreign aromatic amines, (3) there appears to be a direct correlation between the ease of enolization of the ketones and the ease of indole formation from the phenylhydrazone, and (4) the nitrogen atom eliminated as ammonia is the farthest removed from the aromatic ring:

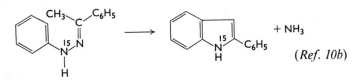

(*Ref. 10b*)

Furthermore, certain of the postulated intermediates have been isolated, as illustrated below:

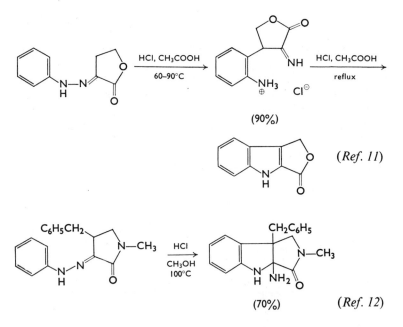

In particular, the proposed mechanism explains why phenyl-hydrazones of unsymmetrical ketones such as [11] give predominantly or exclusively the indole derived from prototropic shift to the more highly substituted enamine. If, however, the original carbonyl group is flanked by a secondary carbon atom, it can be seen that normal indole formation is not possible, and the resulting product is an indolenine.

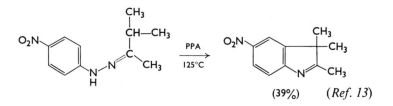

(39%)   (*Ref. 13*)

The Madelung Indole Synthesis[14]

The cyclic dehydration of acyl *o*-toluidines with strong bases at elevated temperatures yields indoles.[15]   This procedure is useful because of the ready accessibility of the starting materials.   The

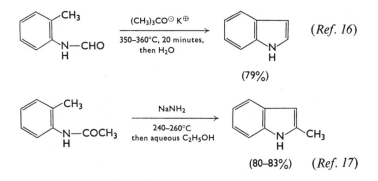

mechanism of the Madelung reaction is not well understood.   Although the function of the base is to abstract a proton from the methyl group, it is believed that the preceding and ensuing steps are more complex than would be required by a simple intramolecular Claisen condensation.   This conclusion is derived from the fact that one-half of the *o*-toluide generally is recovered as *o*-toluidine,[18a] that carbon monoxide frequently is evolved during the reaction, and that the addition of potassium formate to the reaction mixture often can reverse the deleterious effect of the loss of carbon monoxide on the yield.[18b]   Furthermore, when the nitrogen atom carries a substituent, the yields of indole are very poor.[19]

A recent innovation in which formamidines (e.g., [12]) are cyclized with sodium N-methylanilide in refluxing N-methylaniline has been found quite promising.[15a]   The following pathway has been advanced for this modification of the Madelung synthesis.

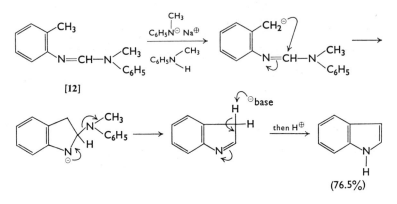

[12]

(76.5%)

The Reissert Indole Synthesis[20]

The reduction of o-nitrophenylpyruvic acid and its derivatives with a variety of reagents such as zinc in acetic acid,[20] ferrous sulfate in ammonium hydroxide,[21] and sodium hydrosulfite,[22] leads via the cyclodehydration of the intermediate o-aminophenylpyruvic acids to the formation of indole-2-carboxylic acids which can readily be decarboxylated by heating at 200–250°C.   The procedure is suited especially for the preparation of indoles which are substituted on the

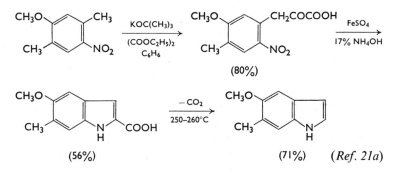

(80%)

(56%)   (71%)   (Ref. 21a)

benzenoid ring because the pyruvic acids are easily prepared by condensation of o-nitrotoluenes with diethyl oxalate in the presence of a basic catalyst.

The Nenitzescu Indole Synthesis[23]

The condensation of 1,4-benzoquinones with 3-aminocrotonates usually at the reflux temperature of a solvent such as acetone represents an indole synthesis of some importance.[24] The indole-3-carboxylic esters which result are easily decarboxylated by refluxing in 20% hydrochloric acid. When a 2-substituted 1,4-benzoquinone

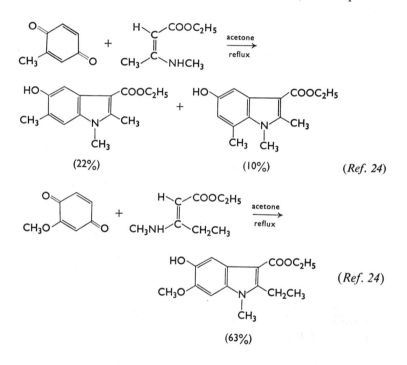

is employed (as in the above examples), the formation of three isomeric 5-hydroxyindole-3-carboxylates (substituent at 4-, 6-, or 7-position) is theoretically possible; however, the 6-substituted derivative generally predominates or is formed exclusively, the 7-substituted derivative usually is present in small quantity (the ratio of the two products is dependent upon the bulk of the substituents), but the 4-isomer has never been observed.

These observations, in addition to other appropriate experiments,[24] suggest a mechanism in which the enamine component adds via its customarily nucleophilic β-carbon atom in a Michael-type reaction to the benzoquinone.[25] Because electronic effects would be expected to be important at this early stage of the process, benzoquinone substituents such as methyl and methoxy would direct addition predominantly to the other side of the molecule (as depicted). The ratio

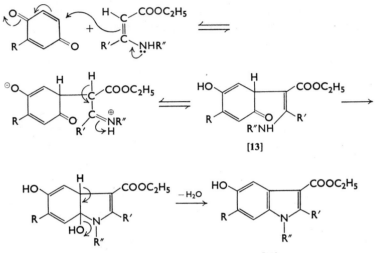

[13]

[14]   **[15]**

of 6-isomer to 7-isomer presumably is a manifestation of steric influences during the final cyclization step in which the heterocyclic ring is formed.

Generally, the Nenitzescu reaction provides indole derivatives in low yields. This phenomenon has been attributed[24] to the fact that a portion of the enamine-benzoquinone adduct is of the wrong

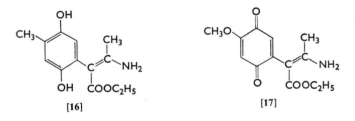

[16]   **[17]**

stereochemistry for cyclization as in **[16]** and **[17]**, and that cis,trans isomerization does not occur under the reaction conditions (**[16]** and **[17]** actually have been isolated from such reactions).

The Bischler Indole Synthesis[26]

The Bischler reaction is another general indole synthesis which involves the reaction of an arylamine with an α-halo-, α-hydroxy-, or α-arylaminoketone in the presence of an acidic reagent. The

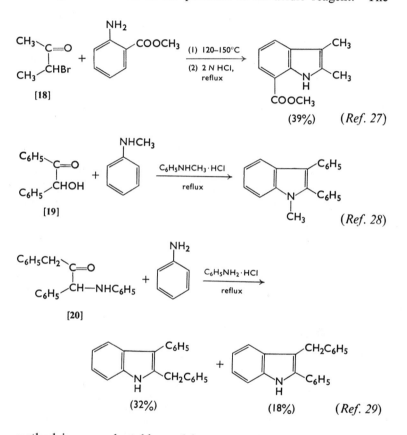

(39%)   (*Ref. 27*)

(*Ref. 28*)

(32%)   (18%)   (*Ref. 29*)

method is very adaptable, and in cases such as [18] and [19], no ambiguity in the structure of the indole is possible. However, in an unsymmetrical example (e.g., [20]) a complication is encountered whereby two isomeric products may result.[30]

It has been shown that the first product of the reaction which can be isolated at low temperatures is an α-ketoamine; however, because of the rapid interconvertibility of α-ketoamines such as [21] and [22] under acidic[29] or purely thermal conditions,[31] a mixture of such

$$C_6H_5CH_2-CH-Br$$
$$C_6H_5-C=O$$

$\longrightarrow$

$$C_6H_5CH_2-CH-NHC_6H_5 \qquad\qquad C_6H_5CH_2C=O$$
$$C_6H_5-C=O \qquad\qquad\qquad C_6H_5-CHNHC_6H_5$$

[21] ⇌ [22]

ketones generally is obtained. Furthermore, because the rates of such rearrangements can be expected to be a function of the structure of the substrate involved, the structure of the particular anilino ketone which leads to the observed indole cannot be ascertained with certainty.

Benzofuran and Benzo[b]thiophene Syntheses[32]

A classic synthesis of benzofurans which remains convenient and generally applicable consists in the bromination of coumarin [23] or a coumarin derivative followed by treatment of the resulting dibromide by base and decarboxylation of the coumarilic acid.[33] The probable mechanism of the process is outlined below.

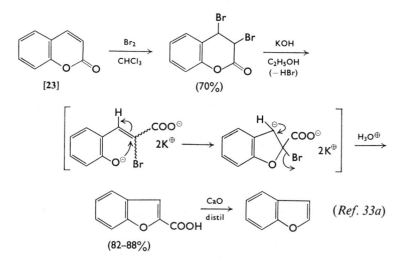

(Ref. 33a)

Benzo[b]thiophene, on the other hand, is prepared commercially by the simple expedient of passing styrene and hydrogen sulfide in the gas phase at 600°C over an iron sulfide-alumina catalyst.[34] The

cyclodehydrogenation of *o*-alkylthiophenols at 445°C over a CuO–
Cr₂O₃ catalyst represents a more general benzo[b]thiophene
synthesis.[35]

A wide variety of alternative syntheses of these ring systems closely
parallel each other. For example, cyclization of appropriate
α-phenoxy or α-thiophenoxy carbonyl compounds under mild

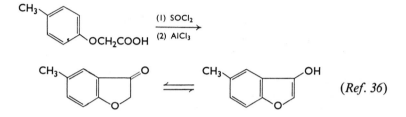

(*Ref. 36*)

Friedel-Crafts conditions readily leads to cyclized products. Syntheses involving formation of the 2,3-bond may be exemplified by the
internal aldol or Claisen condensation of properly substituted

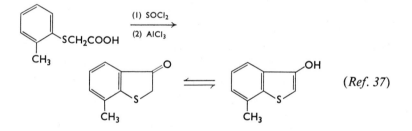

(*Ref. 37*)

aromatic aldehydes or ketones. Such a procedure has found wide
application and is limited only by the accessibility of the starting
materials.[40]

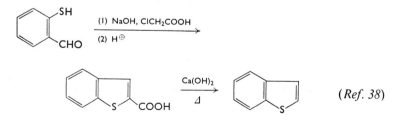

(*Ref. 38*)

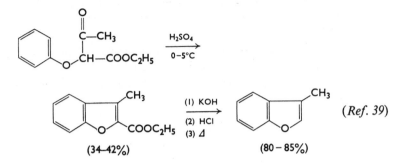

(34–42%) (80 – 85%) (*Ref. 39*)

REACTIONS
Electrophilic Substitution

Allusion has already been made to the fact that the properties of [1], [2], [3], and their derivatives suggest a lower degree of reactivity for these molecules than is manifested by the corresponding mono-cyclic systems (see Chapter 4).   However, the chemistry of the title compounds, especially in the cases of [1] and [3], is not understood well enough to permit sweeping generalizations to be made through-out the series.   In fact, in many instances the title compounds display widely divergent chemical behavior under similar conditions.   To illustrate, although benzofuran is less reactive than furan, the former substance still displays some of the characteristics of a reactive vinyl ether under certain conditions, whereas indole exhibits no such tendency and in fact undergoes electrophilic substitution with great ease.   Benzo[b]thiophene on the other hand, does not undergo formylation under the Vilsmeier conditions[41] or the Mannich reaction,[42] processes which occur readily with thiophene itself.

Certain precautions must be taken when handling these compounds in acid medium.   For example, resinification results upon treating benzofuran with sulfuric acid or aluminum chloride.   Indole forms the dimer [24] when treated with hydrogen chloride in aprotic solvents,

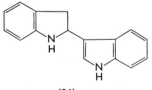

[24]

whereas in aqueous acid an equilibrium is established between indole, its dimer, its trimer, and their salts.[43]   Of interest is the fact that indole, in contrast to pyrrole which polymerizes under these conditions (see p. 105), does not self-condense beyond the trimer stage.[43] That the principal conjugate acid of an indole in acidic solution is the 3-protonated isomer has been established by ultraviolet and n.m.r. studies,[44] and by deuterium exchange.[45]

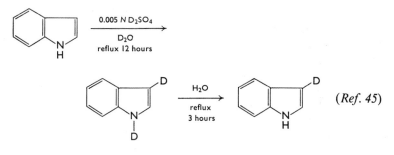

(*Ref. 45*)

Thus, it can be seen that electrophilic substitution of indole occurs at the 3-position as predicted from theoretical considerations (see p. 151).   Benzo[b]thiophene behaves similarly as [2] to yield, in general, 3-derivatives (lesser amounts of 2-derivatives are frequently found), but benzofuran is substituted almost exclusively at the 2-position.   Although this major difference in orientation has been attributed[46] to the relative difference in electronegativity between oxygen on the one hand and sulfur and nitrogen on the other hand, it seems unlikely that this consideration could be the sole causative factor, and the nature of all of the contributing influences to this phenomenon remains an open question.

Various electrophilic substitution processes are exemplified below:

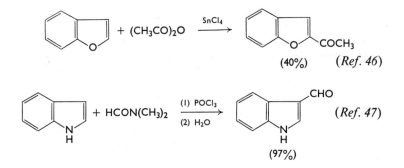

(40%)   (*Ref. 46*)

(97%)   (*Ref. 47*)

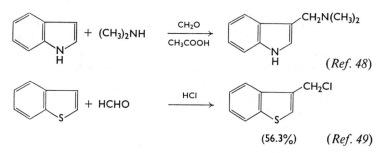

(56.3%)   (*Ref. 49*)

When the position most reactive to electrophilic conditions is blocked by an electron-donating group, substitution generally occurs at the other available ring position:

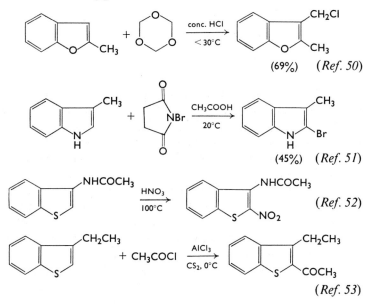

The presence of an electron-withdrawing substituent on the hetero-cyclic ring deactivates that ring to further substitution and attack occurs on the benzenoid portion of the molecule:

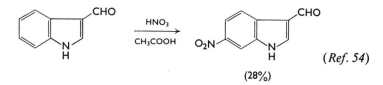

(28%)

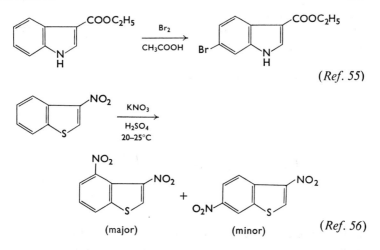

(Ref. 55)

(major)   (minor)   (Ref. 56)

When both positions of the heterocyclic moiety are blocked, substitution in the benzene ring generally is observed:

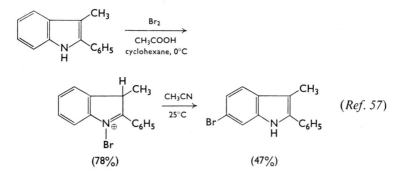

(Ref. 57)

(78%)   (47%)

Sometimes, as with furan, pyrrole, and thiophene, a substituent on the heterocyclic portion of the molecule is displaced:

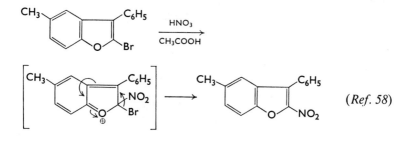

(Ref. 58)

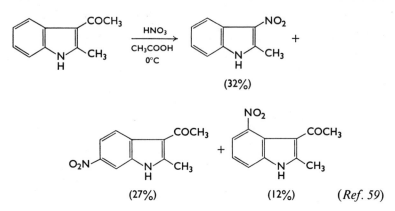

(32%)

(27%)   (12%)   (*Ref. 59*)

The presence of an amino or hydroxyl function on the benzene ring
of these heteroaromatics will direct substitution exclusively to the
benzene ring even when the otherwise reactive positions are vacant.
The overriding directive influence of these substituents is thus aptly
demonstrated:

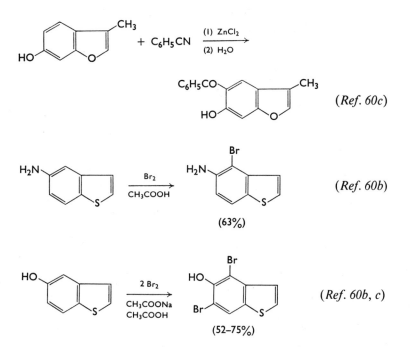

(*Ref. 60c*)

(*Ref. 60b*)

(63%)

(*Ref. 60b, c*)

(52–75%)

Two electrophilic processes, namely nitration and halogenation, have been studied in some detail. Nitration of benzofuran with nitric acid in acetic acid gives predominantly the 2-nitro derivative,[61] whereas benzo[b]thiophene yields the 3-nitro isomer. The nitration of indole derivatives, however, has been found to be especially sensitive to the reaction medium.[54, 62] When nitrations are effected in concentrated nitric or glacial acetic acids, the expected substitution pattern is observed. However, nitration in sulfuric acid yields 5-nitro derivatives almost exclusively. It has been proposed[51, 62]

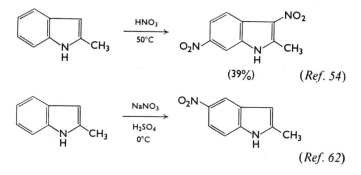

(39%) (*Ref. 54*)

(*Ref. 62*)

that whereas nitration under the first set of conditions presumably involves free indole, nitration in sulfuric acid probably proceeds via the conjugate acid (e.g., [25]) which inhibits normal substitution but permits attack at the 5-position, although it is not clear why the

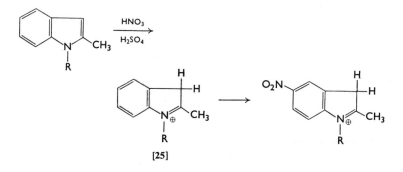

[25]

nitronium ion would prefer to attack para to the positively charged nitrogen substituent.

The direct halogenation of benzofuran with chlorine or bromine results in addition to the 2,3-bond; these unstable addition products may undergo loss of hydrogen halide under purely thermal conditions or upon treatment with alkali to provide mixtures of 2- and 3-halobenzofurans.[63]　In contrast, bromination[64] and iodination[65] of benzo[b]thiophene give the 3-halo derivatives.　As with nitration, the bromination of indoles is solvent dependent.[66]　In nonnucleophilic solvents such as glacial acetic acid or dioxane, normal substitution is evident.　However, in aqueous systems or solvents of appreciable nucleophilicity such as *tert*-butyl alcohol, oxidation to oxindoles

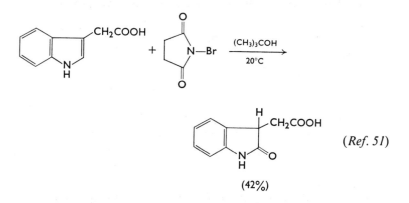

(*Ref. 51*)

(42%)

occurs if the 2-position is vacant.　It is believed[51] that a 3-bromoindolenine intermediate (e.g., [26]) is common to both pathways, but that in the presence of water or a similar nucleophile, [26] is partitioned as shown in the equation.

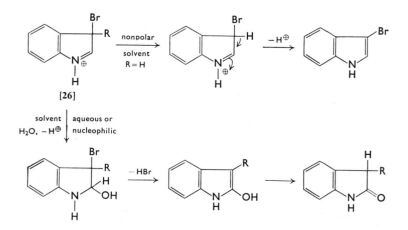

The high reactivity of the indole ring system in electrophilic substitution processes is further demonstrated by its unique behaviour toward electrophilic olefins such as nitroethylene,[67] toward reagents such as lead tetraacetate,[68] and by the ready oxidation of many substituted derivatives.[69]

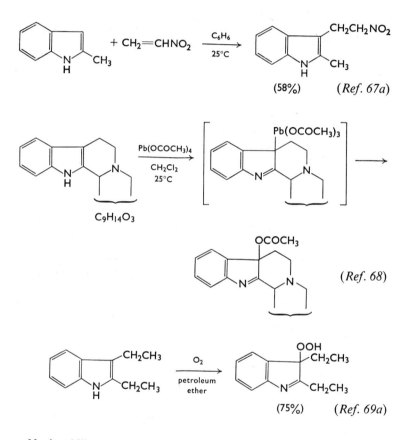

(58%)   (*Ref. 67a*)

(*Ref. 68*)

(75%)   (*Ref. 69a*)

Nucleophilic and Radical Substitutions

Nucleophilic and radical substitution reactions of the title compounds have been little studied and in general are not well understood. However, it is known that direct nucleophilic displacement of a nuclear bound halogen atom is difficult to achieve, unless the halogen is activated by a neighboring electron-withdrawing substituent. Sometimes, as in the case of [27] a complex reaction results.

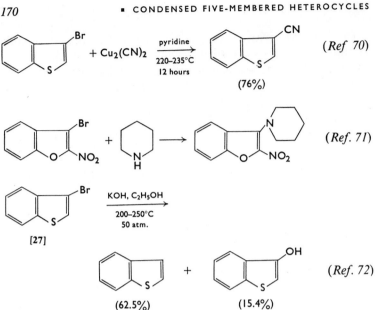

Whereas benzofuran reacts with dichlorocarbene in hexane solution, benzo[b]thiophene does not react and is recovered unchanged.[73] Under the conditions of the Reimer-Tiemann reaction (which are known to generate dichlorocarbene), indole gives both indole-3-

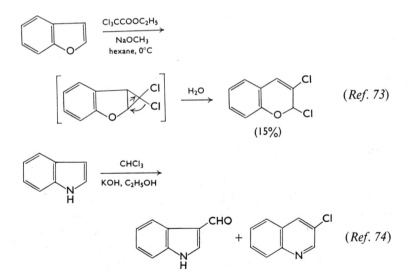

aldehyde and 3-chloroquinoline.[74, 75]   This result is identical to that obtained with pyrrole (see p. 132).   The reaction of benzofuran, indole, and benzo[b]thiophene with diazoacetic ester has been examined, but further systematic work is needed.[75]

Metalation of benzofuran, 1-alkylindoles, and benzo[b]thiophene can be quite readily effected in numerous cases.   When treated with *n*-butyllithium, for example, these compounds give rise to the corre-

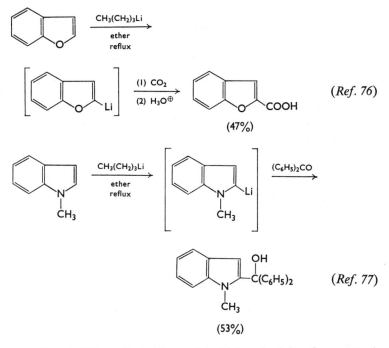

(*Ref. 76*)

(47%)

(*Ref. 77*)

(53%)

sponding 2-lithium derivatives; this high selectivity for α-attack parallels the observations made with their monocyclic counterparts (see p. 133).   Because in the case of the indole and benzo[b]thiophene systems the overall process involves substitution at a site other than that achieved in electrophilic substitution, such metalation reactions possess considerable synthetic utility.

The N—H proton of indole, being appreciably acidic, is readily abstracted by such reagents as metallic sodium, potassium hydroxide at elevated temperatures, *n*-butyllithium, and Grignard reagents. The reactions of the resulting anionic substances appear to vary with the nature of the metal ion, the experimental conditions, and the

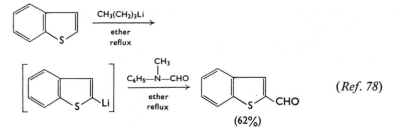

(*Ref. 78*)

nature of the coreactant. The causative factors behind these observed effects have not been elucidated as well as in the case of pyrrole (see p. 134). In contrast to pyrrole, however, the indole derivatives react at the 1- and/or 3-positions. In broad and over-generalized terms, it may be stated that sodium, potassium, and lithium salts yield predominantly products of N-alkylation, whereas magnesium salts of indole lead to substitution at the 3-position, although many exceptions are known.[79, 80]

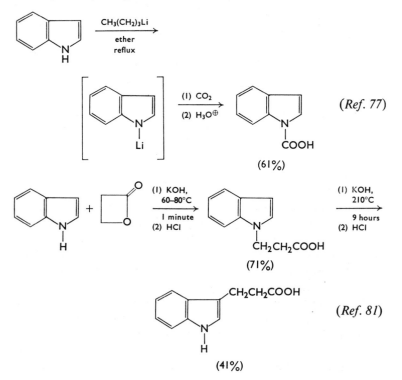

(*Ref. 77*)

(*Ref. 81*)

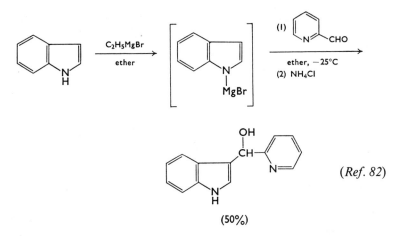

(*Ref. 82*)

(50%)

Although the 2- and 3-bromobenzofurans have been reported not to form a Grignard reagent under conventional conditions,[83] the corresponding benzo[b]thiophene derivatives do undergo such conversions (haloindoles are unstable and therefore are not useful intermediates).

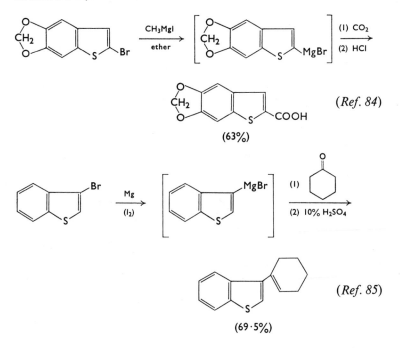

(*Ref. 84*)

(63%)

(*Ref. 85*)

(69·5%)

Halogen-metal interconversion reactions, however, proceed very well and in good yields, except in the case of 3-benzofuryllithium, where low temperatures and very short reaction times (on the order

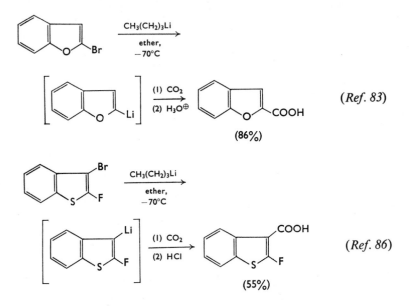

(Ref. 83)

(Ref. 86)

of 2 minutes or less) are necessary to obtain products of 3-substitution.[83]   If such precautions are not observed, ring cleavage occurs as depicted in [28], and acetylenic phenols result.

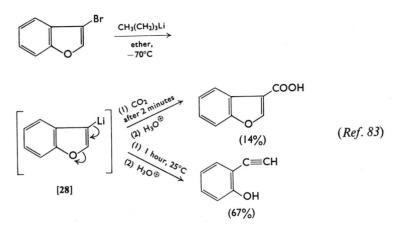

(Ref. 83)

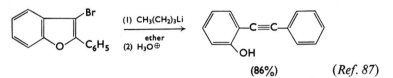

(86%)   (*Ref. 87*)

Exercises

1. Predict the major product of the following reactions:

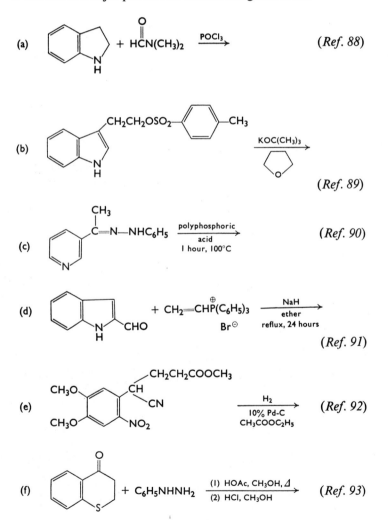

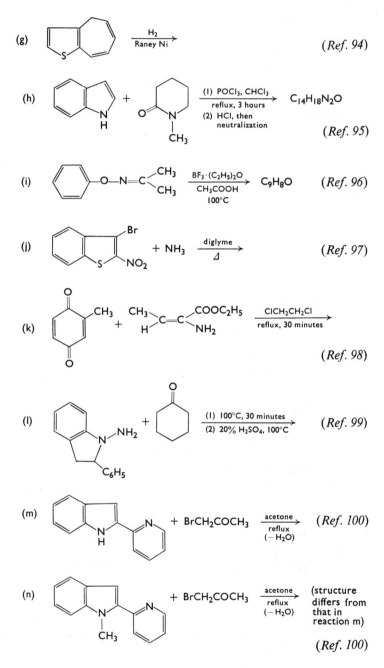

2. Suggest a reasonable mechanism for each of the following transformations:

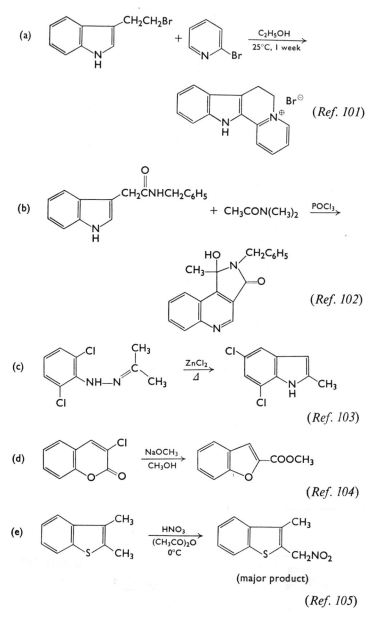

(a)

(*Ref. 101*)

(b)

(*Ref. 102*)

(c)

(*Ref. 103*)

(d)

(*Ref. 104*)

(e)

(major product)

(*Ref. 105*)

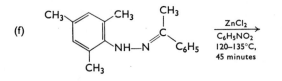

(f)

(Ref. 106)

(major product)

References and Notes

(1) (a) P. Wagner, *Ann. Chem.*, **242**, 388 (1887); (b) K. A. Hofmann, A. Metzler, and K. Hobold, *Chem. Ber.*, **43**, 1082 (1910); (c) B. Oddo, *Gazz. Chim. Ital.*, **43I**, 385 (1913).

(2) R. L. Hinman and J. Lang, *J. Org. Chem.*, **29**, 1449 (1964).

(3) (a) F. G. Bordwell, B. B. Lampert, and W. H. McKellin, *J. Am. Chem. Soc.*, **71**, 1702 (1949); (b) W. Davies, N. W. Gamble, and W. E. Savige, *J. Chem. Soc.*, **1952**, 4678; (c) H. D. Hartough and S. L. Meisel, *Compounds with Condensed Thiophene Rings*, in A. Weissberger (ed.), *The Chemistry of Heterocyclic Compounds*, Interscience, New York, 1954, pp. 156–166.

(4) F. Challenger and P. H. Clapham, *J. Chem. Soc.*, **1948**, 1615.

(5) W. Davies and Q. N. Porter, *ibid.*, **1957**, 459.

(6) For extensive reviews of this topic, see (a) R. B. Van Order and H. G. Lindwall, *Chem. Rev.*, **30**, 69 (1942); (b) P. I. Julian, E. W. Meyer, and H. C. Printy, in R. C. Elderfield, (ed.), *Heterocyclic Compounds*, Vol. 3, Wiley, New York, 1952, Chapter 1; (c) W. C. Sumpter and F. M. Miller, *Heterocyclic Compounds with Indole and Carbazole Systems*, in A. Weissberger (ed.), *The Chemistry of Heterocyclic Compounds*, Interscience, New York, 1954.

(7) H. R. Snyder and C. W. Smith, *J. Am. Chem. Soc.*, **65**, 2452 (1943).

(8) H. M. Kissman, D. W. Farnsworth, and B. Witkop, *ibid.*, **74**, 3948 (1952).

(9) A. E. Arbusow, J. A. Saizew, and A. J. Rasumow, *Chem. Ber.*, **68**, 1792 (1935).

(10) (a) G. M. Robinson and R. Robinson, *J. Chem. Soc.*, **1918**, 639; **1924**, 827; (b) C. F. H. Allen and C. V. Wilson, *J. Am. Chem. Soc.*, **65**, 611 (1943); (c) R. B. Carlin, A. J. Magistro, and G. J. Mains, *ibid.*, **86**, 5300 (1964) and earlier references in this series.

(11) H. Plieninger and I. Nogradi, *Chem. Ber.*, **83**, 273 (1950); **88**, 1964 (1955).

(12) P. L. Southwick, B. McGrew, R. R. Engel, G. E. Milliman, and R. J. Owellen, *J. Org. Chem.*, **28**, 3058 (1963).

(13) W. E. Noland, L. R. Smith, and K. R. Rush, *ibid.*, **30**, 3457 (1965).

(14) W. Madelung, *Chem. Ber.*, **45**, 1128 (1912).

(15) (a) R. R. Lorenz, B. F. Tullar, C. F. Koelsch, and S. Archer, *J. Org. Chem.*, **30**, 2531 (1965); (b) W. Hertz and D. R. K. Murty, *ibid.*, **25**, 2242 (1960); (c) M. M. Robison and B. L. Robison, *J. Am. Chem. Soc.*, **77**, 457, 6554 (1955); (d) F. T. Tyson, *ibid.*, **63**, 2024 (1941).

(16) F. T. Tyson, *Org. Syn.*, **Coll. Vol. 3**, 479 (1955).

(17) C. F. H. Allen and J. Van Allan, *ibid.*, 597 (1955).

(18) (a) A. Galat and H. L. Friedman, *J. Am. Chem. Soc.*, **70**, 1280 (1948); (b) F. T. Tyson, *ibid.*, **72**, 2801 (1950).

(19) L. Marion and W. R. Ashford, *Can. J. Res.*, **23B**, 26 (1945).

(20) (a) A. Reissert, *Chem. Ber.*, **30**, 1030 (1897); (b) W. O. Kermack, W. H. Perkin, and R. Robinson, *J. Chem. Soc.*, **119**, 1602 (1921).

(21) (a) G. R. Allen, Jr., J. F. Poletto, and M. J. Weiss, *J. Org. Chem.*, **30**, 2897 (1965); (b) F. Bergel and A. L. Morrison, *J. Chem. Soc.*, **1943**, 49; (c) F. Mayer and E. Alken, *Chem. Ber.*, **55**, 2278 (1952).

(22) R. H. Cornforth and R. Robinson, *J. Chem. Soc.*, **1942**, 680.

(23) C. D. Nenitzescu, *Bull. Soc. Chim. Romania*, **11**, 37 (1929); *Chem. Abstr.*, **24**, 110 (1930).

(24) G. R. Allen, Jr., C. Pidacks, and M. J. Weiss, *J. Am. Chem. Soc.*, **88**, 2536 (1966). Footnote 4 of this paper constitutes a rather comprehensive listing of work in this area.

(25) The mechanistic diagram describes only the formation of the 6-substituted derivative.

(26) A. Bischler, *Chem. Ber.*, **25**, 2860 (1892); A. Bischler and P. Fireman, *ibid.*, **26**, 1336 (1893).

(27) P. E. Verkade and J. Lieste, *Rec. Trav. Chim.*, **65**, 912 (1946).

(28) M. B. Richards, *J. Chem. Soc.*, **97**, 977 (1910).

(29) P. L. Julian, E. W. Meyer, A. Magnani, and W. Cole, *J. Am. Chem. Soc.*, **67**, 1203 (1945).

(30) For a tabulation of many examples of the Bischler reaction, see ref. 6b, pp. 26–28.

(31) (a) R. M. Cowper and T. S. Stevens, *J. Chem. Soc.*, **1947**, 1041; (b) F. Brown and F. G. Mann, *ibid.*, **1948**, 847, 858; (c) A. F. Crowther, F. G. Mann, and D. Purdie, *ibid.*, **1943**, 58.

(32) For extensive reviews of this topic, see (a) R. C. Elderfield and V. B. Meyer, in R. C. Elderfield (ed.), *Heterocyclic Compounds*, Vol. 2, Wiley, New York, 1951, Chapter 1; (b) D. K. Fukushima, *ibid.*, Vol. 2, Chapter 4; (c) ref. 3, pp. 20–29.

(33) (a) R. C. Fuson, J. W. Kneisley, and E. W. Kaiser, *Org. Syn.*, **Coll. Vol. III**, 209 (1955); (b) W. H. Perkin, *J. Chem. Soc.*, **23**, 368 (1870); **24**, 37 (1871).

(34) R. J. Moore and B. S. Greensfelder, *J. Am. Chem. Soc.*, **69**, 2008 (1946).

(35) C. Hansch and B. Schmidhalter, *J. Org. Chem.*, **20**, 1056 (1955); C. Hansch, B. Schmidhalter, F. Reiter, and W. Saltonstall, *ibid.*, **21**, 265 (1956).

(36) L. Higginbotham and H. Stephen, *J. Chem. Soc.*, **117**, 1534 (1920).

(37) C. E. Dalgliesh and F. G. Mann, *ibid.*, **1945**, 893.

(38) P. Friedländer and E. Lenic, *Chem. Ber.*, **45**, 2083 (1912).

(39) W. R. Boehme, *Org. Syn.*, **Coll. Vol. IV**, 590 (1963).

(40) For example, see R. Adams and I. Levine, *J. Am. Chem. Soc.*, **45**, 2373 (1923).

(41) W. J. King and F. F. Nord, *J. Org. Chem.*, **13**, 635 (1948); M. Bisagni, N. P. Buu-Höi, and R. Royer, *J. Chem. Soc.*, **1955**, 3688.

(42) C. Hansch and H. G. Lindwall, *J. Org. Chem.*, **10**, 381 (1945).

(43) G. F. Smith, *Adv. Heterocyclic Chem.*, **2**, 300 (1963), and references cited therein.

(44) R. L. Hinman and E. B. Whipple, *J. Am. Chem. Soc.*, **84**, 2534 (1962).

(45) R. L. Hinman and C. P. Baumann, *J. Org. Chem.*, **29**, 2437 (1964).

(46) M. W. Farrar and R. Levine, *J. Am. Chem. Soc.*, **72**, 4433 (1950).

(47) P. N. James and H. R. Snyder, *Org. Syn.*, **Coll. Vol. IV**, 539 (1963).

(48) H. R. Snyder, C. W. Smith, and J. M. Stewart, *J. Am. Chem. Soc.*, **66**, 200 (1944).

(49) S. Avakian, J. Moss, and G. J. Martin, *ibid.*, **70**, 3075 (1948).

(50) R. Gaertner, *ibid.*, **74**, 5319 (1952).

(51) R. L. Hinman and C. P. Baumann, *J. Org. Chem.*, **29**, 1206 (1964).

(52) J. L. D'Silva and E. W. McClelland, *J. Chem. Soc.*, **1932**, 2883.

(53) N. P. Buu-Höi and P. Cagniant, *Chem. Ber.*, **76**, 1269 (1943).

(54) W. E. Noland and R. D. Rieke, *J. Org. Chem.*, **27**, 2250 (1962).

(55) R. Magima and M. Kotake, *Chem. Ber.*, **63**, 2237 (1930).

(56) K. Fries, H. Heering, E. Hemmecke, and G. Siebert, *Ann. Chem.*, **527**, 83 (1936).

(57) W. B. Lawson, A. Patchornik, and B. Witkop, *J. Am. Chem. Soc.*, **82**, 5918 (1960).

(58) R. Stoermer, *Chem. Ber.*, **44**, 1853 (1911).

(59) W. E. Noland, L. R. Smith, and K. R. Rush, *J. Org. Chem.*, **30**, 3457 (1965).

(60) (a) P. Karrer and F. Widmer, *Helv. Chim. Acta*, **2**, 454 (1919); (b) F. G. Bordwell and H. Stange, *J. Am. Chem. Soc.*, **77**, 5939 (1955); (c) M. Martin-Smith and M. Gates, *ibid.*, **78**, 5351, 6177 (1956).

(61) R. Stoermer and B. Kahlert, *Chem. Ber.*, **35**, 1640 (1902).

(62) W. E. Noland, L. R. Smith, and D. C. Johnson, *J. Org. Chem.*, **28**, 2262 (1963).

(63) R. Stoermer, *Ann. Chem.*, **312**, 237 (1900); R. Stoermer and B. Kahlert, *Chem. Ber.*, **35**, 1633 (1902); R. Fittig and G. Ebert, *Ann. Chem.*, **216**, 162 (1882); G. Kraemer and A. Spilker, *Chem. Ber.*, **23**, 78 (1890); H. Simonis and G. Wenzel, *ibid.*, **33**, 1961 (1900).

(64) G. Komppa, *J. Prakt. Chem.*, **122**, 319 (1929).

(65) R. Gaertner, *J. Am. Chem. Soc.*, **74**, 4950 (1952).

(66) Refs. 51 and 57, and references cited therein.

(67) (a) W. E. Noland and R. F. Lange, *J. Am. Chem. Soc.*, **81**, 1203 (1959); (b) W. E. Noland, G. M. Christensen, G. L. Sauer, and G. G. S. Dutton, *ibid.*, **77**, 456 (1955); (c) W. E. Noland and P. J. Hartman, *ibid.*, **76**, 3227 (1954).

(68) N. Finch, C. W. Gemenden, I. H. Hsu, and W. I. Taylor, *ibid.*, **85**, 1520 (1963).

(69) (a) E. Leete, *ibid.*, **83**, 3645 (1961); (b) B. Witkop, *et al.*, *ibid.*, **74**, 3855 (1952); **73**, 2641, 2188 (1951); (c) R. J. S. Beer, *et al.*, *J. Chem. Soc.*, **1945**, 4139; **1950**, 3283, 2118.

(70) M. Martynoff, *Compt. Rend.*, **236**, 385 (1953).

(71) R. Stoermer, *Chem. Ber.*, **42**, 199 (1909); R. Stoermer and K. Brachmann, *ibid.*, **44**, 316 (1911).

(72) G. Komppa and S. Weckman, *J. Prakt. Chem.*, **138**, 109 (1933).

(73) W. E. Parham, C. G. Fritz, R. W. Soeder, and R. M. Dodson, *J. Org. Chem.*, **28**, 577 (1963).

(74) A. Ellinger, *Chem. Ber.*, **39**, 2515 (1906).

(75) For an extensive review on the reactions of heterocyclic compounds with carbenes, see C. W. Rees and C. E. Smithen, *Adv. Heterocyclic Chem.*, **3**, 57 (1964).

(76) H. Gilman and J. W. Morton, Jr., *Org. Reactions*, **8**, 258 (1954).

(77) D. A. Shirley and P. A. Roussel, *J. Am. Chem. Soc.*, **75**, 375 (1953).

(78) D. A. Shirley and M. J. Danzig, *ibid.*, **74**, 2935 (1952).

(79) M. S. Kharasch and O. Reinmuth, *Grignard Reactions of Non-metallic Substances*, Prentice-Hall, Inc., New York, 1954, pp. 80–84.

(80) A. R. Katritzky and R. Robinson, *J. Chem. Soc.*, **1955**, 2481.

(81) H. E. Fritz, *J. Org. Chem.*, **28**, 1384 (1963).

(82) H. Bader and W. Oroshnik, *J. Am. Chem. Soc.*, **81**, 163 (1959).

(83) H. Gilman and D. S. Melstrom, *ibid.*, **70**, 1655 (1948).

(84) E. Campaigne and W. E. Kreighbaum, *J. Org. Chem.*, **26**, 359 (1961).

(85) J. Szmuszkovicz and E. J. Modest, *J. Am. Chem. Soc.*, **72**, 571 (1950).

(86) R. D. Schuetz, D. D. Taft, J. P. O'Brien, J. L. Shea, and H. M. Mork, *J. Org. Chem.*, **28**, 1420 (1963).

(87) A. S. Angeloni and M. Tramontini, *Boll. Sci. Fac. Chim. Ind. Bologna*, **21**, 243 (1963); *Chem. Abstr.*, **60**, 15808 (1964).

(88) H. Behringer and P. Duesberg, *Chem. Ber.*, **96**, 377 (1963).

(89) W. D. Closson, S. A. Roman, G. T. Kwiatkowski, and D. A. Corwin, *Tetrahedron Letters*, No. **21**, 2271 (1966).

(90) J. W. Huffman, *J. Org. Chem.*, **27**, 503 (1962).

(91) E. E. Schweizer and K. K. Light, *ibid.*, **31**, 870 (1966).

(92) G. N. Walker, *J. Am. Chem. Soc.*, **78**, 3698 (1956).

(93) T. E. Young and P. H. Scott, *J. Org. Chem.*, **30**, 3613 (1965).

(94) D. Sullivan and R. Pettit, *Tetrahedron Letters*, No. **6**, 401 (1963).

(95) J. C. Powers, *J. Org. Chem.*, **30**, 2534 (1965).

(96) T. Sheradsky, *Tetrahedron Letters*, No. **43**, 5225 (1966).

(97) G. Van Zyl, C. J. Bredeweg, R. H. Rynbrandt, and D. C. Neckers, *Can. J. Chem.*, **44**, 2283 (1966).

(98) S. A. Monti, *J. Org. Chem.*, **31**, 2669 (1966).

(99) A. N. Kost, L. G. Yudin, Y. A. Berlin, and A. P. Terent'ev, *Zh. Obshch. Khim.*, **29**, 3820 (1959); *Chem. Abstr.*, **54**, 19641 (1960).

(100) C. K. Bradsher and E. F. Litzinger, Jr., *J. Org. Chem.*, **29**, 3584 (1964).

(101) Y. Ban, R. Sakaguchi, and M. Nagai, *Chem. Pharm. Bull. (Tokyo)*, **13**, 931 (1965).

(102) L. J. Dolby and S. Furukawa, *J. Org. Chem.*, **28**, 2512 (1963).

(103) R. B. Carlin, J. G. Wallace, and E. E. Fisher, *J. Am. Chem. Soc.*, **74**, 990 (1952).

(104) M. S. Newman and C. K. Dalton, *J. Org. Chem.*, **30**, 4126 (1965).

(105) F. G. Bordwell and T. W. Cutshall, *ibid.*, **29**, 2020 (1964).

(106) R. B. Carlin and J. W. Harrison, *ibid.*, **30**, 563 (1965).

6

▪ THE AZOLES

THE AZOLES ARE A GROUP of heterocycles which are formally derived from furan, pyrrole, and thiophene by substitution of one of the ring =CH— groups by a nitrogen atom.   If this replacement is achieved at the 3-position, then oxazole [1], imidazole [2], and thiazole [3] are generated, whereas insertion of the nitrogen atom at the 2-position leads to isoxazole [4], pyrazole [5], and isothiazole [6].   For the most

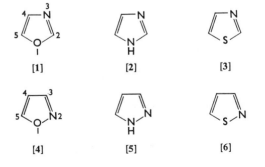

part, this group of heterocycles displays many properties and reactions typical of aromatic compounds. In general, it may be stated that the various azole ring systems are more stable than furan, pyrrole, and thiophene (for example, all are stable to acid at moderate temperatures), and are less reactive. However, there is sometimes a wide variability of chemical reactivity within the series as demonstrated by the fact that whereas isothiazole is stable to permanganate

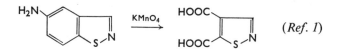

(*Ref. 1*)

oxidation, thiazole is not; also, while oxazoles are generally stable to alkalies, the isoxazole ring is cleaved by bases and other nucleophiles (see p. 201).

In considering the molecular orbital diagram of these substances, each of the three carbon atoms is seen to contribute 1 p_z-electron to the molecular orbital, while the azole nitrogen donates one, and the second hetero atom 2 electrons to complete the aromatic sextet, as depicted in [7] and [8]. In addition to the fact that a stable, closed

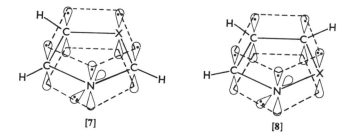

[7]   [8]

shell of six delocalized π-electrons results from such an electronic arrangement, it may be seen that the azole nitrogen atom possesses an additional pair of electrons which are situated in orthogonal fashion to the molecular π-cloud. It is this pair of electrons which allows the azoles to function as bases, and to possess a certain degree of nucleophilic character.[2]

Because of the aromaticity conferred on the azoles by virtue of the "aromatic sextet," these molecules cannot be described adequately by single valence bond structures; rather, they are considered as resonance hybrids of a number of contributing structures. This approach also clearly demonstrates the availability of the azole nitrogen pair for chemical reaction. Furthermore, because each valence bond structure does not contribute equally to the resonance

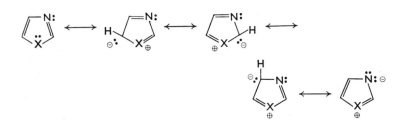

hybrid, the carbon atoms of the azoles are seen not to be equivalent in terms of π-electron density, and this effect is reflected in their chemical behavior.

As demonstrated above, the azole nitrogen possesses a pair of electrons not involved in ring stabilization but available for bonding. However, the basicity of the azoles ranges from the strongly basic imidazole ($pK_a = 7$) to the weakly basic heterocycles thiazole ($pK_a = 2.5$), pyrazole ($pK_a = 2.5$), and isoxazole ($pK_a = 1.3$).[3] Thus, whereas imidazole forms stable crystalline salts with many acidic reagents, the weak bases also can be protonated, but these salts generally dissociate quite readily. In general, however, quaternary salts have been obtained from derivatives of all the azoles upon treatment with alkylating agents (see p. 205). The high stability of

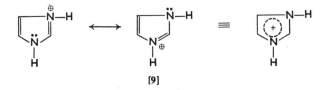

[9]

the imidazolium cation [9] relative to the other azole cations can be attributed to the high degree of symmetry of [9] (which is not available to the other azoles).

In addition to their basic characteristics, imidazole and pyrazole also have an acidic proton and, like pyrrole, readily form salts with metal ions. In fact, [2] and [5] are slightly more acidic than pyrrole because of the electron-withdrawing effect of the azole nitrogen.

   Examination of the physical properties of imidazole and pyrazole has shown that their boiling points, 256° and 187°C at 760 mm, respectively, are much higher than anticipated, because of extensive hydrogen bonding.   Due to the absence of this causative factor, N-alkyl derivatives (but not C-alkyl substituents) have much lower boiling points.   In fact, closer study has demonstrated that in solution imidazole exists as aggregates of 20 or more molecules, for example, [10],[4] and pyrazole exists largely as dimers of type [11].[4a, 5]   On the

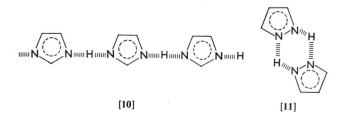

[10]   [11]

basis of these considerations, it becomes apparent that when an imidazole or pyrazole is unsubstituted at the 1-position (i.e., the molecule possesses a free imino hydrogen) a mixture of two tautomeric forms is possible for each system.   These tautomers are in rapid

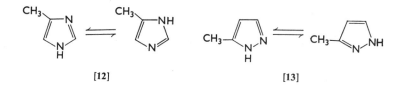

[12]   [13]

equilibrium with each other, most probably via the appropriate hydrogen-bonded species.   Thus, the two nitrogen atoms are indistinguishable and in the event of unsymmetrical substitution such as in [12] and [13], two tautomeric structures are possible, and each substance in fact behaves as a mixture upon chemical reaction. Therefore 4-methylimidazole is identical with 5-methylimidazole [12], and 3-methylpyrazole is the same as the 5-methyl derivative [13]. This phenomenon is denoted by giving the alternative numbering in parenthesis, that is, [12] is named 4(5)-methylimidazole and [13] is designated as 3(5)-methylpyrazole.   With N-substituted derivatives, this problem of tautomerism, of course, no longer exists.[6]

SYNTHETIC APPROACHES
The 1,2-Azoles

The methods of formation of isoxazoles [4] and pyrazoles [5] are all based upon the addition of a species containing the preformed O—N or N—N bond to an acceptor molecule of the desired oxidation level. The most general and widely applicable method for the preparation of derivatives of [4] and [5] consists in the addition of hydroxylamine, hydrazine or a monosubstituted hydrazine to a 1,3-dicarbonyl compound, or to a precursor of such a species. The reaction proceeds via the intermediacy of a ketoxime or hydrazone

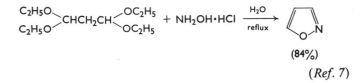

(84%)

(*Ref. 7*)

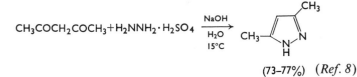

(73–77%) (*Ref. 8*)

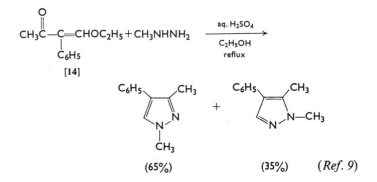

(65%)   (35%)   (*Ref. 9*)

which subsequently undergoes cyclization. When an unsymmetrical dicarbonyl component is employed with hydroxylamine or a monosubstituted hydrazine as in the case of [14], a mixture of two isomeric products frequently is obtained. The formation of such mixtures in these instances is recognized as the chief disadvantage of the method; however, this approach has seen widespread use because of the ease with which these heterocycles readily can be produced.[10, 11]

Isoxazoles and pyrazoles also can be obtained by the condensation of hydroxylamine or a hydrazine with an α,β-acetylenic carbonyl compound or with an α,β-olefinic carbonyl component substituted at either the α- or β-carbon with a readily displaceable group. This rather useful preparative method likewise suffers from the occurrence of mixtures of the two possible tautomers in some instances. The reason for this observed divergence in reaction pathway in certain of

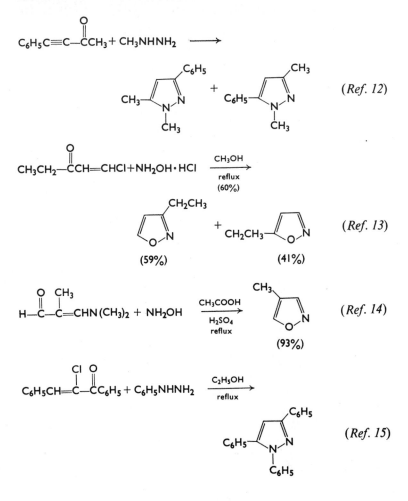

the above cases is that there exists a direct rate competition between the process which involves initial oxime or hydrazone formation followed by cyclization and the process in which preliminary Michael-type addition of hydroxylamine or the hydrazine to the electron-deficient unsaturated linkage occurs.   Obviously, the preferred mode of reaction will be dictated by the nature of the molecules undergoing reaction, but it also is frequently affected by solvent and temperature with the net result that no general predictions can be made.

A third principal method of isoxazole and pyrazole synthesis consists in the 1,3-dipolar addition[16] of a nitrile oxide (often generated *in situ* by the dehydrohalogenation of the corresponding hydroxamic acid chloride (e.g., [15])) or a diazoalkane to an acetylene, the triple bond of which frequently is activated by an electron-withdrawing substituent.   In brief, such condensation reactions proceed by virtue of the fact that nitrile oxides and diazoalkanes may be considered as

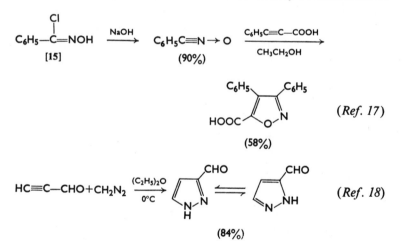

ambivalent compounds which display electrophilic and nucleophilic reactivity at the 1- and 3-positions.   For example, in nitrile oxides such as [16], the oxygen atom forms the negative terminus of the 1,3-dipole and the structure of the resulting cycloaddition product is governed by the energetically most favorable mode of addition of such 1,3-dipoles to the acetylenic dipolarophile.   In the example cited below, the reaction may be considered to proceed formally by a Michael-type addition followed by collapse of dipolar species [17], or in a completely concerted fashion.

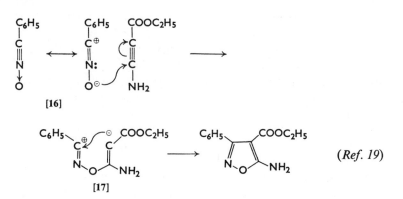

[16]

[17]   (*Ref. 19*)

A necessary condition for the application of the synthetic methods discussed above to the preparation of isothiazoles is the availability of thiohydroxylamine (H_2NSH) and/or nitrile sulfides ($RC\equiv N \rightarrow S$). Thiohydroxylamine has only very recently been obtained[20] and has been found to be very unstable, whereas nitrile sulfides remain unknown. Without the aid of such substances in which the S—N link is preformed, alternative synthetic approaches had to be developed, and several of these are presented below.[21]

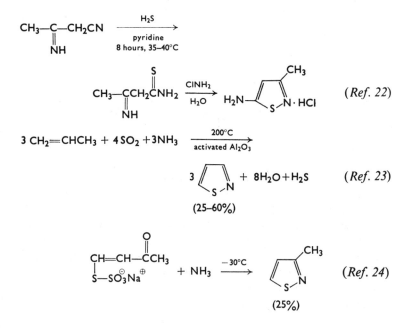

(*Ref. 22*)

(*Ref. 23*)

(25–60%)

(*Ref. 24*)

(25%)

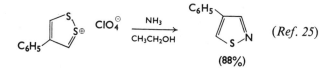

(Ref. 25)

(88%)

The 1,3-Azoles

The synthetic procedures involved in the preparation of the 1,3-azoles are not as general as in the 1,2-azole series.[26] A process which is, however, applicable throughout the series centers about the cyclization of appropriately functionalized 1,4-dicarbonyl compounds. The sequence is formally analogous to the Paal-Knorr

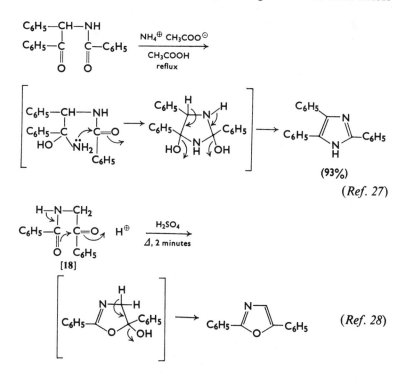

(93%)

(Ref. 27)

(Ref. 28)

synthesis (see p. 109). Cyclization of α-acyl aminoketones [18] is one of the most reliable methods of constructing oxazoles, but the method is generally restricted to derivatives which are at least 2,5-disubstituted. In contrast, no such restriction appears to exist in the thiazole series.[31]

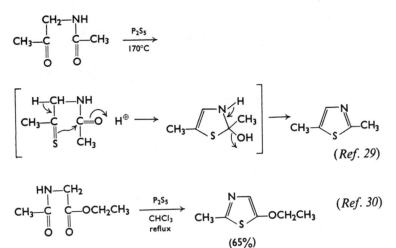

(Ref. 29)

(Ref. 30)

(65%)

On the other hand, the process has seen very limited use as a route to imidazoles.

The interaction of α-halocarbonyl compounds with amidines [19] and thioamides can serve as preparative routes to imidazoles and thiazoles, respectively. Whereas the method has not been widely

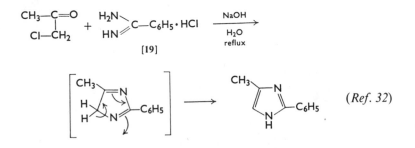

(Ref. 32)

applied to imidazole syntheses because of side reactions and the difficulties encountered in the isolation of pure end products, this has been the source of a large variety of thiazoles.

A somewhat related cyclization by which oxazoles can be prepared involves the addition of imino ethers to α-aminocarbonyl compounds. This modification can be applied directly to the synthesis of oxazole itself.

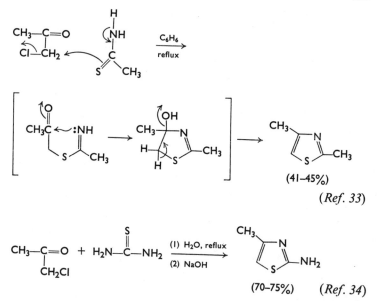

(41–45%)

(*Ref. 33*)

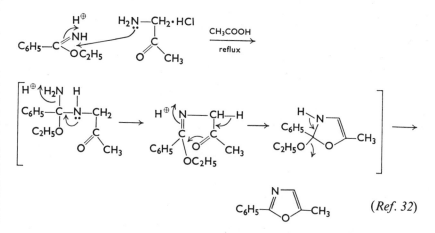

(70–75%)   (*Ref. 34*)

The mechanistic scheme is given some element of factuality in the present instance because of the several intermediates which have been isolated in the course of the oxazole preparation.

(*Ref. 32*)

α-Aminocarbonyl compounds or their precursors have also been condensed with potassium isothiocyanate or alkyl isothiocyanates to give 2-mercaptoimidazoles, the mercapto group of which can be

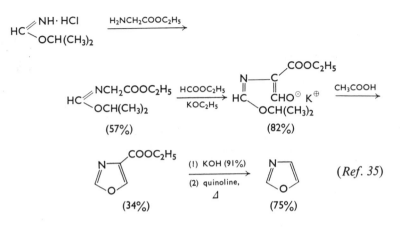

(57%)   (82%)

(34%)   (75%)   (*Ref. 35*)

removed readily by a variety of oxidative methods. The process constitutes a much utilized imidazole synthesis.

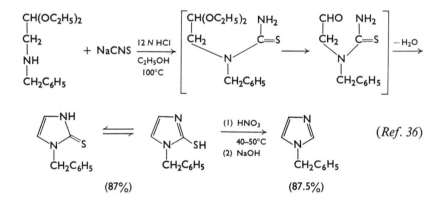

(87%)   (87.5%)   (*Ref. 36*)

Many other syntheses of limited scope are available for the preparation of the azoles, but will not be discussed here.

REACTIONS
Electrophilic Substitution

In general, the reactivity of the azoles toward electrophilic reagents lies intermediate between the high reactivity of the monohetero atomic five-membered heterocycles (Chapter 5) and pyridine (Chapter 7). This reduced susceptibility to electrophilic attack may be attributed to effective electron withdrawal from the ring by the electronegative azole nitrogen atom and to the fact that under the conditions of many such processes (strong acid), the azole ring is protonated and exists as the corresponding azolium cation. This cation is, of course, resistant to further attack by a positively charged electrophile. Evidence which bears on the latter point is derived from the observation that halogenation (which proceeds in the absence of strong acid) occurs more readily than nitration or sulfonation (where strong acids are employed).

Although a direct comparison of the relative ease of substitution of the 1,2-azoles has not been made, it is evident from the conditions

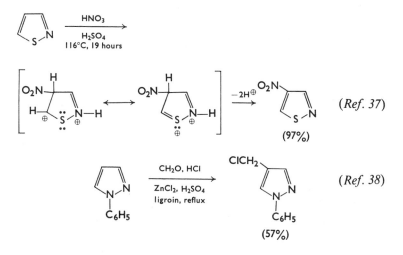

necessary to achieve reaction that the following reactivity order exists: pyrazole > isothiazole > isoxazole. Throughout this series, the electrophile becomes bonded to the 4-position because of the

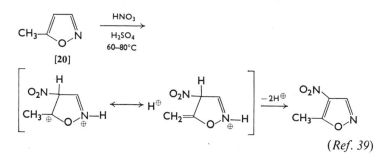

higher stability of the transition state for this pathway. In agreement with the proposed mechanism is the fact that 5-methylisoxazole [20] is more easily nitrated and sulfonated than the corresponding 3-isomer because of added hyperconjugative assistance which the methyl group in the 5-position (but not the 3-methyl) can provide to stabilize the transition state.

Phenyl-substituted pyrazoles undergo substitution at two sites depending upon the acidity of the medium. For example, whereas bromination of [21] results in heterocyclic substitution, nitration

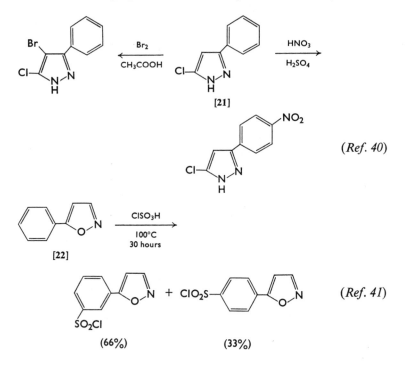

(*Ref. 40*)

(*Ref. 41*)

causes the nitro group to enter the para position of the benzene ring. Somewhat related are the interesting observations that chloro-sulfonation of [22][41] and nitration of [23][42] occur exclusively in the benzene ring. Although one must be cautious not to assign a relative order of reactivity on the basis of such data because of the unknown activating influence of the heterocycle moiety upon the benzenoid ring, it is obvious that formation of an azolium cation strongly deactivates the heterocyclic ring.

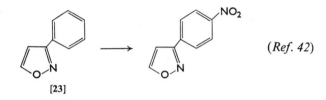

(*Ref. 42*)

The 1,2-azoles appear not to be sufficiently active to react with the weaker electrophiles such as generated in Friedel-Crafts, Vilsmeier, and diazo coupling processes, and as a result few applications of such methods have been successful with these substrates.

The reactivity of the 1,3-azoles toward electrophiles is not amenable to simple correlation, although the following reactivity order suggests itself: imidazole > thiazole > oxazole. Thus, imidazole can be halogenated quite readily in the absence of catalysts (such as those required with benzene), whereas bromination of thiazole under ordinary conditions results only in perbromide formation (other electrophilic processes occur only under forcing conditions) and oxazole does not undergo normal electrophilic substitution at all. The presence of an activating substituent on the thiazole ring causes substitution to become very facile, however.

In reality, imidazole [2] represents one of the very few heterocyclic systems for which detailed observations are available on the orientation in electrophilic substitution over a wide acidity range.[43] Thus, nitration,[44] sulfonation,[44] and deuterium exchange in concentrated D_2SO_4,[45] reactions which proceed via the symmetrical conjugate

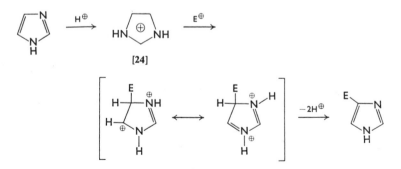

acid [24], lead exclusively to 4(5)-substitution.[46] Bromination in organic solvents, which presumably involves attack by bromonium ion upon the neutral molecule also results in 4(5)-substitution.[44a] In contrast, diazo coupling[47] and deuterium exchange in alkaline media[48] involve electrophilic attack on the anion and give rise to 2-substitution. Iodination also involves the imidazole anion,[49] but is complicated by the fact that a σ-complex probably occurs,[49, 50] 4-iodo-imidazole being formed.

Should the 4-position be blocked by an electron-releasing substituent as in [25], 5-substitution occurs. When both of these positions are occupied, 2-substitution can frequently be achieved.

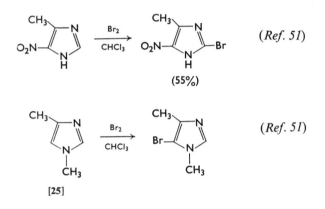

(*Ref. 51*)

(55%)

(*Ref. 51*)

[25]

The observation that substitution reactions of activated thiazoles lead to products in which the electrophile has entered the 5-position (rather than the anticipated 4-position) appears initially to be an

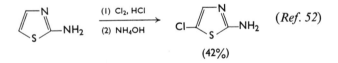

(*Ref. 52*)

(42%)

anomaly. However, it has recently been demonstrated[53] that the best representation of thiazolium ions is not [26a], but rather [26b] in which most of the positive charge resides on sulfur. In light of this evidence, therefore, it becomes obvious that the transition state for

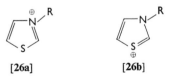

[26a]   [26b]

5-substitution is of lower energy than that of the alternative pathway leading to 4-substitution.

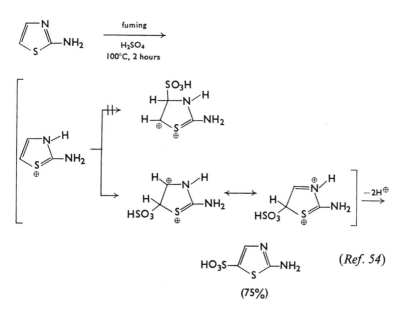

(*Ref. 54*)

(75%)

In contrast with the earlier examples, phenyl-substituted imidazoles,[55] thiazoles,[56] and oxazoles[57] are all nitrated in the benzene ring. Similarly, Friedel-Crafts and Vilsmeier reactions are generally unsuccessful.

Nucleophilic and Radical Substitutions

Because neutral 1,2-azole molecules are endowed with their highest electron density at the 4-position [the preferred site of electrophilic attack], it is to be expected that a halogen atom in this position would be less susceptible to S_N2 displacement, and this is observed. In the more favorable positions, the rates of displacement are in general faster than in the benzene series, although the speed of the particular reaction is, as expected, dependent upon the particular heterocyclic ring and upon the nature of the substituents. Electron-withdrawing groups greatly facilitate the replacement of halogen, and in many cases such as [27] represent necessary requirements for displacements to occur at all. The relative position of the activating substituent is of considerable importance; for example, in **[28]** the 5-chlorine is replaced exclusively, presumably because the negative charge accumulation in the transition state can be dispersed easily by the cyano group. S_N2 displacement at the 3-position cannot be accommodated in a similar fashion and therefore lacks this added stabilization.

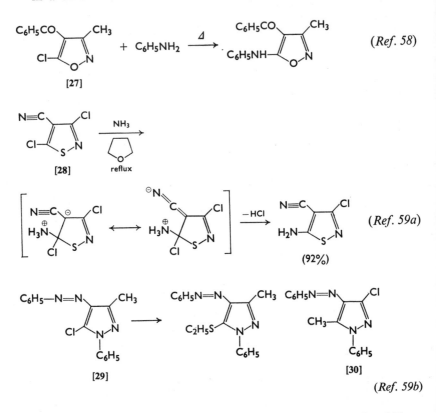

Similarly, whereas **[29]** undergoes ready bimolecular nucleophilic displacement, **[30]** is inert to these reaction conditions.[59b]

In contrast, haloimidazoles and halooxazoles (few are known) resemble halobenzenes in their chemical inertness, and are not generally susceptible to displacement under ordinary conditions. The same is true of thiazoles, except for the 2-halogen derivatives which are quite reactive.[62] Of course, activating groups render the halogen atom considerably more susceptible to displacement.

The isoxazole nucleus is especially labile toward nucleophilic

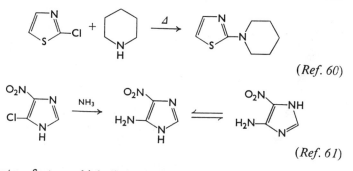

(*Ref. 60*)

(*Ref. 61*)

reagents; a feature which distinguishes this ring system from the other azoles.[10]   Although the N—O bond of the isoxazole ring is invariably severed, the products of ring cleavage are found to vary with the position and nature of the substituents present.   Generally, when the 3-position is unsubstituted, cleavage occurs by abstraction of the

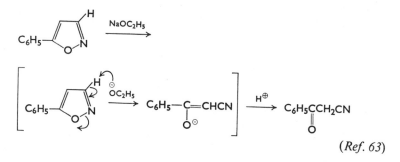

(*Ref. 63*)

3-proton by the nucleophile and a subsequent, or concurrent, flow of electrons as shown; β-ketonitriles, or their subsequent transformation products are obtained.   The yields in such reactions are excellent and the conversion has been utilized as a facile means of changing a ketone to an α-cyanoketone, as exemplified in the case of [30].

When a substituent is present at the 3-position, ring cleavage proceeds differently and can take various courses depending upon the nature of the attached groups.   The various modes of degradation, together with probable mechanistic pathways, are illustrated below.   It can be seen that, except with 3-acylisoxazoles such as [31], proton abstraction at the 5-position initiates rupture of the ring.

Scant attention has been paid to radical substitution processes in the azole series.   Whereas it is known that vapor phase bromination of thiazole at 250–400°C gives principally 2-bromothiazole,[69] and

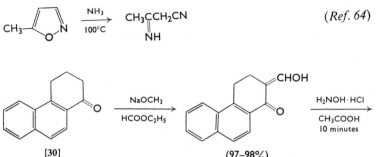

(*Ref. 64*)

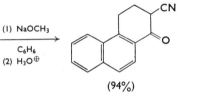

[30]　　(97–98%)

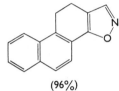

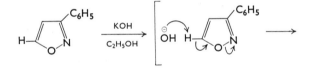

(96%)　　(94%)　　(*Ref. 65*)

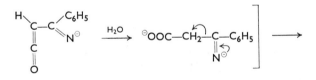

$C_6H_5C{\equiv}N$ + $CH_3COO^{\ominus}$　　(*Ref. 66*)

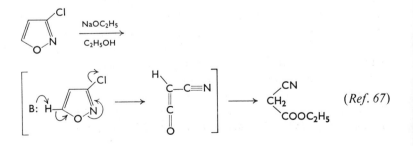

(*Ref. 67*)

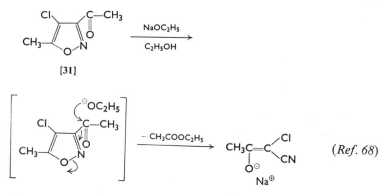

[31]

(*Ref. 68*)

that decomposition of benzoyl peroxide in the presence of isothiazole yields all three isomeric phenylisothiazoles,[23] other examples of homolytic attack at a ring carbon atom are virtually unknown in the case of the remaining azoles. Free radical side chain halogenation has been observed in a few instances.

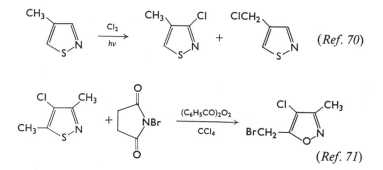

(*Ref. 70*)

(*Ref. 71*)

A few examples of the metalation of 1,2-azoles have been reported, and it appears that high selectivity for attack at the 5-position exists; alternatively, the 2-position is generally favored in the case of 1,3-azoles.

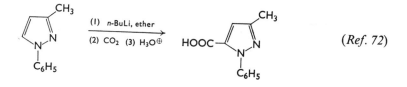

(*Ref. 72*)

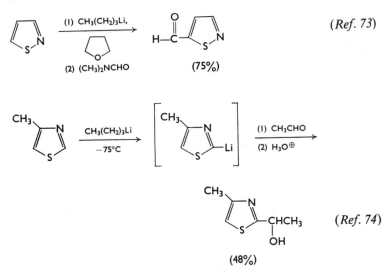

(Ref. 73)

(Ref. 74)

Imidazoles and pyrazoles which are unsubstituted on nitrogen react with such metallic reagents and active metals, like the corresponding pyrroles; however, in contrast to pyrroles (see p. 134), only N-substituted compounds result upon further reaction. For this reason, such intermediates have proved of minimal synthetic value. It should be noted that isoxazoles undergo ring cleavage under conditions of transmetalation or when treated with Grignard reagents for the reasons discussed above.

Halogen-metal interconversion reactions have also been employed with considerable success, subject only to the limitations discussed earlier.

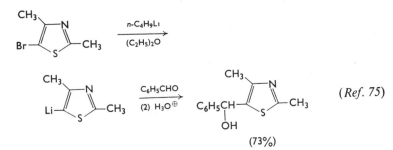

(Ref. 75)

Quaternary Azolium Salts

Quaternization of 1-substituted imidazoles[76] and pyrazoles[77] proceeds to give salts resulting from exclusive nucleophilic attack by the azole nitrogen, that is [31] and [33], respectively. Species of the

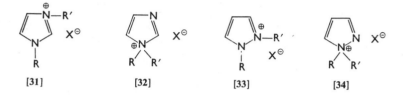

[31]   [32]   [33]   [34]

type [32] and [34] have not been observed. The remaining azoles react with alkylating agents in a similar fashion. However, in the thiazoles (and presumably also in the isothiazoles), the positioning of charge has been shown to reside most predominantly on the sulfur atom and that structure [26b] best represents thiazolium cations. This

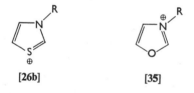

[26b]   [35]

observation contrasts with [35] which illustrates the preferred charge distribution in oxazolium cations.[53]

In the course of studies on the mechanism of thiamine action,[74, 78] it was observed that the C-2 hydrogen of 1,3-azolium salts underwent rapid deuterium exchange via a heterocyclic ylid such as [36]. The

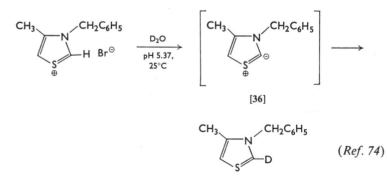

[36]

(Ref. 74)

lability of this proton can be attributed to a combination of a number of factors including high s-character of the C—H bond (the reason acetylene is a stronger acid than ethane), a favorable inductive effect (the reason HCN is a stronger acid than acetylene), stabilization of ylids such as [36] via other resonance forms, and possible d-σ overlap of the ylid electron pair with an empty d-orbital of sulfur. The inductive factor has been clearly demonstrated in the comparative study of [37] and [38]; in [38], the incipient carbanion is located between two α-nitrogen atoms which share the positive charge, a condition not operative in [37]. This influence leads the former to undergo deuterium exchange 30,000 times faster than [37] at 31°C.[79]

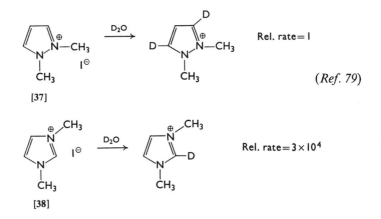

(*Ref. 79*)

[37]

[38]

Similarly, it has been observed[53] that exchange of the 2-hydrogen in the 3,4-dimethyloxazolium cation is 40 times more rapid than in the corresponding thiazolium ion.

3-Substituted isoxazolium salts react very rapidly with a wide variety of bases to give N-substituted ketoketimines such as [39]. Only

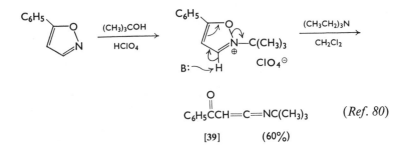

$$C_6H_5\overset{\overset{\displaystyle O}{\|}}{C}CH{=}C{=}NC(CH_3)_3$$ (*Ref. 80*)

[39]   (60%)

a few examples of the latter class of compounds are known, for they are very reactive and are not usually isolable. The utilization of carboxylate anions as bases in these decomposition processes has resulted in a valuable synthesis of peptides.[41, 81] The method consists essentially in the initial activation of a protected amino acid or peptide by combination with an isoxazolium salt ([40] is preferred to other oxazolium salts). This process which gives initially an α-ketoketimine such as [41] is followed by the addition of the car-

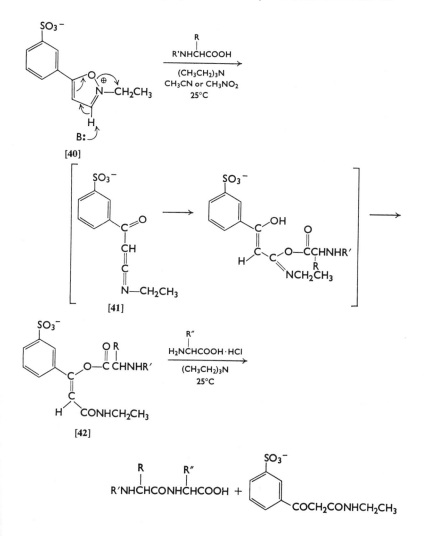

boxylic acid to **[41]** to generate an activated ester of type **[42]**. Combination of this not isolated activated ester with an amino acid ester or peptide ester completes the synthesis. In most cases, the water soluble by-product can be readily removed by mere trituration of the resulting peptide with water. Yields vary from 80–95%.

Certain azolium salts can be reduced with sodium borohydride. For example, treatment of thiazolium salts with aqueous borohydride leads to the formation of tetrahydro derivatives.[82] The presumed mechanism of this transformation is outlined on p. 209.

Side Chain Reactivity

1,2-Azoles with potential hydroxyl groups exist in equilibrium with the corresponding keto forms. However, when in particular positions on the heterocyclic ring, a single form often is preferred[83]; thus

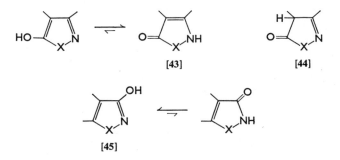

[43]   [44]

[45]

5-isomers rarely appear in the hydroxy form (except when the —OH group is chelated) and the keto forms **[43]** and/or **[44]** predominate. In the case of 3-hydroxy derivatives (e.g., **[45]**), the reverse is true.

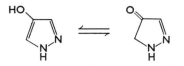

4-Hydroxyl substitution has been little studied, but 4-hydroxy-pyrazoles appear to exist as equilibrium mixtures containing both the hydroxy and keto forms.

A potential hydroxyl group at the 2-position of a 1,3-azole exists predominantly in the keto form. Hydroxyl substituents in the 4-

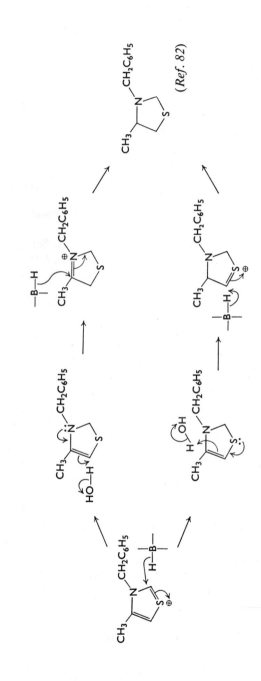

(Ref. 82)

(or 5)- position likewise exist in the keto form except when a neighboring electron-withdrawing substituent is present.

It must be borne in mind, however, that the rate of interconversion of the tautomers generally is very much greater than that of their reaction with an approaching reagent and that reaction via the less populous tautomer may actually predominate. Some examples of this behavior are given below.

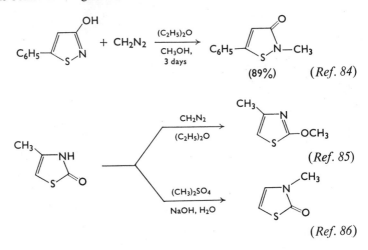

The great majority of azoles possessing potential amino groups are believed to exist as the amino tautomer. These data are in line with the known tendency of amino groups to resist tautomerism to a greater extent than hydroxyl functions. Therefore, many amino-azoles exhibit aromatic character and can undergo successful diazotization to give stable diazonium salts which display the customary coupling and replacement reactions.

Azolecarboxylic acids display the usual reactions of aromatic carboxylic acids. However, they generally undergo smooth decarboxylation upon heating to 200°C or above. Carboxyl groups bonded to a ring carbon atom that is adjacent to a ring hetero atom are found to decarboxylate most readily. Thiazole-2-carboxylic acid has been studied in some detail and has been found to decompose

at an appreciable rate simply by dissolution in quinoline at room temperature.[87] The decarboxylation is much slower in acid, and thus probably proceeds via the zwitterion [46] rather than by an alternative route involving prior protonation.

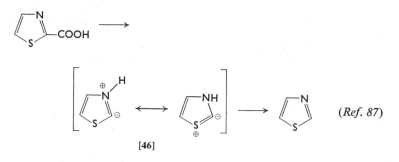

(*Ref. 87*)

[46]

The major discrepancy to the general behavior discussed above lies in the isoxazole series wherein decarboxylation of isoxazole-3-carboxylic acids gives rise to products which parallel those formed during nucleophilic ring cleavage (see pp. 201–3).

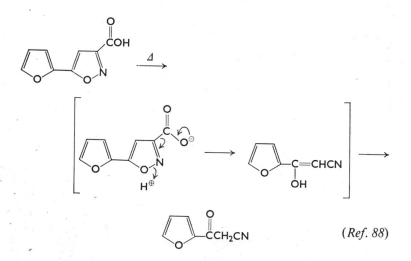

(*Ref. 88*)

Enhanced reactivity of alkyl groups, particularly methyl groups, that are attached to an azole ring is not seen except for 2-methylthiazoles and 5-methylisothiazoles which condense somewhat readily with aldehydes. Facile Claisen condensations of this type do occur

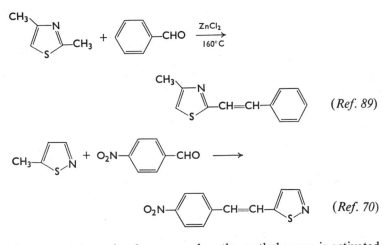

(Ref. 89)

(Ref. 70)

throughout the series, however, when the methyl group is activated by quaternary salt formation or by a neighboring nitro group. As in the case of displacement reactions (see p. 199), the position of the activating nitro group on the ring is important; thus, whereas [47] undergoes ready condensation with an aldehyde, [48] does not.[90] The failure of the reaction in the latter example may be attributed to the inability of the nitro group to stabilize the intermediate carbanion which is required for reaction with the aldehyde.

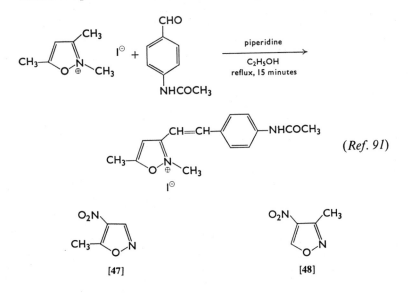

(Ref. 91)

[47]   [48]

N-Acyl derivatives of five-membered nitrogen-containing hetero-cycles, particularly N-acetyl derivatives, display a great tendency to hydrolyze readily under conditions of neutral pH when the ring system contains more than one nitrogen atom (Table 6–1).   The

TABLE 6–I   ▪

Half-Lives for the Hydrolysis of N-Acetylazoles in Water at pH 7.0 and 25°C[92]

Compound	Half-life, minutes	Compound	Half-life, minutes	Compound	Half-life, minutes
pyrrole-COCH₃	∞	pyrazole-COCH₃	908	imidazole-COCH₃	41
triazole-COCH₃	26.6	triazole-COCH₃	6.4	tetrazole-COCH₃	<0.5

(Ref. 93b)

(95%)

driving force for this process is linked to the aromaticity of the ring and the influence exerted by the various electron-withdrawing nitrogen atoms in increasing the electron deficiency at the nitrogen bearing the acetyl group.   From the data in Table 6–1, it can be seen that the effect is cumulative.   This property has been utilized in a wide variety of synthetic procedures most particularly in the case of N,N′ carbonyl diimidazole [49].[92]   Perhaps its most useful application resides in the field of peptide syntheses of the type outlined on the previous page.[93]

Exercises

1. Predict the major product of the following reactions:

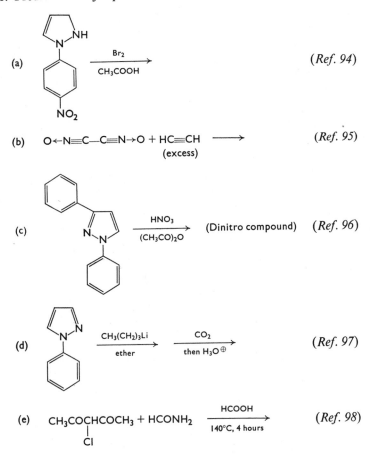

(a) $\xrightarrow[\text{CH}_3\text{COOH}]{\text{Br}_2}$ (*Ref. 94*)

(b) $O \leftarrow N \equiv C - C \equiv N \rightarrow O + HC \equiv CH \longrightarrow$ (*Ref. 95*)
                                    (excess)

(c) $\xrightarrow[\text{(CH}_3\text{CO)}_2\text{O}]{\text{HNO}_3}$ (Dinitro compound)   (*Ref. 96*)

(d) $\xrightarrow[\text{ether}]{\text{CH}_3\text{(CH}_2\text{)}_3\text{Li}}$ $\xrightarrow[\text{then H}_3\text{O}^{\oplus}]{\text{CO}_2}$ (*Ref. 97*)

(e) $CH_3COCHCOCH_3 + HCONH_2$ $\xrightarrow[\text{140°C, 4 hours}]{\text{HCOOH}}$ (*Ref. 98*)
              |
              Cl

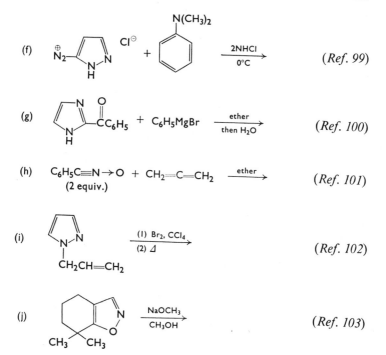

(f) + $\xrightarrow[\text{0°C}]{\text{2NHCl}}$ (*Ref. 99*)

(g) + C_6H_5MgBr $\xrightarrow[\text{then } H_2O]{\text{ether}}$ (*Ref. 100*)

(h) $C_6H_5C\equiv N\rightarrow O$ + $CH_2\!\!=\!\!C\!\!=\!\!CH_2$ $\xrightarrow{\text{ether}}$ (*Ref. 101*)
  (2 equiv.)

(i) $\xrightarrow[\text{(2) }\Delta]{\text{(1) Br}_2, \text{CCl}_4}$ (*Ref. 102*)

(j) $\xrightarrow[\text{CH}_3\text{OH}]{\text{NaOCH}_3}$ (*Ref. 103*)

2. Suggest a reasonable mechanism for each of the following transformations:

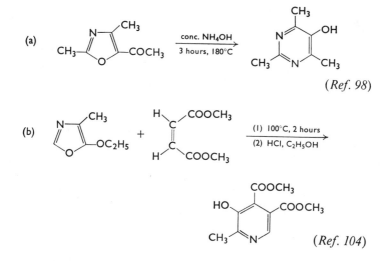

(a) $\xrightarrow[\text{3 hours, 180°C}]{\text{conc. NH}_4\text{OH}}$ (*Ref. 98*)

(b) + $\xrightarrow[\text{(2) HCl, C}_2\text{H}_5\text{OH}]{\text{(1) 100°C, 2 hours}}$

(*Ref. 104*)

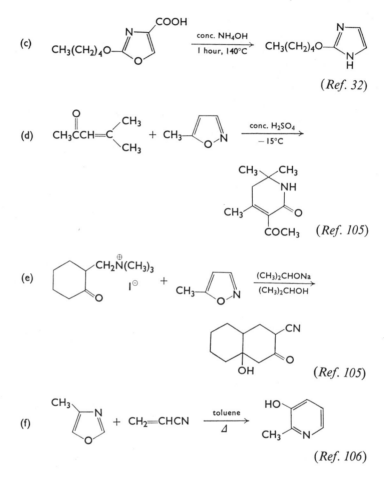

(c) ... $\xrightarrow[\text{I hour, 140°C}]{\text{conc. NH}_4\text{OH}}$ ... (*Ref. 32*)

(d) ... $\xrightarrow[- 15°C]{\text{conc. H}_2\text{SO}_4}$ ... (*Ref. 105*)

(e) ... $\xrightarrow[\text{(CH}_3)_2\text{CHOH}]{\text{(CH}_3)_2\text{CHONa}}$ ... (*Ref. 105*)

(f) ... $\xrightarrow[\Delta]{\text{toluene}}$ ... (*Ref. 106*)

References and Notes

(1) A. Adams and R. Slack, *J. Chem. Soc.*, **1959**, 3061; *Chem. Ind. (London)*, **1956**, 1232.

(2) It is obvious that if X in [7] and [8] is oxygen or sulfur, these atoms will also possess an orthogonal electron pair. However, the relative basicity of nitrogen will, as usual, take precedence.

(3) It is of interest to compare these values with the pK_a's of ammonia (9.2) and pyridine (5.2).

(4) (a) W. Hückel, J. Datow, and E. Simersbach, *Z. Physik. Chem. (Leipzig)*, **186A**, 129 (1940); (b) L. Hunter and J. A. Marriott, *J. Chem. Soc.*, **1941**, 777.

(5) H. Hayes and L. Hunter, *ibid.*, **1941**, 1; L. Hunter, *ibid.*, **1945**, 806.

(6) For more extensive discussions of the tautomeric character of imidazoles and pyrazoles, refer to (a) A. R. Katritzky and J. M. Lagowski, *Adv. Heterocyclic Chem.*, **2**, 27 (1963); (b) K. Hofmann, *Imidazole and Its Derivatives, Part 1*, in A. Weissberger (ed.), *The Chemistry of Heterocyclic Compounds*, Interscience, New York, 1953, pp. 26–30.

(7) R. Justoni and R. Pessina, *Gazz. Chim. Ital.*, **85**, 34 (1955).

(8) R. H. Wiley and P. E. Hexner, *Org. Syn.*, **Coll. Vol. 4**, 351 (1963).

(9) C. L. Habraken and J. A. Moore, *J. Org. Chem.*, **30**, 1892 (1965).

(10) Fur further extensive discussions of isoxazole syntheses, see (a) A. Quilico, *Five- and Six-Membered Compounds with Nitrogen and Oxygen*, in A. Weissberger (ed.), *The Chemistry of Heterocyclic Compounds*, Interscience, New York, 1962, Chapter 1; (b) R. A. Barnes in R. C. Elderfield (ed.), *Heterocyclic Compounds*, Vol. 5, Wiley, New York, 1957, Chapter 7; (c) N. K. Kochetkov and S. D. Sokolov, *Adv. Heterocyclic Chem.*, **2**, 365 (1963).

(11) For further extensive discussions of pyrazole syntheses, see T. L. Jacobs in R. C. Elderfield (ed.), *Heterocyclic Compounds*, Vol. 5, Wiley, New York, 1957, Chapter 2.

(12) K. v. Auwers and W. Schmidt, *Chem. Ber.*, **58**, 528 (1925).

(13) N. K. Kochetkov, A. N. Nesmeyanov, and N. S. Semenov, *Izv. Akad. Nauk SSSR, Otd. Khim. Nauk*, **1952**, 87; *Chem. Abstr.*, **47**, 2167 (1953).

(14) H. Bredereck, H. Herlinger, and E. H. Schweizer, *Chem. Ber.*, **93**, 1208 (1960).

(15) K. v. Auwers and R. Hügel, *J. Prakt. Chem.*, **143**, 157 (1935).

(16) For a generalized discussion of 1,3-dipolar additions, see Chapter 10.

(17) A. Quilico and G. Speroni, *Gazz. Chim. Ital.*, **76**, 148 (1946).

(18) R. Hüttel, *Chem. Ber.*, **74**, 1680 (1941).

(19) See footnote 5 of ref. 18.

(20) R. Gösl and A. Meuwsen, *Z. Anorg. Allgem. Chem.*, **314**, 334 (1962).

(21) For an extensive discussion pertaining to isothiazole syntheses, see R. Slack and K. R. H. Wooldridge, *Adv. Heterocyclic Chem.*, **4**, 107 (1965).

(22) A. Adams and R. Slack, *J. Chem. Soc.*, **1959**, 3061. For extensions of this reaction, see J. Goerdeler, *et al.*, *Chem. Ber.*, **94**, 2950 (1961); **96**, 526, 944, 1551 (1963).

(23) F. Hübenett, F. H. Flock, and H. Hofmann, *Angew. Chem. Intern. Ed.*, **1**, 508 (1962); F. Hübenett and H. Hofmann, *ibid.*, **2**, 325 (1963).

(24) F. Wille, L. Capeller, and A. Steiner, *ibid.*, **1**, 335 (1962).

(25) R. A. Olofson, J. M. Landesberg, R. O. Berry, D. Leaver, W. A. H. Robertson, and D. M. McKinnon, *Tetrahedron*, **22**, 2119 (1966).

(26) For detailed reviews on the synthesis of *imidazoles*, see (a) Ref. 6b; (b) E. S. Schipper and A. R. Day, in R. C. Elderfield (ed.), *Heterocyclic Compounds*, Vol. 5, Wiley, New York, 1957, Chapter 4. *Oxazoles:* (c) J. W. Cornforth, *ibid.*, Vol. 5, Chapter 5. *Thiazoles:* (d) J. M. Sprague and A. H. Land, *ibid.*, Vol. 5, Chapter 8; (e) R. H. Wiley, D. C. England, and L. C. Behr, *Org. Reactions*, **6**, 367 (1951).

(27) D. Davidson, M. Weiss, and M. Jelling, *J. Org. Chem.*, **2**, 319 (1938).

(28) R. Robinson, *J. Chem. Soc.*, **95**, 2167 (1909).

(29) S. Gabriel, *Chem. Ber.*, **43**, 1283 (1910).

(30) D. S. Tartell, H. P. Hirschler, and R. B. Carlin, *J. Am. Chem. Soc.*, **72**, 3138 (1950).

(31) M. Bachstez, *Chem. Ber.*, **47**, 3163 (1914); see also ref. 25e, p. 379.

(32) J. W. Cornforth and H. T. Huang, *J. Chem. Soc.*, **1948**, 1960.

(33) G. Schwarz, *Org Syn.*, **Coll. Vol. 3**, 332 (1955).

(34) J. R. Byers and J. B. Dickey, *ibid.*, **Coll. Vol. 2**, 31 (1943).

(35) J. W. Cornforth and R. H. Cornforth, *ibid.*, **1947**, 96.

(36) R. G. Jones, *J. Am. Chem. Soc.*, **71**, 383 (1949).

(37) M. P. L. Caton, D. H. Jones, R. Slack, and K. R. H. Wooldridge, *J. Chem. Soc.*, **1964**, 446.

(38) I. L. Finar and K. E. Godfrey, *ibid.*, **1954**, 2293.

(39) A. Quilico and C. Musante, *Gazz. Chim. Ital.*, **71**, 327 (1941).

(40) W. Rassmann, *Ann. Chem.*, **352**, 158 (1907).

(41) R. B. Woodward, R. A. Olofson, and H. Mayer, *J. Am. Chem. Soc.*, **83**, 1010 (1961).

(42) (a) C. Musante, *Farmaco (Pavia) Ed. Sci.*, **6**, 32 (1951); *Chem. Abstr.*, **45**, 5879 (1951); (b) N. K. Kochetkov and E. D. Khomutova, *Zh. Obshch. Khim.*, **28**, 359 (1958).

(43) J. H. Ridd, *Physical Methods in Heterocyclic Chem.*, **1**, 109 (1963).

(44) (a) I. E. Bababan and F. L. Pyman, *J. Chem. Soc.*, **121**, 947 (1922); (b) R. G. Fargher and F. L. Pyman, *ibid.*, **115**, 217 (1919); (c) M. Brickman, M. W. Austin, J. H. Ridd, and B. V. Smith, *Chem. Ind. (London)*, **1962**, 1057.

(45) T. D. Breese and J. H. Ridd, personal communication as cited in W. Adam and A. Grimison, *Tetrahedron*, **22**, 835 (1966), footnote 4.

(46) The 4- and 5-positions are obviously equivalent in the symmetrical cation [**24**].

(47) J. H. Ridd, *J. Chem. Soc.*, **1955**, 1238.

(48) R. T. Gillespie, A. Grimison, J. H. Ridd, and R. F. White, *ibid.*, **1958**, 3228.

(49) R. D. Brown, H. C. Duffin, J. C. Mayhard, and J. H. Ridd, *ibid.*, **1953**, 3937.

(50) A. Grimison and J. H. Ridd, *ibid.*, **1959**, 3019; *Proc. Chem. Soc.*, **1958**, 256.

(51) F. L. Pyman and G. M. Timmis, *J. Chem. Soc.*, **123**, 494 (1923).

(52) J. P. English, J. H. Clark, J. W. Clapp, D. Seeger, and R. H. Ebel, *J. Am. Chem. Soc.*, **68**, 453 (1946).

(53) P. Haake and W. B. Miller, *ibid.*, **85**, 4044 (1963).

(54) J. H. Clark, J. P. English, P. S. Winnek, H. W. Marson, Q. P. Cole, and J. W. Clapp, *ibid.*, **68**, 96 (1946).

(55) R. Forsyth and F. L. Pyman, *J. Chem. Soc.*, **1930**, 397; F. L. Pyman and E. Stanley, *ibid.*, **125**, 2484 (1924); R. L. Grant and F. L. Pyman, *ibid.*, **119**, 1893 (1921).

(56) M. T. Bogert and E. M. Abrahamson, *J. Am. Chem. Soc.*, **44**, 826 (1922); M. T. Bogert and M. Meyer, *ibid.*, **44**, 1568 (1922); M. T. Bogert and H. B. Corbitt, *ibid.*, **48**, 783 (1926).

(57) J. Lester and R. Robinson, *J. Chem. Soc.*, **101**, 1297 (1912); C. Gränacher and G. Wolf, *Helv. Chim. Acta*, **10**, 815 (1927).

(58) G. Speroni and E. Giachetti, *Gazz. Chim. Ital.*, **83**, 192 (1953).

(59) (a) W. R. Hatchard, *J. Org. Chem.*, **29**, 660 (1964); (b) A. Michaelis, *Ann. Chem.*, **338**, 183 (1905).

(60) T. E. Young and E. D. Amstutz, *J. Am. Chem. Soc.*, **73**, 4773 (1951); K. R. Brower, J. W. Way, W. P. Samuels, and E. D. Amstutz, *J. Org. Chem.*, **19**, 1830 (1954).

(61) I. E. Balaban, *J. Chem. Soc.*, **1930**, 268.

(62) For an extensive discussion of the properties of 2-halothiazoles, see ref. 25d, pp. 542–4.

(63) L. Claisen and R. Stock, *Chem. Ber.*, **24**, 130 (1891).

(64) L. Claisen, *ibid.*, **42**, 59 (1909).

(65) W. S. Johnson and W. E. Shelberg, *J. Am. Chem. Soc.*, **67**, 1745 (1945); W. S. Johnson, J. W. Petersen, and C. D. Gutsche, *ibid.*, **69**, 2942 (1947).

(66) L. Claisen, *Chem. Ber.*, **36**, 3664 (1903).

(67) P. Bravo, G. Gaudiano, A. Quilico, and A. Ricca, *Gazz. Chim. Ital.*, **91**, 47 (1961).

(68) A. Quilico, R. Fusco, and V. Rosnati, *ibid.*, **76**, 30 (1946).

(69) J. P. Wibaut, *Chem. Ber.*, **72**, 1708 (1939); J. P. Wibaut and H. E. Hansen, *Rec. Trav. Chim.*, **53**, 77 (1934).

(70) F. Hübenett, F. H. Flock, W. Hansel, H. Heinze, and H. Hofmann, *Angew. Chem. Intern. Ed.*, **2**, 714 (1963).

(71) S. D. Sokolov and N. K. Kochetkov, *Zh. Obshch. Khim.*, **33**, 1192 (1963).

(72) H. R. Snyder, F. Verbanac, and D. B. Bright, *J. Am. Chem. Soc.*, **74**, 3243 (1952).

(73) D. Buttimore, D. H. Jones, R. Slack, and K. R. H. Wooldridge, *J. Chem. Soc.*, **1963**, 2032; D. H. Jones, R. Slack, and K. R. H. Wooldridge, *ibid.*, **1964**, 3114.

(74) R. Breslow and E. McNelis, *J. Am. Chem. Soc.*, **81**, 3080 (1959).

(75) R. P. Kurkjy and E. V. Brown, *ibid.*, **74**, 6260 (1952).

(76) C. G. Overberger, J. C. Salamone, and S. Yaroslavsky, *J. Org. Chem.*, **30**, 3580 (1965).

(77) G. F. Duffin, *Adv. Heterocyclic Chem.*, **3**, 1 (1964).

(78) R. Breslow and E. McNelis, *J. Am. Chem. Soc.*, **82**, 2394 (1960); R. Breslow, *ibid.*, **80**, 3719 (1958), and earlier papers in this series.

(79) R. A. Olofson, W. R. Thompson, and J. S. Michelman, *ibid.*, **86**, 1865 (1964).

(80) (a) R. B. Woodward and D. J. Woodman, *J. Org. Chem.*, **31**, 2039 (1966); (b) R. B. Woodward and D. J. Woodman, *J. Am. Chem. Soc.*, **88**, 3169 (1966).

(81) (a) R. B. Woodward and R. A. Olofson, *ibid.*, **83**, 1007 (1961); (b) C. H. Li, D. Chung, J. Ramachandran, and B. Gorup, *ibid.*, **84**, 2460 (1962); (c) P. G. Katsoyannis and M. Tilak, *ibid.*, **85**, 4028 (1963).

(82) G. M. Clarke and P. Sykes, *Chem. Commun.*, **1966**, 370.

(83) For a recent summary of the existing data on this subject, see A. R. Katritzky and J. M. Lagowski, *Adv. Heterocyclic Chem.*, **2**, 27 (1963).

(84) J. Goerdeler, *Angew. Chem.*, **74**, 498 (1962); J. Goerdeler and W. Mittler, *Chem. Ber.*, **96**, 944 (1963).

(85) A. Hantzsch, *ibid.*, **60**, 2537 (1927).

(86) J. Tcherniac, *J. Chem. Soc.*, **115**, 1071 (1919).

(87) H. Schenkel and M. Schenkel-Rudin, *Helv. Chim. Acta*, **31**, 924 (1948).

(88) C. Musante and S. Fatutta, *Gazz. Chim. Ital.*, **88**, 879 (1958).

(89) H. Erlemeyer, O. Weber, P. Schmidt, G. Küng, C. Zinsstag, and B. Prijs, *Helv. Chim. Acta*, **31**, 1142 (1948).

(90) A. Quilico and C. Musante, *Gazz. Chim. Ital.*, **72**, 399 (1942).

(91) W. Lampe and J. Smolinska, *Bull. Acad. Polon. Sci.*, **5**, 835 (1957); *Chem. Abstr.*, **52**, 6319 (1958).

(92) H. A. Staab, *Angew. Chem. Intern. Ed.*, **1**, 351 (1961).

(93) (a) R. Paul and G. W. Anderson, *J. Org. Chem.*, **27**, 2094 (1962); (b) *J. Am. Chem. Soc.*, **82**, 4569 (1960).

(94) J. Elguero and R. Jacquier, *Bull. Soc. Chim. France*, **1966**, 610.

(95) R. Cramer and W. R. McClellan, *J. Org. Chem.*, **26**, 2976 (1961).

(96) B. M. Lynch and Y. Hung, *Can. J. Chem.*, **42**, 1605 (1964).

(97) P. W. Alley and D. A. Shirley, *J. Am. Chem. Soc.*, **80**, 6271 (1958).

(98) A. Dornow and H. Hell, *Chem. Ber.*, **93**, 1998 (1960).

(99) H. Reimlinger and A. Van Overstraeten, *ibid.*, **99**, 3350 (1966).

(100) W. Rohr and H. A. Staab, *Angew. Chem.*, **77**, 1077 (1965).

(101) G. S. d'Alcontres and G. LoVecchio, *Gazz. Chim. Ital.*, **90**, 1239 (1960).

(102) S. Trofimenko, *J. Am. Chem. Soc.*, **87**, 4393 (1965).

(103) W. L. Meyer, G. B. Clemans, and R. W. Huffman, *Tetrahedron Letters*, No. **36**, 4255 (1966).

(104) E. E. Harris *et al.*, *J. Org. Chem.*, **27**, 2705 (1962).

(105) C. H. Eugster, L. Leichner, and E. Jenny, *Helv. Chim. Acta*, **46**, 543 (1963).

(106) T. Naito, T. Yoshikawa, F. Ishikawa, S. Isoda, Y. Omura, and I. Takamura, *Chem. Pharm. Bull.* (*Tokyo*), **13**, 869 (1965).

7

■ THE PYRIDINE GROUP

PYRIDINE [1] IS THE HETEROCYCLIC system which most closely resembles benzene in terms of structure and overall stability. For example, pyridine, like benzene, is extremely resistant to oxidation and is

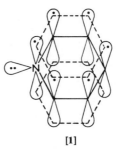

[1]

frequently employed as a solvent in conjunction with such oxidizing agents as chromium trioxide to effect the oxidation of organic molecules.[1]   Cyclic conjugation in [1] is apparent from its stabilization energy of 21 kcal/mole[2] and from the measured C—C and C—N bond lengths which lie intermediate between those known for authentic single and double bonds.[3] Such molecular dimensions denote that the five carbon and lone nitrogen atoms are situated in a planar hexagonal framework wherein all of the atoms are trigonally (sp^2) hybridized in order that 6 p-π electrons may be available to form the stable, delocalized molecular orbital as shown in [1]. In this arrangement, the remaining $2p$ orbital of the nitrogen atom is perpendicular to this molecular orbital; therefore, an electron pair is available for additional bonding. Indeed, pyridine is weakly basic ($pK_a = 5.2$), a fact which profoundly affects its chemical properties.

In the alternative valence-bond description of pyridine, structures [2]–[6] are considered to contribute to the resonance hybrid. The

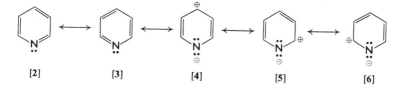

[2]   [3]   [4]   [5]   [6]

zwitterionic forms in the present instance are believed to contribute substantially to the hybrid, chiefly on the basis of the large dipole moment for this substance, 2.26 D,[4] which is appreciably greater than that of piperidine (1.17 D), its perhydro counterpart. On the basis of these resonance structures, it must be noticed that the relatively more electronegative nitrogen atom produces by electron attraction a deficiency of charge in the ring carbon atoms. This effect is in direct contrast to the observations previously discussed in the case of pyrroles and azoles where the ring carbon atoms acquire increased electron density (see pp. 103, 185). This electron-withdrawing influence of the hetero atom is the major factor in the observed reactivity differences of pyridines.

The pyridine nitrogen atom possesses an electron pair not required for stabilization of the aromatic system; consequently, pyridines can become protonated to form the corresponding conjugate acids, the pyridinium ions. The base strength of various pyridines would be expected to vary according to the nature of the ring substituents, with electron-donating groups increasing, and electron-withdrawing groups decreasing, the pK_a value, and this is observed.[5] By the same token, pyridines may form complexes with a variety of Lewis acids, react with alkylating agents to form pyridinium salts such as [7],[6] and be oxidized to pyridine-N-oxides (e.g., [8]) upon treatment with a peracid.

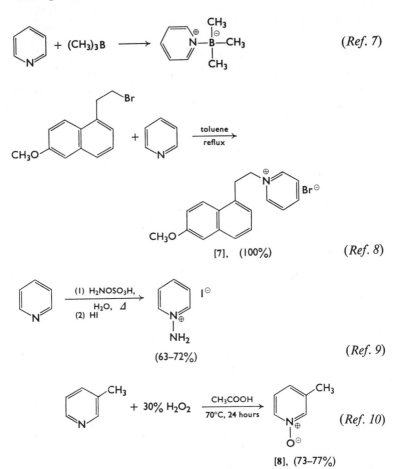

[7], (100%)   (Ref. 8)

(63–72%)   (Ref. 9)

[8], (73–77%)

    From the structural viewpoint, pyridine-N-oxides represent par-
ticularly interesting entities because they are endowed with the
capability of increasing electron density at the various ring positions
or in the reverse direction, upon demand of the reagent to which they
are exposed.   This phenomenon is evident from structures [9]–[15]
which contribute to the resonance hybrid.   As in the case of pyridine,

the dipolar forms appear to be of considerable significance; further-more, the dipole moment (4.24 D)[11] and the pK_a (0.79)[12] of pyridine-N-oxide suggest that structures [13]–[15] are comparable in importance to formulas [9]–[12].

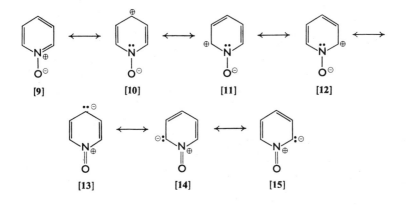

[9]   [10]   [11]   [12]

[13]   [14]   [15]

Ring substitution reactions of pyridine-N-oxides will be considered later in this chapter. As seen from structures [9]–[12], the N-oxide oxygen atom should be capable of functioning as a nucleophilic terminus; this capability is observed in the reactions of pyridine-N-oxides with a wide variety of alkylating agents which result in an S_N2-type displacement to form N-alkoxypyridinium salts.

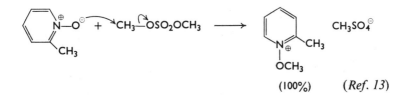

(100%)   (Ref. 13)

SYNTHETIC APPROACHES

Pyridine and many of its derivatives are available from coal tar sources.[14]   This is fortunate for, at present, there exists no feasible large-scale practical synthesis of pyridine.   Although a large variety of miscellaneous synthetic approaches to pyridine derivatives are known,[14] many pyridines are more readily available by direct substitution of simpler pyridines[15]; however, a number of these first methods are of broad synthetic interest.

Perhaps the only exception to this conclusion is the so-called Hantzsch synthesis[16] which, with its many ramifications, represents a reaction scheme of considerable generality. In its original version, the Hantzsch synthesis involves the condensation of a β-keto ester, an aldehyde, and ammonia to give a dihydropyridine which is subsequently oxidized to the corresponding pyridine. The initial condensation which leads to the dihydropyridine is believed to

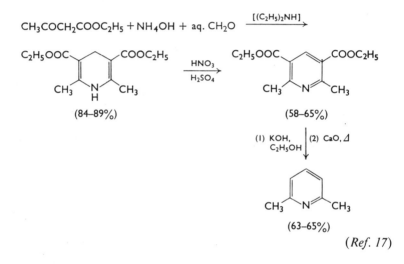

(Ref. 17)

proceed by the initial formation of a β-amino-α,β-unsaturated carbonyl component [16] and an alkylidine or arylidene 1,3-dicarbonyl compound [17]; the formation of these components is followed by a Michael-type addition involving the electron-rich β-carbon of the enamine moiety as the nucleophile; the reaction is completed as shown in the equation. Although structures of the type [16] and [17] have not been isolated from such a process, such species are known to interact in a manner which results in the formation of 1,4-dihydropyridines.

Many variations of the Hantzsch reaction are known, several of which are exemplified on page 228.

The mechanism of the oxidation of dihydropyridines has only recently been somewhat clarified.[18] It has been observed that, if the

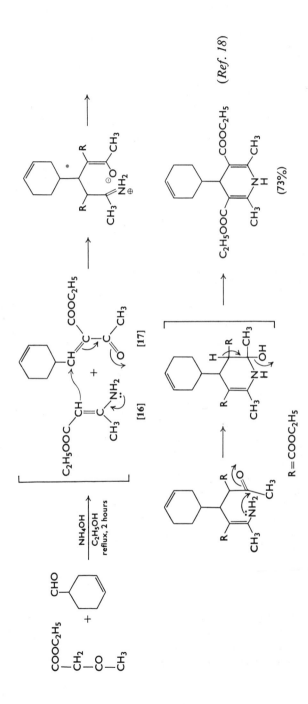

(Ref. 18)

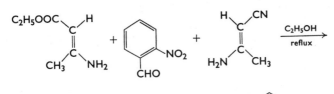

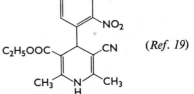

(Ref. 19)

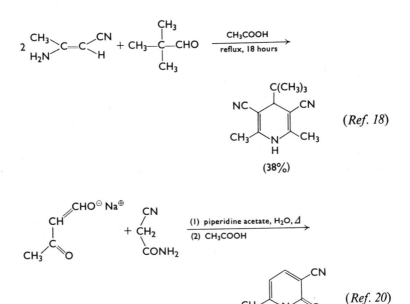

(Ref. 18)

(38%)

(Ref. 20)

(55–62%)

dihydropyridine is substituted in the 4-position by a group which possesses a moderate to strong electron-releasing capability, this group is eliminated during the course of the oxidation. Such results appear to be consistent with a mechanism which involves ejection of

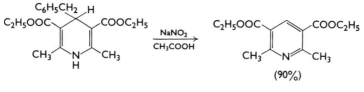

(Ref. 18)

this substituent as a positively charged species (carbonium ion). A likely pathway is indicated in the following equation:

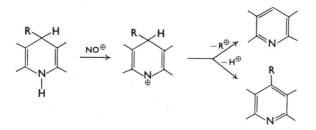

Whether dealkylation or proton loss will occur appears to be governed by the stability of the incipient carbonium ion and the steric size of the groups in the 3-, 4-, and 5-positions.[18]

REACTIONS

Electrophilic Substitution

The electrophilic substitution of pyridine generally can be accomplished only under drastic conditions. Although the possibility exists that a pyridine may react with an electrophile either as the neutral molecule or as the conjugate acid, this option is rarely exercised because the unshared electron pair on the nitrogen atom is the singularly most reactive site relative to a positively charged species, and the initial formation of a pyridinium salt is kinetically favored. For example, the action of dinitrogen pentoxide upon pyridine under neutral conditions leads solely to [18].[21] The substitution of an

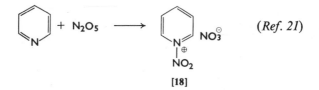

(Ref. 21)

[18]

$\overset{\oplus}{=}$NH group for a ring =CH— moiety of benzene has been estimated to result in a deactivation toward electrophilic attack of the order of 10^{-12} to 10^{-18} fold.[22]   This decrease in the reactivity of pyridine is indeed reflected in the conditions required to effect its reaction with positively charged entities as exemplified below.   However, when the 2- and 6-positions of the pyridine ring are substituted with bulky groups as in [19], coordination at the nitrogen atom is sterically

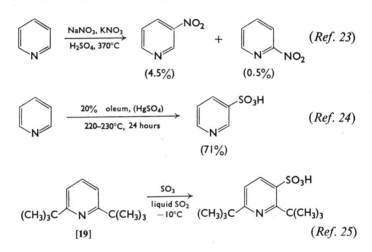

prevented and substitution occurs on the free pyridine base under rather mild conditions.   The strongly deactivating effect of coordination is thus demonstrated.

Electrophilic substitution of pyridines and pyridinium ions occurs preferentially at the 3-position due to the energetically more favorable

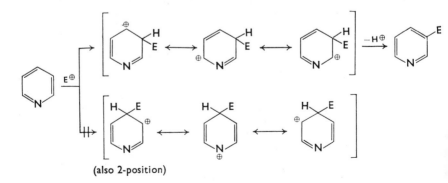

(also 2-position)

transition state encountered when attack occurs at that site. Thus, the localization of a partial positive charge upon the electronegative and often positively charged nitrogen atom (which would occur in 2- and 4-substitution) can serve only to increase the energy of that particular transition state relative to the 3-substitution pathway where this phenomenon is obviated.

Electrophilic attack on pyridine-N-oxide may occur either at the 3- or the 4-position depending upon whether reaction involves the free base or the conjugate acid. Nitration of this substance proceeds

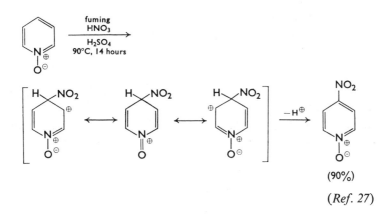

(90%)

(*Ref. 27*)

by attack upon the free base[26] and results in the ready formation of the 4-nitro derivative. If this position is occupied, nitration is usually not observed. Sulfonation, on the contrary, occurs with difficulty

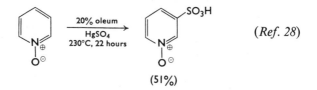

(*Ref. 28*)

(51%)

and at the 3-position; apparently in fuming sulfuric acid coordination of the N-oxide with sulfur trioxide occurs and this substrate behaves as a typical pyridinium salt.[29]

Alkyl substituents are observed to activate the pyridine group toward electrophilic substitution. In general, the heterocyclic nitrogen atom remains the dominating orienting influence as seen in

the case of [20].   The same is true in the case of the N-oxides.[31]
Further substitution of halogenated pyridines likewise is controlled
by the heterocyclic center.

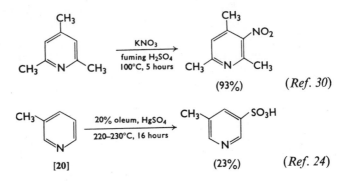

(*Ref. 30*)

(*Ref. 24*)

An analysis of the known electrophilic processes performed on
aminopyridines indicates that amino substituents exert the dominating orienting effect.   A 2-amino group directs the incoming electrophile predominantly to the 5-position, whereas a 3-amino group

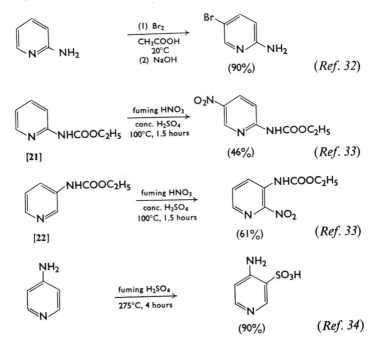

(*Ref. 32*)

(*Ref. 33*)

(*Ref. 33*)

(*Ref. 34*)

leads chiefly to 2-substitution, and a 4-amino group directs attack to the 3-position. It can be seen from compounds [21] and [22] that carbamyl (and also acetamido) groups are equally effective in controlling the substitution process. Such is not the case in the corresponding N-oxides where the order of directive power appears to be

$$NR_2 > \overset{\oplus}{N}\!\!-\!\!\overset{\ominus}{O} > NHCOR,$$ as illustrated by the following examples.

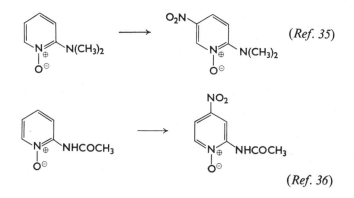

(*Ref. 35*)

(*Ref. 36*)

Pyridine rings bearing alkoxy groups behave similarly.[37] However, whereas the ether substituent controls further substitution in the pyridine series, the directing capability of the N-oxide group exceeds that of the alkoxy group in the oxidized counterparts such as [23].

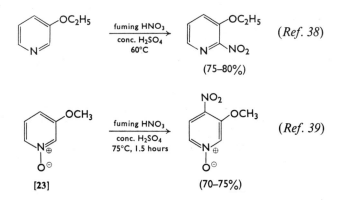

(*Ref. 38*)

(75–80%)

(*Ref. 39*)

[23]

(70–75%)

In the case of the 3-hydroxy group, this substituent is sufficiently powerful in its directive influence to dominate matters in both series.

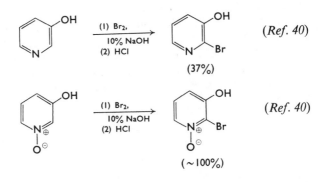

(Ref. 40)

(37%)

(Ref. 40)

(~100%)

As will be seen (see p. 248), the 2- and 4-hydroxypyridines and their N-oxides are unique because in their ground state these substances exist predominantly in their tautomeric pyridone forms. As would be expected, this precondition is reflected in their reactivity and in the possibility that they may react from either structural species. For example, 2-pyridones undergo preferential attack at the 3-position in marked contrast to the behavior of the related 2-alkoxy derivatives (where 5-substitution is generally observed).

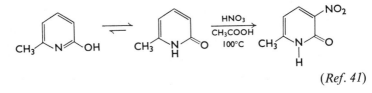

(Ref. 41)

N-Alkyl-2-pyridones (which cannot tautomerize) are likewise substituted at the 3-position.[42]

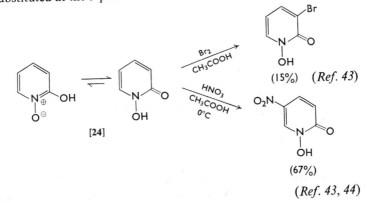

(15%)   (Ref. 43)

(67%)

(Ref. 43, 44)

N-Hydroxy-2-pyridone (2-hydroxypyridine-N-oxide) [24] undergoes bromination to give the 3-bromo derivative, whereas nitration
results in 5-substitution. In the latter reaction, it is likely that the
conjugate acid of [24] is involved.

4-Pyridones and N-hydroxy-4-pyridones behave as expected, and
usually undergo substitution in the 3- and 5-positions.[31]

Electron-withdrawing substituents such as nitro and carboxyl
deactivate the pyridine ring sufficiently so that no additional electrophilic attack will occur. The lack of reactivity can be reversed, if
there is present in addition to the deactivating function an activating
group such as hydroxy or amino. Pyridines and their N-oxides are
obviously insufficiently reactive to interact with the weaker electrophiles of the type generated in Friedel-Crafts and Vilsmeier reactions.

Nucleophilic Substitution

In any discussion of nucleophilic substitution of pyridine and its
derivatives, it is important to recognize by which of two possible
mechanistic pathways the process at hand is occurring, that is, via the
addition-elimination mechanism[31,45] or the elimination-addition, or
hetaryne, mechanism.[46] These two mechanistic types will be
discussed in turn.

Nucleophilic displacement reactions of the pyridine nucleus take
place with relative ease. A useful reaction of this type involves the
synthesis of aminopyridines from pyridines and alkali metal amides
(the Tschitschibabin[47] reaction).[48] Attack at the 2- or 6-positions
is observed unless these positions are occupied, whereby 4-amino-
pyridines are formed (higher temperatures are generally required in
such instances). The pronounced reactivity of the α- and γ-positions
is attributable to the fact that addition at these sites permits the
negative charge to reside partially on the electronegative nitrogen

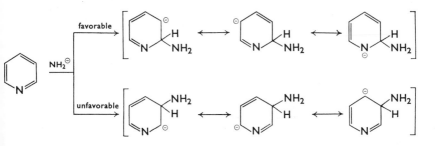

atom. The detailed nature of the ensuing steps in this amination reaction remains under discussion.[49] The illustrated mechanism denotes, however, one possible manner in which the reaction can

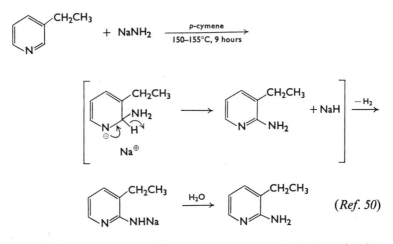

terminate and hydrogen be liberated. The utility of the amination reaction lies in the great variety of derivatives which can be obtained readily from aminopyridines.

Grignard and organolithium reagents react similarly with pyridines; the lithium compounds are preferred because of their greater nucleophilicity. The interaction of pyridine-N-oxides and alkoxy-

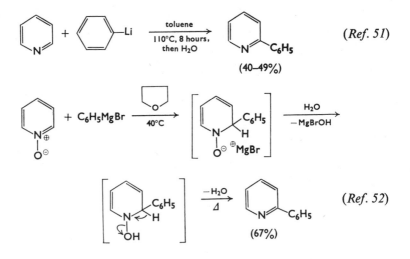

pyridinium salts with such organometallics likewise gives substituted pyridines. In general, the products derived from attack of the nucleophile at the 2-position again predominate.

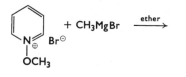

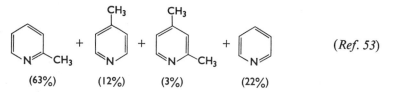

(63%)   (12%)   (3%)   (22%)   (Ref. 53)

Certain weaker nucleophiles such as hydroxide ion have been found to react with pyridines only under forcing conditions. Still weaker nucleophiles such as cyanide or halide ions are unreactive toward pyridines, but attack pyridinium and alkoxypyridinium salts quite readily. The best known application of hydroxide as nucleophile resides in conjunction with the alkaline ferricyanide oxidation of pyridinium salts to 2-pyridones. Such conversions proceed by initial nucleophilic attack at the highly electron-deficient 2-position of the pyridinium salt to afford a pseudobase (e.g., [25]) which is subsequently oxidized by the ferricyanide ion in a series of 1-electron

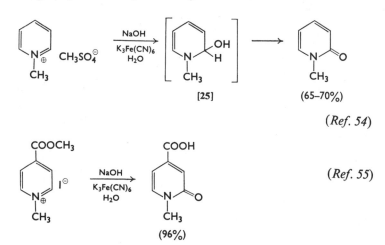

[25]   (65–70%)

(Ref. 54)

(96%)

(Ref. 55)

transfers. This reaction, however, is not applicable to α-alkyl-pyridinium salts. It is due to the fact that attack by hydroxide ion at the carbon bearing the alkyl substituent appears to be kinetically favored and the intermediate [26] readily eliminates water to give rise to the anhydro base [27], which subsequently polymerizes.

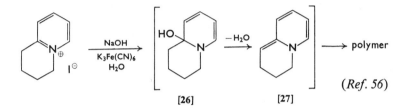

(*Ref. 56*)

In contrast, N-alkoxypyridinium salts decompose in the presence of alkali to give an aldehyde and the parent pyridine. In this instance, the hydroxide ion functions not as a nucleophile, but as a base which abstracts a proton from the carbon atom adjacent to the oxygen.

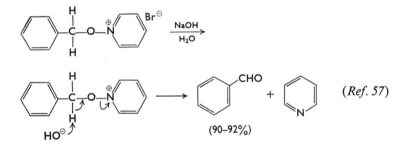

(*Ref. 57*)

Other bases sometimes act in similar fashion.[58] Nucleophilic substitution does result in the case of cyanide ion. In general, attack at the 2-position predominates except when the 1-substituent is large as in [28] or in the case of 3-substituted derivatives where 4-cyano-pyridines are formed in highest yield.[59-61] This reversal in trend in the latter examples can be attributed to the combined steric influence of the 1- and 3-substituents which greatly retards the rate of attack by the nucleophile at the α-position. If, as is believed, the initial attack of cyanide ion is reversible, then the structures of the nitriles reflect the relative stabilities of the transition states leading to them.

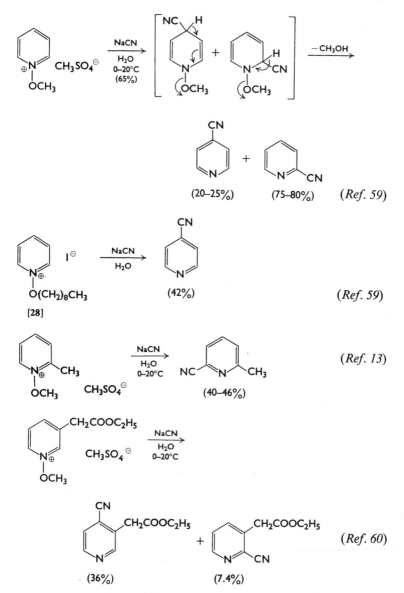

(20–25%) (75–80%) (*Ref. 59*)

(42%) (*Ref. 59*)

(*Ref. 13*)

(40–46%)

(*Ref. 60*)

(36%) (7.4%)

Alkoxypyridinium salts sometimes react with nucleophiles such as thiophenoxide and acetate ions, and anilines, in a manner which involves displacement of the N-oxide.[62]

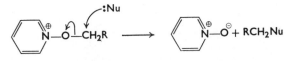

Pyridinium ions are rapidly reduced by borohydride ions to yield 1,2,5,6-tetrahydropyridines such as [29], although in some cases 1,2- and/or 1,4-dihydropyridines have been found to result.[63] The

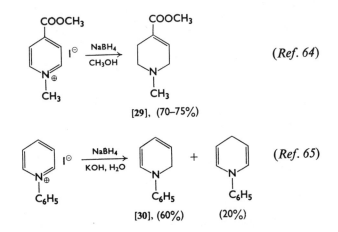

mechanism for these conversions involves initial irreversible nucleophilic attack by hydride ion generally at the 2-position (kinetically favored) to generate a 1,2-dihydropyridine.   In the absence of over-riding steric factors, these dienamines undergo protonation by the

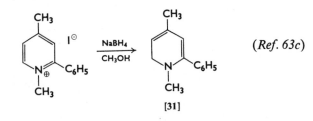

solvent at the center of the conjugated system,[63c] as illustrated, to give rise to an immonium salt which in turn is rapidly reduced by the borohydride present.   The rate of electrophilic attack by solvent upon the 1,2-dihydropyridine intermediate is apparently retarded considerably by electronic and steric factors.   For example, in the

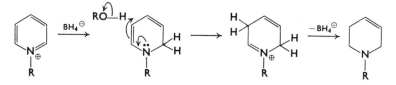

case of [30], the pair of electrons on nitrogen are sufficiently stabilized by the phenyl substituent to render the energetics of solvent attack unfavorable. Steric bulk such as is offered by the methyl and phenyl substituents in [31] prevents the approach of solvent at the 3-position thereby allowing for isolation of this dihydro intermediate.

The displacement of halide ions in substituted pyridines also reflects the activating effects of the pyridine nitrogen atom toward nucleophilic substitution. Whereas 3-halopyridines are very inert to direct substitution, 2- and 4-halogen substituents are quite reactive. The data of Table 7–1 indicate that the 4-position is more reactive by a slight margin.

TABLE 7–I •

Reaction of Chloropyridines with Sodium Ethoxide in Ethanol at 20°C [66]

Isomer	k, liter mole^{-1} second^{-1}	E^*, kcal/mole
2-Chloropyridine	2.2×10^{-9}	26.8
4-Chloropyridine	8.7×10^{-8}	20.9

As anticipated, appropriately substituted pyridinium salts and pyridine-N-oxides are yet of higher reactivity. The ease with which such processes occur is shown in the following examples. 3-Substituted derivatives are unreactive under these conditions.

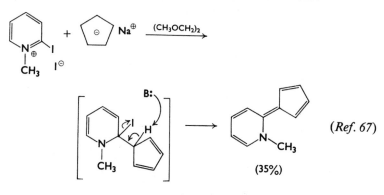

(Ref. 67)

(35%)

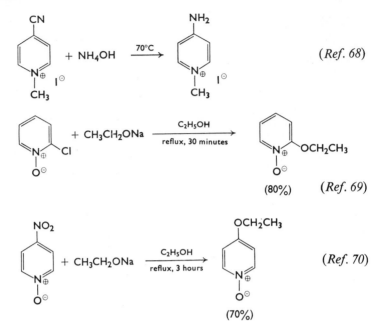

(*Ref. 68*)

(80%)   (*Ref. 69*)

(*Ref. 70*)

(70%)

As has been discussed above, 2-halopyridines appear to undergo nucleophilic substitution exclusively by the addition-elimination mechanism to afford unrearranged products. When certain 3- and 4-halopyridines are treated with strongly basic nucleophiles, however, rearrangement products are frequently observed. Such results have been interpreted in terms of pyridyne intermediates,[46] which are formally analogous to benzyne.[71] In the examples cited, certain

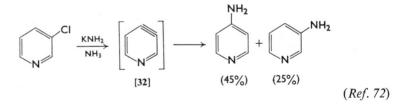

[32]   (45%)   (25%)

(*Ref. 72*)

generalities are obvious; 3,4-pyridynes, but not 2,3-pyridynes, are generated in the amination of 3-halopyridines (e.g., [32], [34], and [35]) except when the former type of species cannot form as in the case of [36]. The addition ratios for [33] and [34] can be associated

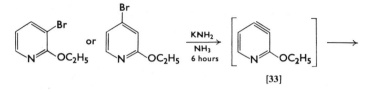

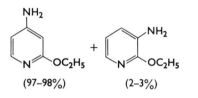

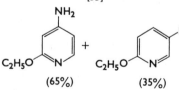

(*Ref. 73*)

(97–98%)   (2–3%)

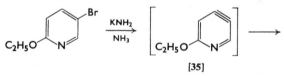

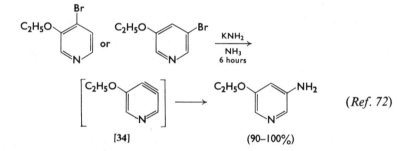

(*Ref. 72*)

[34]   (90–100%)

(*Ref. 72*)

[35]

(65%)   (35%)

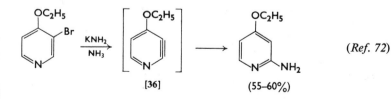

(*Ref. 72*)

[36]   (55–60%)

with a strong meta-directing effect of the alkoxy group; 2,3-pyridynes are attacked at C-2 irrespective of the electronic character of the C-4 substituent.

A similar mechanistic rationalization has been used to explain certain rearrangements observed in the pyridine-N-oxide series.   In

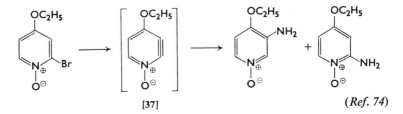

[37]   (Ref. 74)

the case of [37], the addition of amide ion to the pyridyne-N-oxide is influenced not only by the inductive effect of the ethoxy group, but also by the N-oxide function, which results in addition to both the 2- and 3-positions.

Radical Substitution[75]

Although the free radical phenylation of pyridine has been studied in some detail (Table 7–2), few other studies are available.[31]   With reference to Table 7–2, it can be seen that the ratios of phenylated pyridines are quite comparable irrespective of the source of the phenyl

TABLE 7–2 ■

Free Radical Phenylations of Pyridine

Radical source	Temp., °C	Isomer ratio, %			Partial rate factors			Rate ratio, k py/C_6H_6
		2-	3-	4-	f_2	f_3	f_4	
Benzoyl peroxide[76]	80	58	28	14	1.8	0.87	0.87	1.04
Benzoyl peroxide[77]	105	54	32	14	Not determined			
Lead tetrabenzoate[77]	105	52	32	14	Not determined			
Electrolysis of benzoic acid[78]	15–20	56	35	9	Not determined			
Photolysis of triphenylbismuth[79]	100	48	31	21	1.7	1.1	1.5	1.18 (80°)
Gomberg-Hey reaction[80]	40	53.6	29.3	17.1	1.83	1.00	1.18	1.14

radicals and that the 2-position is somewhat favored. Bromination of pyridine at 500°C, a process believed to be radical in nature, leads to a mixture of 2-bromo- and 2,6-dibromopyridines.[81] Thus, although the directive effect of the nitrogen atom in radical substitution is less than in electrophilic substitution, the specificity of attack is frequently sufficiently large to permit the utilization of such processes for the synthesis of 2-substituted pyridines.

The phenylation of pyridine-N-oxide with diazoaminobenzene has been found to give a mixture of phenylated pyridine-N-oxides in the ratio shown in [38].[82]

[38]

Side Chain Reactivity

Pyridine rings substituted with alkyl groups can be oxidized to the corresponding carboxylic acids with a wide variety of reagents.[83] This behavior is similar to that observed in the benzene series.

Because of the electron-attracting inductive and resonance effects of the nitrogen atom, protons at the α-positions of 2- and 4-alkyl-pyridines are quite acidic and are readily removed by numerous strong bases. The resulting carbanions undergo condensation reactions which are characteristic of such intermediates.[83, 84] Although 3-alkylpyridines are deprived of resonance stabilization of

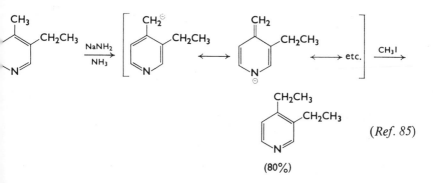

(Ref. 85)

(80%)

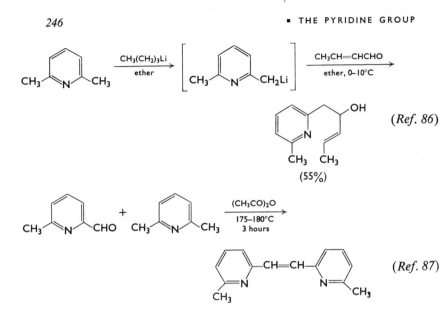

(Ref. 86)

(55%)

(Ref. 87)

the incipient carbanion, the inductive effect remains sufficient to allow metalation reactions to occur. However, the weak acidity of these latter hydrogens often allows for the possibility of an alternative reaction involving nucleophilic attack upon the ring (see p. 235). In the case of [39], it can be seen that the reaction pathway which results is a direct function of the base employed.

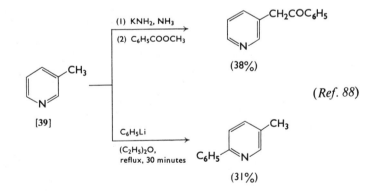

(38%)

(Ref. 88)

(31%)

The reactivity of a 2- or 4-alkylpyridine can be increased by conversion to the corresponding pyridinium salt or N-oxide. The result of this side chain activation is generally reflected in the need of a much milder base to effect similar condensations.

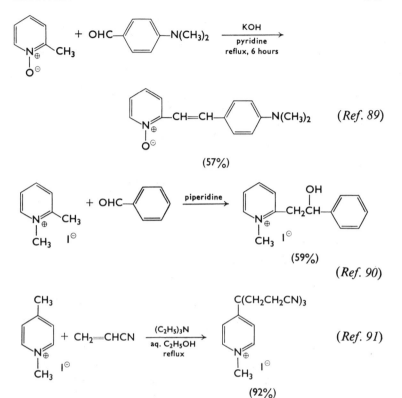

(*Ref. 89*)

(57%)

(59%)

(*Ref. 90*)

(*Ref. 91*)

(92%)

The electron deficiency imposed by the electronegative nitrogen atom at the 2- and 4-positions of the pyridine ring also permits nucleophilic reagents to add in a Michael-type fashion to vinyl substituents attached at these sites, but not at the 3-position.[92]   Prior conversion of such vinylpyridines to their N-oxides enhances the electron deficiency of the double bond, as expected.

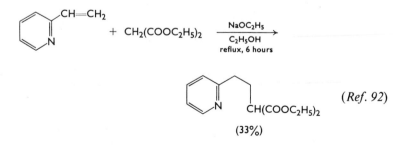

(*Ref. 92*)

(33%)

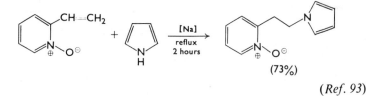

(73%)

(*Ref. 93*)

That the 2- and 4-hydroxypyridines exist predominantly as pyridones [40] and [41], respectively, is now well established.[94] In contrast, 3-hydroxypyridine is totally enolic and phenol-like in character; however, the hydroxy form predominates only in solvents

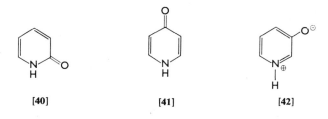

[40]   [41]   [42]

of low dielectric constant. In other media, the occurrence of zwitterion [42] has been observed.[94] This tautomeric behavior is reflected in the chemical behavior of these molecules.[95] For example, whereas alkylation of salts of 3-pyridinol results in ether formation, alkali metal salts of the 2- and 4-pyridones give rise predominantly

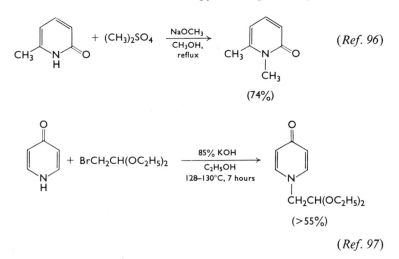

(*Ref. 96*)

(74%)

(>55%)

(*Ref. 97*)

to products of N-alkylation. In the latter cases, replacement of the alkali metal salts by silver salts results in a preponderance of O-alkylation; the pyridones are thus examples of a group of compounds called "ambident anions" because of their inherent property of possessing two nucleophilic sites. This dichotomy of reaction pathways has been explained[98] on the basis of transition state characteristics. Thus, when alkali metal salts are employed, reaction proceeds by an S_N2 mechanism and the more nucleophilic center (N) is alkylated; the use of silver salts increases the S_N1 character of the transition state, carbonium ion character is evidenced in the alkylating agent, and the more electronegative center (O) is attacked. On this basis, reaction of the pyridones with diazoalkanes would be expected to proceed as in the case of the silver salts; however, a graded S_N1–S_N2 spectrum of reactivity appears to be operative and the ratio of O/N alkylated product varies with the diazoalkane employed.[99]

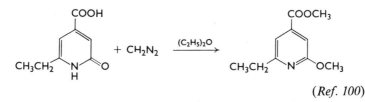

(*Ref. 100*)

Although the 2- and 4-aminopyridines are potentially tautomeric, these substances exist chiefly in the amino form in consonance with the observations in the azole series (see p. 210).[94] However, because of the electronic effects operating at the 2- and 4-carbon atoms (due to the electronegativity of the ring nitrogen), the chemical properties of these amines differ from those observed with anilines or 3-aminopyridines. 3-Aminopyridine behaves as a typical aromatic amine and can, for example, be diazotized readily. Attempted diazotization of the 2- and 4-isomers leads to the corresponding pyridones, unless special precautions are observed.[101] The diazonium salts cannot be detected; the high reactivity of these entities (e.g., [**43**]) may

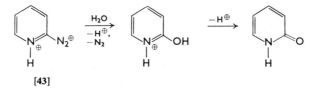

[**43**]

be attributed to the rapid nucleophilic displacement of nitrogen by water or a similar nucleophile.   This behavior is characteristic of the aliphatic diazonium salts.

In contrast, 2- and 4-aminopyridine-1-oxides, which also exist largely in the amino form, diazotize readily and undergo coupling reactions.[102]   The greater stability of these diazonium salts, relative to those derived from pyridine, may be attributed to the capability of the N-oxide oxygen atom to increase electron density at the α- and

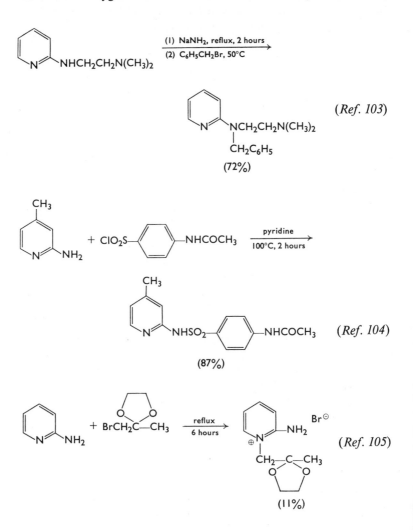

(Ref. 103)

(72%)

(Ref. 104)

(87%)

(Ref. 105)

(11%)

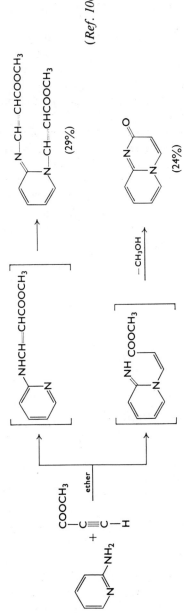

(Ref. 106)

γ-positions (see p. 225), thereby stabilizing the cationic species and diminishing significantly the rate of attack by water or similar nucleophiles.

The aminopyridines are capable of undergoing reaction at either of the two nitrogen atoms. In general, when the aminopyridine is initially converted to its anion with a strong base, alkylation of the side chain is observed. Acylation generally gives a similar product, but alkylation of the free base frequently yields a mixture of products. Examples are given on pages 250 and 251.

The nucleophilic displacement reactions of the halopyridines have already been discussed (see p. 241), but certain other aspects of their chemistry merit attention. Firstly, 2- and 4-halopyridines are most readily obtained by the treatment of 2- or 4-pyridones with a wide variety of halogenating agents such as the phosphorus halides, phosgene, or thionyl chloride. This process has considerable synthetic value.[107]   3-Hydroxypyridine does not give 3-halopyridines under any of these conditions.

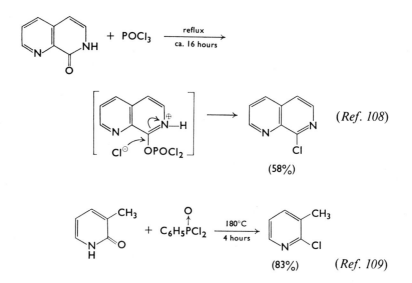

(Ref. 108)

(58%)

(83%)   *(Ref. 109)*

Halogen atoms which are attached at the 2- or 4-position of the pyridine ring are readily hydrogenolyzed in the presence of hydrogen and a suitable catalyst.

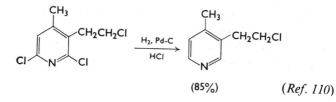

(85%)　　　　　*(Ref. 110)*

Because the bromopyridines can be converted to their Grignard reagents only by means of the entrainment method, it has generally proved more efficacious to resort to the respective lithium derivatives which are formed quite readily upon reaction with *n*-butyllithium.[84] These derivatives react as expected.

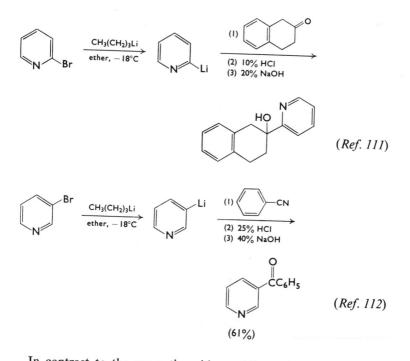

(Ref. 111)

(Ref. 112)

(61%)

In contrast to the aromatic acids, pyridinecarboxylic acids lose carbon dioxide with relative facility. The ease of decarboxylation follows the order: 2->3->4-.[113] In fact, when picolinic acid [44] is decarboxylated in the presence of aldehydes or ketones, coupling occurs and a pyridyl carbinol is formed. This conversion is known as the Hammick reaction.[114]   Studies of the influence of pH on the decarboxylation of [44][114b, 117] suggest that the intermediate in these conversions is the dipolar ion [45].   Moreover, quaternization of the nitrogen leads to compounds which decarboxylate especially easily,

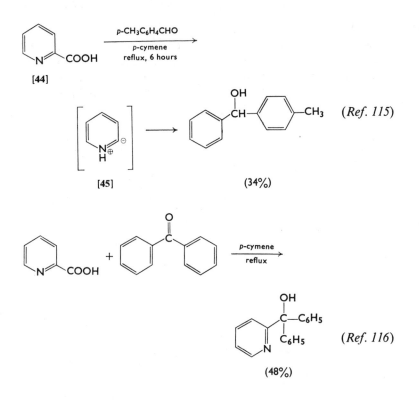

(*Ref. 115*)

(34%)

(*Ref. 116*)

(48%)

which suggests that the carbanion in [45] is markedly stabilized by the inductive effect of the positively charged nitrogen.   Similar factors have already been suggested to explain the ease of formation of heterocyclic ylides in the azoles (see p. 205).

2- and 4-Alkoxypyridines and their N-oxides are particularly sensitive to acidic reagents and to attempted quaternization reactions. Under these conditions, the 2- and 4-pyridone ring systems are generated because of the ready cleavage of the alkoxy substituent.[8, 118] As illustrated in the case of [46] and [47], the observed products arise via nucleophilic attack by halide ion at the alkoxy group of the

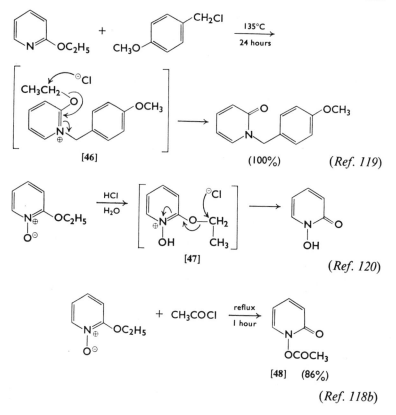

[46] (100%) (*Ref. 119*)

[47] (*Ref. 120*)

[48] (86%)

(*Ref. 118b*)

positively charged pyridinium ring. Carboxylate esters of 1-hydroxy-2-pyridone such as [48] and [49] display high reactivity in nucleophilic reactions and have found application in peptide synthesis.[118b]

Finally, pyridine-N-oxides undergo a number of reactions which have not yet been discussed, but which are of considerable significance. As mentioned earlier, the N—O bond of a pyridine-N-oxide is stabilized and therefore might be expected to display comparatively strong resistance to reduction; indeed, many other substituents may be reduced selectively in the presence of the N-oxide grouping. The N—O bond, however, may be cleaved by reduction with 5 % palladium on carbon[121] in ethanol or Raney nickel in acetic anhydride or methanol.[122]

Deoxygenation also results upon treatment of an N-oxide with a phosphorus trihalide in an inert solvent[102] or with a trisubstituted

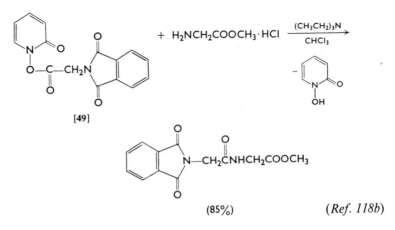

[49]

(85%)   (Ref. 118b)

phosphine.[123]   Dichlorocarbene can also be employed for the same purpose.[124]

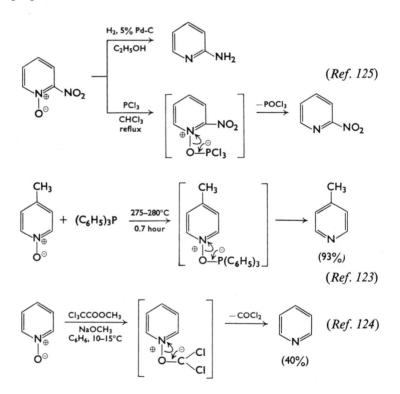

If phosphorus pentahalides, phosphorus oxychloride, or other active halides are caused to react with pyridine-N-oxides, ring substitution accompanies deoxygenation.[102] The position of entry of the halogen atom depends to a large extent on the nature and number of the ring substituents. Thus, if the N-oxide possesses a 2-alkyl group, side chain chlorination is encountered. Possible mechanistic pathways for these conversions are outlined below.

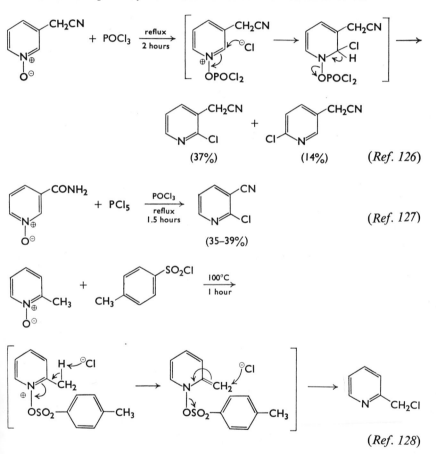

Perhaps the most interesting, and certainly the most exhaustively studied, deoxygenation-substitution reaction of pyridine-N-oxides is found in their reaction with acid anhydrides. For example, when pyridine-N-oxides which possess no alkyl groups in the α- or γ-position

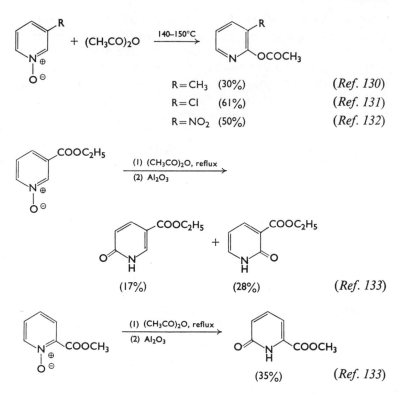

R=CH₃ (30%)   (*Ref. 130*)

R=Cl (61%)   (*Ref. 131*)

R=NO₂ (50%)   (*Ref. 132*)

(17%)   (28%)   (*Ref. 133*)

(35%)   (*Ref. 133*)

are heated with acetic anhydride, 2-pyridylacetates result[129]; acid hydrolysis of these materials affords 2-pyridones.

With alkyl substituents in the 2- or 4-positions, however, the reaction generally leads to side chain acetylation. Several examples are described below:

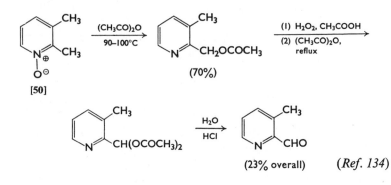

(70%)

(23% overall)   (*Ref. 134*)

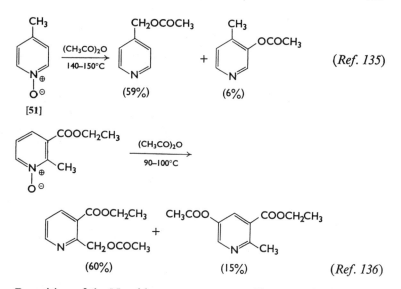

(*Ref. 135*)

(*Ref. 136*)

Repetition of the N-oxide rearrangement as illustrated in the case of [50] can be successfully employed as a route to 2-pyridylaldehydes. However, it appears that it is necessary to have at least two α-hydrogens available for replacement in order for the rearrangement to occur in good yield.[130]

Careful kinetic studies of the reaction of pyridine-N-oxide with acetic anhydride have shown that the process exhibits pseudo first-order kinetics, that the rate is slightly decreased upon the addition of sodium acetate, and that no gaseous products such as methane or carbon dioxide are obtained from the reaction.[137] These results, in conjunction with deuterium labelling (utilizing pyridine-2,6-d_2-N-oxide) which gave rise to a secondary isotope effect (k_H/k_D) of 0.92 and O^{18} isotopic tracer experiments,[138] strongly suggests the operation of the following mechanism.

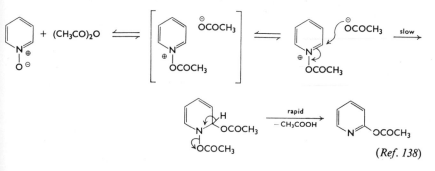

(*Ref. 138*)

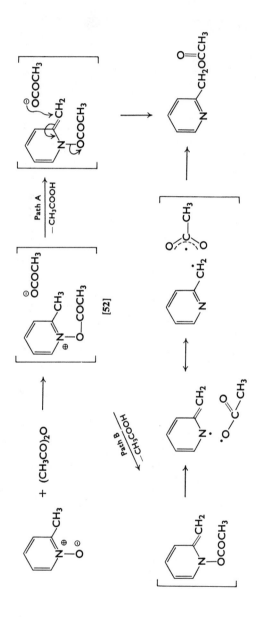

[52]

The mechanism of the rearrangement of the picoline-N-oxide remains controversial. Although it is generally agreed that the first step of the reaction is the formation of [52],[139] conclusive evidence pertaining to the subsequent fate of [52] remains to be provided. Two mechanisms, the ion-pair (Path A)[129, 140] and the radical-pair (Path B),[141] are being considered by current investigators.

The formation of small quantities of 3-acetoxypyridines during these rearrangement reactions as in the case of [51] can also be rationalized in terms of polar or radical intermediates.

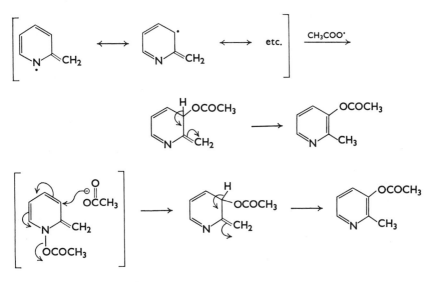

Exercises

1. Predict the major product of the following reactions:

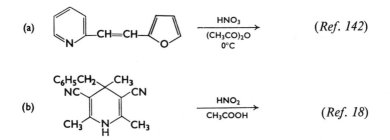

(a) ——— $\dfrac{HNO_3}{(CH_3CO)_2O}$ ———→   (*Ref. 142*)
            0°C

(b) ——— $\dfrac{HNO_2}{CH_3COOH}$ ———→   (*Ref. 18*)

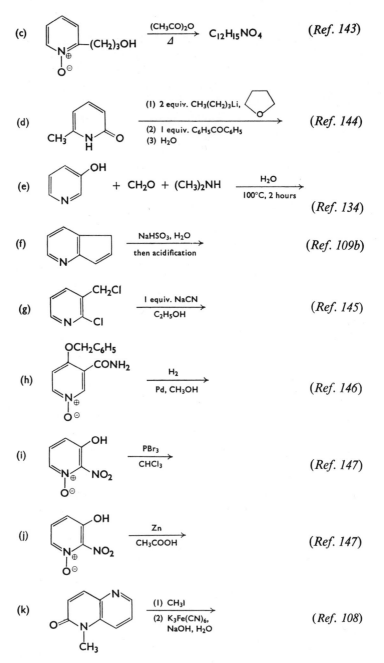

(c) $\xrightarrow{\underset{\Delta}{(CH_3CO)_2O}}$ $C_{12}H_{15}NO_4$ (*Ref. 143*)

(d) $\xrightarrow{\begin{array}{l}\text{(1) 2 equiv. } CH_3(CH_2)_3Li, \\ \text{(2) 1 equiv. } C_6H_5COC_6H_5 \\ \text{(3) } H_2O\end{array}}$ (*Ref. 144*)

(e) $+ CH_2O + (CH_3)_2NH$ $\xrightarrow[100°C,\ 2\ hours]{H_2O}$ (*Ref. 134*)

(f) $\xrightarrow[\text{then acidification}]{NaHSO_3,\ H_2O}$ (*Ref. 109b*)

(g) $\xrightarrow[C_2H_5OH]{1\ equiv.\ NaCN}$ (*Ref. 145*)

(h) $\xrightarrow[Pd,\ CH_3OH]{H_2}$ (*Ref. 146*)

(i) $\xrightarrow[CHCl_3]{PBr_3}$ (*Ref. 147*)

(j) $\xrightarrow[CH_3COOH]{Zn}$ (*Ref. 147*)

(k) $\xrightarrow[\begin{array}{l}\text{(2) } K_3Fe(CN)_6, \\ NaOH,\ H_2O\end{array}]{\text{(1) } CH_3I}$ (*Ref. 108*) (l)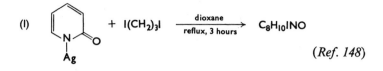

$$+ I(CH_2)_3I \xrightarrow[\text{reflux, 3 hours}]{\text{dioxane}} C_8H_{10}INO$$

(*Ref. 148*)

(m)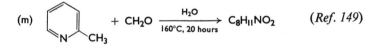

$$+ CH_2O \xrightarrow[\text{160°C, 20 hours}]{H_2O} C_8H_{11}NO_2$$

(*Ref. 149*)

(n)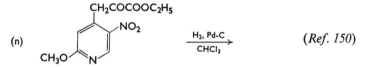

$$\xrightarrow[\text{CHCl}_3]{H_2, \text{Pd-C}}$$

(*Ref. 150*)

(o)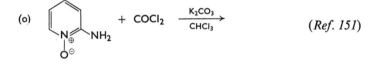

$$+ COCl_2 \xrightarrow[\text{CHCl}_3]{K_2CO_3}$$

(*Ref. 151*)

(p)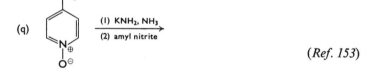

$$\xrightarrow[\text{H}_2\text{SO}_4]{\text{HNO}_3}$$

(*Ref. 152*)

(q)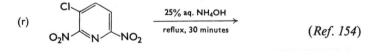

$$\xrightarrow[\text{(2) amyl nitrite}]{\text{(1) KNH}_2, \text{NH}_3}$$

(*Ref. 153*)

(r)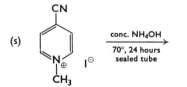

$$\xrightarrow[\text{reflux, 30 minutes}]{\text{25\% aq. NH}_4\text{OH}}$$

(*Ref. 154*)

(s)

$$\xrightarrow[\substack{\text{70°, 24 hours} \\ \text{sealed tube}}]{\text{conc. NH}_4\text{OH}}$$

(*Ref. 155*)

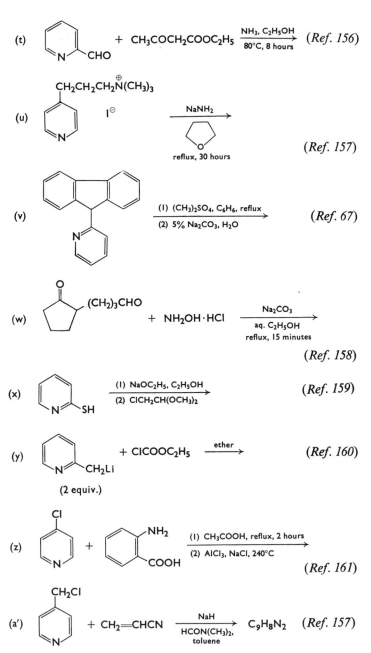

(t) [pyridine-2-CHO] + CH₃COCH₂COOC₂H₅ $\xrightarrow[80°C, 8 \text{ hours}]{NH_3, C_2H_5OH}$ (*Ref. 156*)

(u) [4-substituted pyridine] CH₂CH₂CH₂N⁺(CH₃)₃ I⁻ $\xrightarrow[\text{reflux, 30 hours}]{NaNH_2 / \text{THF}}$ (*Ref. 157*)

(v) [9-(pyridin-2-yl)fluorene] $\xrightarrow{(1) (CH_3)_2SO_4, C_6H_6, \text{reflux} \\ (2) 5\% Na_2CO_3, H_2O}$ (*Ref. 67*)

(w) [cyclopentanone with (CH₂)₃CHO substituent] + NH₂OH·HCl $\xrightarrow[\text{reflux, 15 minutes}]{Na_2CO_3 \\ \text{aq. } C_2H_5OH}$ (*Ref. 158*)

(x) [pyridine-2-SH] $\xrightarrow{(1) NaOC_2H_5, C_2H_5OH \\ (2) ClCH_2CH(OCH_3)_2}$ (*Ref. 159*)

(y) [pyridine-2-CH₂Li] (2 equiv.) + ClCOOC₂H₅ $\xrightarrow{\text{ether}}$ (*Ref. 160*)

(z) [4-chloropyridine] + [2-aminobenzoic acid] $\xrightarrow{(1) CH_3COOH, \text{reflux, 2 hours} \\ (2) AlCl_3, NaCl, 240°C}$ (*Ref. 161*)

(a') [4-(CH₂Cl)pyridine] + CH₂=CHCN $\xrightarrow[\text{toluene}]{NaH \\ HCON(CH_3)_2,}$ C₉H₈N₂ (*Ref. 157*)

2. Suggest a reasonable mechanism for each of the following transformations:

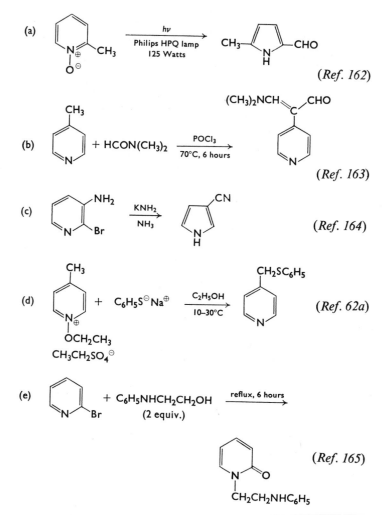

(a) ![reaction](hv / Philips HPQ lamp / 125 Watts) → CH₃—pyrrole—CHO

(*Ref. 162*)

(b) 4-methylpyridine + HCON(CH₃)₂ $\xrightarrow[\text{70°C, 6 hours}]{POCl_3}$ → (CH₃)₂NCH=C(CHO)(pyridyl)

(*Ref. 163*)

(c) 3-amino-2-bromopyridine $\xrightarrow[\text{NH}_3]{\text{KNH}_2}$ → 3-cyanopyrrole

(*Ref. 164*)

(d) 4-methylpyridinium (N-OCH₂CH₃ CH₃CH₂SO₄⁻) + C₆H₅S⁻Na⁺ $\xrightarrow[\text{10–30°C}]{C_2H_5OH}$ → 4-(CH₂SC₆H₅)pyridine

(*Ref. 62a*)

(e) 2-bromopyridine + C₆H₅NHCH₂CH₂OH (2 equiv.) $\xrightarrow{\text{reflux, 6 hours}}$ → 1-(CH₂CH₂NHC₆H₅)pyridin-2-one

(*Ref. 165*)

References and Notes

(1) G. I. Poos, G. E. Arth, R. E. Beyler, and L. H. Sarett, *J. Am. Chem. Soc.*, **75**, 422 (1953).

(2) J. D. Roberts and M. C. Caserio, *Basic Principles of Organic Chemistry*, W. A. Benjamin, Inc., New York, 1964, p. 981.

(3) V. Schomaker and L. Pauling, *J. Am. Chem. Soc.*, **61**, 1769 (1939); B. B. DeMore, W. S. Wilcox, and J. H. Goldstein, *J. Chem. Phys.*, **32**, 876 (1954); B. Bak, L. Hansen, and J. Rastrup-Andersen, *ibid.*, **22**, 2013 (1954).

(4) B. A. Middleton and J. R. Partington, *Nature*, **141**, 516 (1938); L. E. Orgel, T. L. Cottrell, W. Dick, and L. E. Sutton, *Trans. Faraday Soc.*, **47**, 113 (1951).

(5) H. C. Brown, D. H. McDaniel, and O. Häfliger, in E. A. Braude and F. C. Nachod (eds.), *Determination of Organic Structures by Physical Methods*, Vol. 1, Academic Press, New York, 1955, p. 597.

(6) For studies relating to the mechanistic details by which pyridine undergoes quaternization, cf. *inter alia*, C. G. Swain and R. W. Eddy, *J. Am. Chem. Soc.*, **70**, 2989 (1948); Y. Pocker, *J. Chem. Soc.*, **1957**, 1279; M. L. Bender and D. F. Hoeg, *J. Am. Chem. Soc.*, **79**, 5649 (1957).

(7) H. C. Brown and G. K. Barbaras, *J. Am. Chem. Soc.*, **69**, 1137 (1947).

(8) L. A. Paquette and N. A. Nelson, *J. Org. Chem.*, **27**, 1085 (1962).

(9) R. Gösl and A. Meuwsen, *Org. Syn.*, **43**, 1 (1963).

(10) E. C. Taylor, Jr., and A. J. Crovetti, *ibid.*, **Coll. Vol. 4**, 654 (1963); for additional examples, see *ibid.*, **Coll. Vol. 4**, 704 (1963); H. S. Mosher, L. Turner, and A. Carlsmith, *ibid.*, **Coll. Vol. 4**, 828 (1963).

(11) E. P. Linton, *J. Am. Chem. Soc.*, **62**, 1945 (1940).

(12) H. H. Jaffe and G. O. Doak, *ibid.*, **77**, 4441 (1955).

(13) W. E. Feely, G. Evanega, and E. M. Beavers, *Org. Syn.*, **42**, 30 (1962).

(14) F. Brody and P. R. Ruby in E. Klingsberg (ed.), *Pyridine and Its Derivatives*, Part 1, Interscience, New York, 1960, Chapter II.

(15) (a) K. Thomas and D. Jerchel, *Angew. Chem.*, **70**, 719 (1958); for English translation, see W. Foerst (ed.), *Newer Methods of Preparative Organic Chemistry*, **3**, 53 (1964); (b) H. S. Mosher in R. C. Elderfield (ed.), *Heterocyclic Compounds*, Vol. 1, Wiley, New York, 1950, Chapter 8; (c) N. Campbell in E. H. Rodd (ed.), *Chemistry of Carbon Compounds*, Vol. 4A, Elsevier, New York, 1957, Chapter 7.

(16) A. Hantzsch, *Ann. Chem.*, **251**, 1 (1882).

(17) A. Singer and S. M. McElvain, *Org. Syn.*, **Coll. Vol. 2**, 214 (1943).

(18) B. Loev and K. M. Snader, *J. Org. Chem.*, **30**, 1914 (1965).

(19) V. A. Petrow, *J. Chem. Soc.*, **1946**, 884.

(20) R. P. Mariella, *Org. Syn.*, **Coll. Vol. 4**, 210 (1963).

(21) R. W. Foster, Ph.D. Thesis, London, 1954, see also J. Jones and J. Jones, *Tetrahedron Letters*, **No. 31**, 2117 (1964).

(22) J. H. Ridd, *Physical Methods in Heterocyclic Chem.*, **1**, 109 (1963); A. R. Katritzky and B. J. Ridgewell, *J. Chem. Soc.*, **1963**, 3743.

(23) H. J. den Hertog and J. Overhoff, *Rec. Trav. Chim.*, **49**, 552 (1930).

(24) S. M. McElvain and M. A. Goese, *J. Am. Chem. Soc.*, **65**, 2233 (1943).

(25) H. C. Brown and B. Kanner, *ibid.*, **75**, 3865 (1953); H. C. vander Plas and H. J. den Hertog, *Tetrahedron Letters*, **No. 1**, 13 (1960).

(26) R. B. Moodie, K. Schofield, and M. J. Williamson, *Chem. Ind. (London)*, **1964**, 1577.

(27) H. J. den Hertog and J. Overhoff, *Rec. Trav. Chim.*, **69**, 468 (1950); E. Ochiai, *J. Org. Chem.*, **18**, 534 (1953); for an example of application to 3-methylpyridine-N-oxide, see E. C. Taylor, Jr., and A. J. Crovetti, *Org. Syn.*, **Coll. Vol. 4**, 654 (1963).

(28) H. S. Mosher and F. J. Welsh, *J. Am. Chem. Soc.*, **77**, 2902 (1955), see also M. van Ammers and H. J. den Hertog, *Rec. Trav. Chim.*, **78**, 586 (1959).

(29) A. R. Katritzky, *Quart. Rev. (London)*, **10**, 395 (1955).

(30) E. V. Brown and R. H. Neil, *J. Org. Chem.*, **26**, 3546 (1961).

(31) R. A. Abramovitch and J. G. Saha, *Adv. Heterocyclic Chem.*, **6**, 229 (1966); refer especially to pp. 266 ff.

(32) B. A. Fox and T. L. Threlfall, *Org. Syn.*, **44**, 34 (1964).

(33) H. M. Curry and J. P. Mason, *J. Am. Chem. Soc.*, **73**, 5043 (1951).

(34) E. Koenigs and O. Jungfer, *Chem. Ber.*, **57**, 2080 (1924).

(35) Footnote 62 of ref. 31.

(36) E. V. Brown and P. L. Malloy, *Abstr. Papers 126th Meeting Am. Chem. Soc.*, *New York*, 1954, p. 61–0.

(37) Refer, however, to p. 255 for a discussion of the fate of 2-pyridyl ethers in acidic media.

(38) H. J. den Hertog, C. Jouwersma, A. A. vander Wal, and E. C. Willebrands-Schogt, *Rec. Trav. Chim.*, **68**, 275 (1949).

(39) H. J. den Hertog and M. van Ammers, *ibid.*, **74**, 1160 (1955).

(40) K. Lewicka and E. Plazek, *Rocznicki Chem.*, **40**, 405 (1966); *Chem. Abstr.*, **65**, 7134 (1966); for additional data on the electrophilic substitution of 3-hydroxypyridine, see J. A. Moore and F. J. Marascia, *J. Am. Chem. Soc.*, **81**, 6049 (1959).

(41) C. A. Salemink and G. M. vander Want, *Rec. Trav. Chim.*, **68**, 1013 (1949).

(42) For example, N-methyl-2-pyridone undergoes nitration to yield mainly the 3-nitro derivative: R. A. Abramovitch and C. S. Giam, *Can. J. Chem.*, **40**, 231 (1962); A. H. Berrie, G. T. Newbold, and F. S. Spring, *J. Chem. Soc.*, **1951**, 2590.

(43) W. A. Lott and E. Shaw, *J. Am. Chem. Soc.*, **71**, 70 (1949).

(44) M. van Ammers and H. J. den Hertog, *Rec. Trav. Chim.*, **75**, 1259 (1956).

(45) G. Illuminati, *Adv. Heterocyclic Chem.*, **3**, 285 (1964).

(46) (a) H. J. den Hertog and H. C. vander Plas, *ibid.*, **4**, 121 (1965); (b) T. Kauffmann, *Angew. Chem. Intern. Ed.*, **4**, 543 (1965).

(47) A. E. Tschitschibabin and O. A. Seide, *J. Russ. Phys. Chem. Soc.*, **46**, 1216 (1914); *Chem. Abstr.*, **9**, 1901 (1915).

(48) M. T. Leffler, *Org. Reactions*, **1**, 91 (1942).

(49) R. A. Abramovitch, F. Helmer, and J. G. Saha, *Can. J. Chem.*, **43**, 725 (1965) and references cited therein.

(50) M. M. Robison and B. L. Robison, *J. Am. Chem. Soc.*, **77**, 457 (1955).

(51) J. C. W. Evans and C. F. H. Allen, *Org. Syn.*, **Coll. Vol. 2**, 517 (1957), see also R. A. Abramovitch and C. S. Giam, *Can. J. Chem.*, **40**, 231 (1962).

(52) T. Kato and H. Yamanaka, *J. Org. Chem.*, **30**, 910 (1965).

(53) O. Cervinka, *Collection Czech. Chem. Commun.*, **27**, 567 (1962).

(54) E. A. Prill and S. M. McElvain, *Org. Syn.*, **Coll. Vol. 2**, 419 (1957).

(55) M. H. Fronk and H. S. Mosher, *J. Org. Chem.*, **24**, 196 (1959).

(56) F. Bohlmann, N. Ottawa, and R. Keller, *Ann. Chem.*, **587**, 162 (1954).

(57) W. E. Feeley, W. L. Lehn, and V. Boekelheide, *J. Org. Chem.*, **22**, 1135 (1957).

(58) (a) N. A. Coats and A. R. Katritzky, *ibid.*, **24**, 1836 (1959); (b) L. Bauer and L. A. Gardella, *ibid.*, **28**, 1320 (1963).

(59) W. E. Feeley and E. M. Beavers, *J. Am. Chem. Soc.*, **81**, 4004 (1959).

(60) R. Tan and A. Taurins, *Tetrahedron Letters*, **No. 31**, 2737 (1965).

(61) G. Büchi, R. E. Manning, and F. A. Hochstein, *J. Am. Chem. Soc.*, **84**, 3393 (1962); H. Tani, *Chem. Pharm. Bull. (Tokyo)*, **7**, 930 (1959); M. Marti, M. Viscontini, and P. Karrer, *Helv. Chim. Acta*, **39**, 1451 (1956) A. San Pietro, *J. Biol. Chem.*, **217**, 579 (1955); A. G. Anderson, Jr., and G. Berkelhammer, *J. Org. Chem.*, **23**, 1109 (1958).

(62) L. Bauer and L. A. Gardella, *ibid.*, **28**, 1323 (1963); R. Eisenthal and A. R. Katritzky, *Tetrahedron*, **21**, 2205 (1965).

(63) For a summary of references in this area, see (a) E. N. Shaw in E. Klingsberg (ed.), *Pyridine and Its Derivatives*, Part 2, Interscience, New York, pp. 47–55; (b) R. E. Lyle, D. A. Nelson, and P. S. Anderson, *Tetrahedron Letters*, **No. 13**, 553 (1962); (c) P. S. Anderson and R. E. Lyle, *ibid.*, **No. 3**, 153 (1964).

(64) R. E. Lyle, E. F. Perlowski, H. J. Troscianiec, and G. C. Lyle, *J. Org. Chem.*, **20**, 1761 (1955).

(65) M. Saunders and E. H. Gold, *ibid.*, **27**, 1439 (1962).

(66) (a) N. B. Chapman and D. Q. Russell-Hill, *J. Chem. Soc.*, **1956**, 1563; (b) R. R. Bishop, E. A. S. Cavell, and N. B. Chapman, *ibid.*, **1952**, 437.

(67) J. A. Berson, E. M. Evleth, Jr., and Z. Hamlet, *J. Am. Chem. Soc.*, **87**, 2887 (1965).

(68) E. J. Poziomek, *J. Org. Chem.*, **28**, 590 (1963).

(69) J. N. Gardner and A. R. Katritzky, *J. Chem. Soc.*, 4375 (1957).

(70) H. J. den Hertog and W. P. Combe, *Rec. Trav. Chim.*, **70**, 581 (1951).

(71) H. Heany, *Chem. Rev.*, **62**, 81 (1962).

(72) M. Pieterse and H. J. den Hertog, *Rec. Trav. Chim.*, **80**, 1376 (1961).

(73) H. J. den Hertog, M. J. Pieterse, and D. J. Buurman, *ibid*, **82**, 1173 (1963).

(74) R. J. Martens and H. J. den Hertog, *ibid.*, **83**, 621 (1964).

(75) R. O. C. Norman and G. K. Radda, *Adv. Heterocyclic Chem.*, **2**, 131 (1963), see also R. A. Abramovitch and M. Saha, *Can. J. Chem.*, **44**, 1765 (1966).

(76) D. R. Angood, D. H. Hey, and G. H. Williams, *J. Chem. Soc.*, **1952**, 2094; R. L. Dannby and E. C. Gregg, *J. Am. Chem. Soc.*, **76**, 2997 (1954).

(77) D. H. Hey, C. J. M. Stirling, and G. H. Williams, *J. Chem. Soc.*, **1955**, 3963.

(78) P. J. Bunyan and D. H. Hey, *ibid.*, **1960**, 3787.

(79) D. H. Hey, D. A. Shingleton, and G. H. Williams, *ibid.*, **1963**, 5612.

(80) R. A. Abramovitch and J. G. Saha, *Tetrahedron Letters*, **No. 5**, 301 (1963); *J. Chem. Soc.*, **1964**, 2175.

(81) H. J. den Hertog and J. P. Wibaut, *Rec. Trav. Chim.*, **51**, 385 (1932).

(82) L. K. Dyall and K. H. Pausacker, *J. Chem. Soc.*, **1961**, 18.

(83) L. E. Tenenbaum, in E. Klingsberg (ed.), *Pyridine and Its Derivatives*, Part 2, Interscience, New York, 1961, Chapter 5.

(84) H. L. Yale, *ibid.*, Part 2, 1961, Chapter 7.

(85) D. Taub, R. D. Hoffsommer, C. H. Kuo, and N. L. Wendler, *J. Org. Chem.*, **30**, 3229 (1965).

(86) V. Boekelheide, H. Fritz, J. M. Ross, and H. X. Kaempfen, *Tetrahedron*, **20**, 33 (1964).

(87) W. Baker, K. M. Buggle, J. F. W. McOmie, and D. A. M. Watkins, *J. Chem. Soc.*, **1958**, 3594.

(88) A. D. Miller, C. Osuch, N. N. Goldberg, and R. Levine, *J. Am. Chem. Soc.*, **78**, 674 (1956).

(89) L. Pentimalli, *Tetrahedron*, **14**, 151 (1961).

(90) H. C. Beyerman, J. Eenshnistra, E. Eveleens, and A. Zweistra, *Rec. Trav. Chim.*, **78**, 43 (1959).

(91) J. A. Adamcik and R. J. Flores, *J. Org. Chem.*, **29**, 572 (1964).

(92) W. E. Doering and R. A. N. Weil, *J. Am. Chem. Soc.*, **69**, 2461 (1947); for a review of the application of this reaction, see E. D. Bergmann, D. Ginsburg, and R. Pappo, *Org. Syn.*, **10**, 179 (1959).

(93) V. Boekelheide and R. Scharrer, *J. Org. Chem.*, **26**, 3802 (1961).

(94) A. R. Katritzky and J. M. Lagowski, *Adv. Heterocyclic Chem.*, **1**, 339 (1963).

(95) H. Meislich, in E. Klingsberg (ed.), *Pyridine and Its Derivatives*, Part 3, Interscience, New York, 1962, Chapter 12.

(96) R. Adams and A. W. Schrecker, *J. Am. Chem. Soc.*, **71**, 1186 (1949).

(97) A. F. Bickel, *ibid.*, **70**, 328 (1948).

(98) N. Kornblum, R. A. Smiley, R. K. Blackwood, and D. C. Iffland, *ibid.*, **77**, 6269 (1955).

(99) N. Kornblum and G. P. Coffey, *J. Org. Chem.*, **31**, 3447 (1966).

(100) A. H. Tracy and R. C. Elderfield, *J. Org. Chem.*, **6**, 70 (1941).

(101) A. S. Tomcufcik and L. N. Starker, in E. Klingsberg (ed.), *Pyridine and Its Derivatives*, Part 3, Interscience, New York, 1962, Chapter 9.

(102) E. N. Shaw, *ibid.*, Part 2, 1961, Chapter 4.

(103) C. P. Huttrer, C. Djerassi, W. L. Beears, R. L. Mayer, and C. R. Scholz, *J. Am. Chem. Soc.*, **68**, 1999 (1946).

(104) J. Bernstein, E. J. Pribyl, K. Losee, and W. A. Lott, *ibid.*, **69**, 1158 (1947).

(105) R. Adams and J. S. Dix, *ibid.*, **80**, 4618 (1958).

(106) G. R. Lappin, *J. Org. Chem.*, **26**, 2350 (1961).

(107) H. E. Martel, in E. Klingsberg (ed.), *Pyridine and Its Derivatives*, Part 2, Interscience, New York, 1961, Chapter 6.

(108) H. Rapoport and A. D. Batcho, *J. Org. Chem.*, **28**, 1753 (1963).

(109) (a) M. M. Robison, *J. Am. Chem. Soc.*, **80**, 5481 (1958), (b) *ibid.*, **80**, 6254 (1958).

(110) J. R. Stevens, R. H. Bentel, and E. Chamberlain, *ibid.*, **64**, 1093 (1942).

(111) N. A. Nelson and L. A. Paquette, *J. Org. Chem.*, **27**, 964 (1962).

(112) H. E. French and K. Sears, *J. Am. Chem. Soc.*, **73**, 469 (1951).

(113) (a) E. P. Oliveto, in E. Klingsberg (ed.), *Pyridine and Its Derivatives*, Part 3, Interscience, New York, 1962, Chapter 10; (b) P. Haake and J. Mantecon, *J. Am. Chem. Soc.*, **86**, 5230 (1964).

(114) (a) M. R. F. Ashworth, R. P. Daffern, and D. L. Hammick, *J. Chem. Soc.*, **1939**, 809; (b) B. Brown and D. Hammick, *ibid.*, **1949**, 659.

(115) N. Sperber, D. Papa, E. Schwenk, and M. Sherlock, *J. Am. Chem. Soc.*, **71**, 887 (1949).

(116) N. H. Cantwell and E. V. Brown, *ibid.*, **75**, 1489 (1953).

(117) N. H. Cantwell and E. V. Brown, *ibid.*, **74**, 5967 (1952); *ibid.*, **75**, 4466 (1953).

(118) (a) L. A. Paquette, *Tetrahedron*, **22**, 25 (1966); (b) L. A. Paquette, *J. Am. Chem. Soc.*, **87**, 5186 (1965), and references cited in these papers.

(119) L. A. Paquette and G. Slomp, *ibid.*, **85**, 765 (1963).

(120) G. T. Newbold and F. S. Spring, *J. Chem. Soc.*, **1948**, 1864.

(121) A. R. Katritzky and A. M. Monro, *ibid.*, **1958**, 1263; H. Biener and T. Wieland, *Chem. Ber.*, **95**, 277 (1962).

(122) D. Jerchel and W. Melloh, *Ann. Chem.*, **613**, 144 (1958); E. Hayashi, H. Yamanaka, *et al.*, *Chem. Pharm. Bull. (Tokyo)*, **7**, 141, 146, 149, 650 (1959).

(123) E. Howard, Jr., and W. F. Olszewski, *J. Am. Chem. Soc.*, **81**, 1483 (1959).

(124) E. E. Schweizer and G. J. O'Neill, *J. Org. Chem.*, **28**, 2460 (1963).

(125) E. V. Brown, *J. Am. Chem. Soc.*, **79**, 3565 (1957).

(126) S. Okuda and M. M. Robison, *ibid.*, **81**, 740 (1959).

(127) E. C. Taylor, Jr., and A. J. Crovetti, *Org. Syn.*, **Coll. Vol. 4**, 166 (1963).

(128) E. Matsumura, *J. Chem. Soc. Japan*, **74**, 363 (1953); *Chem. Abstr.*, **48**, 6642 (1954), see also J. F. Vozza, *J. Org. Chem.*, **27**, 3856 (1962).

(129) M. Katada, *J. Pharm. Soc. Japan*, **67**, 51 (1947); *Chem. Abstr.*, **45**, 9536 (1951).

(130) V. Boekelheide and W. J. Linn, *J. Am. Chem. Soc.*, **76**, 1286 (1954).

(131) M. P. Cava and B. Weinstein, *J. Org. Chem.*, **23**, 1616 (1958).

(132) E. C. Taylor, Jr., and J. S. Driscoll, *ibid.*, **25**, 1716 (1960).

(133) V. Boekelheide and W. J. Lehn, *ibid.*, **26**, 428 (1961).

(134) S. Ginsburg and I. B. Wilson, *J. Am. Chem. Soc.*, **79**, 481 (1957).

(135) J. A. Berson and T. Cohen, *ibid.*, **77**, 1281 (1951); V. J. Traynelis and R. F. Martello, *ibid.*, **82**, 2744 (1960).

(136) H. J. Rimek, *Ann. Chem.*, **670**, 69 (1963).

(137) J. H. Markgraf, H. B. Brown, Jr., S. C. Mohr, and R. G. Peterson, *J. Am. Chem. Soc.*, **85**, 958 (1963).

(138) S. Oae and S. Kozuka, *Tetrahedron*, **21**, 1971 (1965).

(139) T. Koenig, *J. Am. Chem. Soc.*, **88**, 4045 (1966).

(140) (a) I. J. Pachter, *ibid.*, **75**, 3026 (1953); (b) S. Oae, T. Kitao, and Y. Kitaoka, *ibid.*, **84**, 3362 (1962); (c) T. Cohen and J. Fager, *ibid.*, **87**, 5701 (1965); (d) V. J. Traynelis and P. L. Pacini, *ibid.*, **86**, 4917 (1964), and additional references cited in these papers.

(141) (a) V. J. Traynelis and R. F. Martello, *ibid.*, **80**, 6590 (1958); (b) S. Oae, T. Kitao, and Y. Kitaoka, *ibid.*, **84**, 3359 (1962); S. Oae, Y. Kitaoka, and T. Kitao, *Tetrahedron*, **20**, 2691 (1964), and references cited in these papers.

(142) Ciba Ltd., Swiss Pat. 396,909 dated Jan. 31, 1966.

(143) V. Boekelheide and W. Feely, *J. Org. Chem.*, **22**, 589 (1957).

(144) R. L. Gay, S. Boatman, and C. R. Hauser, *Chem. Ind. (London)*, **1965**, 1789.

(145) F. Gadient, E. Jucker, A. Lindemann, and M. Taeschler, *Helv. Chim. Acta*, **45**, 1860 (1962).

(146) H. Biener and T. Wieland, *Chem. Ber.*, **95**, 277 (1962).

(147) K. Lewicka and E. Plazek, *Rec. Trav. Chim.*, **78**, 644 (1959).

(148) K. Winterfeld and H. Michael, *Chem. Ber.*, **93**, 61 (1960).

(149) M. Kotake, I. Kawasaki, T. Okamoto, S. Kusumoto, and T. Kaneko, *Ann. Chem.*, **636**, 158 (1960).

(150) B. Frydman, M. E. Despuy, and H. Rapoport, *J. Am. Chem. Soc.*, **87**, 3530 (1965).

(151) K. Hoegerle, *Helv. Chim. Acta*, **41**, 549 (1958).

(152) M. M. Robison, B. L. Robison, and F. P. Butler, *J. Am. Chem. Soc.*, **81**, 743 (1959).

(153) T. Kato and Y. Goto, *Chem. Pharm. Bull. (Tokyo)*, **11**, 461 (1963).

(154) W. Czuba and E. Plazek, *Rec. Trav. Chim.*, **77**, 92 (1958).

(155) E. J. Poziomek, *J. Org. Chem.*, **28**, 590 (1963).

(156) R. F. Homer, *J. Chem. Soc.*, **1958**, 1574.

(157) A. P. Gray and H. Kraus, *J. Org. Chem.*, **31**, 399 (1966).

(158) J. Cologne, J. Dreux, and M. Thiers, *Bull. Soc. Chim. France*, **1959**, 1461.

(159) C. K. Bradsher and D. F. Lohr, Jr., *Chem. Ind. (London)*, **1964**, 1801.

(160) A. Rother, J. M. Bobbitt, and A. E. Schwarting, *ibid.*, **1962**, 654.

(161) B. M. Ferrier and N. Campbell, *ibid.*, **1958**, 1089.

(162) J. Streith and C. Sigwalt, *Tetrahedron Letters*, **No. 13**, 1347 (1966).

(163) Z. Arnold, *Collection Czech. Chem. Commun.*, **28**, 863 (1963).

(164) H. J. den Hertog, R. J. Martens, H. C. vander Plas, and J. Bon, *Tetrahedron Letters*, **No. 36**, 4325 (1966).

(165) R. G. Hiskey and J. Hollander, *J. Org. Chem.*, **29**, 3687 (1964).

8

■ QUINOLINE AND ISOQUINOLINE

FUSION OF A BENZENE RING to the pyridine nucleus gives rise to two uncharged bicyclic molecules, namely, quinoline [1] and isoquinoline [2]. Like pyridine, [1] and [2] are obtainable from coal tar. These

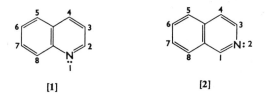

[1]   [2]

weakly basic heterocycles[1] are somewhat similar to pyridine in their stability to chemical attack, but certain basic differences in their overall reactivity do exist.

It was recognized long ago, in the course of the structure proof of [1], that on oxidation with potassium permanganate the benzene ring is attacked preferentially. Similar oxidation of [2] yields approximately equal quantities of phthalic and cinchomeronic [3] acids.

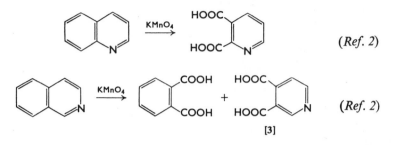

(Ref. 2)

(Ref. 2)

[3]

Although quinoline and isoquinoline are best regarded as aromatic delocalized 10π-electron systems, experimental observations of the type obtained in the oxidation experiments suggest that these molecules resemble naphthalene in having greater double bond character in the 1,2-, 3,4-, 5,6-, and 7,8-bonds than in the remaining bonds. The increased electron density at these sites exerts a profound influence not only upon the reactions of [1] and [2], but also upon the reactivity of substituents attached to various positions of the ring.   For instance, as will be seen later in this chapter, the electronegativity of the nitrogen atom in isoquinoline is much more readily transmitted to a methyl group attached at the 1-position than to the same substituent in the 3-position.

As with pyridine, the pair of 2p electrons on nitrogen which are orthogonal to the molecular π-cloud in [1] and [2] are not required for aromatic stabilization and, therefore, these substances readily undergo quaternization and conversion to N-oxides.   The resulting quaternary salts and N-oxides have chemical properties similar to those of the related pyridine derivatives.

SYNTHETIC APPROACHES
The Skraup Quinoline Synthesis[3, 4]

The general procedure by which a primary aromatic amine possessing at least one vacant ortho position is condensed with an α,β-unsaturated carbonyl compound, or a suitable precursor, in the

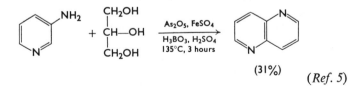

(31%)

(Ref. 5)

presence of a condensing agent and an oxidant, represents a widely used synthetic route to quinoline and many of its derivatives. Amines which fail to yield the desired quinolines generally are those endowed

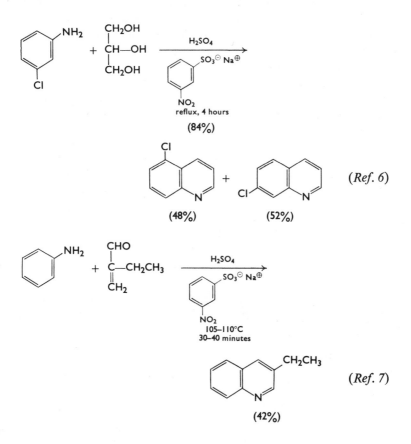

(84%)

(48%)   (52%)   (Ref. 6)

(42%)   (Ref. 7)

with labile substituents. If a meta-substituted aromatic amine is employed, a mixture of 5- and 7-substituted quinolines generally results. In such cases the nature of the reaction mixture has been found to be sometimes quite important in determining the resultant product ratios.

In the preparation of pyridine ring-unsubstituted compounds, glycerol is utilized to generate acrolein *in situ*, in order to minimize the polymerization of the latter. The formation of acrolein can be achieved conveniently with concentrated sulfuric acid which also may function as the condensing agent. Many oxidizing agents have been conveniently employed, among which may be cited nitrobenzene (generally as its sulfonated derivative), stannous chloride, oxygen, and arsenic pentoxide. Ferrous sulfate is frequently utilized to control the initial vigorous reaction, and the presence of boric acid has been found to improve yields. The mode of action of these latter two reagents is not clear.

From a mechanistic viewpoint, the Skraup reaction may be considered to consist of four successive reactions: the dehydration of glycerol to acrolein, Michael addition of the aromatic amine to the α,β-unsaturated carbonyl component to give rise to [4], electrophilic

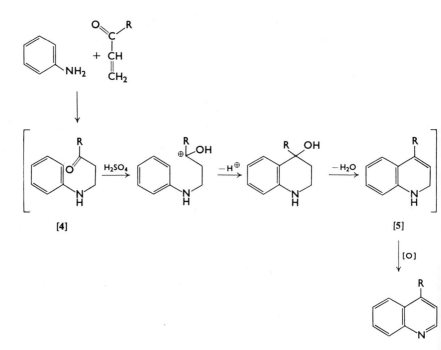

substitution of protonated [4] upon the aromatic ring followed by dehydration and finally, dehydrogenation of dihydroquinoline [5] by the oxidizing agent.

Several modifications of the Skraup synthesis exist, the most important of which is the so-called Doebner-von Miller synthesis.[8, 9] In this closely related process, a primary aromatic amine is heated with an aldehyde in the presence of hydrochloric acid; although the reaction proceeds satisfactorily with air as an oxidant, better yields are observed if *m*-nitrobenzenesulfonic acid is added for this purpose. The accepted mechanism involves self-condensation of the aldehyde to an α,β-unsaturated aldehyde which reacts with the amine as described above.

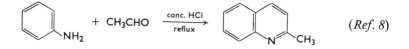

$$(Ref.\ 8)$$

The Friedlander[10] and Pfitzinger[11] Syntheses

A second generally useful method of preparing substituted quinolines involves the condensation of an *o*-amino aromatic aldehyde or ketone with a carbonyl compound having the grouping —CH₂CO—.[9, 12] The

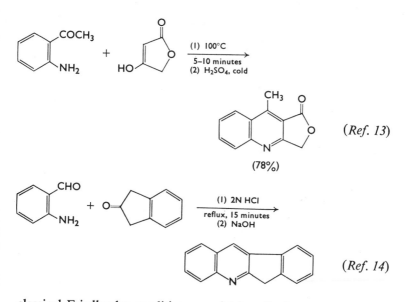

$$(Ref.\ 13)$$

(78%)

$$(Ref.\ 14)$$

classical Friedlander conditions consist in refluxing an aqueous or alcoholic solution of the reactants in the presence of a base, or merely in heating the reactants in the absence of base to 150–200°C.[9] More recently, however, it has become evident that acids are particularly effective catalysts for this reaction.[14–16] Unsymmetrical ketones

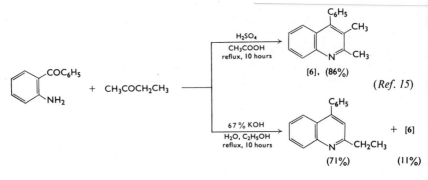

(Ref. 15)

which possess two α-methylene groups appear to condense at different α-carbon atoms as the catalyst is changed.[15]

Mechanistically, this ring closure proceeds by virtue of initial Schiff base formation followed by an internal aldol-type condensation[17] between the aryl carbonyl and the activated methylene groups.

The o-amino aromatic aldehydes or ketones are difficult to prepare and are frequently unstable. For these reasons, the Friedlander synthesis is not readily adaptable to the preparation of quinolines carrying substituents in the benzene ring. These practical difficulties can be overcome by the use of isatins such as [7]; this modification constitutes the Pfitzinger synthesis.[9, 11] Many isatins are available and their condensation with carbonyl compounds represents a general

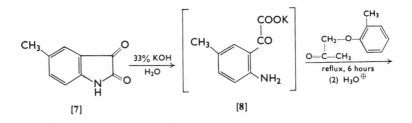

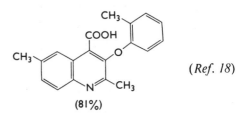

(Ref. 18)

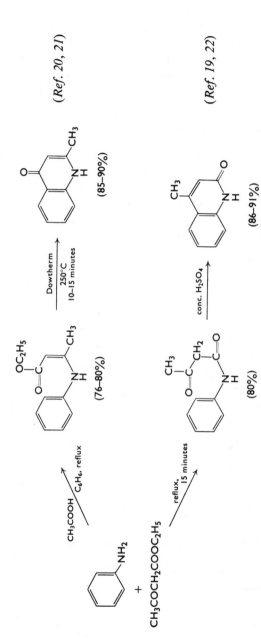

(Ref. 20, 21)

(Ref. 19, 22)

reaction.   The resulting quinoline-4-carboxylic acids can be easily decarboxylated to the corresponding quinolines.

The Pfitzinger reaction involves preliminary ring cleavage of the isatin molecule by base to afford an isatic acid derivative such as [8] which subsequently reacts with the ketone component in a manner presumably analogous to the mechanism of the Friedlander process.

Other Quinoline Syntheses

The most widely employed quinoline syntheses, which are of wide utility because of the broad range of ring substitution which can be readily achieved, consist in the condensation of anilines with β-dicarbonyl compounds (Conrad-Limpach, Knorr, and Combes reactions) or ethoxymethylenemalonic ester (Gould-Jacobs reaction).

When aniline is treated with ethyl acetoacetate, for example, nucleophilic attack may occur at either the ketone or ester carbonyl group to produce an enamide or an anilide, respectively.   Actually, the reactions concerned are equilibrium reactions and either reaction pathway may be followed depending on the conditions.[19]   Whereas the enamide gives rise to a 4-quinolone derivative, a 2-quinolone is produced from the anilide.   In the first case, cyclization is best achieved by merely heating the enamide at 240–250°C in an inert medium such as mineral oil for a few minutes.   Ring closure to 2-quinolones is achieved in concentrated sulfuric acid at 80–100°C for approximately 2 hours.   The versatility of the method is due to

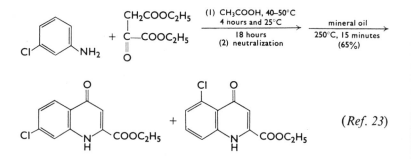

the fact that the aniline and β-keto ester components may be structurally varied almost without limitation.   The intermediate enamides may also be alkylated in order to achieve additional substitution.

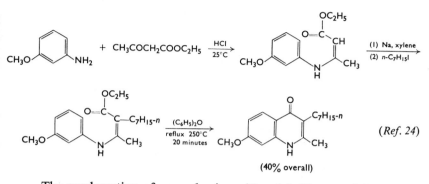

(*Ref. 24*)

(40% overall)

The condensation of an arylamine with a 1,3-diketone, followed by cyclodehydration with concentrated sulfuric acid, is often a convenient route to substituted quinolines.

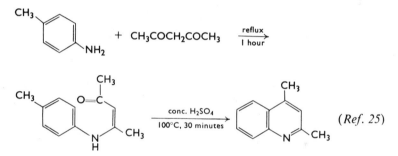

(*Ref. 25*)

4-Quinolones result when anilines are treated with ethoxymethylene-malonic ester and the resulting α-carbethoxy-β-anilinoacrylates are cyclized by heating at 250°C in mineral oil. The synthesis can be applied to almost any aromatic amine.

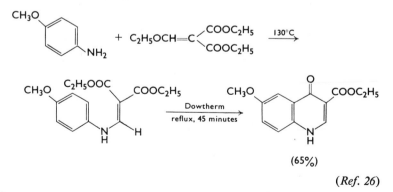

(65%)

(*Ref. 26*)

Several less general quinoline syntheses are known, but will not be discussed here.[27]

The major differentiating factor between the preparation of quinolines and isoquinolines is the fact that whereas most quinoline syntheses lead directly to the aromatic species, two of the most widely applicable isoquinoline syntheses lead initially to partially reduced bases. However, several good dehydrogenative methods are available for the ultimate conversion of the perhydroisoquinolines to the corresponding aromatic counterparts, and so these methods may formally be considered as preparative routes to derivatives of [2].

The Bischler-Napieralski Synthesis[28-30]

The cyclodehydration of acyl derivatives of β-phenethylamine, usually effected by heating with a dehydrating agent in an inert solvent, results in the formation of 3,4-dihydroisoquinolines. This reaction is of considerable generality. The cyclodehydration process may be regarded as an intramolecular electrophilic substitution of the aromatic ring induced by initial attack of the dehydrating agent at the oxygen atom of the amide linkage. The mechanistic sequence is illustrated below for the case of [9]. Because the mode of cycliza-

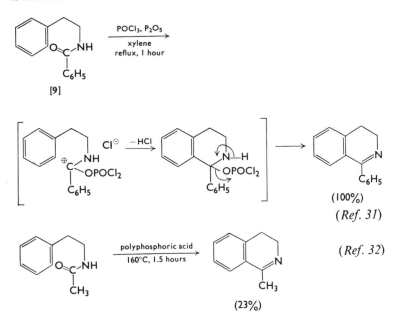

tion is electrophilic in nature, the rate may be expected to be enhanced or retarded by the nature and number of substituents present on the aromatic ring. This effect is frequently reflected in the yields

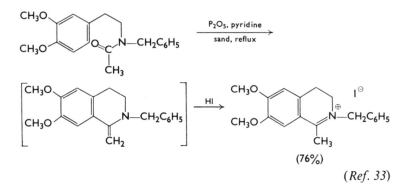

(Ref. 33)

obtained. The successful ring closure of [10] illustrates, however, that a powerful electronegative substituent does not prevent the reaction altogether.

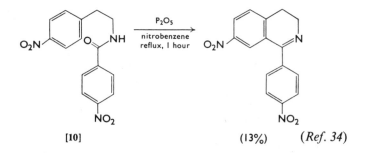

[10]   (13%)   (Ref. 34)

Furthermore, such substituents would be expected to exert the usual directive effects which are normally operative under such conditions. Thus, [11] cyclizes only para to the methoxyl group to give [12] and no [13] is formed. Ring closure ortho to the substituent invariably does not occur.

An important extension of this reaction is the Pictet-Gams modification[36] wherein the β-phenethylamide is replaced by an α-hydroxy-β-phenethylamide such as [13]. Such materials undergo rapid dehydration under the reaction conditions, and the styrylamide so

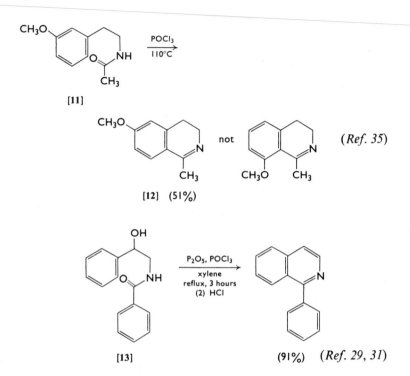

[11]

[12] (51%)   not   (Ref. 35)

[13]   (91%)   (Ref. 29, 31)

formed undergoes cyclization to give an isoquinoline directly. In this manner the dehydrogenation step may be bypassed, and in some cases this has proved to be quite advantageous.

The Pictet-Spengler Synthesis[30, 37, 38]

The condensation of a β-arylethylamine with a carbonyl compound under acidic conditions represents a tetrahydroisoquinoline synthesis of some importance, especially in the alkaloid field. The overall conversion is a special example of the Mannich reaction. The process proceeds equally well with primary as well as secondary amines.

The conditions required for reaction suggest initial formation of an imine (or enamine in the case of a secondary amine), followed by protonation of this intermediate. This positively charged species subsequently effects intramolecular electrophilic substitution. This sequence is illustrated in the case of [14]; it can be seen to be entirely

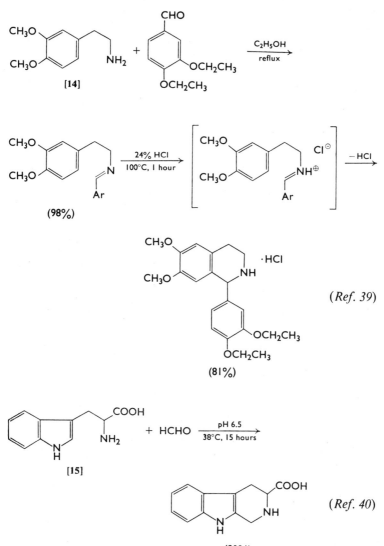

(Ref. 39)

(Ref. 40)

analogous to the mechanism of the Bischler-Napieralski reaction with the exception that the condensing agent is not expelled in the last step (see p. 282). Because of this similarity, the effect of substituents on the rate of cyclization and upon the direction of ring closure exactly

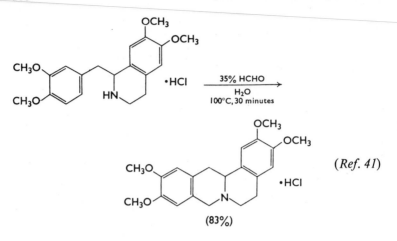

(*Ref. 41*)

(83%)

parallel the phenomena observed in the Bischler-Napieralski process.[38]

When the electrophilic cyclization is to occur at a very reactive center such as the 2-position of indole [15], then conditions which approach the so-called "physiological conditions" of pH, temperature, and concentration are sufficient for reaction.

The Pomeranz-Fritsch Synthesis[42, 43]

The Pomeranz-Fritsch reaction represents a direct synthesis of the isoquinoline ring system and involves the preliminary condensation of an aromatic aldehyde with an aminoacetal to yield a Schiff base such as [16], followed by cyclization with a suitable acidic catalyst.

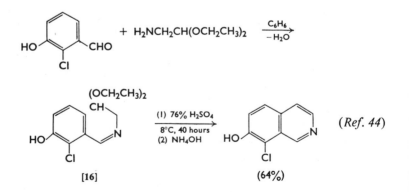

(*Ref. 44*)

[16]　　　　　　　　　　　　(64%)

This synthesis complements the two isoquinoline syntheses discussed earlier, for it offers the possibility of preparing isoquinolines with substituent groups at positions often unattainable by the other routes.

Poor results are usually obtained when aromatic ketones are substituted for the aldehydes. However, by means of the modification exemplified below, the scope of the Pomeranz-Fritsch method has been extended considerably.

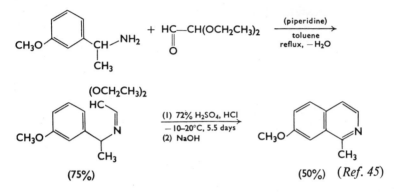

(75%)

(50%) (*Ref. 45*)

Mechanistic details of this reaction are lacking, although the cyclization step is undoubtedly electrophilic in character.

REACTIONS
Electrophilic Substitution

The electrophilic substitution of [1] and [2] and their derivatives can generally be effected under conditions that are considerably less strenuous than those required for the corresponding pyridines. As with pyridine, however, [1] and [2] may undergo electrophilic substitution either through the neutral molecule or through the conjugate acid, although the former option is again believed to be only rarely exercised. Electrophilic substitution of quinoline and isoquinoline

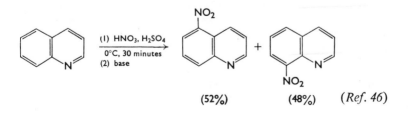

(52%)   (48%)   (*Ref. 46*)

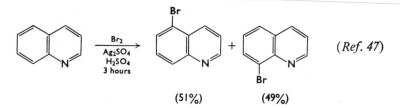

(51%)   (49%)   *(Ref. 47)*

in strongly acidic media proceeds by way of the corresponding conjugate acids and results in substitution at the 5- and 8-positions. This orientational pattern is expected on the basis of pyridine nucleus

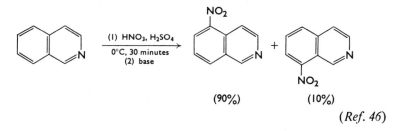

(90%)   (10%)

(Ref. 46)

deactivation due to protonation. At lower acid strengths, however, quinoline undergoes substitution initially at the 3-position, followed by reaction at the 6- and 8-positions. Such results have been interpreted[48] as proceeding by initial formation of an N-substituted quinolinium ion which subsequently reacts with a nucleophile

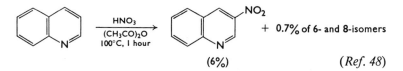

(6%)   *(Ref. 48)*

at the 2-position to give a 1,2-dihydroquinoline. This intermediate is then stated to react with the electrophile at the 3,4-double bond and at the 6- and 8-positions, which processes are followed by rearomatization. Evidence supporting this proposal has been summarized,[49] and has been extended to explain the bromination of isoquinoline at the 3-position.[50]

Nitration of quinoline-N-oxide at 65–70°C, not unlike pyridine-N-oxide, appears to involve the free base and results in substitution at the 4-position.[51] In contrast, nitration of isoquinoline-N-oxide has

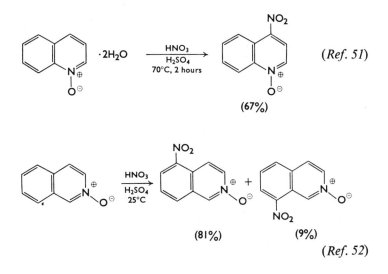

(*Ref. 51*)

(67%)

(81%)   (9%)

(*Ref. 52*)

been shown to proceed through the conjugate acid and to result in 5- and 8-substitution.[52]   Comparison of the available data indicates that the relative reactivities of various N—X-substituted isoquinolinium salts toward nitration[52] follow the order: X=H, 1.0; X=CH$_3$, 1.0; X=OH, 0.47; X=OCH$_3$, 0.13.   Because isomer distributions are similar in this series of compounds, these results indicate that the N-hydroxy and N-methoxy substituents strongly deactivate the 5- and 8-positions.

Nucleophilic and Radical Substitution

In general, attack by a nucleophile at the C-2 of quinoline and at the C-1 of isoquinoline, and their derivatives, is observed unless these positions are occupied.   Both substrates, for example, have been found to undergo the Tschitschibabin reactions[53] (see p. 235); 2-aminoquinoline[46a] and 1-aminoisoquinoline[54b] result. Organometallic reagents react with these heterocycles in a parallel manner. It will be noted from the examples provided that the results duplicate those observed in the pyridine series (see p. 236).   With allylmagnesium bromide as a selective nucleophile, it was observed that quinoline and isoquinoline were of approximately equal reactivity and that both were more reactive than pyridine.[55]

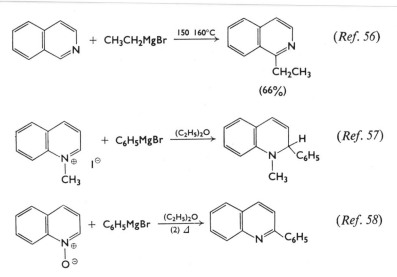

Weaker nucleophiles, although ineffective in achieving substitution of [1] and [2] under ordinary conditions, do react quite readily with the corresponding quaternary salts or N-oxides.   Such behavior may be illustrated by the alkaline ferricyanide oxidation of [17] and by the formation of the Reissert compounds [18] and [19].   Because aldehydes are formed in high yields when Reissert compounds are submitted to acid hydrolysis, considerable effort has been expended in the preparation of such compounds.[62]   The conversion of acid chlorides to aldehydes in good yields is understandably of considerable synthetic value, although the intermediacy of Reissert compounds

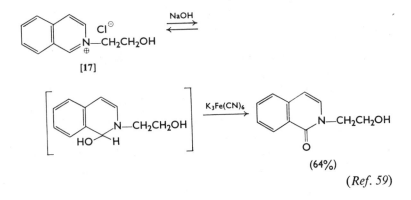

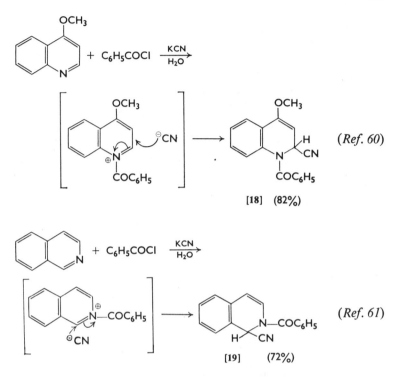

(*Ref. 60*)

[18] (82%)

(*Ref. 61*)

[19] (72%)

does not now represent the sole method of achieving this transformation.

The proposal has been made that hydrolysis occurs by initial protonation of the cyano nitrogen, followed by cyclization, with the result that [20] is formed. This intermediate is subject to a prototropic shift thereby producing [21], which subsequently is attacked by water to give [22], which fragments to the observed products.

Quinolium and isoquinolium salts are also subject to facile reduction by various hydride reducing agents in a manner paralleling the behavior of pyridinium salts (see p. 240).

Because of the low electron density at the 2- and 4-positions of quinoline and the 1- and (less so) 3-positions of isoquinoline, halogen atoms at these sites are capable of replacement by nucleophiles. The kinetics of such reactions have been exhaustively studied.[63] Table 8–1 provides an indication of the relative reactivities of the chloro derivatives in question. Because of the wide difference in the rates

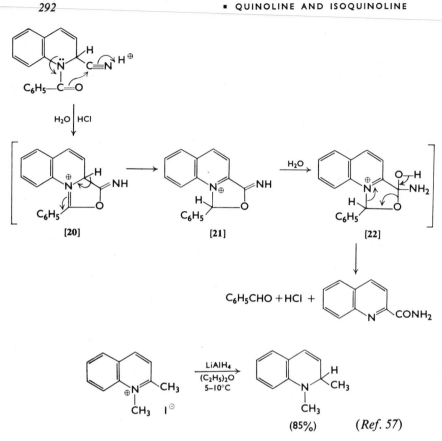

$$C_6H_5CHO + HCl +$$ (quinoline)-2-$CONH_2$

(quinoline derivative) $\xrightarrow[\substack{(C_2H_5)_2O \\ 5-10°C}]{LiAlH_4}$ (dihydroquinoline derivative)

(85%)   (*Ref. 57*)

TABLE 8–I •

Reaction of Some Hetero Atomic Chloro Compounds with Sodium Ethoxide in Ethanol at 20°C[64]

Compound	k, liter mole^{-1} second^{-1}	E, kcal/mole	$-\Delta S^*$
2-Chloroquinoline	6.3×10^{-7}	23.1	10.7
4-Chloroquinoline	6.5×10^{-7}	20.4	19.6
1-Chloroisoquinoline	6.9×10^{-7}	22.5	12.3
3-Chloroisoquinoline	1.2×10^{-11}	32.4	0.7

of displacement of the 1- and 3-chloroisoquinolines, selective sub-stitution at the 1-position can be readily achieved.

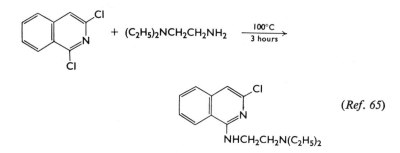

(Ref. 65)

When 1-chloroisoquinoline is heated with alkyl iodides, quaternary salts of 1-iodoisoquinoline are obtained. This process, which presumably occurs by way of nucleophilic attack by iodide at the 1-position to displace chloride ion from the quaternary salt, illustrates the marked enhancement of susceptibility to nucleophilic substitution which arises when the electron-withdrawing capability of nitrogen is increased.

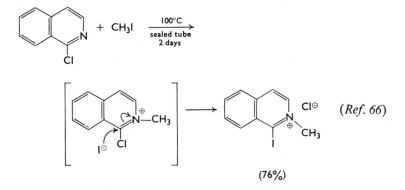

(Ref. 66)

(76%)

Free radical phenylation of quinoline with benzoylperoxide has been found to give rise to phenylation at all the possible nuclear positions, the relative reactivities of the various positions being 8->4->3-, 5->2-, 6->7-.[67]

Side Chain Reactivity

In general, alkyl groups situated ortho or para to the ring nitrogen atom in aromatic nitrogen heterocycles display enhanced reactivity. Alkyl groups located at sites other than these select positions have properties similar to normal alkylbenzenes. Quinaldine [23] and lepidine [24], and their homologs, are no exceptions, and their chemical reactivity resembles closely that of the 2- and 4-alkyl-pyridines (see p. 245). Both 1- and 3-methylisoquinoline might be

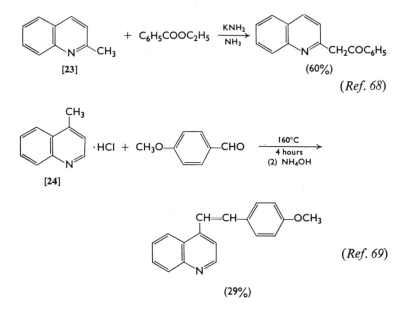

(Ref. 68)

(Ref. 69)

expected to display similar behavior and they do, but because of apparent double bond fixation in such molecules (see p. 274), the 1-methyl substituent is much more reactive than the 3-methyl group. The alkyl group in 3-methylisoquinoline is, however, of a higher order of reactivity than the methyl group of 2-methylnaphthalene, so that the electronegativity of the hetero atom is transmitted to some degree to that site. Thus, 3-methylisoquinoline will condense with benzaldehyde but only under conditions that are more vigorous than those necessary for the 1-isomer.

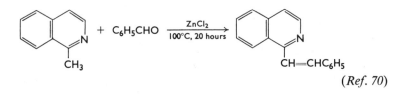

(Ref. 70)

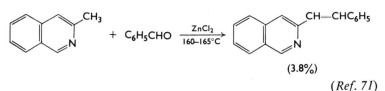

(3.8%)

(*Ref. 71*)

The structural features of the 2- and 4-hydroxyquinolines are analogous to those of the 2- and 4-pyridones; high concentration of the quinolone tautomers is evident in a variety of solvents.[72] This tautomeric behavior is likewise reflected in their chemical properties; for example, when 4-methyl-2-quinolone is methylated with methyl iodide and sodium methoxide, the N—CH$_3$/O—CH$_3$ ratio is 4.5, with potassium ethoxide it increases 10.8, and with (CH$_3$CH$_2$)$_3$$\overset{\oplus}{N}CH_3$(OCH$_3$$^{\ominus}$) only N-methylation occurs.[73] 1-Hydroxyisoquinoline exhibits similar behavior.[74, 75]

The related amino compounds typically exist predominantly in the amino form, although their tautomeric capability is evidenced by their reactions which can occur at either of the two nitrogen atoms. Several examples of this behavior are provided below.

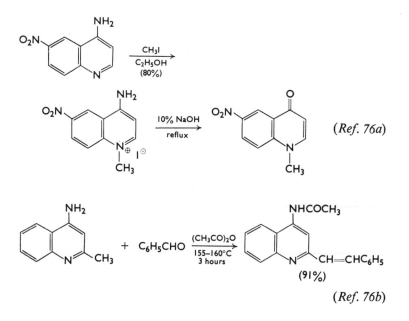

(*Ref. 76a*)

(91%)

(*Ref. 76b*)

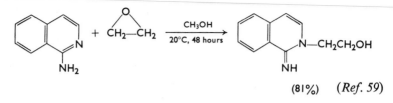

(81%)   (*Ref. 59*)

Quinoline-2-carboxylic acid (quinaldinic acid) [25] is known to undergo facile decarboxylation. When the decarboxylation is effected in the presence of reactive carbonyl compounds, condensation occurs. The overall conversion represents a modification of the Hammick reaction (see p. 253), and the mechanism of decarboxylation probably parallels that encountered in the pyridine series.

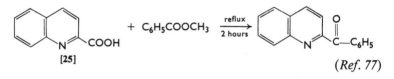

[25]
(*Ref. 77*)

Quinoline- and isoquinoline-N-oxides have been observed to undergo a number of rearrangements of various types. From the reaction of quinoline-N-oxide with sulfuryl chloride, there result 2- and 4-chloroquinoline in the ratio of 1:1.7.[78] The ratio of 2- to 4-isomers interestingly varies as a function of substitution: 6-methoxy-, 1:0.6; 6-nitro-, 1:3.5; 6-chloro-, 1:1.38.[78] The ratios apparently are not affected by changes in the reaction conditions.

When these same N-oxides are heated in acetic anhydride, deoxygenation results and an acetoxy group is incorporated into the molecule. Like the pyridine examples (see p. 258), the position of entry of the acetoxy group is a function of the substitution, or lack of it, in the positions α- or γ- to the nitrogen atom. No rearrangement to the 3-position of isoquinoline is observed in agreement with the concept of double bond fixation. On the basis of various observations, these reactions are believed to proceed by mechanistic routes comparable to those outlined in Chapter 7 for the pyridine-N-oxides.

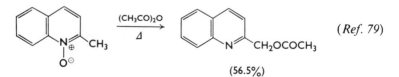

(56.5%)

(*Ref. 79*)

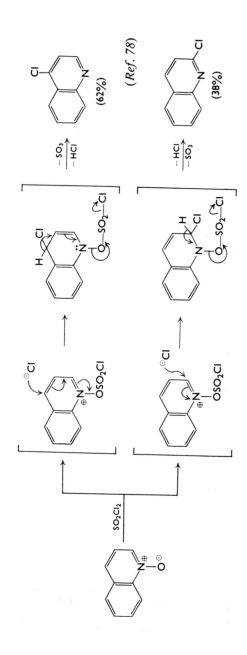

(Ref. 78)

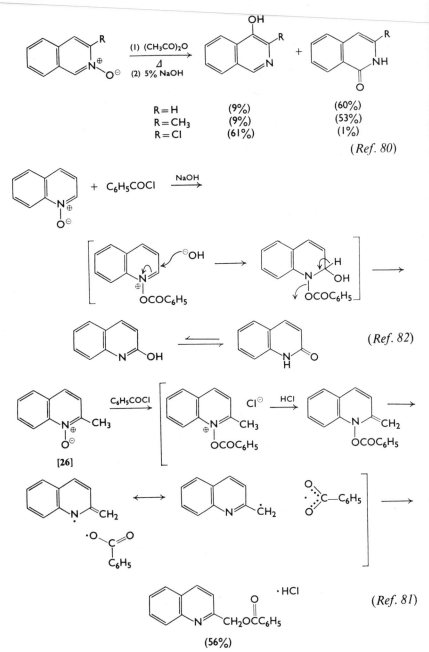

R = H   (9%)   (60%)
R = CH$_3$ (9%)   (53%)
R = Cl   (61%)   (1%)

(Ref. 80)

(Ref. 82)

(Ref. 81)

[26]

(56%)

The reactions of quinoline- and isoquinoline-N-oxides with benzoyl chloride appear to be of a similar mechanistic type. Specifically, in the absence of side chain substituents, the product is formed most probably by means of an ionic pathway. When a substituent is present, however, such as in the case of quinaldine-N-oxide [**26**], evidence favors a radical cage mechanism and rules out an intra-molecular ionic mechanism. This conclusion is based chiefly on the results of O^{18}-labeling experiments and the ineffectiveness of radical scavengers on the reaction.[81]

In contrast, lepidine-N-oxide [**27**] upon treatment with benzoyl chloride gives rise chiefly to 3-benzoyloxylepidine.[83] The mechanism of this rearrangement is still inconclusive, but appears to involve the

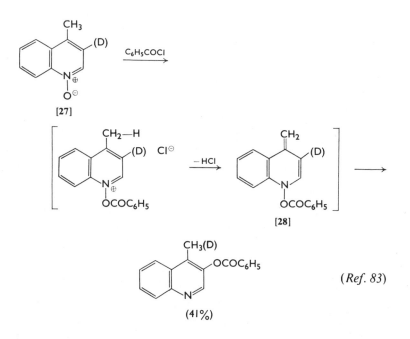

(*Ref. 83*)

anhydro base [**28**]. Deuterium labeling indicates that the proton at C-3 eventuates in the methyl group at C-4. O^{18}-Labeling showed that the carbonyl and ether oxygens of the benzoyl group are completely scrambled. A possible explanation of these results is outlined below.

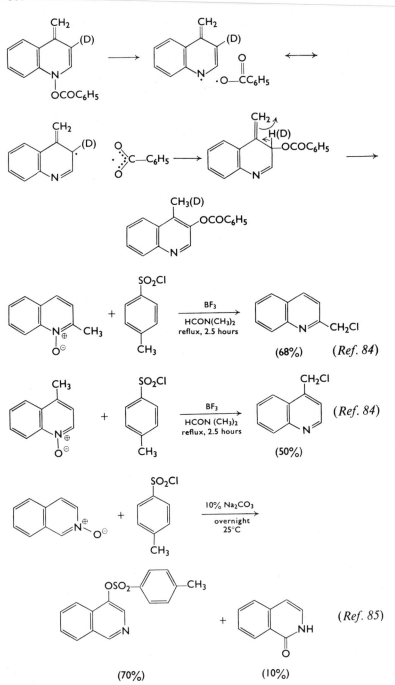

Rearrangement reactions with arylsulfonyl halides have also been observed. The mechanisms of these transformations, although probably analogous to those discussed above, have not been completely elucidated.

Exercises

1. Predict the major product of the following reactions:

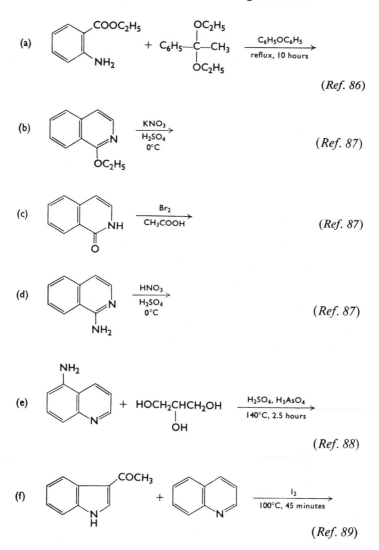

(a) $+$ $C_6H_5-\overset{OC_2H_5}{\underset{OC_2H_5}{C}}-CH_3$ $\xrightarrow[\text{reflux, 10 hours}]{C_6H_5OC_6H_5}$

(*Ref. 86*)

(b) $\xrightarrow[\substack{H_2SO_4 \\ 0°C}]{KNO_3}$

(*Ref. 87*)

(c) $\xrightarrow[CH_3COOH]{Br_2}$

(*Ref. 87*)

(d) $\xrightarrow[\substack{H_2SO_4 \\ 0°C}]{HNO_3}$

(*Ref. 87*)

(e) $+$ $HOCH_2CHCH_2OH$ with OH $\xrightarrow[\text{140°C, 2.5 hours}]{H_2SO_4, H_3AsO_4}$

(*Ref. 88*)

(f) $+$ $\xrightarrow[\text{100°C, 45 minutes}]{I_2}$

(*Ref. 89*)

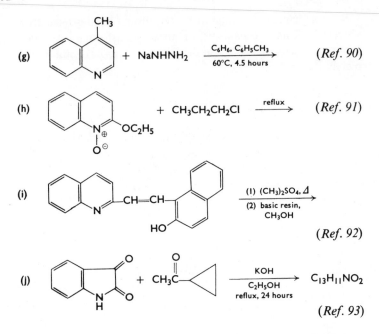

(g) [4-methylquinoline] + NaNHNH₂ $\xrightarrow[60°C, 4.5 \text{ hours}]{C_6H_6, C_6H_5CH_3}$ (*Ref. 90*)

(h) [quinoline N-oxide with OC₂H₅] + CH₃CH₂CH₂Cl $\xrightarrow{\text{reflux}}$ (*Ref. 91*)

(i) [2-styrylquinoline naphthol] $\xrightarrow[\substack{(2) \text{ basic resin,} \\ CH_3OH}]{(1) (CH_3)_2SO_4, \Delta}$ (*Ref. 92*)

(j) [isatin] + CH₃C(O)-cyclopropane $\xrightarrow[\substack{C_2H_5OH \\ \text{reflux, 24 hours}}]{\text{KOH}}$ C₁₃H₁₁NO₂ (*Ref. 93*)

2. Suggest a reasonable mechanism for each of the following transformations:

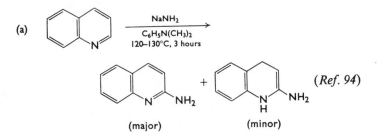

(a) [quinoline] $\xrightarrow[\substack{C_6H_5N(CH_3)_2 \\ 120–130°C, 3 \text{ hours}}]{NaNH_2}$

[2-aminoquinoline] + [2-amino-3,4-dihydroquinoline] (*Ref. 94*)

(major)   (minor)

Explain minor product formation.

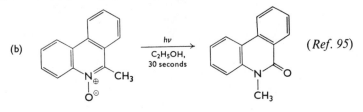

(b) [6-methylphenanthridine N-oxide] $\xrightarrow[\substack{C_2H_5OH, \\ 30 \text{ seconds}}]{h\nu}$ [N-methylphenanthridinone] (*Ref. 95*)

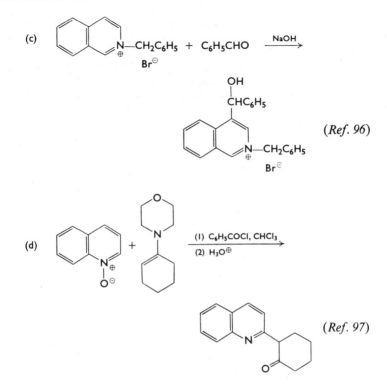

(c) ... + C$_6$H$_5$CHO $\xrightarrow{\text{NaOH}}$ ... (*Ref. 96*)

(d) ... + ... $\xrightarrow[\text{(2) H}_3\text{O}^{\oplus}]{\text{(1) C}_6\text{H}_5\text{COCl, CHCl}_3}$ ... (*Ref. 97*)

References and Notes

(1) The pK$_a$'s of quinoline and isoquinoline in water at 20°C are 4.85 and 5.14 respectively.

(2) S. Hoogewerff and W. A. van Dorp, *Chem. Ber.*, **12**, 747 (1879).

(3) Z. H. Skraup, *Monatsh. Chem.*, **1**, 316 (1880); **2**, 139 (1881).

(4) R. H. F. Manske and M. Kulka, *Org. Reactions*, **7**, 59 (1953).

(5) H. Rapoport and A. D. Batcho, *J. Org. Chem.*, **28**, 1753 (1963).

(6) M. H. Palmer, *J. Chem. Soc.*, **1962**, 3645.

(7) W. P. Utermohlen, Jr., *J. Org. Chem.*, **8**, 544 (1943).

(8) O. Doebner and W. von Miller, *Chem. Ber.*, **14**, 2812 (1881); **16**, 2464 (1883).

(9) R. C. Elderfield, in R. C. Elderfield (ed.), *Heterocyclic Compounds*, Vol. 4, Wiley, New York, 1952, Chapter 1.

(10) P. Friedländer, *Chem. Ber.*, **15**, 2572 (1882).

(11) W. Pfitzinger, *J. Prakt. Chem.*, **33**, 100 (1886).

(12) R. H. Manske, *Chem. Rev.*, **30**, 113 (1942).

(13) S. Oae, S. Tamagaki, and S. Kozuka, *Tetrahedron Letters*, **No. 14,** 1513 (1966); E. A. Fehnel, J. A. Deyrup, and M. B. Davidson, *J. Org. Chem.*, **23,** 1996 (1958).

(14) G. R. Clemo and D. G. I. Felton, *J. Chem. Soc.*, **1952,** 1658.

(15) E. A. Fehnel, *J. Org. Chem.*, **31,** 2899 (1966).

(16) G. Kempter, P. Andratske, D. Heilman, H. Krausman, and M. Mietasch, *Chem. Ber.*, **97,** 16 (1964); G. Kempter and S. Hirschberg, *ibid.*, **98,** 419 (1965).

(17) H. O. House, *Modern Synthetic Reactions*, W. A. Benjamin, Inc., New York, 1965, Chapters 7–9.

(18) A. M. Dowell, Jr., H. S. McCullough, and P. K. Callaway, *J. Am. Chem. Soc.*, **70,** 226 (1948).

(19) C. R. Hauser and G. A. Reynolds, *ibid.*, **70,** 2402 (1948).

(20) G. A. Reynolds and C. R. Hauser, *Org. Synth.*, **Coll. Vol. 3,** 374 (1955).

(21) G. A. Reynolds and C. R. Hauser, *ibid.*, 593 (1955).

(22) W. M. Lauer and C. E. Kaslow, *ibid.*, 580 (1955).

(23) A. R. Surrey and H. F. Hammer, *J. Am. Chem. Soc.*, **68,** 113 (1946).

(24) N. J. Leonard, H. F. Herbrandson, and E. M. Van Heyningen, *ibid.*, **68,** 1279 (1946).

(25) E. Roberts and E. E. Turner, *J. Chem. Soc.*, **1927,** 1832.

(26) C. C. Price and R. M. Roberts, *J. Am. Chem. Soc.*, **68,** 1204 (1946).

(27) See refs. 9 and 12 for a review of these lesser known processes.

(28) A. Bischler and B. Napieralski, *Chem. Ber.*, **26,** 1903 (1893).

(29) W. M. Whaley and T. R. Govindachari, *Org. Reactions*, **6,** 74 (1951).

(30) W. J. Gensler, in R. C. Elderfield (ed.), *Heterocyclic Compounds*, Vol. 4, Wiley, New York, 1952, Chapter 2.

(31) W. M. Whaley and W. H. Hartung, *J. Org. Chem.*, **14,** 650 (1949).

(32) H. R. Snyder and F. X. Werber, *J. Am. Chem. Soc.*, **72,** 2962 (1950).

(33) N. Itoh and S. Sugasawa, *Tetrahedron*, **1,** 45 (1957).

(34) A. McCoubrey and D. W. Mathieson, *J. Chem. Soc.*, **1949,** 696.

(35) See footnote 105 of ref. 21.

(36) A. Pictet and A. Gams, *Chem. Ber.*, **42,** 2943 (1909); *ibid.*, **43,** 2384 (1910).

(37) A. Pictet and T. Spengler, *ibid.*, **44,** 2030 (1911).

(38) W. M. Whaley and T. R. Govindachari, *Org. Reactions*, **6,** 151 (1951).

(39) E. C. Weinbach and W. H. Hartung, *J. Org. Chem.*, **15,** 676 (1950).

(40) D. G. Harvey, E. J. Miller, and W. Robson, *J. Chem. Soc.*, **1941,** 153.

(41) L. E. Craig and D. S. Tarbell, *J. Am. Chem. Soc.*, **70,** 2783 (1948).

(42) C. Pomeranz, *Monatsh. Chem.*, **14**, 116 (1893); **15**, 299 (1894); **18**, 1 (1897); P. Fritsch, *Chem. Ber.*, **26**, 419 (1893); *Ann. Chem.*, **286**, 1 (1895).

(43) W. J. Gensler, *Org. Reactions*, **6**, 191 (1951).

(44) See ref. 35; R. H. F. Manske and M. Kulka, *Can. J. Research*, **27B**, 161 (1949).

(45) See ref. 35; E. Schlittler and J. Müller, *Helv. Chim. Acta*, **31**, 914 (1948).

(46) M. J. S. Dewar and P. M. Maitlis, *J. Chem. Soc.*, **1957**, 2521.

(47) P. B. D. de la Mare, M. Kiamud-din, and J. H. Ridd, *ibid.*, **1960**, 561.

(48) M. J. S. Dewar and P. M. Maitlis, *J. Chem. Soc.*, **1957**, 944.

(49) J. H. Ridd, *Physical Methods in Heterocyclic Chemistry*, **1**, 109 (1963).

(50) See pertinent footnotes in ref. 39.

(51) The position taken by the nitro group on nitration of quinoline-N-oxide is very temperature dependent. At 0–10°C, only the 5- and 8-nitro derivatives are formed, whereas at higher temperatures, the 4-nitro derivative is obtained. This phenomenon, although probably due to thermodynamic factors, has not been totally clarified: E. Ochiai, *J. Org. Chem.*, **18**, 534 (1953).

(52) J. Gleghorn, R. B. Moodie, K. Schofield, and M. J. Williamson, *J. Chem. Soc. (B)*, **1966**, 870.

(53) M. T. Leffler, *Org. Reactions*, **1**, 91 (1942).

(54) (a) F. W. Bergstrom, *J. Am. Chem. Soc.*, **56**, 1748 (1954); *J. Org. Chem.*, **2**, 411 (1937); **3**, 233, 424 (1938); (b) G. W. Ewing and E. A. Steck, *J. Am. Chem. Soc.*, **68**, 2181 (1946); F. W. Bergstrom, *ibid.*, **62**, 3030 (1940); *J. Org. Chem.*, **10**, 479 (1945).

(55) H. Gilman, J. Eisch, and T. Soddy, *J. Am. Chem. Soc.*, **79**, 1245 (1957).

(56) F. W. Bergstrom and E. H. McAllister, *ibid.*, **52**, 2845 (1930).

(57) R. C. Elderfield and B. H. Wark, *J. Org. Chem.*, **27**, 543 (1962).

(58) M. Colonna and A. Risalti, *Gazz. Chim. Ital.*, **83**, 58 (1953).

(59) W. Schneider and B. Müller, *Chem Ber.*, **93**, 1579 (1960).

(60) F. D. Popp, W. Blount, and P. Melvin, *J. Org. Chem.*, **26**, 4930 (1961).

(61) F. D. Popp and W. Blount, *ibid.*, **27**, 297 (1962).

(62) W. E. McEwen and R. L. Cobb, *Chem. Rev.*, **55**, 511 (1955).

(63) G. Illuminati, *Adv. Heterocyclic Chem.*, **3**, 285 (1964).

(64) N. B. Chapman and D. Q. Russell-Hill, *J. Chem. Soc.*, **1956**, 1563.

(65) R. D. Haworth and S. Robinson, *ibid.*, **1948**, 777.

(66) N. I. Fisher and F. M. Hamer, *ibid.*, **1934**, 1905.

(67) K. H. Pausacker, *Australian J. Chem.*, **11**, 200 (1958).

(68) F. W. Bergstrom and A. Moffat, *J. Am. Chem. Soc.*, **59**, 1494 (1937).

(69) C. T. Bahner, H. Kinder, and T. Rigdon, *J. Med. Pharm. Chem.*, **8**, 137 (1965).

(70) W. H. Mills and J. L. B. Smith, *J. Chem. Soc.*, **121**, 2724 (1922).

(71) H. Erlenmeyer, H. Baumann, and E. Sorkin, *Helv. Chim. Acta*, **31**, 1978 (1948).

(72) For a summary of this evidence, see N. Campbell in E. H. Rodd (ed.), *Chemistry of Carbon Compounds*, Vol. 4A, Elsevier, New York, 1957, p. 621; S. F. Mason, *J. Chem. Soc.*, **1957**, 4874, 5010.

(73) O. L. Brady and J. Jakobovits, *ibid.*, **1950**, 767.

(74) See ref. 64, p. 660.

(75) For the properties of 3-hydroxyquinoline, see J. H. Boyer and L. T. Wolford, *J. Org. Chem.*, **21**, 1297 (1956).

(76) (a) J. C. E. Simpson and P. H. Wright, *J. Chem. Soc.*, **1948**, 1707; (b) R. Royer, *ibid.*, **1949**, 1803.

(77) B. R. Brown and D. L. Hammick, *ibid.*, **1949**, 173, 659.

(78) G. B. Bachman and D. E. Cooper, *J. Org. Chem.*, **9**, 302 (1944).

(79) V. Boekelheide and W. J. Linn, *J. Am. Chem. Soc.*, **76**, 1286 (1954).

(80) M. M. Robison and B. L. Robison, *J. Org. Chem.*, **21**, 1337 (1956); *J. Am. Chem. Soc.*, **80**, 3443 (1958).

(81) S. Oae and S. Kozuka, *Tetrahedron*, **20**, 2671 (1964).

(82) M. Henze, *Chem. Ber.*, **69**, 1566 (1936).

(83) S. Oae, S. Tamagaki, and S. Kozuka, *Tetrahedron Letters*, No. 14, 1513 (1966).

(84) H. Tanida, *Yakugaku Zasshi*, **78**, 611 (1958); *Chem. Abstr.*, **52**, 18420 (1958); *Chem. Pharm. Bull.* (*Tokyo*), **7**, 887 (1959).

(85) E. Ochiai and M. Ikehara, *Pharm. Bull.* (*Tokyo*), **3**, 454 (1955).

(86) R. C. Fuson and D. M. Burgess, *J. Am. Chem. Soc.*, **68**, 1270 (1946).

(87) E. Ochiai and Y. Kawazoe, *Chem. Pharm. Bull.* (*Tokyo*), **8**, 24 (1960).

(88) R. F. Homer, *J. Chem. Soc.*, **1958**, 1574.

(89) D. R. Liljegren and K. T. Potts, *J. Org. Chem.*, **27**, 377 (1962).

(90) T. Kauffmann, J. Hansen, C. Kosel, and W. Schoeneck, *Ann. Chem.*, **656**, 103 (1962).

(91) L. A. Paquette, *Tetrahedron*, **22**, 25 (1966).

(92) C. Schiele and H. O. Kalinowski, *Angew. Chem.*, **78**, 389 (1966).

(93) N. P. Buu-Höi, R. Boyer, N. D. Xuong, and P. Jacquinon, *J. Org. Chem.*, **18**, 1209 (1953).

(94) T. Kametani, K. Kigasawa, G. Iwabuchi, and T. Hayasaka, *J. Heterocyclic Chem.*, **2**, 330 (1965).

(95) E. C. Taylor and G. G. Spence, *Chem. Commun.*, **1966**, 767.

(96) E. E. Betts, D. W. Brown, S. F. Dyke, and M. Sainsbury, *Tetrahedron Letters*, **No. 31**, 3755 (1966).

(97) M. Hamana and H. Noda, *Chem. Pharm. Bull.* (*Tokyo*), **13**, 912 (1965).

9

■ THE DIAZINES AND S-TRIAZINE

THE DIAZINES ARE A GROUP of compounds formally derived from benzene and naphthalene by replacement of two carbon atoms of a six-membered ring by nitrogen. Similarly, triazabenzenes such as [4] are termed triazines. The parent diazine ring systems all of which have common names, are known as pyridazine [1], pyrimidine [2], pyrazine [3], cinnoline [5], phthalazine [6], quinazoline [7], and quinoxaline [8]. All of these compounds may be regarded as

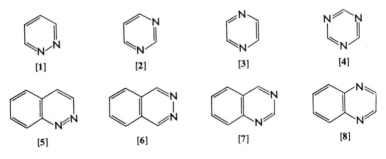

[1]   [2]   [3]   [4]

[5]   [6]   [7]   [8]

aromatic; this conclusion has been derived from experimental observations of the C—C and C—N bond lengths which have been found to be intermediate in length between the values expected for the characteristic single and double bonds in question.

The diazines are basic, but weakly so because of the added electron deficiency which the second nitrogen atom conveys to the heterocyclic system. The basic strengths of the important diazines are summarized in Table 9–1; it is to be noted that the 1,4-diazines are particularly weak bases.

TABLE 9–I ▪

pKa's of Diazines (H₂O, 20–25°C)¹

Compound	pK$_a$	Compound	pK$_a$
Pyridazine	2.3	Cinnoline	2.3
Pyrimidine	1.3	Phthalazine	3.5
Pyrazine	0.6	Quinazoline	3.5
		Quinoxaline	0.7

The quaternization of these substances has been studied to a limited extent.[2] Thus, pyridazine reacts quite readily with alkylating agents, and the position of quaternization is determined by the ring substituents. For example, 3-substituted pyridazines such as [9] are generally quaternized at N-1 presumably due to a steric effect. On the other hand, whereas electropositive 4-substituents lead to attack

(Ref. 3)

[9]

(75%)

(Ref. 4)

(88%)

at N-1, similarly positioned electronegative groups generally give rise to quaternization at N-2. The reaction of pyrimidines with alkylating agents also appears to be subject to direction by the

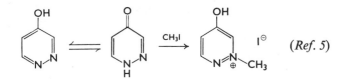

(*Ref. 5*)

attached groups as exemplified by 4-aminopyrimidines which are quaternized slowly at N-1. The few examples which have been studied in the pyrazine series indicate that electronic effects are also

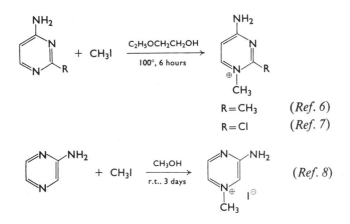

R=CH₃　　(*Ref. 6*)
R=Cl　　(*Ref. 7*)

(*Ref. 8*)

important in that ring system.　Although the quaternization reactions of the benzo derivatives of these heterocycles have not been studied in detail, some correlations are presently available which, in general, parallel the behavior observed in the monocyclic counterparts.[2]

Diquaternary salts have recently been obtained with pyrazines and pyrimidines.[9] All of the pyrazinium diquaternary salts exhibit strong electron paramagnetic resonance signals upon solution in alcohols. This facile electron abstraction which leads to radical cations such as [10] is believed to result because of the strong tendency for reduction of the unfavorable charge interaction in the dications.

Mono-N-oxides are known for all the diazines, and several of them are known to be capable of di-N-oxide formation.

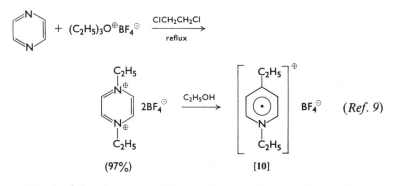

(*Ref. 9*)

Much of the chemistry of the *s*-triazines relates to the transformation of substituent groups on a heterocyclic ring which is not often involved in reactions save for its effect on charge distribution.[10]

SYNTHETIC APPROACHES

The most direct synthesis of pyridazines[11] involves the addition of hydrazine to unsaturated 1,4-diketones (generally obtainable from furans, see p. 135); an interesting modification makes use of hydroxy diketones. The utilization of saturated diketones gives dihydropyridazines which can be dehydrogenated to the aromatic heterocycles.

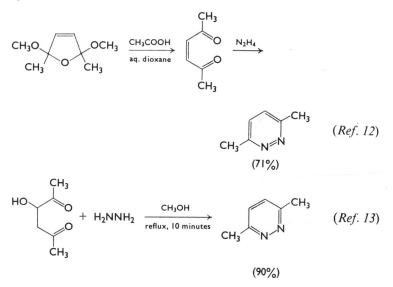

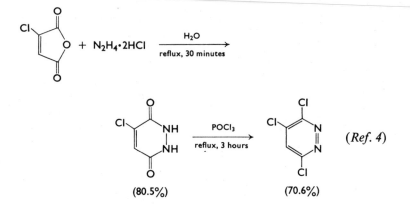

(80.5%)   (70.6%)

Maleic anhydride and its derivatives also react with hydrazine to yield the hydrazide of the derived dicarboxylic acid which may in turn be converted to pyridazines.

The important syntheses of phthalazines[14] are designed along similar lines and involve the condensation of hydrazines with o-diaroyl benzenes, o-acylbenzoic acids, and phthalic anhydrides or acids.

The pyrimidines greatly exceed in importance all of the other diazines because many pyrimidine derivatives play key roles in

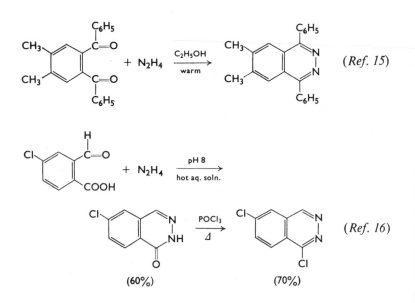

(60%)   (70%)

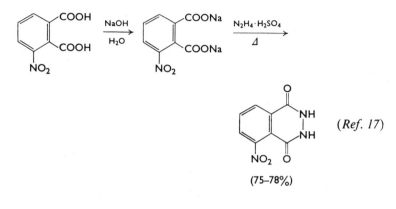

(*Ref. 17*)

(75–78%)

numerous biological processes. For this reason, many synthetic approaches to the pyrimidine nucleus are available[18]; however, most of them fall into three broad categories. The most common pyrimidine synthesis involves the condensation of a three-carbon unit to a species having an N—C—N linkage. This general method is extremely versatile because of the large variety of molecules which undergo the cyclization. For example, the three-carbon unit may be a β-dialdehyde, β-ketoaldehyde, β-keto ester, malonic ester, β-ketonitrile, or other combinations of these functional groups. The nitrogen-containing unit may be a thiourea, amidine, urea, or guanidine. Several examples are illustrated below.

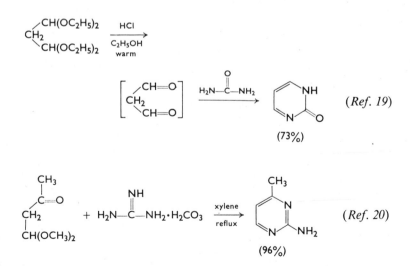

(*Ref. 19*)

(73%)

(*Ref. 20*)

(96%)

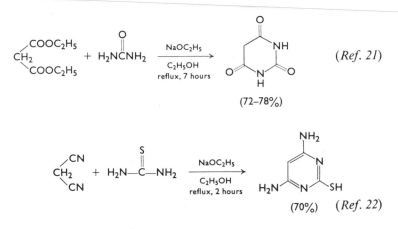

(72–78%)   (*Ref. 21*)

(70%)   (*Ref. 22*)

A second pyrimidine synthesis, of considerable use because it affords pyrimidines which are unsubstituted at the 2-position, involves the condensation of formamide with β-dicarbonyl compounds or their precursors at elevated temperatures. The mechanism by which the pyrimidines are formed in this reaction has not been completely clarified.

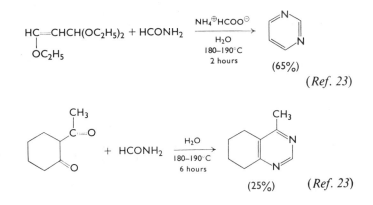

$HC{=}CHCH(OC_2H_5)_2 + HCONH_2$
$\overset{OC_2H_5}{|}$

$\xrightarrow[\substack{H_2O \\ 180-190°C \\ 2 \text{ hours}}]{NH_4^{\oplus}HCOO^{\ominus}}$

(65%)

(*Ref. 23*)

$+ HCONH_2 \xrightarrow[\substack{180-190°C \\ 6 \text{ hours}}]{H_2O}$

(25%)   (*Ref. 23*)

The third important method of pyrimidine synthesis, likewise is complementary to the major synthetic approach and consists in the addition of a C—N fragment to a molecule containing the sequence C—C—C—N. These structural requirements typify a large number of molecules, and indeed this synthesis has a broad scope.

The preparations of quinazolines[27] bear many resemblances to the

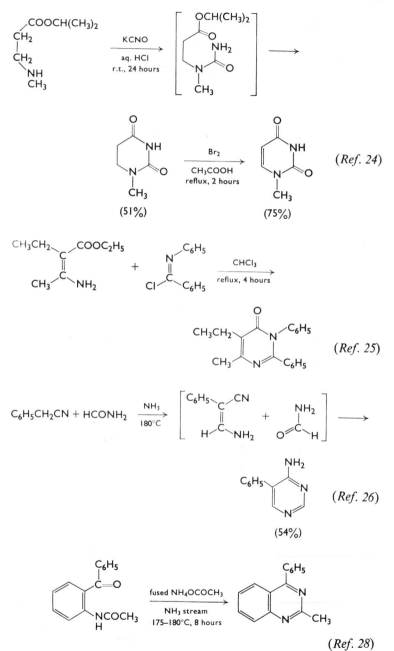

(51%) (75%) (*Ref. 24*)

(*Ref. 25*)

(*Ref. 26*)

(54%)

(*Ref. 28*)

synthetic approaches which lead to the pyrimidine ring system, but the number of satisfactory methods is much more limited. Perhaps, the most important of these methods are found in the reaction of *o*-acylamino-benzaldehydes or -phenylketones with ammonia, and in

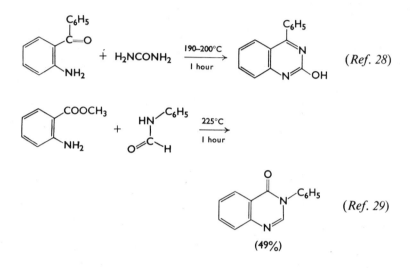

(*Ref. 28*)

(*Ref. 29*)

(49%)

the condensation of anthranilic acid and its derivatives with a variety of amides.

The most significant method for the synthesis of substituted pyrazines[30] centers about the rapid (in solution) self-condensation of α-aminocarbonyl compounds to dihydropyrazines, which in turn may be readily oxidized by air or other mild oxidizing agents (see p. 111 for various means of producing β-aminocarbonyl compounds).

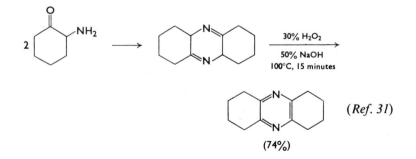

(*Ref. 31*)

(74%)

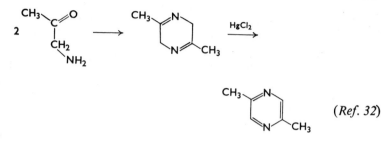

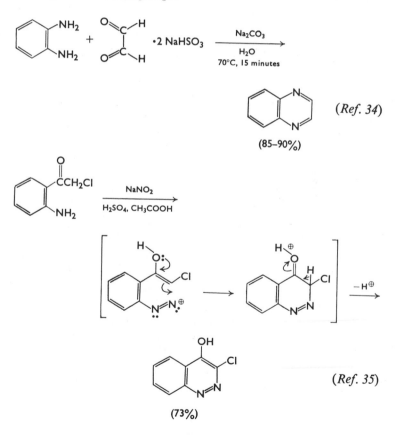

The classical synthesis of quinoxalines,[33] which consists in the condensation of *o*-phenylenediamines with 1,2-dicarbonyl compounds, is sufficiently general, simple, and straightforward that the reaction is widely used as a diagnostic test for compounds containing two adjacent carbonyl groups.

The cinnoline nucleus is most frequently prepared by the intra-molecular cyclization of an aryldiazonium salt which contains a reactive unsaturated *o*-substituent. These cyclizations result from electrophilic attack of the diazonium function upon the unsaturated linkage, followed by proton loss which leads to the aromatic system.

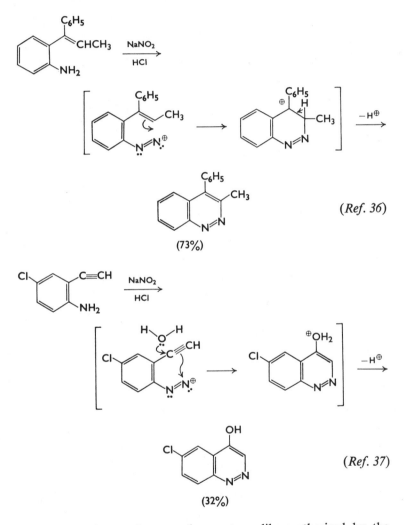

(*Ref. 36*)

(73%)

(*Ref. 37*)

(32%)

The *s*-triazine nucleus can be most readily synthesized by the trimerization of nitriles, generally under conditions of acid catalysis.

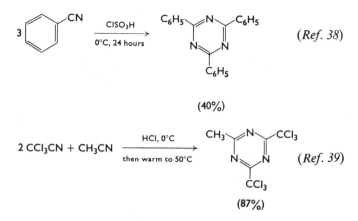

(Ref. 38)

(40%)

2 CCl₃CN + CH₃CN →(HCl, 0°C / then warm to 50°C)→

(Ref. 39)

(87%)

The mechanism which has been proposed[40] for this acid-catalyzed trimerization process is outlined below.

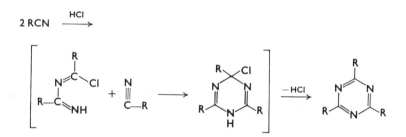

REACTIONS

Electrophilic Substitution

The presence of the second nitrogen atom in the monocyclic diazines would be expected to increase significantly the electron deficiency of these heterocycles relative to pyridine, and render compounds [1], [2], and [3] extremely resistant to attack by positively charged entities. This unreactivity is, in fact, very pronounced and the ring systems are often destroyed under the vigorous conditions which have been unsuccessfully employed. If activating groups such as hydroxyl and amino substituents, or even the N-oxide oxygen in the case of pyridazine, are present in the molecule, then electrophilic substitution has been found to occur. Pyrimidines are invariably attacked at the 5-position, the site which is least deactivated by the hetero atoms.

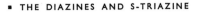

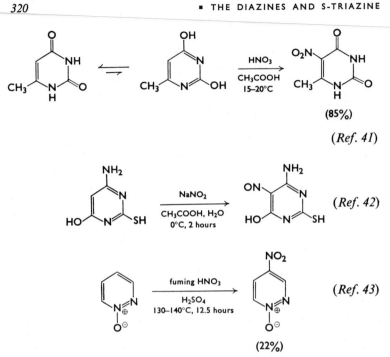

(85%)

(Ref. 41)

(Ref. 42)

(Ref. 43)

(22%)

The benzo derivatives [5], [6], [7], and [8], as anticipated, are somewhat more reactive than the monocyclic diazines, and have been found to undergo direct electrophilic substitution. Attack by the electro-

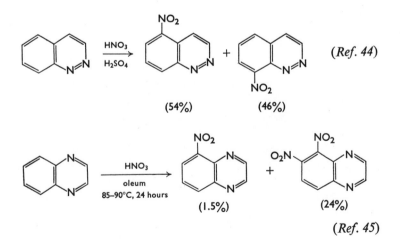

(54%)   (46%)

(Ref. 44)

(1.5%)   (24%)

(Ref. 45)

philic reagents at the 5- and 8-positions, anticipated on the basis of the orientation effects observed with quinoline and isoquinoline, is encountered except in the case of quinazoline [7]. Evidence has been presented[47] to substantiate the fact that the conjugate acid of quinazoline reacts rapidly with water to form cation [11]. This species

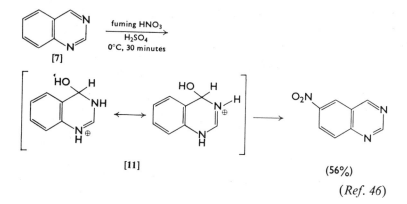

[7]   fuming HNO₃, H₂SO₄, 0°C, 30 minutes

[11]

(56%)

(*Ref. 46*)

would be expected to be subject to electrophilic substitution at the position para to the N—H function. The intermediacy of [11] in the reactions of quinazoline is believed to be the cause of the anomalous substitution pattern.[47] The conjugate acids of all of these heterocycles appear to be involved in these processes.[48] Because of the equivalency of the 5- and 8-positions in quinoxaline [8], only one isomer is formed.

The nitration of cinnoline-1- and -2-oxides interestingly parallels the observations made with quinoline- and isoquinoline-N-oxides (see p. 288). Thus, whereas the 1-oxide undergoes substitution in the heterocyclic ring at the 4-position, the 2-oxide is nitrated exclusively in the benzenoid ring.

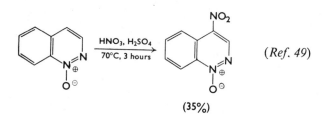

HNO₃, H₂SO₄, 70°C, 3 hours

(*Ref. 49*)

(35%)

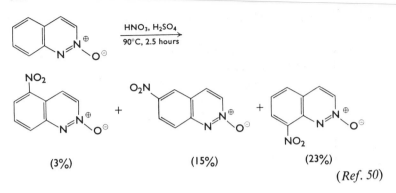

(3%) (15%) (23%)

(*Ref. 50*)

Nucleophilic Substitution

In the diazine series, the positions alpha and gamma to the nitrogen atoms are reactive toward nucleophilic reagents in a manner paralleling the behavior of the analogous positions in pyridine, quinoline, and isoquinoline. Table 9–2, which not only summarizes certain rate data for representative activated chlorodiazines, but also includes the significant pyridine and benzopyridine analogs, provides an indication of the enhancing effect which the second nitrogen of the diazines exerts on the bimolecular displacement process. The most striking results derivable from Table 9–2 are those which reveal that a halogen atom para to an activating nitrogen atom is more reactive

TABLE 9–2 ▪

Reaction of Some Heteroaromatic Chloro Compounds with Piperidine in Ethanol at 20°C [51]

Compound	k, liter mole^{-1} second^{-1}	E, kcal/mole	$-\Delta S^*$, e.u.
2-Chloropyrimidine	3.34×10^{-4}	12.4	34.3
4-Chloropyrimidine	1.5×10^{-3}	~10.5	~35.7
2-Chloroquinoxaline	6.36×10^{-5}	11.3	40.9
2-Chloroquinazoline	4.79×10^{-4}	11.1	37.8
1-Chlorophthalazine	2.5×10^{-5}	11.8	42.0
4-Chloroquinazoline	3.1	7	37.5
2-Chloropyridine	4.8×10^{-10}	19.9	35.8
2-Chloroquinoline	1.5×10^{-7}	15.6	38.9
1-Chloroisoquinoline	2.5×10^{-7}	14.5	41.9

than a similar ortho substituent (unless specific ortho-directing effects intervene). Such results have been attributed predominantly to differences in electron repulsion effects and in coulombic interactions of several kinds in several transition states.[52] It must be borne in mind that relative positional reactivity is a reflection of the ratio of relative rates. In other words, the nucleophile attacks at all the possible positions but at greatly different speeds. Because the rate of a reaction is controlled by the magnitude of the energy of activation, the greater reactivity at the γ- than at the α-position can be attributed to small differences in transition state energy. To illustrate, 3,4,6-trichloropyridazine [12] reacts with one equivalent

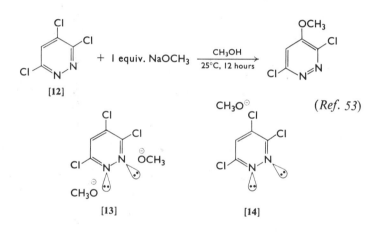

of sodium methoxide in methanol to afford the 4-methoxy derivative in good yield. Structures [13] and [14] illustrate the fact that considerable electron repulsion is to be expected when the negatively charged nucleophile approaches the β-positions which are in close proximity to the electron-rich lone pair orbitals of the nitrogen atoms; no such repulsion is present in the approach of the nucleophile to the γ-position, as in [14]. The magnitude of this electrostatic barrier may well be sufficient to cause small differences in the energies of the three transition states involved and thus affect the relative rates in a manner which favors γ-substitution.

These differences in reactivity have been of significant utility in the synthetic manipulations of the diazines, two examples of which are provided below.

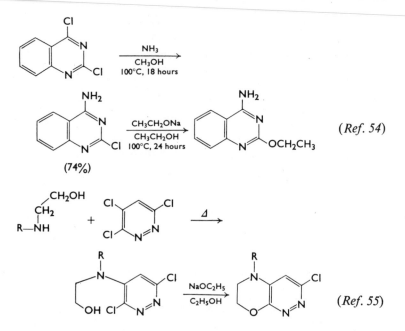

(*Ref. 54*)

(*Ref. 55*)

Hydrogen bonding of a protic solvent to the heterocyclic center occasionally assumes importance in the distribution of products. For example, 2,4-dichloropyrimidine [15] reacts with one equivalent of sodium methoxide in methanol to give only the 4-methoxy derivative (72% yield); however, when [15] is heated alone in methanol

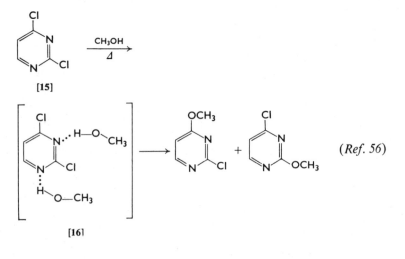

(*Ref. 56*)

solution, approximately equal amounts of 2- and 4-methoxy derivatives have been isolated. Such alterations in product ratios have been attributed to the fact that hydrogen bonding as in [16] permits the formation of methoxide ion in close proximity to C-2, a phenomenon which would enhance the rate of substitution at the site (note that only minimal nucleophile-Nπ interaction is likely under these circumstances).

Nucleophilic substitution in diazine mono-N-oxides has been studied only to a limited extent, except for the pyridazine-N-oxides which have been examined in some detail. In this series, N-oxidation dramatically increases the reactivity of the 3- and 5-positions toward anionic reagents[57] (Table 9–3). The 4- and 6-positions are much less

TABLE 9–3 •

Reaction of Halogenopyridazine 1-Oxides with Piperidine (50°C)[58]

Pyridazine 1-oxide	$k \times 10^5$, liter mole^{-1} second^{-1}	E, kcal/mole	$-\Delta S^*$, e.u.
5-Chloro	288	12.1	-33
3-Chloro	126	12.2	-34
6-Chloro	39.4	13.0	-34
4-Chloro	7.08	13.0	-37

affected by the added N-oxide substituent. The magnitude of this activating influence may be gauged somewhat by the susceptibility of the two chlorine atoms of [17] to nucleophilic reagents. These

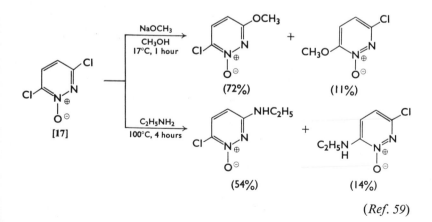

(*Ref. 59*)

results are in direct contrast to the behavior of pyridine- and quinoline-N-oxides where the highest reactivity in nucleophilic substitution is shown at the position para to the N-oxide function (see p. 242). This apparent anomaly may be attributed to a certain degree of added activation at the 3- and 5-positions caused by the azine nitrogen, an influence which is absent at the 4- and 6-position and in the monoazines.

Nucleophilic additions to diazine rings are frequently encountered. In some cases, the charge deficiency on the carbon atoms is sufficiently pronounced that addition reactions can occur with reagents such as sodium bisulfite, hydrogen cyanide, and the like. Quinazoline 3-oxide [18] shows the same reactivity as quinazoline toward nucleophilic reagents, but the addition products frequently eliminate water with the net effect that 4-substituted quinazoline results.

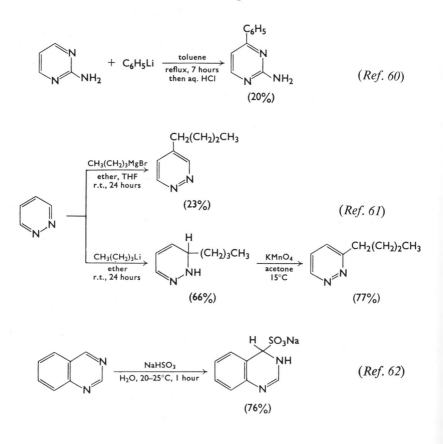

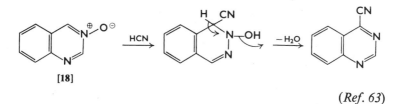

(*Ref. 63*)

Side Chain Reactivity

In general, the chemical properties of substituents at the so-called "activated" α- and γ-positions of the diazine molecules display reactions similar to those discussed in Chapters 7 and 8. For example, alkyl groups at these sites possess acidic hydrogens and undergo condensation reactions in the presence of appropriate bases or Lewis acids.

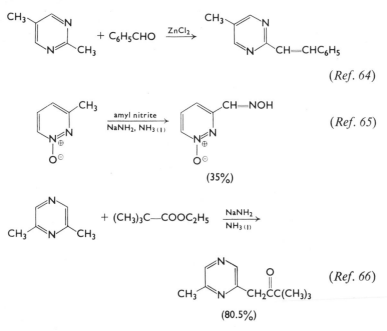

(*Ref. 64*)

(*Ref. 65*)

(35%)

(*Ref. 66*)

(80.5%)

In accordance with the established pattern of behavior, hydroxydiazines exist predominantly as their keto tautomers. However, in such molecules the number of possible keto tautomers is greater than one, and it becomes difficult to assess the relative importance of the various structures.[67]　Aminodiazines generally exist predominantly in the amino form.

Carboxyl groups situated at the α- and γ-positions are prone to decarboxylation at somewhat elevated temperatures, a phenomenon which is diagnostic of this substitution pattern (see pp. 253, 296).

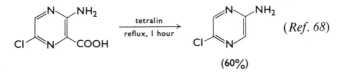

(*Ref. 68*)

(60%)

Diazine-N-oxides in general react as do their monoazine-N-oxide counterparts.　For example, deoxygenation occurs in the presence of phosphorus trichloride, and deoxygenation-ring chlorination are

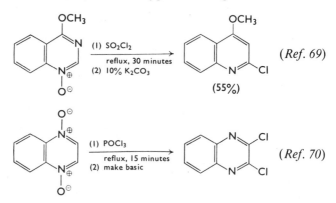

(*Ref. 69*)

(55%)

(*Ref. 70*)

observed upon reaction with sulfuryl chloride or phosphorus oxychloride.　In warm acetic anhydride, rearrangements occur and the nature of the product is again a function of the substitution at the α-carbon atom (see pp. 258, 296).　Because of the similarity of these reactions with those of the related pyridine- and quinoline-N-oxides, it is likely that similar mechanisms are operative in both instances; however, the diazine-N-oxide rearrangements have not been examined for mechanistic detail.

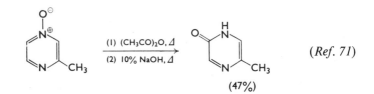

(*Ref. 71*)

(47%)

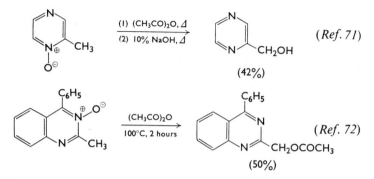

(*Ref. 71*)

(42%)

(*Ref. 72*)

(50%)

The major exception to the general pattern of behavior is quinazoline-3-oxide, whose behavior is modified by the fact that ring fission or ring enlargement frequently accompanies reaction. Some of these reactions are illustrated below.

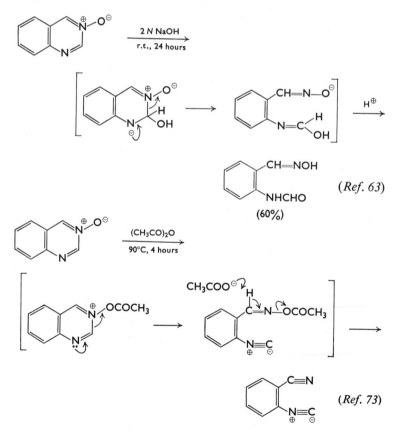

(*Ref. 63*)

(60%)

(*Ref. 73*)

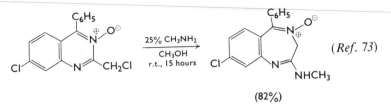

(Ref. 73)

(82%)

Exercises

1. Predict the major product of the following reactions:

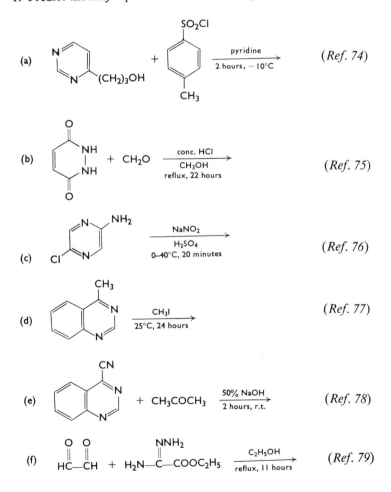

(a)   (Ref. 74)

(b)   (Ref. 75)

(c)   (Ref. 76)

(d)   (Ref. 77)

(e)   (Ref. 78)

(f)   (Ref. 79)

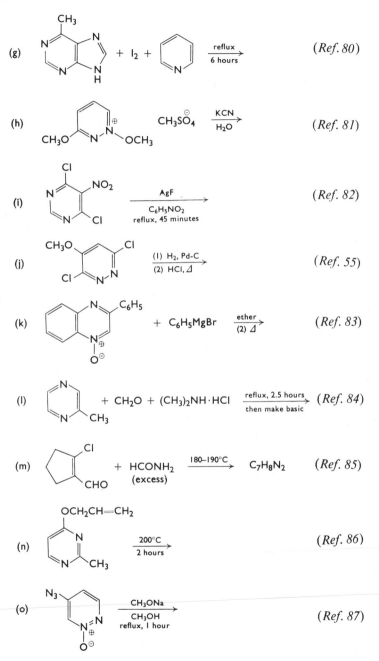

(g) [reflux, 6 hours] (*Ref. 80*)

(h) [KCN, H₂O] (*Ref. 81*)

(i) [AgF, C₆H₅NO₂, reflux, 45 minutes] (*Ref. 82*)

(j) [(1) H₂, Pd-C, (2) HCl, Δ] (*Ref. 55*)

(k) [ether, (2) Δ] (*Ref. 83*)

(l) [reflux, 2.5 hours, then make basic] (*Ref. 84*)

(m) [180–190°C] (*Ref. 85*)

(n) [200°C, 2 hours] (*Ref. 86*)

(o) [CH₃ONa, CH₃OH, reflux, 1 hour] (*Ref. 87*)

2. Suggest a reasonable mechanism for each of the following transformations:

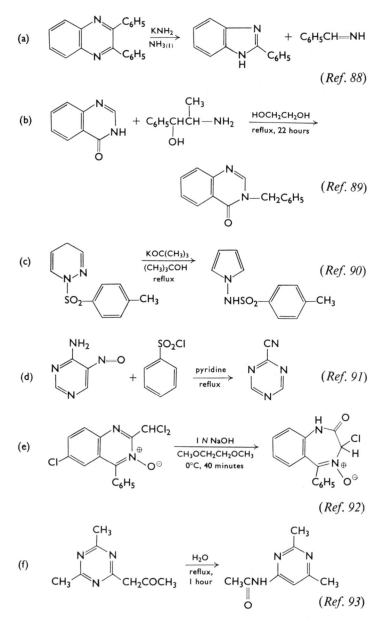

(a)   (Ref. 88)

(b)   (Ref. 89)

(c)   (Ref. 90)

(d)   (Ref. 91)

(e)   (Ref. 92)

(f)   (Ref. 93)

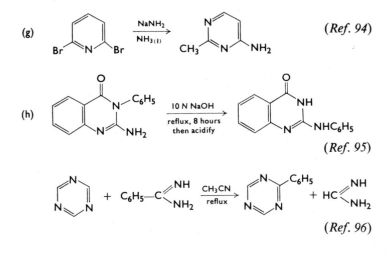

(g)   (*Ref. 94*)

(h)   (*Ref. 95*)

(*Ref. 96*)

References and Notes

(1) A. Albert, *Heterocyclic Chemistry*, Athlone Press, London, 1959.

(2) G. F. Duffin, *Adv. Heterocyclic Chem.*, **3**, 19 (1964).

(3) (a) G. F. Duffin and J. D. Kendall, *J. Chem. Soc.*, **1959**, 3789; (b) see, however: M. S. Bale, A. B. Simmonds, and W. F. Trager, *ibid.*, (*B*), **1966**, 867.

(4) R. H. Mizzoni and P. E. Spoerri, *J. Am. Chem. Soc.*, **76**, 2201 (1954).

(5) S. F. Mason, *J. Chem. Soc.*, **1958**, 674.

(6) F. H. S. Curd and D. N. Richardson, *ibid.*, **1955**, 1853.

(7) F. H. S. Curd and D. N. Richardson, *ibid.*, **1955**, 1850.

(8) G. W. H. Cheeseman, *ibid.*, **1960**, 242.

(9) T. J. Curphey, *J. Am. Chem. Soc.*, **87**, 2063 (1965).

(10) (a) E. M. Smolin and L. Rapoport, *s-Triazines and Derivatives*, in A. Weissberger (ed.), *The Chemistry of Heterocyclic Compounds*, Interscience, New York, 1959; (b) E. J. Modest, in R. C. Elderfield (ed.), *Heterocyclic Compounds*, Vol. 7, Wiley, New York, 1961, Chapter 7.

(11) T. L. Jacobs, in R. C. Elderfield (ed.), *ibid.*, Vol. 6, 1957, Chapter 4.

(12) J. Levisailles, *Bull. Soc. Chim. France*, **1957**, 1004.

(13) J. Levisailles, *ibid.*, **1957**, 1009.

(14) (a) R. C. Elderfield and S. L. Wythe, in R. C. Elderfield (ed.), *Heterocyclic Compounds*, Vol. 6, Wiley, New York, 1957, Chapter 6; (b) J. C. E. Simpson, *Condensed Pyridazine and Pyrazine Rings*, in A. Weissberger (ed.), *The Chemistry of Heterocyclic Compounds*, Interscience, New York, 1955; (c) W. R. Vaughan, *Chem. Rev.*, **43**, 447 (1948).

(15) G. O. Schenk, *Chem. Ber.*, **80**, 289 (1947).

(16) W. R. Vaughan and S. L. Baird, Jr., *J. Am. Chem. Soc.*, **68**, 1314 (1946).

(17) C. T. Redemann and C. E. Redemann, *Org. Syn.*, **Coll. Vol. 3**, 656 (1955).

(18) (a) D. J. Brown, *The Pyrimidines*, in A. Weissberger (ed.), *The Chemistry of Heterocyclic Compounds*, Interscience, New York, 1962; (b) G. W. Kenner and A. Todd, in R. C. Elderfield (ed.), *Heterocyclic Compounds*, Vol. 6, Wiley, New York, 1957, Chapter 7.

(19) R. R. Hunt, J. F. W. McOmie, and E. R. Sayer, *J. Chem. Soc.*, **1959**, 525.

(20) D. M. Burness, *J. Org. Chem.*, **21**, 97 (1956).

(21) J. B. Dickey and A. R. Gray, *Org. Syn.*, **Coll. Vol. 2**, 60 (1943).

(22) A. Bendich, J. F. Tinker, and G. B. Brown, *J. Am. Chem. Soc.*, **70**, 3109 (1948).

(23) H. Bredereck, R. Gompper, and G. Morlock, *Chem. Ber.*, **90**, 942 (1957).

(24) R. C. Smith and S. B. Binkley, *J. Org. Chem.*, **24**, 249 (1959).

(25) B. Staskun and H. Stephen, *J. Chem. Soc.*, **1956**, 4708.

(26) W. H. Davies and H. A. Piggott, *ibid.*, **1945**, 347.

(27) (a) T. A. Williamson, in R. C. Elderfield (ed.), *Heterocyclic Compounds*, Vol. 6, Wiley, New York, 1957, Chapter 8; (b) W. L. F. Amarego, *Adv. Heterocyclic Chem.*, **1**, 253 (1963).

(28) K. Schofield, *J. Chem. Soc.*, **1952**, 1927.

(29) J. F. Meyer and E. C. Wagner, *J. Org. Chem.*, **8**, 239 (1943).

(30) Y. T. Pratt, in R. C. Elderfield (ed.), *Heterocyclic Compounds*, Vol. 6, Wiley, New York, 1957, Chapter 9.

(31) G. H. Alt and W. S. Knowles, *J. Org. Chem.*, **25**, 2047 (1960).

(32) For a survey of such reactions, see G. R. Ramage and J. K. Landquist in E. H. Rodd (ed.), *Chemistry of Carbon Compounds*, Vol. 4B, Elsevier, New York, 1959, Chapter XV.

(33) Y. T. Pratt, and R. C. Elderfield (ed.), *Heterocyclic Compounds*, Vol. 6, Wiley, New York, 1957, Chapter 10.

(34) R. G. Jones and K. C. McLaughlin, *Org. Syn.*, **Coll. Vol. 4**, 824 (1963).

(35) K. Schofield and J. C. E. Simpson, *J. Chem. Soc.*, **1948**, 1170.

(36) J. C. E. Simpson, *ibid.*, **1946**, 673.

(37) K. Schofield and T. Swain, *ibid.*, **1949**, 2393.

(38) A. H. Cook and D. G. Jones, *ibid.*, **1941**, 278.

(39) C. Grundmann, G. Weisse, and S. Seide, *Ann. Chem.*, **577**, 77 (1952).

(40) C. Grundmann and A. Kreutzberger, *J. Am. Chem. Soc.*, **76**, 5646 (1954).

(41) A. Albert, D. J. Brown, and H. C. S. Wood, *J. Chem. Soc.*, **1954**, 3832.

(42) J. Baddiley, B. Lythgoe, D. McNeil, and A. R. Todd, *ibid.*, **1943**, 383.

(43) T. Itai and S. Natsume, *Chem. Pharm. Bull.* (*Tokyo*), **11**, 83 (1963).

(44) M. J. S. Dewar and P. M. Maitlis, *J. Chem. Soc.*, **1957**, 2521.

(45) M. J. S. Dewar and P. M. Maitlis, *ibid.*, **1957**, 2518.

(46) R. C. Elderfield, T. A. Williamson, W. J. Gensler, and C. B. Kremer, *J. Org. Chem.*, **12**, 405 (1947).

(47) K. Schofield, *Chem. Ind.* (*London*), **1957**, 1068.

(48) J. H. Ridd, *Physical Methods in Heterocyclic Chem.*, **1**, 109 (1963).

(49) I. Suzuki, T. Nakashima, and T. Itai, *Chem. Pharm. Bull.* (*Tokyo*), **11**, 268 (1963).

(50) I. Suzuki, T. Nakashima, and N. Nagasawa, *ibid.*, **14**, 816 (1966).

(51) N. B. Chapman and D. Q. Russell-Hill, *J. Chem. Soc.*, **1956**, 1563.

(52) R. G. Shepherd and J. L. Fedrick, *Adv. Heterocyclic Chem.*, **4**, 145 (1965).

(53) K. Eichenberger, R. Rometsch, and J. Druey, *Helv. Chim. Acta*, **39**, 1755 (1956).

(54) M. Claesen and H. Vanderhaeghe, *Bull. Soc. Chim. Belges*, **68**, 220 (1959); F. G. Wolf, R. H. Beutel, and J. R. Stevens, *J. Am. Chem. Soc.*, **70**, 4264 (1948).

(55) J. Druey, *Angew. Chem.*, **70**, 5 (1958).

(56) H. Yamanaka, *Chem. Pharm. Bull.* (*Tokyo*), **7**, 297 (1959).

(57) T. Nakagome, *Yakugaku Zasshi*, **82**, 244, 253 (1962).

(58) S. Sako and T. Itai, *Chem. Pharm. Bull.* (*Tokyo*), **14**, 269 (1966).

(59) S. Sako, *ibid.*, **10**, 957 (1962).

(60) W. K. Detweiler and E. D. Amstutz, *J. Am. Chem. Soc.*, **73**, 5451 (1951).

(61) R. L. Letsinger and R. Lasco, *J. Org. Chem.*, **21**, 812 (1956).

(62) A. Albert, W. L. F. Amarego, and E. Spinner, *J. Chem. Soc.*, **1961**, 2689.

(63) T. Higashino, *Chem. Pharm. Bull.* (*Tokyo*), **9**, 635 (1961).

(64) A. Holland, *Chem. Ind.* (*London*), **1954**, 786.

(65) M. Ogata, *Chem. Pharm. Bull.* (*Tokyo*), **11**, 1517 (1963).

(66) M. R. Kamal and R. Levine, *J. Org. Chem.*, **27**, 1355 (1962).

(67) A. R. Katritzky and J. M. Lagowski, *Adv. Heterocyclic Chem.*, **1**, 329 (1963).

(68) G. Palamidessi and L. Bernardi, *J. Org. Chem.*, **29**, 2491 (1964).

(69) T. Higashino, *Yakugaku Zasshi*, **79**, 699 (1959); *Chem. Abstr.*, **53**, 21997 (1959).

(70) J. K. Landquist, *J. Chem. Soc.*, **1953**, 2816.

(71) C. F. Koelsch and W. H. Gumprecht, *J. Org. Chem.*, **23**, 1603 (1958).

(72) L. H. Sternbach, S. Kaiser, and E. Reeder, *J. Am. Chem. Soc.*, **92**, 475 (1960).

(73) L. H. Sternbach and E. Reeder, *J. Org. Chem.*, **26**, 1111 (1961).

(74) J. L. Wong, M. S. Brown, and H. Rapoport, *ibid.*, **30**, 2398 (1965).

(75) H. Feuer and R. Harmetz, *ibid.*, **24**, 1501 (1959).

(76) G. Palamidessi and L. Bernardi, *ibid.*, **29**, 2491 (1964).

(77) D. J. Fry, J. D. Kendall, and A. J. Morgan, *J. Chem. Soc.*, **1960**, 5062.

(78) T. Higashino, *Chem. Pharm. Bull.* (*Tokyo*), **10**, 1048 (1962).

(79) W. W. Paudler and J. M. Barton, *J. Org. Chem.*, **31**, 1720 (1966).

(80) A. Giner-Sorolla, I. Zimmerman, and A. Bendich, *J. Am. Chem. Soc.*, **81**, 2515 (1959).

(81) H. Igeta, *Chem. Pharm. Bull.* (*Tokyo*), **11**, 1472 (1963).

(82) A. G. Beaman and R. K. Robins, *J. Med. Pharm. Chem.*, **5**, 1067 (1962).

(83) E. Hayashi and C. Iijima, *Yakugaku Zasshi*, **86**, 571 (1966).

(84) M. R. Kamal, M. Neubert, and R. Levine, *J. Org. Chem.*, **27**, 1363 (1962).

(85) W. Ziegenbein and W. Franke, *Angew. Chem.*, **71**, 628 (1959).

(86) H. J. Minnemeyer, P. B. Clarke, and H. Tieckelmann, *J. Org. Chem.*, **31**, 406 (1966).

(87) T. Itai and S. Kamiya, *Chem. Pharm. Bull.* (*Tokyo*), **11**, 1059 (1963).

(88) E. C. Taylor and A. McKillop, *J. Org. Chem.*, **30**, 2858 (1965).

(89) L. J. Chinn, *J. Heterocyclic Chem.*, **2**, 475 (1965).

(90) D. M. Lemal and T. W. Rave, *Tetrahedron*, **19**, 1119 (1963).

(91) E. C. Taylor and C. W. Jefford, *J. Am. Chem. Soc.*, **84**, 3744 (1962).

(92) A. Stempel, E. Reeder, and L. Sternbach, *J. Org. Chem.*, **30**, 4267 (1965).

(93) D. R. Osborne, W. T. Wieder, and R. Levine, *J. Heterocyclic Chem.*, **1**, 145 (1964).

(94) H. J. den Hertog, H. C. van der Plas, M. J. Pieterse, and J. W. Streef, *Rec. Trav. Chim.*, **84**, 1569 (1965).

(95) R. J. Grant and M. W. Partridge, *J. Chem. Soc.*, **1960**, 3540.

(96) F. C. Schaefer and G. A. Peters, *J. Am. Chem. Soc.*, **81**, 1470 (1959).

10

■ FURTHER PRINCIPLES OF
HETEROCYCLIC SYNTHESIS

DURING THE PAST DECADE OR TWO, several general synthetic routes to heterocyclic molecules have been investigated in some detail and, because of their utility and inherently broad scope, are of considerable importance. In this chapter, an outline of three such synthetic principles has been undertaken; they are (a) cycloaddition reactions, (b) valence-bond isomerizations, and (c) enamine condensations.

Cycloaddition Reactions

Cycloaddition reactions may be regarded collectively as processes by which two reactants combine to form a stable cyclic molecule, and during which no small fragments are eliminated and σ-bonds are formed but not broken.[1] The most commonly encountered of the cycloaddition reactions are those in which two new σ-bonds are formed, and this reaction type will therefore be discussed in some

detail. These cycloadditions may be conveniently classified according to the number of ring atoms contributed by each of the reactants
and the ultimate size of the ring formed. For example, the cycloaddition which occurs when carbethoxynitrene [1] is generated in the

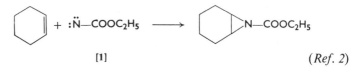

[1]   (*Ref. 2*)

presence of cyclohexene (see p. 6) is a $2+1 \rightarrow 3$ process. It is
obvious that for reactions of this type to be possible, the component
which contributes one ring atom must be endowed with electrophilic
and nucleophilic characteristics, as is the case with nitrenes. The
cycloaddition concept is employed in cases where the new σ-bonds
are formed simultaneously as well as in those examples where bond
formation is not synchronous.

The $2+2 \rightarrow 4$ group encompasses a rapidly expanding class of
reactions of which several new examples are being uncovered yearly.
To this class belong numerous syntheses of heterocyclic four-
membered rings, some of which were discussed earlier in Chapter 3.
The formation of β-lactams upon the addition of ketenes to imines
(see p. 85, 86) or upon the addition of chlorosulfonyl isocyanate to
alkenes (see p. 86) are exemplary.

Although cycloadditions of the $3+1 \rightarrow 4$ variety are not yet known,
the $3+2 \rightarrow 5$ classification contains an extremely large number of
examples, the major portion of which have been investigated by
Huisgen and his co-workers.[3] This group of transformations is
more commonly referred to as 1,3-*dipolar reactions*. In this reaction,
a neutral five-membered ring is formed by the combination of a

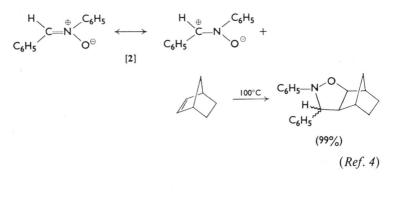

[2]

(99%)

(*Ref. 4*)

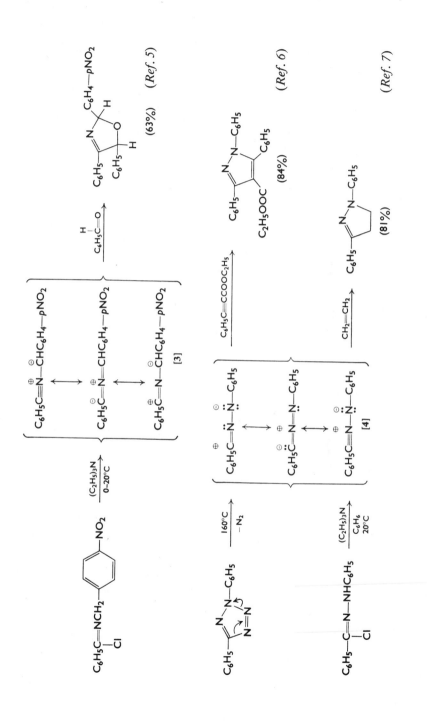

dipolar species (generally a triatomic 1,3-dipole such as [2]) and an unsaturated acceptor or dipolarophile.

Because a large variety of structural types qualify as suitable 1,3-dipoles, the $3+2 \rightarrow 5$ cycloaddition is subject to extensive variation, and lends itself to the synthesis of many five-membered heterocyclic systems. Some representative 1,3-dipoles are the nitrile ylides (e.g., [3]), the nitrile imines (e.g., [4]), nitrile oxides (see p. 189), diazo-

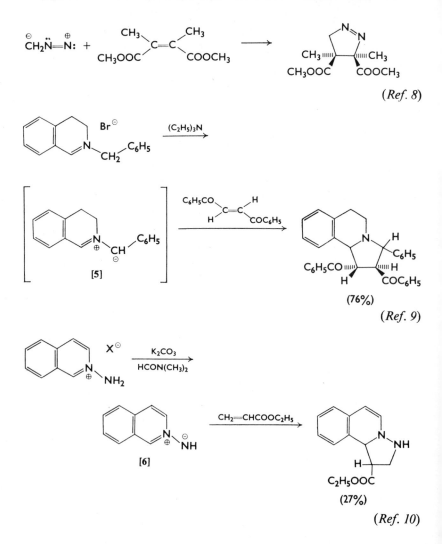

(*Ref. 8*)

(76%)

(*Ref. 9*)

(27%)

(*Ref. 10*)

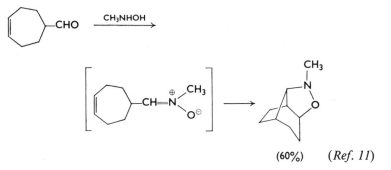

(60%)   (*Ref. 11*)

alkanes, azides, azomethine ylides (e.g., [5]), azomethine imines (e.g., [6]), and nitrones. The range of synthetic possibilities is enormous.

A study of the relative rates of addition of diphenyl nitrilimine to various olefinic substrates has been made (Table 10–1)[12]; the observed differences in reactivity demonstrate the profound rate-enhancing

TABLE 10–I   ▪

Relative Rates of Addition of [4] *in Refluxing Benzene*[1]

Compound	Relative rate	Compound	Relative rate
Dimethyl fumarate	283	*trans*-Stilbene	0.274
Ethyl acrylate	48.2	I-Heptene	0.146
Methyl methacrylate	16.6	I,I-Diphenylethylene	0.112
Norbornene	3.12	*cis*-Stilbene	0.011
Ethyl crotonate	1.00	Cyclohexene	0.011

effect of conjugation with one or more electron-withdrawing substituents, and suggest that partial charges are produced at the dipolarophile in the transition state. The 1,3-dipolar additions are generally stereospecific and therefore fully charged centers cannot be implicated in the reaction mechanism. Rather the rate differences probably reflect the fact that both σ-bonds have not formed to an equal degree in the activated complex.

Olefins which lack symmetry can add 1,3-dipoles in either of two directions. Frequently, a single orientation is observed. In the absence of overriding electronic effects, it appears that steric effects dictate the orientation.

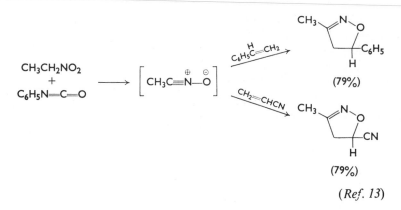

(*Ref. 13*)

The best known examples of the $4+1 \rightarrow 5$ cycloaddition reaction center about the 1,4-addition of sulfur dioxide to 1,3-dienes. The reaction is subject to steric rate retardation as evidenced by the fact that *trans,trans*-2,4-hexadiene reacts rapidly and stereospecifically with sulfur dioxide while *cis,trans*-2,4-hexadiene adds SO_2 much more slowly; the higher temperatures required in the latter case cause a certain amount of isomerization.[14]

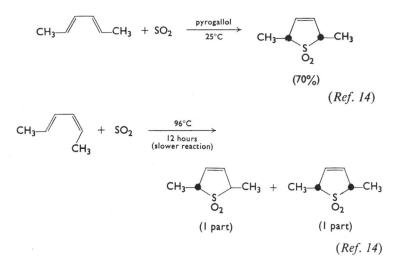

The Diels-Alder reaction, or diene synthesis, consists in the addition of a dienophile possessing a double or triple bond to the 1,4-positions of a conjugated diene with the formation of a six-membered ring.

This general process may be considered a reaction of the $4+2 \rightarrow 6$ type. When dienophiles possessing a hetero atom as a segment of the unsaturated linkage are utilized, a variety of heterocyclic compounds result.[15] Some of the hetero atomic dienophiles which are capable of taking part in the reaction are the carbonyl, imino, nitroso, and nitrile groups, and alkyl azodicarboxylates. Several examples are illustrated below.

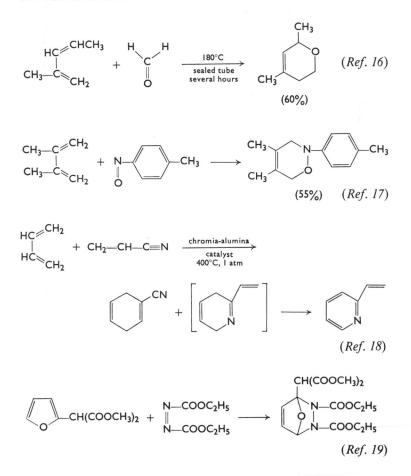

(*Ref. 16*)

(*Ref. 17*)

(*Ref. 18*)

(*Ref. 19*)

The diene component may also be the source of the hetero atom; α,β-unsaturated carbonyl compounds have been found to be of the greatest utility.

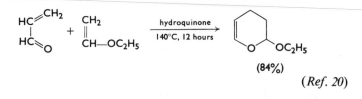

(84%)

(*Ref. 20*)

Methods of cycloaddition which would lead to heterocyclic compounds of ring sizes larger than six members have not yet been devised. At this point in time, these larger rings are available to a limited extent through synthetic approaches involving valence-bond isomerization.

Valence-Bond Isomerizations

In recent years, a sizeable number of isomerization reactions have been reported which differ mechanistically from the majority of the common molecular rearrangements. These reactions characteristically proceed without migration of atoms or groups of atoms and consist solely in a reorganization of the σ- and π-electrons within the framework of the molecule. Such reorganizations, which are accompanied by corresponding changes in atomic distances and bond angles, are known as valence-bond isomerizations. Although such isomerizations were first uncovered and more thoroughly studied in all-carbon systems, application of this concept to heterocyclic molecules has led to its utilization as a valuable synthetic tool.

For example, lithium chloride-catalyzed pyrolysis of [7] gives a mixture of *trans*-[8] and *cis*-divinylethylene oxides [9] of which the *cis*-isomer is unstable and rearranges to its valence isomer [10]. The

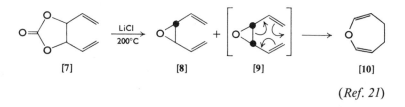

[7]   [8]   [9]   [10]

(*Ref. 21*)

stability of [8] resides in the fact that both ends of the vinyl substituents do not lie in the same plane. The essential prerequisite for valence-bond isomerization, namely that the atoms involved in the bond reorganization lie roughly in a parallel plane, is necessary in order that very small adjustments of angles, bond distances, and electron distribution can be achieved. The same phenomenon has been observed in a nitrogen case.

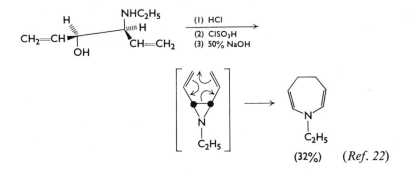

The valence-bond approach has been especially successful in the synthesis of derivatives of azepine (e.g., [12]) and oxepin (e.g., [13]).

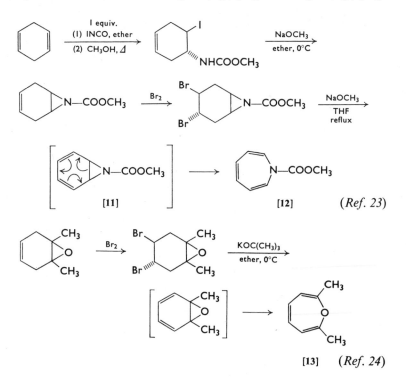

Generation of carbethoxynitrene, either by the photodecomposition[25] or thermolysis[26] of ethyl azidoformate or by the α-elimination of p-nitrobenzenesulfonic acid from its N-hydroxy-urethane ester with triethylamine (each method leads to nitrene[14])[27] in the presence of benzene has been found to proceed via an intermediate such as [11] to afford N-carbethoxyazepine.

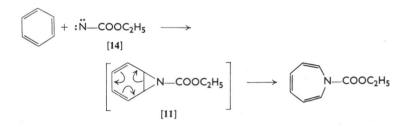

[14]

[11]

Additional applications of the valence-bond isomerization concept to heterocyclic synthesis are outlined in the following equations.

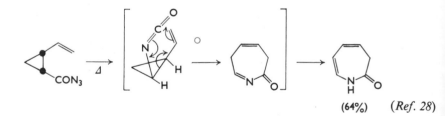

(64%)   (Ref. 28)

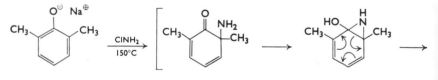

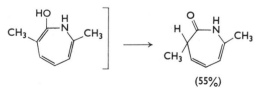

(55%)   (Ref. 29)

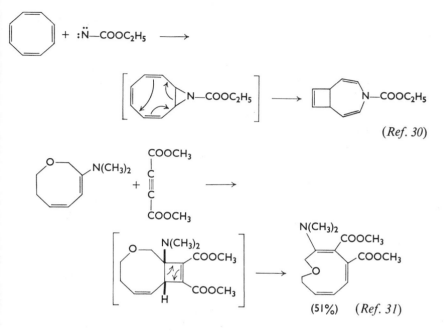

(*Ref. 30*)

(51%)   (*Ref. 31*)

Enamine Condensations

Investigation of the chemical properties of enamines, or α,β-unsaturated amines, has contributed most significantly to the progress of synthetic organic chemistry in recent years.[32, 33] The reactions of enamines are varied and numerous, and a number of these chemical phenomena have found application in the synthesis of heterocyclic compounds.

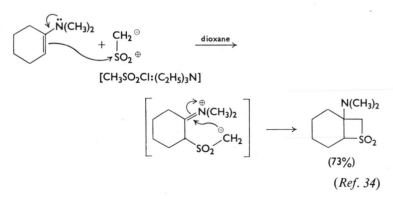

(73%)

(*Ref. 34*)

In this regard, the most general type of reaction perhaps is the cycloaddition of enamines with reactive addends to yield four-, five- or six-membered heterocycles. The four-membered rings result from interaction of the enamine with a diatomic moiety suitably

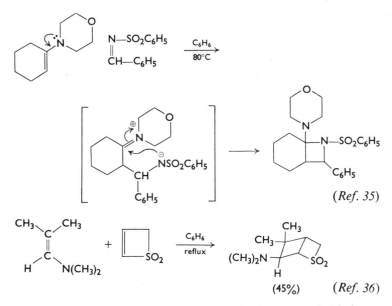

(Ref. 35)

(45%)　　(Ref. 36)

constructed so that stabilized zwitterions (which are probable intermediates) will form readily and subsequently cyclize to produce the strained ring. The five-membered heterocycles result from interaction of the enamines with 1,3-dipoles of the type discussed earlier

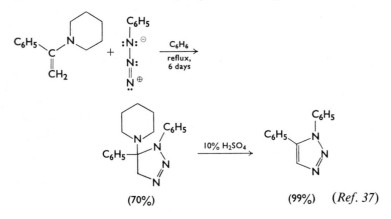

(70%)　　　　(99%)　(Ref. 37)

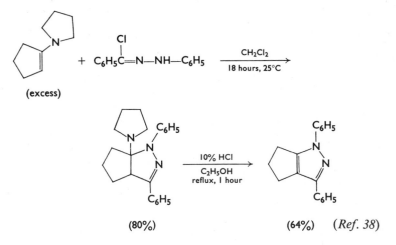

(80%) (64%) (*Ref. 38*)

in this chapter. The facility with which the enamine nitrogen can be removed from the primary adducts, in these latter examples, upon acid treatment further extends the utility of the synthetic sequence.

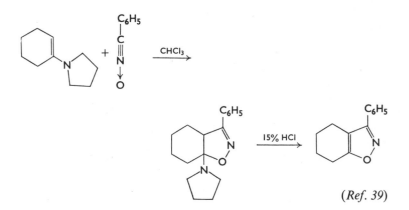

(*Ref. 39*)

The condensation of enamines with a variety of selected carbonyl-containing compounds leads to the formation of six-membered heterocycles. For example, the interaction of enamines with di-ketene [15] proceeds to give chromones; with excess ketene, α-pyrones result. When enamines are admixed with salicyladehydes in an inert solvent such as benzene or hexane, cyclic O,N-ketals such as [16] are

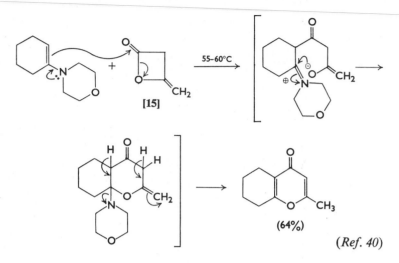

(Ref. 40)

formed in nearly quantitative yield; these substances undergo oxidation with the loss of the enamine nitrogen to produce tetrahydroxanthones. This reaction sequence represents a general synthetic approach to oxygen-containing heterocycles.[42] The following examples illustrate additional enamine reactions in which six-membered rings are formed. The common interlocking aspect of all

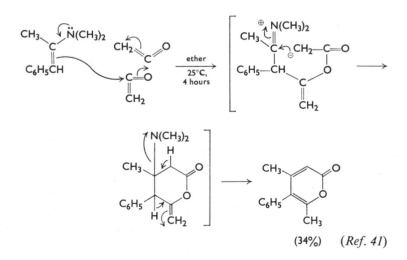

(34%)   (Ref. 41)

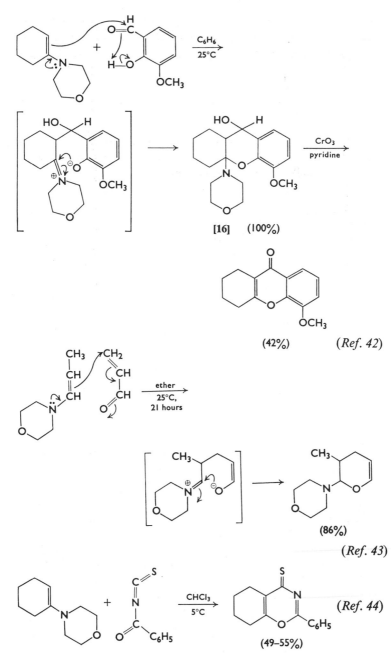

[16]   (100%)

(42%)   (*Ref. 42*)

(86%)

(*Ref. 43*)

(49–55%)   (*Ref. 44*)

the enamine reactions herein presented resides in the fact that the
β-carbon atom of the enamine system is highly nucleophilic and the
driving force for C-alkylation at that site predominates over a variety

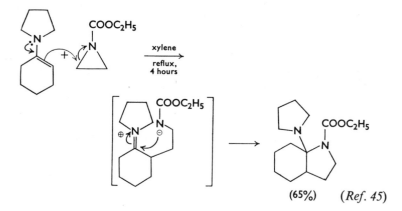

of alternative possible reactions.   This characteristic enamine-type
activation has been used to advantage in the opening of strained rings
such as N-carbalkoxy aziridines as shown below.

(65%)   (*Ref. 45*)

A number of two-step heterocyclic syntheses have been devised
which utilize enamines as starting materials.   For example, the
reaction of a secondary enamine such as [17] with benzoyl isothiocyanate leads to the formation of a benzoylthiocarbamoyl derivative
which can be readily cyclized in refluxing tetrahydrofuran solution.
The products of condensation of enamines with isothiocyanates such
as [18] and [19] can be treated with hydrazines or amidines to produce
aminopyrazoles and aminopyrimidines respectively.

When primary enamines are allowed to react with acetylenic
aldehydes or ketones, pyridine ring formation frequently ensues.

The intramolecular acylation of enamines has found utility in the
preparation of polycyclic nitrogen compounds.   An example is
provided below.   Again, here the powerful nucleophilic character of
the β-carbon atom of the enamine system provides the driving force
necessary to achieve reaction.

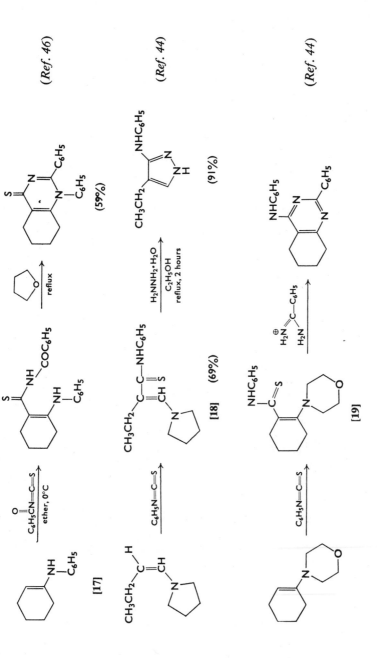

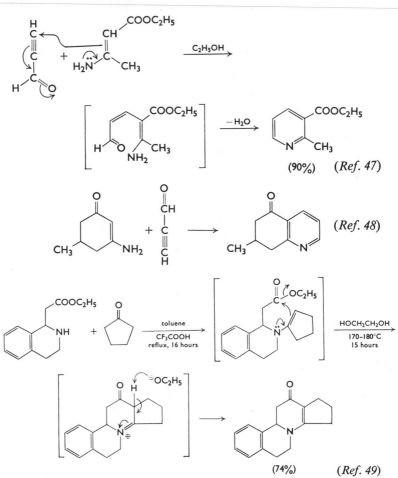

(90%)   (Ref. 47)

(Ref. 48)

(74%)   (Ref. 49)

Exercises

1. Predict the major product of the following reactions:

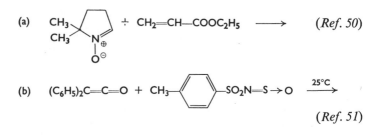

(a) CH_3 ... $+ CH_2=CH-COOC_2H_5 \longrightarrow$ (Ref. 50)

(b) $(C_6H_5)_2C=C=O + CH_3-$⟨ ⟩$-SO_2N=S \rightarrow O$ $\xrightarrow{25°C}$

(Ref. 51)

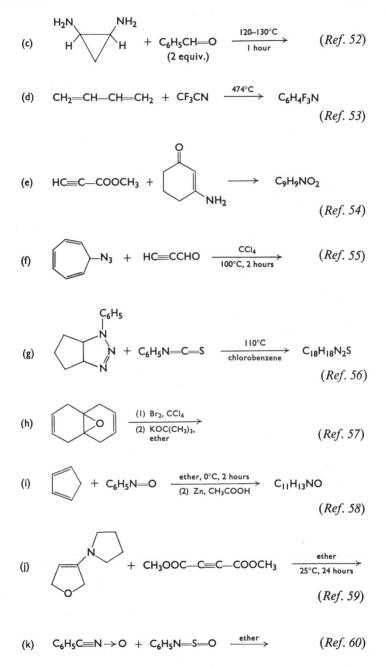

(c) H₂N, NH₂ cyclopropane + C₆H₅CH=O (2 equiv.) →(120-130°C, 1 hour) (Ref. 52)

(d) CH₂=CH—CH=CH₂ + CF₃CN →(474°C) C₆H₄F₃N (Ref. 53)

(e) HC≡C—COOCH₃ + [cyclohexenone-NH₂] → C₉H₉NO₂ (Ref. 54)

(f) [cycloheptatrienyl]—N₃ + HC≡CCHO →(CCl₄, 100°C, 2 hours) (Ref. 55)

(g) [bicyclic triazole with C₆H₅] + C₆H₅N=C=S →(110°C, chlorobenzene) C₁₈H₁₈N₂S (Ref. 56)

(h) [bicyclic epoxide] →(1) Br₂, CCl₄ (2) KOC(CH₃)₃, ether (Ref. 57)

(i) [cyclopentadiene] + C₆H₅N=O →(ether, 0°C, 2 hours) (2) Zn, CH₃COOH → C₁₁H₁₃NO (Ref. 58)

(j) [dihydrofuran-pyrrolidine] + CH₃OOC—C≡C—COOCH₃ →(ether, 25°C, 24 hours) (Ref. 59)

(k) C₆H₅C≡N→O + C₆H₅N=S=O →(ether) (Ref. 60)

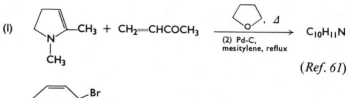

(l) [structure] —CH_3 + CH_2=$CHCOCH_3$ $\xrightarrow[\text{(2) Pd-C, mesitylene, reflux}]{\text{[THF], } \Delta}$ $C_{10}H_{11}N$

(*Ref. 61*)

(m) [cyclooctatetraene-Br structure] + $C_6H_5N_3$ $\xrightarrow[\text{ether-}C_6H_6]{\text{KOC(CH}_3)_3}$ (*Ref. 62*)

(n) $CH_3NCH_2(CH_2)_3CH$=CH_2 / OH $\xrightarrow[\text{25°C, 5 hours}]{\text{HgO, }C_2H_5OH}$ (*Ref. 63*)

(o) $(C_2H_5)_2NCH$=$CHCH_2CH_3$ + $ClCH$=$CHCC_6H_5$ (2 equivalents) $\xrightarrow{\text{ether}}$ $C_{17}H_{23}NO$

(*Ref. 64*)

(p) C_6H_5C≡N→O + C_6H_5CN $\xrightarrow{\text{ether}}$ (*Ref. 65*)

(q) CH_2=$CH(CH_2)_3CH$ + CH_3NHOH $\xrightarrow[\text{ether reflux, 8 hours}]{\text{MgSO}_4}$ (*Ref. 63*)

2. Suggest a reasonable mechanism for each of the following transformations:

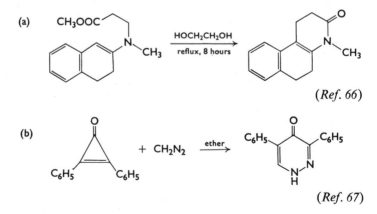

(a) [structure with CH_3OOC and N—CH_3] $\xrightarrow[\text{reflux, 8 hours}]{\text{HOCH}_2CH_2OH}$ [tricyclic product]

(*Ref. 66*)

(b) [diphenylcyclopropenone structure] + CH_2N_2 $\xrightarrow{\text{ether}}$ [pyridazinone structure]

(*Ref. 67*)

References and Notes

(1) R. Huisgen, R. Grashey, and J. Sauer, in S. Patai (ed.), *The Chemistry of Alkenes*, Interscience, New York, 1964, Chapter 11.

(2) Reference 18 of Chapter 1.

(3) R. Huisgen, *Angew. Chem. Intern. Ed.*, **2**, 565, 633 (1963).

(4) G. Wallbillich, Diploma Thesis, University of Munich, Germany, 1959.

(5) R. Huisgen, H. Stangl, H. J. Sturm, and H. Wagenhofer, *Angew. Chem.*, **74**, 31 (1962).

(6) R. Huisgen, M. Seidel, G. Wallbillich, and H. Knupfer, *Tetrahedron*, **17**, 3 (1962).

(7) V. Weberndörfer, Diploma Thesis, University of Munich, Germany, 1961.

(8) K. von Auwers and E. Cauer, *Ann. Chem.*, **470**, 284 (1929); K. von Auwers and F. König, *ibid.*, **496**, 27, 252 (1932).

(9) R. Huisgen, R. Grashey, and E. Steingruber, *Tetrahedron Letters*, No. **22**, 1441 (1963).

(10) R. Huisgen, R. Grashey, and R. Krischke, *ibid.*, 387 (1962).

(11) N. A. LeBel and J. J. Whang, *J. Am. Chem. Soc.*, **81**, 6334 (1959); N. A. LeBel, G. M. J. Slusarczuk, and L. A. Spurlock, *ibid.*, **84**, 4360 (1962).

(12) Each dipolar compound apparently calls for a new specific sequence of dipolarophilic activity, and the sequence developed in Table 10–1 is applicable only to [4].

(13) T. Mukaiyama and T. Hoshino, *J. Am. Chem. Soc.*, **82**, 5339 (1960); G. B. Bachman and L. E. Strom, *J. Org. Chem.*, **28**, 1150 (1963).

(14) S. D. McGregor and D. M. Lemal, *J. Am. Chem. Soc.*, **88**, 2858 (1966).

(15) S. B. Needleman and M. C. Changkno, *Chem. Rev.*, **62**, 405 (1962).

(16) T. L. Gresham and T. R. Steadman, *J. Am. Chem. Soc.*, **71**, 737 (1949).

(17) O. Wichterle and V. Gregor, *Collection Czech. Chem. Commun.*, **24**, 1158 (1959).

(18) G. J. Janz and N. E. Duncan, *J. Am. Chem. Soc.*, **75**, 5389 (1953).

(19) P. Baranger and J. Levisailles, *Bull. Soc. Chim. France*, **1957**, 704.

(20) R. I. Longley, Jr., and W. S. Emerson, *J. Am. Chem. Soc.*, **72**, 3079 (1950); see also C. W. Smith, D. G. Norton, and S. A. Ballard, *ibid.*, **73**, 5273 (1951), and related papers.

(21) R. A. Braun, *J. Org. Chem.*, **28**, 1383 (1963); E. L. Stogryn, M. H. Gianni, and A. J. Passannante, *ibid.*, **29**, 1275 (1964).

(22) E. L. Stogryn and S. J. Brois, *ibid.*, **30**, 88 (1965).

(23) L. A. Paquette and D. E. Kuhla, *Tetrahedron Letters*, No. **45**, 4517 (1967).

(24) E. Vogel, R. Schubart, and W. A. Böll, *Angew. Chem. Intern. Ed.*, **3**, 510 (1964).

(25) K. Hafner and C. König, *Angew. Chem.*, **74**, 89 (1962); *Tetrahedron Letters*, No. **26**, 1733 (1964).

(26) R. J. Cotter and W. F. Beach, *J. Org. Chem.*, **29**, 751 (1964).

(27) W. Lwowski and T. J. Maricich, *J. Am. Chem. Soc.*, **87**, 3630 (1965).

(28) E. Vogel, R. Erb, G. Lenz, and A. A. Bothner-By, *Ann. Chem.*, **682**, 1 (1965).

(29) L. A. Paquette, *J. Am. Chem. Soc.*, **84**, 4987 (1962); **85**, 3288 (1963).

(30) S. Masamune and N. T. Castellucci, *Angew. Chem.*, **76**, 569 (1964).

(31) L. A. Paquette and R. W. Begland, *J. Am. Chem. Soc.*, **88**, 4685 (1966).

(32) J. Szmuszkovicz, in R. A. Raphael, E. C. Taylor, and H. Wynberg (eds.), *Advances in Organic Chemistry, Methods and Results*, **4**, 1 (1963).

(33) G. Stork, A. Brizzolara, H. Landesman, J. Szmuszkovicz, and R. Terrell, *J. Am. Chem. Soc.*, **85**, 207 (1963).

(34) L. A. Paquette, *J. Org. Chem.*, **30**, 629 (1965).

(35) F. Effenberger and R. Maier, *Angew. Chem.*, **78**, 389 (1966).

(36) L. A. Paquette and M. Rosen, The Ohio State University, Columbus, Ohio, unpublished observations.

(37) M. E. Munk and Y. K. Kim, *J. Am. Chem. Soc.*, **86**, 2213 (1964).

(38) M. E. Kuehne, S. J. Weaver, and P. Franz, *J. Org. Chem.* **29**, 1582 (1964).

(39) B. Bianchetti, D. Pocar, and P. Dalla Croce, *Gazz. Chim. Ital.*, **93**, 1726 (1963).

(40) S. Hünig, E. Benzing, and K. Hübner, *Chem. Ber.*, **94**, 486 (1961).

(41) G. A. Berchtold, G. R. Harvey, and G. E. Wilson, Jr., *J. Org. Chem.*, **30**, 2642 (1965).

(42) L. A. Paquette and H. Stucki, *ibid.*, **31**, 1232 (1966).

(43) G. Opitz and I. Löschmann, *Angew. Chem.*, **72**, 523 (1960); G. Opitz and H. Holtmann, *Ann. Chem.*, **684**, 79 (1965).

(44) S. Hünig and K. Hübner, *Chem. Ber.*, **95**, 937 (1962).

(45) J. E. Dolfini and J. D. Simpson, *J. Am. Chem. Soc.*, **87**, 4381 (1965).

(46) R. W. J. Carney, J. Wojtkunski, and G. de Stevens, *J. Org. Chem.*, **29**, 2887 (1964).

(47) F. Bohlmann and D. Rahtz, *Chem. Ber.*, **90**, 2265 (1957).

(48) F. Bohlmann and R. Mayer-Mader, *Tetrahedron Letters*, No. **3**, 171 (1965).

(49) W. Sobotka, W. N. Beverung, G. G. Munoz, J. C. Sircar, and A. I. Meyers, *J. Org. Chem.*, **30**, 3667 (1965).

(50) G. R. Delpierre and M. Lamchen, *Proc. Chem. Soc.*, **1960**, 386.

(51) H. Beecken and F. Korte, *Tetrahedron*, **18**, 1527 (1962).
(52) H. A. Staab and F. Vögtle, *Chem. Ber.*, **98**, 2701 (1965).
(53) J. M. S. Jarvie, W. E. Fitzgerald, and G. J. Janz, *J. Am. Chem. Soc.*, **78**, 978 (1956); G. J. Janz and M. A. DeCrescente, *J. Org. Chem.*, **23**, 765 (1958).
(54) M. A. T. Sluyter, U. K. Pandit, W. N. Speckamp, and H. O. Huisman, *Tetrahedron Letters*, No. **1**, 87 (1966).
(55) J. J. Looker, *J. Org. Chem.*, **30**, 638 (1965).
(56) J. E. Baldwin, G. V. Kaiser, and J. A. Romersberger, *J. Am. Chem. Soc.*, **87**, 4114 (1965).
(57) E. Vogel, M. Biskup, W. Pretzer, and W. A. Böll, *Angew. Chem.*, **76**, 785 (1964); F. Sondheimer and A. Shani, *J. Am. Chem. Soc.*, **86**, 3168 (1964).
(58) G. Kresze and G. Schulz, *Tetrahedron*, **12**, 7 (1961).
(59) K. C. Brannock, R. D. Burpitt, V. W. Goodlett, and J. G. Thweatt, *J. Org. Chem.*, **28**, 1464 (1963).
(60) R. Rajagopalan and H. U. Daenicker, *Angew. Chem.*, **75**, 91 (1963).
(61) R. E. Ireland, *Chem. Ind.* (*London*), **1958**, 979.
(62) A. Krebs, *Angew. Chem.*, **77**, 966 (1965).
(63) N. A. LeBel, M. E. Post, and J. J. Whang, *J. Am. Chem. Soc.*, **86**, 3759 (1965).
(64) W. Schroth and G. Fischer, *Angew. Chem.*, **75**, 574 (1963).
(65) R. Huisgen, W. Mack, and E. Anneser, *Tetrahedron Letters*, No. **17**, 587 (1961).
(66) Z. Horii, C. Iwata, Y. Tamura, N. A. Nelson, and G. H. Rasmusson, *J. Org. Chem.*, **29**, 2768 (1964).
(67) P. T. Izzo and A. S. Kende, *Chem. Ind.* (*London*), **1964**, 839.

11

■ SOME HETEROCYCLES OF
BIOLOGICAL INTEREST

A LARGE NUMBER OF THE HETEROCYCLIC ring systems which have been discussed in earlier chapters derive special interest and importance from the fact that certain of their derivatives are produced in nature by various animals or plants. Frequently, the naturally occurring heterocycles are structurally complex. A limited number of such substances will be described briefly in this chapter. The intended goal is to generate in the reader an awareness of the types of compounds which are of biological or physiological importance and an appreciation of the elegant synthetic capability of living systems.

β-Lactam Antibiotics

The term antibiotic refers to substances, produced in general by microorganisms, which are antagonistic to the growth of other microbes. The penicillins and the cephalosporins represent two examples of powerful antibiotics; both contain the reactive β-lactam unit. There is a variety of penicillins, all of which consist of the basic structure [1] with various substituent R groups. The different

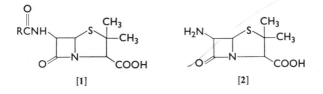

[1]   [2]

penicillins have been produced by various strains of *Penicillin* molds.[1] A very important recent development is the discovery that 6-aminopenicillanic acid [2], the penicillin molecule without the acyl side chain, can be isolated from cultures of *Penicillium chrysogenum* under certain conditions.[2] The availability of [2] has led to the synthesis of penicillin analogs not otherwise available or obtained under difficult conditions merely by performing a careful acylation of the amino function. The first total synthesis of a penicillin, penicillin V [6], was achieved in 1957.[3] Condensation of D-penicillamine [4] with aldehyde [3] yielded a thiazolidine, from which the phthaloyl group was removed by hydrazinolysis. Acylation with phenoxyacetyl chloride and cleavage of the *tert*-butyl ester with anhydrous hydrogen chloride gave the penicilloic acid [5]. Cyclization of [5] under very mild conditions through the agency of dicyclohexylcarbodiimide (which upon hydration during the reaction leads to the inert N,N-dicyclohexylurea) yielded the desired penicillin [6].

The cephalosporins, which substances have been isolated as products of the metabolism of various cephalosporium molds, generally display an antibacterial spectrum which is markedly different from that of many penicillins. The total synthesis of the first member of this group, cephalosporin C [7], was reported in 1966.[4] Especially noteworthy points in this elegant synthesis are the careful steps utilized in the construction of the β-lactam moiety, the unprecedented utilization of important blocking groups, and the novel rearrangement of a thiazolidine to a six-membered ring heterocycle.

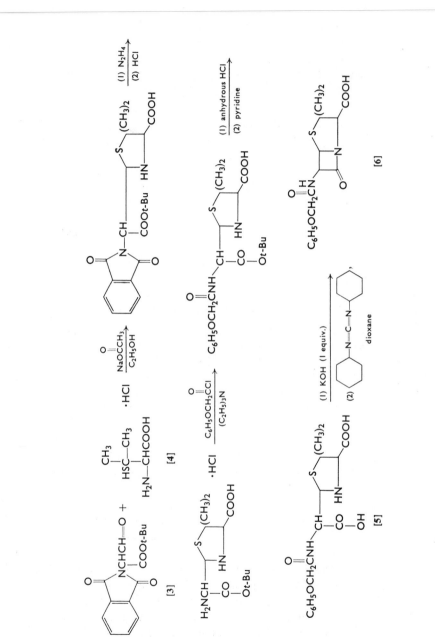

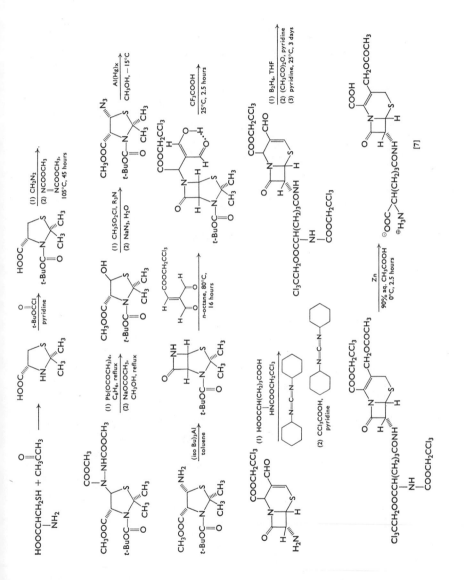

[7]

Porphyrins

The compound formed by linking four pyrrole rings together through their 2- and 5-positions by four methine bridges has been termed porphin [8].   Substituted porphins are known as porphyrins.

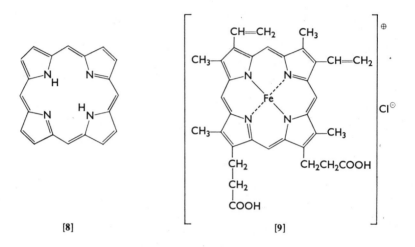

[8]   [9]

Although porphin itself is not found in nature, many porphyrins are known to be widely distributed and certain of these, such as hemin, chlorophyll, and vitamin B_{12}, play very essential roles in life processes.   The porphyrins may occur in the free form or as complexes with metallic cations.

Because many substitution patterns of [8] are possible, many porphyrins are named in a manner indicative of the nature of the substituents.[5, 6]   For example, etioporphyrins are derivatives of [8] which possess four methyl and four ethyl groups.   Four isomeric etioporphyrins are known and are generally referred to as I, II, III, and IV.   Other examples of this nomenclature are provided in Table 11–1.

Hemoglobin is a constituent of the red corpuscles of the blood and serves as the oxygen carrier from the lungs to the body tissue.   Acid treatment of hemoglobin serves to hydrolyze away from the protein (globin) the prosthetic group called heme and the complex ferric salt, hemin [9], is obtained.   The structure of hemin, a protoporphyrin, was firmly established by its synthesis in 1929.[7]

TABLE II-I ■

Nomenclature of Porphyrins

Name	Substitution pattern
Etioporphyrins	Four methyl and four ethyl groups
Protoporphyrins	Four methyl, two vinyl, and two propionic acid groups
Coproporphyrins	Four methyl and four propionic acid groups
Mesoporphyrins	Four methyl, two ethyl, and two propionic acid groups
Hematoporphyrins	Four methyl, two α-hydroxyethyl, and two propionic acid groups
Uroporphyrins	Four propionic acid and four acetic acid groups

Chlorophyll, the agent responsible for the green color in plants, has been shown to be a porphyrin in which the four pyrrole nitrogens are complexed to magnesium. The key role played by chlorophyll in nature is to function as the substance which, during photosynthesis, triggers the transformation of light energy into chemical energy.[8] Although the mechanism of the photosynthetic conversion of carbon dioxide and water to carbohydrates and oxygen has not yet been completely elucidated, the primary reaction is known to be photo-excitation of the chlorophyll, followed by utilization of the derived energy to oxidize water and reduce carbon dioxide. Two chloro-phylls, which differ little in structure and which are termed *a* [12] and *b* [13], are known; the former [12] is believed to be chiefly responsible for photosynthesis. A total synthesis was achieved in 1960.[9]

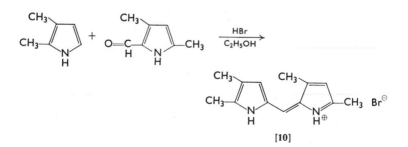

[10]

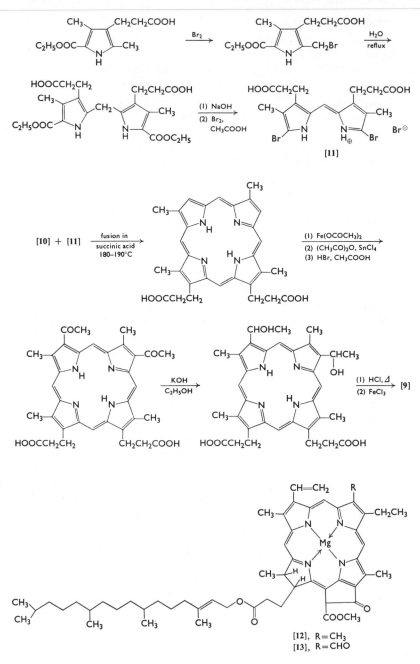

[10] + [11]

[12], R=CH₃
[13], R=CHO

Vitamin B_{12}, also known as cyanocobalamine or the antipernicious anemia factor, is constructed of a partially reduced porphyrin ring lacking one methine bridge [14]. The nitrogen atoms are complexed to cobalt which in turn is covalently bonded to a cyano group. The structure of vitamin B_{12} was elucidated through extensive chemical degradation and by crystallographic studies.

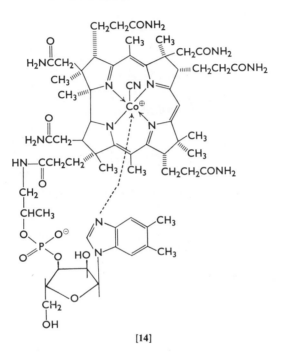

[14]

Natural Products Related to Indole

Many natural products are known in which the indole ring constitutes an important segment of the structural framework. For example, L-tryptophan [15], found in many proteins, is known to be

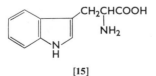

[15]

an essential amino acid.   Because [15] is not synthesized by mammals, it must be provided in the diet.

An important metabolic transformation product of tryptophan is serotonin [16] which is believed to play a significant role in the mental

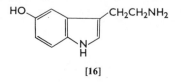

[16]

processes of man.   When the concentration levels of serotonin in the brain are markedly altered, either chemically or physically, severe mental disturbance in the patient is observed.

The greatest variety of indole derivatives are of vegetable origin and form part of a broad class of nitrogen-containing plant products known as alkaloids.   The large number of indole alkaloids are generally classified into five subgroups, namely, (a) the Simple alkaloids, (b) the Harmala alkaloids, (c) the Ergot alkaloids, (d) the Yohimbe alkaloids, and (e) the Strychnos alkaloids.

The Simple alkaloids are closely related structurally to tryptophan. Some examples include serotonin [16] which is very widely distributed in nature, bufotenine [17] which occurs in fungi (mushrooms) and in the seeds of tropical shrubs, and gramine [18] which is produced in sprouting barley.

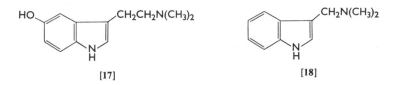

[17]   [18]

Derivatives of indole which have in common the β-carboline ring system are known as the Harmala alkaloids.   Examples are harman [19] and harmine [20].   Such molecules are believed to be synthesized

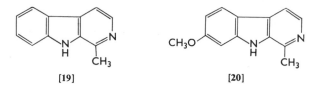

[19]   [20]

in the plant by condensation of decarboxylated tryptophan or its hydroxylated equivalent with acetaldehyde and subsequent oxidation.

The six Ergot alkaloids, all products of a fungus which grows as a parasite on cereals, especially rye, are amides of lysergic acid [21]. The most well-known derivative of [21] is its diethylamide (not naturally occurring), termed LSD, which is known to cause hallucinations in human subjects presumably because it acts to alter the serotonin levels in the brain. The total synthesis of lysergic acid, which was achieved in 1956, is described below.[10]

The partially reduced β-carboline ring system is a structural characteristic of the Yohimbe class of alkaloids, the most important member of which is reserpine [22]. This alkaloid has assumed

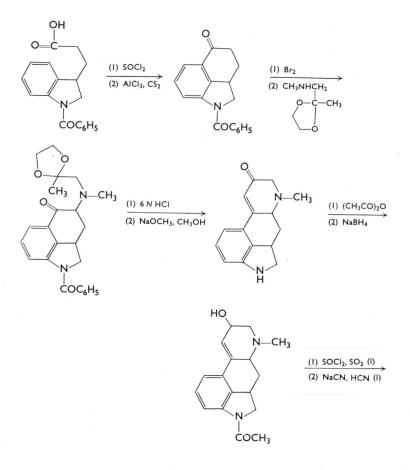

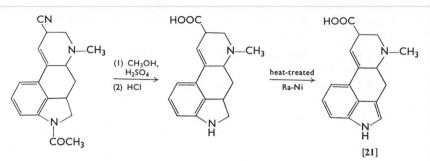

[21]

considerable clinical importance in the treatment of hypertension (high blood pressure) and nervous and mental disorders. The tranquilizing capability of reserpine is believed to arise by virtue of a reduction of serotonin levels in the brain. The total synthesis of this complex molecule has been effected in the manner summarized.[11]

The Strychnos alkaloids, the most outstanding examples of which are strychnine [23a] and brucine [23b], are structurally very complex.

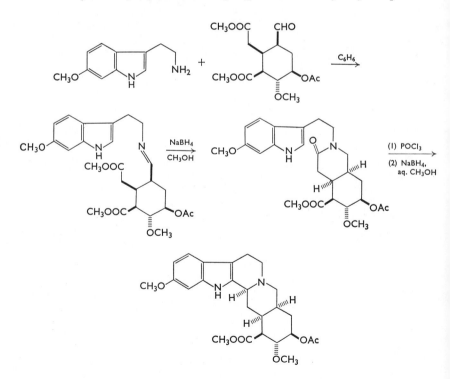

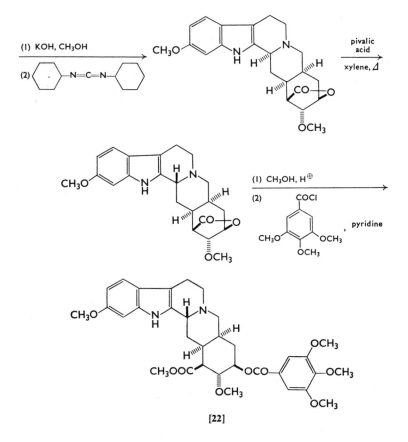

[22]

Investigations which spanned over more than a century led to the final structural assignment. The high point of this vast quantity of research was attained in the total synthesis of the strychnine molecule.[12]

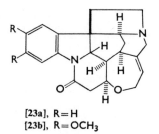

[23a], R=H
[23b], R=OCH₃

Pyridine-Derived Compounds: the Pyridine Coenzymes

Nicotine, a major alkaloidal constituent of tobacco leaves, is known to possess structure [24]. Studies on the biosynthesis of nicotine by the tobacco plant have indicated that the pyridine ring is formed from nicotinic acid [25],[13] which may arise from tryptophan, and that the pyrrolidine ring is derived from ornithine.[14] Nicotinic acid or

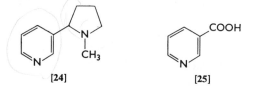

[24]   [25]

niacin [25] and its amide (niacinamide) are of biological importance as specific curative agents for human pellagra and because of their presence in the pyridine nucleotides (see below). Although nicotine was first synthesized by Pictet in 1895,[15] the structure [24] was not considered fully confirmed until Spath's synthesis (less vigorous conditions throughout precluded rearrangements) in 1935.[16]

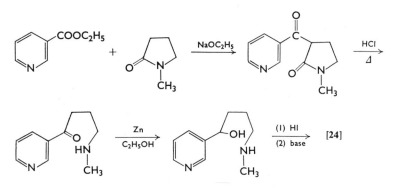

Pyridoxine [26], pyridoxamine [27], and pyridoxal [28] constitute the three members of the vitamin B_6 group, all of which occur in combined form in nature. Whereas [26] and [27] occur principally as the corresponding 3-phosphates, the structure of the combined form of [28] has not been established with certainty. All three are interchangeable in their biological activity for mammals and birds, but not for microorganisms.

The most significant role of these substrates in biological systems centers around transamination and decarboxylation reactions. Thus

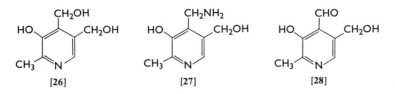

[26] [27] [28]

α-amino acids react with pyridoxal phosphate (as the prosthetic group of enzymes such as amino acid transaminases and decarboxylases) to produce α-keto acids and pyridoxamine phosphate or carbon dioxide and a primary amine, respectively. Pyridoxamine phosphate usually reacts subsequently with a different α-keto acid to produce a new amino acid.

Several syntheses of pyridoxine have been devised. Because the synthetic schemes employed illustrate certain principles of heterocyclic synthesis discussed in earlier chapters, three methods of approach are outlined in Charts 11–1, 11–2, and 11–3.

CHART 11–1 ▪

Harris-Folkers Pyridoxine Synthesis[17]

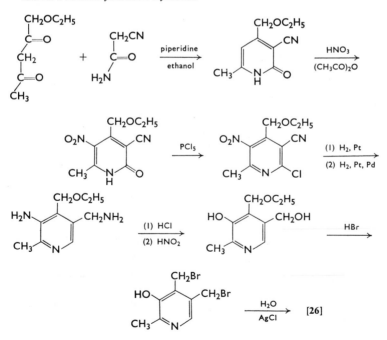

CHART II-2 ▪

Wibaut Pyridoxine Synthesis[18]

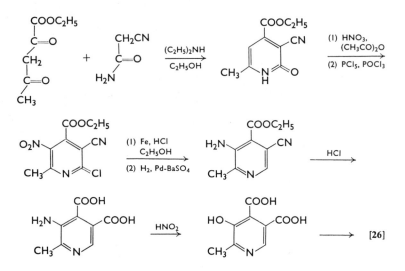

CHART II-3 ▪

Kuhn Pyridoxine Synthesis[19]

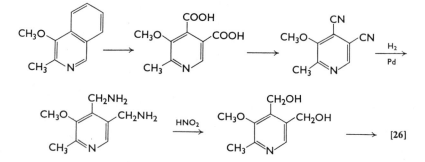

Enzymes, that is, proteins which function as catalysts of chemical reactions in living systems, have been found to react with their substrates in many cases only when a second component termed a coenzyme is also present. In general, coenzymes are relatively simple organic molecules which complex reversibly with enzymes and, in fact, frequently function with more than one enzyme to catalyze reactions of widely differing substrates. One of the more important coenzymes is nicotinamide adenine dinucleotide (NAD) [29]. In conjunction with various enzymes, NAD participates with great

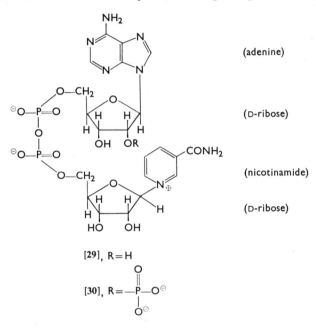

(adenine)

(D-ribose)

(nicotinamide)

(D-ribose)

[29], R = H

[30], R = —P—O⁻

facility in electron transfer reactions, the nicotinamide portion of NAD being reduced to the 1,4-dihydropyridine counterpart (NADH) and the substrate undergoing oxidation. In the reduced form, the coenzyme donates electrons enzymatically to electron acceptors.

To illustrate the action of NAD, let us consider the oxidation of ethanol. In conjunction with the enzyme alcohol dehydrogenase

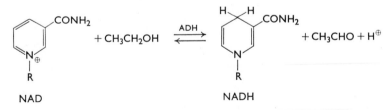

(ADH), ethanol is converted to acetaldehyde and the reduced coenzyme NADH is formed concomitantly. High stereospecificity is operative in the hydride transfer; thus, with CH_3CHDOH only the

D or the H atom is directly transferred to NAD depending on which enantiomer of the labeled ethanol is employed.[20] The participation of hydrogen atoms from the medium was thereby excluded.

NAD occurs in all living cells, and its role is that of a universal electron carrier. Because the NAD molecule contains nicotinamide as one of its structural components, it becomes apparent why this B vitamin must be present in the diet of man and higher animals. As already stated, its absence causes the dietary deficiency disease known as pellagra. It becomes apparent, then, that pellagra results from a deficiency of certain enzymic reactions involving electron transfers to and from NAD caused by the absence in the cell of sufficient nicotinamide to permit construction of NAD molecules.

A second, very closely related, coenzyme is nicotinamide adenine dinucleotide phosphate (NADP) [30]; its structure is identical with that of NAD, with the exception of an additional phosphate group at C-2 of the D-ribose unit adjacent to the adenine ring. Despite the fact that NAD and NADP are quite similar in structure and are found in nearly all living cells, the coenzymes are not interchangeable and have quite different biochemical functions.[21] Whereas NAD is specific for those dehydrogenase enzymes which are normally involved in the transfer of ring electrons to oxygen during the respiration process, NADP is specific for dehydrogenases which function primarily in the realm of biosynthetic reductions, for example, in the formation of glucose during the dark phase of photosynthesis.[21]

Thiamine and Natural Products Related to Pyrimidine and Purine

Thiamine, or vitamin B_1, [31] is an essential component of the human diet; in its absence, the human vitamin deficiency known as beriberi develops. Fortunately, rich sources of thiamine are available in eggs and yeast and the vitamin occurs widely in plants. In the form of its pyrophosphate [32] (also known as cocarboxylase), the substance participates in several biological reactions among which may be cited the enzymic conversion of pyruvate to acetyl coenzyme A and to acetoin, the enzymic decarboxylation of α-ketoglutarate and of other keto acids, and the transformations catalyzed by yeast carboxylase and transketolase. The important chemical role played by thiamine and its pyrophosphate appears to be dependent upon the facility with which the proton at C-2 of the thiazolium ring can undergo ionization to produce the derived heterocyclic ylid which

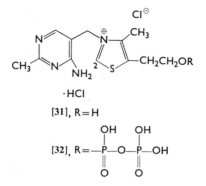

[31], R=H

[32], R=

appears to be the reactive species (see p. 205 for a further discussion of such ylids).

A variety of syntheses of thiamine have been reported; the following scheme[22] is exemplary.

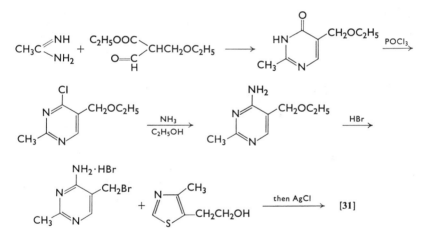

Three pyrimidine derivatives are of considerable biological importance because of their relation to the nucleic acids (see below).

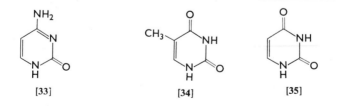

[33]   [34]   [35]

These are cytosine [33], thymine [34], and uracil [35]. The purine ring system [36], a result of the fusion of pyrimidine and imidazole nuclei, likewise derives its importance because certain of its derivatives, specifically adenine [37] and guanine [38], are building blocks of RNA and DNA. The free base [36] is potentially tautomeric in the

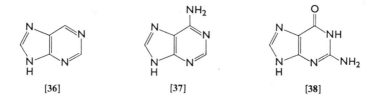

five-membered ring and can give rise to derivatives of both tautomeric forms.

Several other purine-based natural products constitute the alkaloidal components of several plants. To illustrate, hypoxanthine [39] and xanthine [40] occur in tea, whereas caffeine [41] and theophylline [42] are constituents of tea leaves, and theobromine [43] is found in the cocoa bean.

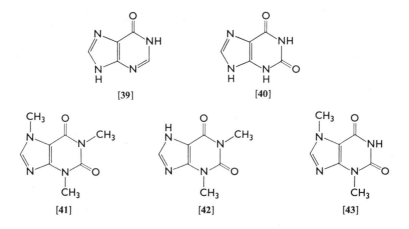

Attachment of either of two sugar residues, D-ribose or D-2-deoxyribose, at N-3 of pyrimidines [33]–[35] or at N-9 of purines [37] and [38] results in the formation of glycosides known as nucleosides. Although nucleosides exist as such in the living cell, they can also be obtained by hydrolysis of nucleotides (the phosphoric acid esters of

nucleosides) and nucleic acids. For example, hydrolysis of ribonucleic acid (RNA) produces cytidine [**44**], uridine [**45**], adenosine
[**46**], and guanosine [**47**]. From inspection of the structures, it can

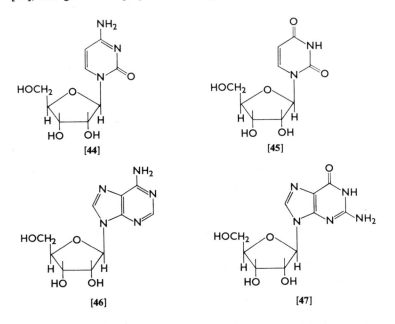

be recognized that these materials are β-D-ribofuranosides of cytosine,
uracil, adenine, and guanine, respectively. Hydrolysis of deoxyribonucleic acid (DNA) affords predominantly deoxycytidine [**48**],

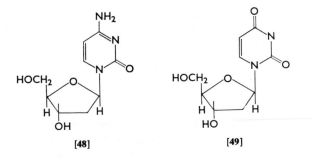

thymidine [**49**], and the corresponding purine nucleosides, deoxy-
adenosine and deoxyguanosine, all of which are β-D-(2'-deoxy)-
ribofuranosides.

The phosphoric acid esters of nucleosides are termed nucleotides. Many coenzymes are nucleotides and nucleotides are found in all living cells; significantly, they play an essential role in many biological reactions. In this regard, adenosine triphosphate (ATP) [52] functions as the key transfer agent linking phosphate donors and phosphate acceptors. Interestingly, ATP as it occurs in the cell

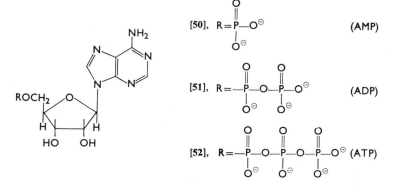

(pH 7.0) is completely ionized and bears four negative charges in the polyphosphate moiety, a fact which is an important feature of the activity of the ATP molecule. The entire function of the ATP-ADP system is to act as an intermediate linking system between phosphate compounds with high phosphate group transfer potential, and compounds lacking in this capacity, by making possible the transfer of phosphate groups from one to the other.

Nucleic acids are molecules which are composed of chains of mononucleotide units adapted for the storage and transcription of biological information. Two main types of nucleic acid have been recognized, deoxyribonucleic acid (DNA) and ribonucleic acid (RNA). DNA is present in the cell nucleus and is the master informational molecule of the cell. Thus, it functions to supply information for the exact reproduction of each type of cell, including the synthesis of the necessary enzymes and additional DNA molecules as required. Since the DNA of a particular organism is not likely to be identical to that of any other, it becomes impossible to be specific about the exact structure of DNA. In general terms, however, DNA molecules are long and chainlike, and occur as a double-stranded helix of two such molecules about 20 Å apart. The molecular weights generally lie in the 100,000,000 to 4,000,000,000 range.

The links of the long chain are four different recurring mononucleotides which constitute the elements of the coding system and are termed the backbone of DNA. The sequential structure of the strands of DNA are shown in Chart 11–4. The backbone is uniform

CHART 11–4 ▪

The Structure of DNA and RNA Polynucleotides

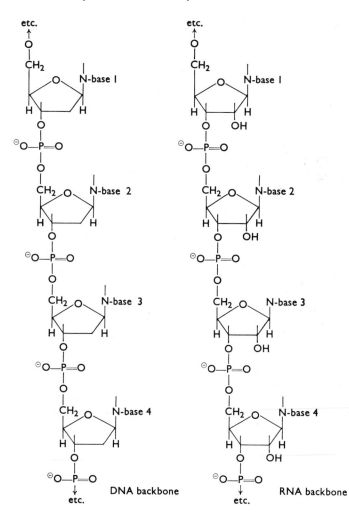

throughout the enormous length of the molecule, and each 2-deoxyribose unit is linked to one of the four bases, adenine, guanine, cytosine, and thymine. DNA molecules generally contain a minimum of 3,000,000 mononucleotide units. The genetic message for which the DNA molecule is responsible is imparted by the particular sequence of the four basic mononucleotides (abbreviated A, T, G, and C) along the entire length of the DNA chain, for example, A-T-G-T-C-A-A-G-C-T-; an enormous variety of sequences is obviously possible. In the cell nucleus, the DNA normally exists as a double-helical structure, both strands of which are mutually intertwined in such a way that the molecules are held together by hydrogen bonding between uniquely fitting pairs of bases. This arrangement causes them to fit each other uniquely in a rigid, rodlike structure.[23, 24]

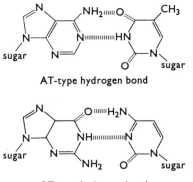

AT-type hydrogen bond

GT-type hydrogen bond

Ribonucleic acids (RNA) are polymeric molecules similar in molecular structure to DNA (see Chart 11-4), except that D-ribofuranose is the carbohydrate component and uracil has replaced thymine. The base sequence along the RNA backbone is not yet known for any naturally occurring RNA; furthermore, in contrast to DNA, RNA consists of a single polynucleotide chain which appears to lack regularity in the sequential makeup of its purine and pyrimidine bases. Presently, the ribonucleic acids are classified into three groups depending upon the functions which each fulfill. Ribosomal RNA, the major RNA component of the cell, is believed to play a structural role, although this is not known with certainty. Messenger RNA is the template for protein synthesis and is considered the synthetically active part of polyribosomes. The determination of which protein is synthesized is accomplished by virtue of the specific arrangement of bases (A, C, U, and G) along the polynucleotide chain. Soluble RNA functions as the amino acid-adaptor molecule which guides the amino acids into their specific places on the protein synthesizing template. Further discussion of the details of the biological function of both DNA and RNA is available in a number of reference sources.[21, 24]

A widely distributed nucleotide derivative that plays a decisive role in many metabolic processes is called coenzyme A [53]. Its im-

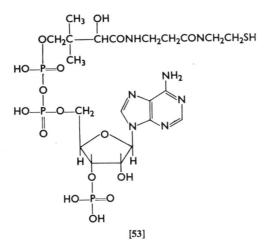

[53]

portance is derived in part from its involvement in transacetylation reactions, fatty acid oxidation, α-ketoacid decarboxylation, and similar important biological syntheses and degradations. Structurally, coenzyme A consists of an adenine-3′,5′-diphosphate fragment linked to phosphopantetheine, a derivative of the vitamin pantothenic acid, by means of a pyrophosphate bond. The synthesis of [53] was reported in 1959.[25]

The Pteridine Ring System: Folic Acid and Riboflavin

The pteridine ring system [54] which may be regarded as a pyrimido-pyrazine is also widely distributed in nature. A variety of pteridine syntheses are available, but frequently a diaminopyrimidine is condensed with a two-carbon fragment to construct the pyrazine

[54]

portion of the molecule.[26]   Leucopterin [55] and xanthopterin [56] have been prepared by such a synthetic route.   Several insect pigments are derivatives of pteridine.

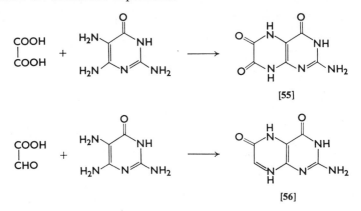

[55]

[56]

The important growth factor folic acid (vitamin B_{10}) [57] is constructed of a pteridine ring, *p*-aminobenzoic acid, and glutamic acid.

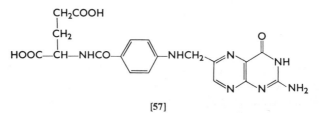

[57]

Another vitamin of the B group, B_2 or riboflavin [58], also contains the basic pteridine ring system.   The substance occurs in many

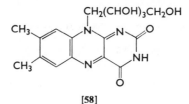

[58]

cellular systems; it is the yellow pigment of egg yolk. The structure of riboflavin was confirmed by synthesis.[27]

Flavin adenine dinucleotide (FAD) [59], the prosthetic group of a number of important flavoprotein enzymes which function as oxidation-reduction catalysts in biological systems, contains the riboflavin-5′-phosphate moiety.

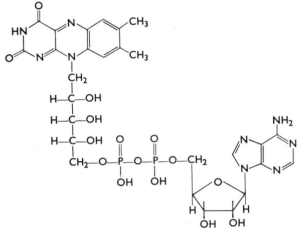

[59]

References and Notes

(1) M. C. Rebstock in A. Burger (ed.), *Medicinal Chemistry*, 2nd ed., Interscience, New York, Chapter 44.

(2) F. R. Batchelor, F. P. Doyle, J. H. C. Naylor, and G. N. Robinson, *Nature*, **183**, 258 (1959).

(3) J. C. Sheehan and K. R. Henery-Logan, *J. Am. Chem. Soc.*, **79**, 1262 (1957); *ibid.*, **81**, 3089 (1959).

(4) R. B. Woodward, K. Heusler, J. Gosteli, P. Naegeli, W. Oppolzer, R. Ramage, S. Ranganathan, and H. Vorbrüggen, *ibid.*, **88**, 852 (1966).

(5) C. Rimington, *Endeavour*, **14**, 126 (1955).

(6) J. M. Orten, *Rec. Chem. Progr.* (*Kresge-Hooker Sci. Lib.*), **17**, 259 (1956).

(7) H. Fischer and K. Zeile, *Ann. Chem.*, **468**, 98 (1929).

(8) For a general review of photosynthesis, see J. S. Fruton and S. Simmonds, *General Biochemistry*, 2nd ed., Wiley, New York, Chapter 22.

(9) R. B. Woodward, *Angew. Chem.*, **72**, 651 (1960); R. B. Woodward, W. A. Ayer, J. M. Beaton, F. Bickelhaupt, R. Bonnett, P. Buchschacher,

G. L. Closs, H. Dutler, J. Hannah, F. P. Hauck, S. Ito, A. Langemann, E. LeGoff, W. Leimgruber, W. Lwowski, J. Sauer, Z. Valenta, and H. Vohy, *J. Am. Chem. Soc.*, **82**, 3800 (1960).

(10) E. C. Kornfeld, E. J. Fornefeld, G. B. Kline, M. J. Mann, D. E. Morrison, R. G. Jones, and R. B. Woodward, *ibid.*, **78**, 3087 (1956).

(11) R. B. Woodward, F. E. Bader, H. Bickel, A. J. Frey, and R. W. Kierstead, *Tetrahedron*, **2**, 1 (1958).

(12) R. B. Woodward, M. P. Cava, W. D. Ollis, A. Hunger, H. V. Daeniker, and K. Schenker, *ibid.*, **19**, 247 (1963).

(13) R. F. Dawson, D. R. Christman, R. C. Anderson, M. L. Solt, A. F. D'Adamo and U. Weiss, *J. Am. Chem. Soc.*, **78**, 2645 (1956); E. Leete *ibid.*, **78**, 3520 (1956).

(14) L. J. Dewey, R. U. Byerrum, and C. D. Ball, *Biochim. Biophys. Acta*, **18**, 141 (1955).

(15) A. Pictet and P. Crepieux, *Chem. Ber.*, **28**, 1904 (1895); **31**, 2018 (1898); A. Pictet and A. Rotschy, *ibid.*, **37**, 1225 (1904).

(16) E. Späth and F. Kuffner, *ibid.*, **68**, 494 (1935).

(17) S. A. Harris and K. Folkers, *J. Am. Chem. Soc.*, **61**, 1245 (1939), see also E. Testa and A. Vecchi, *Gazz. Chim. Ital.*, **87**, 467 (1957).

(18) H. M. Wuest, J. A. Bigot, T. J. deBoer, B. vander Wal, and J. P. Wibaut, *Rec. Trav. Chim.*, **78**, 226 (1959).

(19) R. Kuhn, K. Westphal, G. Wendt, and O. Westphal, *Naturwissenschaften*, **27**, 469 (1939).

(20) B. Vennesland and F. H. Westheimer in W. D. McElroy and B. Glass (eds.), *The Mechanism of Enzyme Action*, Johns Hopkins Press, Baltimore, 1954.

(21) A. L. Lehninger, *Bioenergetics*, W. A. Benjamin, Inc., New York, 1965.

(22) R. R. Williams and J. K. Cline, *J. Am. Chem. Soc.*, **58**, 1504 (1936); J. K. Cline, R. R. Williams, and J. Finkelstein, *ibid.*, **59**, 1052 (1937).

(23) For an extensive discussion of this topic, see ref. 21.

(24) V. M. Ingram, *The Biosynthesis of Macromolecules*, W. A. Benjamin, Inc., New York, 1965.

(25) J. G. Moffatt and H. G. Khorana, *J. Am. Chem. Soc.*, **81**, 1265 (1959).

(26) D. J. Brown, *J. Appl. Chem.*, **2**, 239 (1952).

(27) P. Karrer, B. Becker, F. Benz, P. Frei, H. Salomon, and K. Schöpp, *Helv. Chim. Acta*, **18**, 1435 (1935); W. A. Wisansky and S. Ansbacher, *J. Am. Chem. Soc.*, **63**, 2532 (1941).

APPENDIX

■ NOMENCLATURE OF HETEROCYCLIC

COMPOUNDS

IN AN EFFORT to systematize the naming of heterocyclic compounds, a system has been devised which permits the accurate and intelligible conveyance of information from one chemist to another.[1]

For monocyclic rings, the proper nomenclature is derived by combining an appropriate prefix and suffix to a given stem according to the following rules.

(a) The size of the ring is denoted by the appropriate stem selected from Table A–1.

(b) The nature of the hetero atom is denoted by such prefixes as oxa, thia, or aza for oxygen, sulfur, or nitrogen, respectively. Multiplicity of the same hetero atom is designated by an additional prefix such as di- or tri-, etc. When two or more different hetero atoms are present, they are named in the order $O > S > N$, for example, oxaza and thiaza.

TABLE A–I ■

Stems and Suffix for Three- to Ten-Membered Monocyclic Heterocycles

Stem and suffix

Ring size	Stem	Rings containing nitrogen		Rings without nitrogen	
		Unsaturated[a]	Saturated	Unsaturated[a]	Saturated
3	·ir-	-irine	-iridine	-irene	-irane
4	-et-	-ete	-etidine	-ete	-etane
5	-ol-	-ole	-olidine	-ole	-olane
6	-in-	-ine	[b]	-in	-ane
7	-ep-	-epine	[b]	-epin	-epane
8	-oc-	-ocine	[b]	-ocin	-ocane
9	-on-	-onine	[b]	-onin	-onane
10	-ec-	-ecine	[b]	-ecin	-ecane

[a] Corresponding to the maximum number of double bonds, excluding cumulative double bonds.

[b] Expressed by prefixing "perhydro" to the name of the corresponding unsaturated compound.

(c) The degree of unsaturation is specified in the suffix as given in Table A–1. It is important to note that the suffix is slightly modified when nitrogen is absent from the heterocyclic ring.

(d) The numbering of the ring begins with the hetero atom of highest priority and proceeds around the ring so as to give other hetero atoms or substituents the lowest numbers possible.

These rules may be illustrated by the following examples.

thiirene 1,1-dioxide

3-methyloxepin

oxocane

3-methylhexahydro
1,3-thiazepine

thiete

1,2-oxathiolane

When a name applies equally to two or more isomeric parent ring systems with the maximum number of noncumulative double bonds, and when the name can be made specific by indicating the position of one or more hydrogen atoms in the structure, this is accomplished by modifying the name with a locant followed by italic capital *H* for each of these hydrogen atoms. Such symbols ordinarily precede the name.

2-methoxy-3*H*-azepine   2-methoxy-1*H*-azepine   2-methoxy-4*H*-azepine

Many of the common heterocyclic ring systems have acquired trivial names which are retained in systematic nomenclature. The majority of these have been discussed throughout this text.

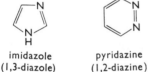

imidazole   pyridazine   tetrahydrofuran
(1,3-diazole)   (1,2-diazine)   (oxolane)

Polycyclic systems are named according to the following rules[1,2]:
(e) The name of the hetero ring is chosen as the parent compound and the name of the fused ring is attached as a prefix. For example,

benzothiazole

(f) In selecting the parent ring when two or more hetero rings are present, a nitrogen-containing ring is given precedence over an oxygen-containing ring (and oxygen over sulfur). However, in numbering the polycyclic compound, an oxygen hetero atom, if such is present, is given the lowest number consistent with rule (i) (see p. 391).

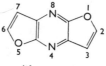

difuropyrazine

(g) Preference is given to the largest hetero ring system which has a simple name. The example that follows is therefore called benzoquinoline rather than naphthopyridine.

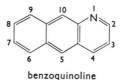

benzoquinoline

(h) The structure given to illustrate rule (g) above is not fully identified by the name benzoquinoline, for it is necessary to indicate in the name the position of the ring junction. To do this, the sides of the parent ring (quinoline) are lettered a, b, c, etc., starting with the 1,2-bond; the benzo grouping is found fused to bond g, and this is so indicated in the name.

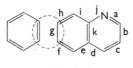

benzo[g]quinoline

In the example given in rule (f) above, there is a further complication, because the position of the ring junction has to be specified for each of three rings. The following breakdown of the structure with appropriate numbering and lettering will serve to illustrate how this is done.

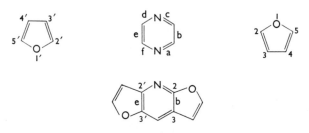

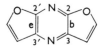

difuro[2,3-b:2',3'-e]pyrazine

Note that the isomeric structure would have to be named as follows; the individual numbering of the parent ring and the subsidiary ring(s) follow the same order through the points of fusion, as in meshing gears.

difuro[2,3-b:3',2'-e]pyrazine

(i) In numbering the periphery of a polycyclic compound, the written structure must first be oriented according to certain rules.

a. The greatest number of rings must lie along a horizontal axis.

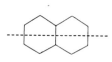

correct orientation   incorrect orientation

b. Of the other rings present, a maximum must lie uppermost to the right above the horizontal axis.

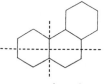   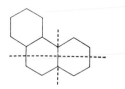

correct orientation   incorrect orientation

Numbering starts with the uppermost ring farthest to the right and proceeds in a clockwise direction, omitting the ring junctions.

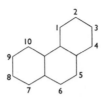

Other things being the same, the orientation of the rings should be such as to lead to the lowest possible number for the hetero atoms.

correct orientation   incorrect orientation

A few commonly encountered examples follow:

isoquinoline   pteridine   phenanthridine

References and Notes

(1) *J. Am. Chem. Soc.*, **82**, 5566 (1960).

(2) (a) A. M. Patterson, L. T. Capell, and D. F. Walker, *The Ring Index*, 2nd ed., 1959; (b) J. D. Roberts and M. C. Caserio, *Basic Principles of Organic Chemistry*, W. A. Benjamin, Inc., New York, 1964, pp. 972–4.

■ INDEX